Frances E. Lee and Bruce I. Oppenheimer

D1429815

Sizing Up the Senate

The Unequal Consequences of Equal Representation

The University of Chicago Press
Chicago and London

Frances E. Lee is assistant professor of political science at Case Western Reserve University.

Bruce I. Oppenheimer is professor of political science at Vanderbilt University.

The University of Chicago Press, Chicago 60637
The University of Chicago Press, Ltd., London
© 1999 by The University of Chicago
All rights reserved. Published 1999
08   07   06   05   04   03   02   01   00   99   1   2   3   4   5
ISBN: 0-226-47005-9 (cloth)
ISBN: 0-226-47006-7 (paper)

Library of Congress Cataloging-in-Publication Data

Lee, Frances E.
  Sizing up the Senate : the unequal consequences of equal representation / Frances E. Lee
and Bruce I. Oppenheimer.
      p.   cm.
  Includes bibliographical references and index.
  ISBN 0-226-47005-9 (cloth : alk. paper). — ISBN 0-226-47006-7 (pbk. : alk. paper)
  1. United States. Congress. Senate. 2. Apportionment (Election law)—United
States. I. Oppenheimer, Bruce Ian. II. Title.
  JK1161.L43   1999
  328.73'07347–dc21   99-20500
                                                                                          CIP

  ♾ The paper used in this publication meets the minimum requirements of the
American National Standard for Information Sciences—Permanence of Paper for Printed
Library Materials, ANSI Z39.48-1992.

Sizing Up the Senate

To Emery
F. E. L.

To Susan and Anne
B. I. O.

It often comes to pass, that in governments, where part of the legislative consists of representatives chosen by the people, that in tract of time this representation becomes very unequal and disproportionate to the reasons it was at first established upon. To what gross absurdities the following of custom, when reason has left it, may lead, we may be satisfied, when we see the fare name of a town, of which there remains not so much as the ruins, where scarce so much housing as a sheepcote, or more inhabitants than a shepherd is to be found, sends as many representatives to the grand assembly of law-makers, as a whole county numerous in people, and powerful in riches. This strangers stand amazed at, and everyone must confess needs a remedy; tho' most think it hard to find one, because the constitution of the legislative being the original and supreme act of the society, antecedent to all positive laws in it, and depending wholly on the people, no inferior power can alter it. And therefore the people, when the legislative is once constituted, having, in such a government as we have been speaking of, no power to act as long as the government stands; this inconvenience is thought incapable of a remedy.

John Locke, *Second Treatise of Government*

Contents

Preface

While working on this book we were constantly amazed that previous scholars had given so little attention to the effects of Senate apportionment. The Senate's unique apportionment scheme, after all, is one of its more distinctive and obvious characteristics. When describing our project we were often asked, Hasn't that been done? Fortunately for us, scholars had left the subject almost untouched. The reasons for this strange omission are difficult to pin down. We have concluded that Senate apportionment is typically just taken for granted. As one of the reviewers of our manuscript noted, "Everyone I know in the Congress field simply 'goes with the flow' with respect to what the framers said about Senate apportionment. Academics . . . talk about the Great Compromise, but . . . few bother to reflect on what consequences arise from this constitutional mandate. It is just 'there' and has been for over two centuries."

At times we felt like detectives investigating a long-unsolved case only to discover that the key piece of evidence had been sitting in plain view all along. Perhaps Senate apportionment has been overlooked for so long simply because it is so obvious, there for anyone to find. Sometimes we think we were just lucky to stumble on it. But there are limits to our modesty.

We hope that *Sizing Up the Senate* changes scholars' minds about the importance of Senate apportionment in at least two ways. First, we argue that one must take its effects into account in order to fully understand the Senate as a representative and legislative institution. Second, we hope our readers conclude that this is a rich area for study. Although we have uncovered many ways that equal representation of states shapes the Senate, we trust it is obvious that we have not fully tapped this subject. Nothing would please us more than for other scholars to extend this exploration and deepen our knowledge of the effects of Senate apportionment. In the concluding chapter we offer some suggestions for future research.

This book is the product of our equal efforts. Although Oppenheimer initiated the project, Lee's contributions were critical to its full conception and completion. As one might expect, there are some parts of the book for which Lee deserves more credit and some for which Oppenheimer is more responsible. The collaborative process, however, makes separating these individual contributions difficult. What is clear to us is that the end product is more than merely the sum of our individual contributions.

Although most of what follows has not previously appeared in print, some of our findings have been reported in journals. Some material in chapter 3 can be found in Oppenheimer's article "The Representational Experience: The Effect of State Population on Senator-Constituent Linkages," *American Journal of Political Science* 40 (1996): 1280–99 (© 1996; reprinted by permission of the University of Wisconsin Press). Chapter 4 builds on Lee and Oppenheimer, "Senate Apportionment: Competitiveness and Partisan Advantage," *Legislative Studies Quarterly* 22 (1997): 3–24. Finally, chapter 6 is a revision of Lee's "Representation and Public Policy: The Consequences of Senate Apportionment for the Geographic Distribution of Federal Funds," *Journal of Politics* 60 (1998): 34–62 (copyright 1998 by the University of Texas Press. All rights reserved). Between writing these articles and completing the book manuscript, however, we did additional research, revised some of our earlier findings, and conducted interviews with senators, Senate staffers, and lobbyists. Chapters 3 and 4 thus include substantial sections that were not part of the journal articles, and all three chapters include interview materials and other new research.

Throughout our work we have benefited significantly from institutional support. The political science department at Vanderbilt University supplied the environment that fostered our collaborative research effort. In addition, Vanderbilt provided Oppenheimer with faculty research funding and Lee with financial support as a graduate student. Both of us are also grateful to the Brookings Institution. Lee was a research fellow in Governmental Studies at Brookings during the 1997–98 academic year, and Oppenheimer was a guest scholar there during the spring and summer of 1997. We both thank Tom Mann, Susan Stewart, and Judith Light, who went out of their way to make our time at Brookings comfortable and productive. Lee thanks Case Western Reserve University for granting her leave so she could spend the year at Brookings.

There are also many individuals to whom we feel indebted. No one can read this book without recognizing its debt to Dick Fenno, particularly to his research on representation and senators. In addition we appreciate Dick's sound advice, friendly encouragement, and tolerance for listening, of which we periodically took advantage. Bob Stein and Ken Bickers kindly shared their data on federal domestic assistance programs and offered valuable criticisms of our analyses of those data. Barbara Sinclair generously supplied us with her data on national media coverage of senators and offered helpful insights on researching the Senate.

A number of scholars read various parts of the manuscript. Emery Lee read and reread the entire thing; his substantive and editorial suggestions proved invaluable. Oppenheimer took advantage of his good friend Larry Dodd's willing ear and useful feedback. Rory Austin, Sarah Binder, George Connor, Jacob Hacker, and Wendy Schiller were kind enough to read various chapters and suggest improvements. Scott Ainsworth, Robert Birkby, John Gilmore, Pat Hurley, John Kaji, Sean Kelley, Michael Malbin, John McAdams, Robb McDaniel, Jim Pfiffner, Barry Rundquist, Kent Weaver, and Joe White offered helpful comments on earlier materials. Geoff Layman, Tom Carsey, Barbara Kilbourne, Richard Odom, and Paul Senese gave us methodological advice. We also thank Betsy Barclay for her willingness to intervene on our behalf. Christine Lipsmeyer and Lan Lou, graduate students at Vanderbilt, were most capable research assistants during various phases of the project.

We especially appreciate the faculty, graduate students, and staff of the political science department at Vanderbilt. In particular, John Geer's sense of humor prevented us from taking ourselves too seriously, and his sound counsel was always available.

Oppenheimer owes special thanks to several longtime close friends in the Washington area. Leah and Rick Schroeder provided a home away from home and helped out in countless ways. Jud Sommer's assistance was priceless. Not only did they ease some of the research burdens, but they had a marked influence on the quality of this book. One feels very lucky to have such loyal friends.

In addition, we are grateful to all those who consented to be interviewed. Their perspectives are an essential part of this book. Their observations and experiences added richness to our findings and raised important issues for us to address.

We want to express our appreciation to our editor John Tryneski. His energy and enthusiasm for the project made it a pleasure to work with the University of Chicago Press. In addition, we are grateful to Alice Bennett for her exceptionally fine copyediting work. Thanks also to others at the Press, including Randy Petilos, Robert Herbst, Toni Ellis, and Robert Williams.

Finally, this book is dedicated to our families—Frances's husband, Emery, and Bruce's wife, Susan, and daughter, Anne. Their love, understanding, and encouragement are our most valued memories of our time working on this book.

1

Introduction

On July 16, 1987, two hundred members of the One Hundredth Congress gathered at Independence Hall in Philadelphia to commemorate the bicentennial of the Great Compromise. Out of that larger group, one congressional delegate from each of the fifty states plus the House and Senate leaders met in a joint session in the assembly room where the Constitution was drafted. Interestingly, of the eleven senators serving as delegates at this joint session, seven represented small states—states with only one or two congressional districts—and none represented any of the largest states.[1] This is fitting when one considers that the Great Compromise—the decision at the Constitutional Convention to apportion states' seats in the House of Representatives based on population while granting each state equal representation in the Senate—was a great victory for the small states. Many of the senators who gathered to celebrate this victory owed their political influence to it, even two centuries later.

After nearly an hour of speeches in which the House and Senate leaders extolled the virtues of the Great Compromise and their separate houses, the session adjourned to Congress Hall, where they were joined by the other House members and senators in simultaneous meetings of the two bodies. More speeches were made, and official photographs were taken. Many of the senators in attendance at this celebration lauded the framers of the Constitution for their wisdom in creating the Senate. Sen. Robert Byrd (D-W.Va.), majority leader at the time, praised the body as "one of the great foundation stones, if not the principal foundation stone, of our constitutional system" (*Congressional Record* 1987, 10100). A few of the senators present even praised the scheme of Senate apportionment agreed to in the Great Compromise.

1

Sen. John Melcher (D-Mont.) was the most effusive in this regard: "On behalf of Montana and all States like it, with small populations, we thank those
Connecticut Yankees for their foresight and their genius; their compromise
permitted great States such as Montana and all the rest of the West, so diverse
in a land of plains, mountains and rivers, so rich in agriculture and minerals
and forests but limited in population, to become partners with other states
on a footing of equality in the Senate" (*Congressional Record* 1987, 10108).

Not surprisingly, none of the members of Congress at this event discussed
the effects that Senate apportionment has had during its two hundred year
history or asked how well equal representation of states had stood the test of
time. They were, after all, gathered to celebrate the Great Compromise, and
thus the setting was not appropriate for raising such questions.

What is surprising is that these senators are not alone in ignoring these
effects. The Great Compromise—the decision to grant each state equal representation in the Senate—has certainly had consequences over the course
of the nation's history. Given the increasing difference in size between the
largest and smallest states, combined with other changes in the American
political context any effects of Senate apportionment are greater today than
in the past. By reference to the one person, one vote standard, the Senate is
the most malapportioned legislature in the world (Lijphart 1984, 174).[2] Currently Wyoming, with fewer than half a million residents, enjoys the same
level of representation as California, with more than 30 million. More than
a quarter of the United States population now lives in three very large, rap-
idly growing states (California, Texas, and Florida), yet they are represented
by only six senators. A mere 7 percent of the total United States population,
on the other hand, resides in the seventeen least populous states and is thus
represented by thirty-four senators.

The Senate's deviation from a population-based standard is all the more
significant in light of the chamber's extensive powers. Unlike other countries
with bicameral legislatures, in the United States the Constitution grants equal
power to the two chambers. The Canadian and French senates and the British House of Lords, which apportion seats by factors other than population,
are weak compared with their population-based counterparts, having at most
a qualified veto over the lower chamber (Lijphart 1984, 96–97). The Senate,
by contrast, is coequal with the House of Representatives in all powers of
legislation, even possessing some powers not granted to the House, the most
important being the right to approve presidential appointments and treaties.

Despite these facts, the public, journalists, legal scholars, and political
scientists have generally ignored the consequences of the Great Compromise
and equal representation of states in the Senate. Ironically, the most intensely
debated issue at the Constitutional Convention—how to apportion representation among the states—has received very little attention since.

We are not claiming, of course, to be the first since 1787 to have noticed the unusual apportionment scheme of the Senate. Nor are we the first to suspect that this scheme has had consequences for the Senate as a representative and policymaking institution. A few observers—senators, journalists, scholars—have noted and commented on it. Sen. Daniel Patrick Moynihan (D-N.Y.), for example, has openly criticized the equal representation of states in the Senate (1995, xxi). Moynihan's concern, of course, is that his state and its millions of residents suffer because of this system. Similarly, Fareed Zakaria, editor of *Foreign Affairs,* has pointed out that the "Senate is the most unrepresentative upper house in the world, with the lone exception of the House of Lords, which is powerless" (1997, 39). In a survey of legal scholars in the journal *Constitutional Commentary* (1995), two legal scholars (out of nineteen) selected Senate apportionment as "the stupidest part of the Constitution," and three others listed it as "one of the stupidest."

In recent years several muckraking journalists have also attacked Senate apportionment. In "The Infernal Senate," for example, Tom Geoghegan (1994, 17) complains that the Senate deprives the United States of majority rule, especially in terms of progressive reforms: "We can't raise our wages. We can't get health insurance. No aid to the cities. And why? The Senate votes it down. By a weighted vote, for small-town whites in pickup trucks with gun racks all out there shooting these things down. We have a Louisiana Purchase of Rotten Burroughs, full of senators who are horse doctors, or in rifle clubs, targeting our bills." Michael Lind (1998) has called for breaking up the largest states to balance out the effects of Senate apportionment. If all states must be represented equally, then why not subdivide the most populous ones to make the Senate more representative? Instead of having just one state called California, with its 30 million people, for example, Lind facetiously proposes a total of eight states in the same territory: San Diego, Los Angeles, Santa Barbara, Orange, Reagan, Siliconia, Marin, and Vineland. Daniel Lazare (1996) goes even further in his book *The Frozen Republic,* describing a futuristic scenario in which California, fed up with its underrepresented status in the Senate, secedes from the Union and ignites a second American revolution. These sharp attacks on the Senate, however, have spurred little public interest in the topic.

Although other scholars have noticed Senate apportionment, we are the first political scientists in a very long time to engage in a systematic inquiry into its political and policy effects. Some political scientists of an earlier era' were interested in the effects of Senate apportionment, at least to a limited extent. Moffett (1895), for example, studied key Senate votes from 1789 through 1893, finding no evidence that senators representing a minority of the population tended to vote together against senators representing a majority. In the 1920s and 1930s a number of scholars addressed the issue of

Senate apportionment (Haynes 1938, 1006–19; Luce 1930; Merriam 1931, 34–61; Rogers 1926; Woody 1926). Charles Merriam argued in 1931 that Senate representation was so out of step with current economic and industrial development that "a reorganization of state boundaries" would be necessary "in the near future" (61). After the 1930s, however, interest in the topic waned, despite a few brief mentions, as in Dahl's classic *Preface to Democratic Theory* (1956, 118) and Holcombe's *Our More Perfect Union* (1967, 209).

Political scientists' general lack of interest in Senate apportionment is difficult to explain, especially when one considers the amount of research conducted in the 1950s and 1960s into the effects of legislative malapportionment at the state level (Adrian 1960; Dye 1966; Frost 1959; Jacob 1964; Jewell 1962; Schubert and Press 1964). These political scientists were particularly concerned that state legislative malapportionment—especially the underrepresentation of urban areas and the overrepresentation of rural areas—caused a number of problems and undesirable policy outcomes, including low levels of party competition in many states, inequitable distribution of state transportation and education funds, and failure to adopt or expand social welfare programs, among others (Baker 1955b; Havard and Beth 1962; Jewell 1962; Key 1956; Sorauf 1962). Interest in apportionment ebbed, however, after the Supreme Court mandated the reapportionment of all legislative chambers in the United States, other than the Senate, based on the standard of one person, one vote.[3]

In recent years political scientists concerned with issues of representation have instead studied the effects of different electoral systems and districting on minority representation in the aftermath of the Voting Rights Act and subsequent legislation. Almost every legislative body has received attention in this literature—the House of Representatives, state legislatures, city councils, and school boards—with one exception, the Senate.[4] It is strange that political scientists interested in representation have focused so exclusively on the House and have ignored the Senate, an equally powerful national legislature. This choice of focus becomes even more curious when one considers that House apportionment raised relatively few concerns with the framers, whereas the success or failure of the Constitutional Convention itself hinged on the issue of Senate apportionment.

More generally, reading the scholarly literature on the Senate might lead one to conclude that apportionment is not a particularly important feature of that institution. When Senate apportionment is mentioned at all, the subject is typically passed over with little comment, generally in the context of a discussion of the Great Compromise (Davidson and Oleszek 1998; Matthews 1960). Political scientists instead tend to study the Senate as a legislative rather than a representative institution, placing a much heavier emphasis on the chamber's distinctive rules, procedures, norms, and leadership than on its unusual basis of representation (Baker 1989; Evans 1994; Foley 1980; Matthews 1960; Oleszek 1996; Price 1972; Ripley 1969; Sinclair 1989, 1997; Smith 1989). Even when they have studied the Senate as a representative institution, scholars have generally focused on the "dyadic" relationship (Weisberg 1978) between individual senators and their constituencies rather than on the representational character of the institution as a whole (Bernstein 1988; Erikson 1990; Fenno 1996; Wright and Berkman 1986). Surprisingly, then, the scholars studying legislative apportionment have been uninterested in the Senate, and those studying the Senate have been uninterested in its basis of apportionment.

This lack of concern with the effects of Senate apportionment among political scientists is difficult to understand, especially when one takes into account two additional considerations. First, political scientists have not hesitated to question many other aspects of American constitutional design and governmental structure, especially those that conflict with widely held democratic values. Criticism of the entire constitutional system of separation of powers and checks and balances, for example, has been a long-standing tradition in American political science (Burns 1963; Hardin 1974; Schattschneider 1942, 1960; Sundquist 1986; Wilson 1911). Other aspects of American government have not escaped similar treatment, including the electoral college (Glennon 1992; Peirce and Longley 1981; Polsby and Wildavsky 1996, 291–99), length of legislative and presidential terms (Sundquist 1986), legislative term limits (Gilmour and Rothstein 1994; Mondak 1995; Reed and Schansberg 1995), and single-member, plurality districts (Amy 1993; Lijphart 1998; Lind 1995; Zimmerman and Rule 1998). In short, scholars have questioned and investigated virtually every aspect of American political institutions but have inexplicably overlooked Senate apportionment.

Second, political scientists and others often assume that the population-based House and nationally elected presidency counterbalance the effects of Senate apportionment. We were surprised how often this perspective came up when we discussed this research with others. This apparently widely held belief has not been subjected to empirical scrutiny. Although there are a number of studies of conference committees (Fenno 1966; Ferejohn 1974; Longley and Oleszek 1989; Manley 1970; Pressman 1966; Steiner 1951; Van Beek 1995; Vogler 1971), political scientists have neglected to examine how Senate apportionment shapes the preferences of the Senate, creates a source of conflict with the House, and in turn affects congressional policymaking. In fact, congressional scholars have recently been criticized for their failure to study interchamber negotiations more fully (Tsebelis and Money 1997). As a result, scholars have not assessed whether the House really does counterbalance the effects of Senate apportionment in national policymaking, a topic we take up in chapters 6 and 7.

This book addresses the ignored but important effects of Senate apportionment. We ask, How does equal representation of states shape and influence the Senate as a representative, electoral institution? Similarly, how does it affect the Senate as a legislative and policymaking institution? What follows can be understood as a response to Donald Matthews's observation that equal representation of states in the Senate is an understudied topic. Matthews (1990, 401–2) notes, "I should think that [equal representation of states of vastly different size] might result in systematic differences between small and large state senators, how they relate to their constituencies, how they behave in the chamber, and so on. . . . Then there is the matter of who wins and who loses, in public policy terms."

We examine the impact of Senate apportionment on four interrelated aspects of the institution: representation, election, strategic behavior, and policymaking. These are the fundamental aspects of any legislative institution, and recognizing how equal representation of states affects them is essential for a complete understanding of the Senate. Granting equal representation to all states (and thus having senators represent constituencies that vary greatly in population size) has enormous consequences. We will show that variation in Senate constituency size affects

- the nature of senators' representational relationships with their constituents,

- the competitiveness, conduct, and partisan outcomes of Senate elections,

- the strategic behavior of senators within the institution, and

- the Senate's making of public policy, especially in terms of its distribution of federal funds and its interactions with the House of Representatives.

Senate apportionment shapes all these aspects of the institution because, as we will demonstrate, it has three closely related consequences. First, the immense variation in Senate constituency size contextualizes the work that all senators do—representing their constituents, running for reelection, and raising campaign funds, among others. In this sense there is no such thing as the "average" senator. Representing California or New York is much different from representing Wyoming or a median-sized state like Connecticut. Second, these contextual differences in constituency size shape the incentives of individual senators as they pursue a number of career goals, particularly reelection. The strategy that advances the goals of a senator from North Dakota is not the same strategic behavior a senator from California employs. As a result, senators from large and small states tend to pursue different strategies in Washington, in large part because of differences in constituency size.

Third, the effects of constituency size on individual senators in turn shape the Senate's preferences as a body. The way the Senate makes policy and interacts with the House is in this sense the sum of its parts—the incentives of individual senators. Given that a majority of senators represent small states, or states that are overrepresented in the Senate (according to a population-based standard), the effect of constituency size on the incentives of small-state senators is particularly important. Taken together, the distribution of constituencies (states) represented in the Senate and the different incentives of senators from small and large states result in an institution that prefers certain types of policies and that interacts in certain ways with the House.

Approach and Methods

Our approach is based on the recognition that the immense variation in constituency size shapes the Senate as both a representative and a policymaking institution. At the outset, then, it is important to differentiate our approach to this topic from three other possible ones. First, we are not directly concerned with the ways Senate apportionment overrepresents some interests and underrepresents others. Students of legislative districting have generally concluded that any system of geographic districts advantages certain interests and disadvantages others, depending on how district lines are drawn. In effect, as Dixon (1968, 462) concludes, "All districting is gerrymandering." To show that Senate apportionment affects the representation of interests would be to demonstrate the obvious. More important are its effects independent of its representation of particular interests—the effects it has simply by representing groups of people of greatly different numbers.

Second, it should also be clear that we are not simply pointing to the Senate's deviation from a one person, one vote standard. The concern of political theorists, muckraking journalists, and Supreme Court justices alike has been the abstract philosophical or legal weight of an individual's vote. What really matters in terms of the practical import of equal representation of states, however, is not a mathematical ratio, but the difference of millions of constituents between states like California, New York, and Texas, on the one hand, and states like Wyoming, Vermont, and North Dakota on the other. It is these large absolute differences in the size of constituencies, not merely the disparity in the relative weights of votes, that affect the Senate as a representative and policymaking institution.

Third, past studies of the effects of Senate apportionment, like the early work of Moffett (1895) and Wooddy (1926) as well as that of many contemporary critics of Senate apportionment (Baker and Dinkin 1997, 24–30; Eskridge 1995, 159–60; Geoghegan 1994; Lind 1998, 46–47), have focused on the effects of the equal representation of states on Senate roll-call votes. The idea behind this emphasis is that Senate apportionment matters only if important decisions are made by a majority of senators representing a minority of the population outvoting a minority of senators representing a majority of the population, thus subverting majority rule. In such situations, Tocqueville (1990, 1:119) observed, "the minority of the nation in the Senate may paralyze the decisions of the majority represented in the other house, which is contrary to the spirit of constitutional government."

Although this does happen from time to time (for some examples, see Lind 1998 and Eskridge 1995), constituency size is not an important variable for understanding the outcomes of Senate roll-call votes generally because the size of the constituency a senator represents has no direct effect on voting behavior. Studies of roll-call voting have shown that party, ideology, cue taking, presidential leadership, and constituency interests are the important determinants (Davidson and Oleszek 1998, 259–69; Kingdon 1989; Matthews and Stimson 1975). This is hardly surprising, because other than the controversy over Senate apportionment at the Constitutional Convention, no major political issue has divided small states from large states per se at any point in United States history (Moffett 1895; Rogers 1926; Tocqueville 1990; Wooddy 1926). To emphasize roll-call votes, then, is to miss the more important and pervasive ways that apportionment affects the Senate as an institution. In the following chapters we will demonstrate that this variation in constituency size affects the representational relationships of senators and their constituents, the competitiveness and partisan outcomes of Senate elections, campaign fund-raising, the strategies senators pursue in Washington, the distribution of federal funds to the states, and the bicameral interactions of the Senate and the House. An analysis of Senate roll-call votes would not uncover any of these important effects of apportionment.

To study the effects of Senate apportionment in all these contexts, we have employed multiple research methods. The research we present includes statistical analyses of survey data, election results, Federal Election Commission records, and data on federal outlays as well as extensive archival research and interviews with Senate insiders. This multiple-method approach is one of the greatest strengths of this project. We are able to show, from a number of vantage points, the effects of Senate apportionment on the Senate as an institution. This wealth of information, drawn and analyzed from a wide variety of sources, lends additional weight to our evidence and arguments. In the end, we believe this book makes a very strong case for the importance of Senate apportionment.

Approaching this broad topic with these different research methods, we do not rely on a single theoretical framework throughout. In the later chapters (5–7) we draw on "soft" rational choice theory, emphasizing the strategic calculations of senators as they pursue reelection. We argue, for example, that constituency size influences their incentives to engage in different Washington behaviors because the same strategies do not have the same electoral payoff in large and small states. These chapters, however, are set within a larger theoretical framework emphasizing the important place of institutions in structuring the incentives of and constraints on political actors. In chapter 2, for example, we emphasize the path-dependent nature of Senate apportionment. Senate apportionment is the result of a number of historical contingencies, including but not limited to the strategic calculations of earlier political actors (at the Constitutional Convention). Although the reasons the delegates agreed to the equal representation of states in the Senate are no longer at issue, the decision cannot be revisited by political actors today who find that it imposes costs on them. In fact, because Senate apportionment also determines who the relevant political actors are, most senators do not find that it does impose costs on them. Thus we regard it as a self-perpetuating arrangement, even if it no longer serves any particularly important contemporary function. In chapters 3 and 4 our approach is more inductive as we examine how this self-perpetuating arrangement contextualizes the work that all senators do, including representation, running for re-election, and campaign fund-raising.

A few brief comments are in order on the interviews we conducted. We interviewed senators, former senators, lobbyists, Senate staffers, and other political consultants with some Senate experience (several had experience in more than one capacity). This group was not a random sample, but in the end it did turn out to be fairly representative. Our subject group included an equal number of Democrats and Republicans, persons of various ideological persuasions, and most important for this project, senators and former senators from large, medium-sized, and small states. Most of these interviews were conducted after the bulk of our research was complete.

These interviews served a number of purposes. Most important, we hoped to discover how sensitive these individuals with intimate knowledge of the Senate were to the effects of Senate apportionment. In general we found that senators were aware of its effects in some, but not all, contexts. We discovered, for example, that almost all our subjects recognized that apportionment affects the quality of Senate representation. The small-state senators we interviewed spoke of answering some of their own mail, meeting with constituents one-on-one, and attending even relatively obscure civic events in their home states; at the same time, they were aware that their colleagues from larger states could not maintain this close connection with their constituents. In other contexts, however, we found senators and other insiders less conscious of the effects of Senate apportionment. In these instances we were interested in the reactions of senators to our findings. Did our findings make sense to them? In addition, we believe these interviews add depth and richness to our analyses of quantitative and archival data.

Senate Apportionment Today

Although the equal representation of states in the Senate has been with us for more than two hundred years, Senate apportionment deviates further from a population-based system than ever before in the nation's history. Senate malapportionment, of course, is not new. James Madison and others opposed equal representation of states in the Senate at the Constitutional Convention precisely because they feared its effects (discussed in chapter 2). In his final speech on this matter at the Constitutional Convention, Madison predicted that the unequal representation of people in the large and small states caused by the Senate's equal representation would increase over time (Farrand 1937, 2:10). History has proved Madison correct—the first Senate did not conform to the one person, one vote standard, and subsequent Senates have deviated further and further.

Just how malapportioned is the Senate? There are a number of measures of legislative malapportionment, most of them developed by political scientists studying state legislatures in the 1950s and 1960s. One of the most widely used, developed by Dauer and Kelsay (1955), simply measures the theoretical minimum percentage of the population able to elect a majority of the legislative body. In other words, legislative districts (in this case states) are ranged from smallest in population to largest, and then the populations of the smallest districts (states) are summed until the number of districts constitutes a majority of the legislative body. This sum is then transformed into a percentage of the total population.

Figure 1.1 plots this percentage for the Senate at ten-year intervals from 1790 through 1990. The overall pattern confirms Madison's prediction at the Constitutional Convention that the Senate would grow more malapportioned over time. Historically, territorial expansion and the admission of new states to the Union have generally increased the Senate's deviation from a population-based standard. In fact the greatest decreases in the theoretical minimum percentage of the nation's population needed to elect a Senate majority occurred during periods of rapid national expansion, such as 1810 to 1820. In 1810 the theoretical minimum to elect a Senate majority was 33 percent; by 1820, with the admission of six new states (Louisiana, Indiana, Mississippi, Illinois, Alabama, and Maine), it had fallen to 18.6 percent. Similarly, in 1860, 25.8 percent of the nation's population was theoretically necessary to elect a Senate majority; by 1890, with the admission of nine new states, only 20 percent was needed.

With a few brief exceptions, the Senate has progressively become more malapportioned, and therefore less representative, over the course of American history. At no point since 1810 has the theoretical minimum percentage of the nation's population necessary to elect a majority of senators been

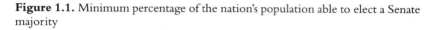

Figure 1.1. Minimum percentage of the nation's population able to elect a Senate majority

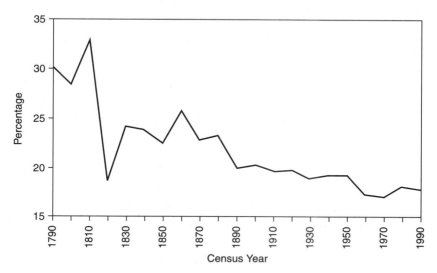

greater than 30 percent, and at no point since 1900 has it been greater than 20 percent. The historical trend in figure 1.1 is clear, despite the increase in the theoretical minimum since 1970 (the all-time low, at 17 percent). A more sophisticated measure of legislative malapportionment developed by Schubert and Press (1964)—which takes into account the entire distribution of state size in order to assess the extent and kind of legislative malapportionment—reveals that Senate malapportionment is more serious today than at any point in history. The Schubert-Press measure (described in some depth in appendix A) reveals that since 1970 the largest states have grown even larger and the number of overrepresented states has increased. With current demographic trends, moreover, malapportionment is going to increase further. With a few exceptions, the fastest-growing states in the Union are the largest. California, Texas, and Florida, for example, are all among the seven fastest-growing states. The small states, on the other hand, tend to have relatively low population growth rates.[5] These trends are likely to continue.

If malapportionment is an important topic for study because it affects the Senate in fundamental ways, then those effects have never been greater than during the past few decades, and they promise to increase in the future. These trends have not escaped the attention of everyone. As Senator Moynihan of New York, for one, has suggested: "Sometime in the next century the United States is going to have to address the question of apportionment in the Senate. Already we have seven states with two senators and one representative. The Senate is beginning to look like the pre-reform British House of Commons" (1995, xxi). The implication here is that the trends we have noted—toward a few increasingly large states and a large number of small states—will continue. If so, and if as Moynihan predicts this becomes a problem to be addressed by policymakers and the broader public, the research presented in this book should be of particular interest.

Our purpose, however, is not to argue for reform but rather to advance our understanding of the Senate as a representative and legislative institution. Equal representation of states is, for all practical purposes, a permanent feature of American government. Because of the language of article 5—"No state, without its consent, shall be deprived of equal suffrage in the Senate"—Senate apportionment may be the one part of the Constitution that cannot be changed by an ordinary constitutional amendment. Depending on how the courts interpret this provision, unanimity among the states seems to be necessary to change it. Regardless of whether unanimity or the standard amending procedures pertain, however, any alteration would require that many of those who benefit from the existing structure consent to a change that would reduce their individual power, in the case of senators, or their representation in Congress, in the case of states. In short, the chances of any reform are slim to none.

Organization of the Book

The four central aspects of any legislative body that we referred to above—representation, elections, strategic behavior, and policymaking—are the subjects of chapters 3–7 as we investigate how Senate apportionment affects various facets of each.

In chapter 3 we explore how Senate apportionment shapes the representational experiences of senators and their constituents. Using the National Election Study Pooled Senate Election Study, 1988–92 (Inter-University Consortium 1993), we demonstrate that state population dramatically affects both the quantity of contact that constituents have with their senators and the perceived quality of those interactions. Constituents in less populous states report more contact with their senators and also rate them more favorably than constituents in more populous states. In addition, we find that state population affects the reasons constituents contact their senators. Constituents in populous states do so mainly to express an opinion on an issue. Constituents in less populous states are much more likely than constituents in larger states to ask senators for help with problems. This suggests that constituents' expectations of the representational experience are shaped by state size: constituents in large states appear to recognize that their senators' relationships with constituents must necessarily be less personal and more remote. Based on our interview material, we also extend some of our findings to interest groups' access to senators.

Analyzing the three separate effects of variation in constituency size on Senate elections is the focus of chapter 4. First, we hypothesize that Senate elections should be more competitive in large states than in small ones because of the more distant representational ties between senators and constituents in large states and, more important, the greater diversity of political interests there. Using a modified version of the *Candidate and Constituency Statistics of Elections* data set (Inter-University Consortium 1990), we find a negative relationship between state population and the margin of victory in all Senate elections—regardless of whether an incumbent is running—for the entire period since popular election of senators was instituted in 1914. In the chapter's second part we examine the effects of Senate apportionment on campaign fund-raising. Although political scientists have long recognized that Senate elections are generally more expensive in larger states, they have not considered that state size may also affect the sources from which senators raise campaign funds and the amount of time they commit to fund-raising. We devote the final section of chapter 4 to examining the influence of apportionment on the Senate's partisan composition. Comparing the actual outcomes of elections over time with hypothetical outcomes derived by holding state population constant, we find that Senate apportionment frequently leads to one party's receiving more seats than if all states were equal in population.

In chapter 5 we study the link between apportionment and the strategic behavior of senators in office. We argue that small-state senators have greater incentives to pursue particularized benefits for their states than their large-state colleagues because in a small state any given benefit will have a greater impact on the state's economy and the senator's visibility. Large-state senators, by contrast, have enhanced incentives to pursue policy activism to further their reelection goals because they need to use the media to communicate with their larger constituencies. To analyze the relation between state population and Senate strategies, we examine senators' committee assignments (80th Congress to 105th Congress), finding that small-state senators are more likely to obtain assignment to "constituency" committees whereas large-state senators are more likely to be on "policy" committees. Similarly, we find that large-state senators receive more national media coverage than their colleagues from less populous states, all else being equal (103d and 104th Congresses).

In the later sections of the chapter we investigate other ways constituency size affects senators' behavior in Washington. We present evidence—drawn from a sample of thirty-one close votes—that senators from the small-population states often cast the decisive votes on closely fought legislation. This pattern of late deciding and vote switching may indicate both that coalition leaders tend to seek out senators from small states to find needed votes and that these senators—who know that their demands are less costly and thus more likely to be accommodated—delay committing themselves to a side, expecting to be courted by coalition leaders. Finally, we argue that Senate apportionment affects senators' ability to seek leadership positions in the contemporary Senate. For a number of reasons, we contend that it may no longer be possible for senators from the most populous states to hold floor leadership positions.

We analyze the effects of Senate apportionment on public policy and policymaking in chapters 6 and 7. In chapter 6 we employ Bickers and Stein's *U.S. Domestic Assistance Programs Database* (1992) to show that coalition building in the Senate produces distributions of federal funds to states that reflect the representational advantages of small-population states. First, federal distributive programs are typically constructed so that a majority, frequently an overwhelming majority, of states benefit. Second, small states benefit disproportionately, receiving higher per capita allocations of federal funds than large states across a broad range of domestic distributive programs, even after controlling for differences in state need. The least populous states, those most overrepresented in the Senate, receive the greatest windfall from Senate apportionment. As one would expect, this small-state advantage is most pronounced in the type of program for which Congress writes the distributional formula.

To determine whether Senate apportionment is in fact the origin of the small-state advantage revealed in chapter 6, in chapter 7 we examine House-Senate politics for a sample of forty-two federal formula-grant programs. We find that House-Senate conflict over funding formulas is common and that the issues in these disputes stem from the differing bases of representation in the two chambers. Because a majority of senators represent small states, the Senate consistently prefers formulas that distribute federal funds more generously to small states, and less generously to large ones, than the formulas the House prefers. Small states are advantaged in federal outlays because the Senate prefers distributions of funds reflecting its basis of apportionment and because Senate preferences tend to win out in conference when there is House-Senate conflict. The Senate's dominance over funding formulas is the result, in large part, of the incentives of small-state senators, which are in turn directly linked to their constituency contexts. These findings demonstrate that neither the House nor the presidency (institutions more attuned to population-based concerns) exerts sufficient influence to counterbalance the effects of equal representation of states in the Senate in distributive policymaking.

In the concluding chapter we examine the collective implications of our findings, addressing the normative issues that our research raises and the dim prospects for reform of Senate apportionment. More important, we discuss the implications of our findings for scholarly research on the Senate. In addition, we suggest several subjects for further research, topics that have yet to be explored but that are important to understanding the Senate and the operation of American democracy.

Before turning to the contemporary effects of Senate apportionment, we need to establish the appropriate theoretical and historical perspectives. Thus in chapter 2 we explore the reasons typically given for the equal representation of states in the Senate. Rejecting as inadequate the standard functionalist explanations of Senate apportionment, we put forward a new interpretation of the Great Compromise based on a historical-institutional, path-dependent perspective. The Great Compromise is best understood, we argue, as the result of several historical contingencies rather than as the product of functional design. Equal representation of states persists not because it serves any current function—other than that described by Senator Melcher above—but as a consequence of historical contingencies more than two centuries ago. Chapter 2 is meant to counteract the tendency among students of American politics to take the institutions of American government for granted. If we simply accept Senate apportionment as one of the "givens" of American politics, we have no frame of reference for evaluating its contemporary effects. Before proceeding to examine the effects of Senate apportionment, then, we ask—and answer—the following questions: Why do we have a Senate constructed in this way? What purpose, if any, was equal representation of states intended to perform in American government?

2

Senate Apportionment in Theoretical and Historical Perspective

At least since *The Federalist Papers,* Americans have tended to believe that their political institutions are the product of rational design rather than the result of historical contingency. "It has been frequently remarked," Hamilton writes in the opening paragraph of *The Federalist Papers,* that "the people of this country" will "by their conduct and example . . . decide the important question whether societies of men are really capable or not of establishing good government from reflection and choice" or "whether they are forever destined to depend for their political constitutions on accident and force" (Hamilton, Jay, and Madison 1987, 87). Hamilton flatters his audience, telling them that it is up to them, "by their conduct and example," to rise above "accident and force" and show the world that men really are capable "of establishing good government from reflection and choice." Today Americans view the resulting United States Constitution in much the same light. One telling indication of this is the ubiquity of appeals to the framers' intent in American political discourse. Whether the subject is term limits or campaign finance reform, debates about institutional reform in America regularly devolve into disputes about what the framers of the Constitution intended more than two hundred years ago.

Every American government textbook teaches that the framers designed the United States Congress to represent the people of the nation. As we discussed in the previous chapter, however, Senate apportionment represents "the people" in an increasingly odd way. Over time it has grown more and more out of alignment with population. How are we to understand the meaning and significance of this fundamental characteristic of our national representative institutions?

In this chapter we explore the theoretical and historical reasons for equal state apportionment in the Senate. If we simply take Senate apportionment as one of the "givens" of American politics, we lack a frame of reference for understanding and evaluating the significance of its effects on contemporary politics and policy. We first need to examine the role of the Senate and apportionment's place within it; failing to think about Senate apportionment prevents us from grasping its importance for our national representative institutions. Accordingly, we cannot inquire into its effects without taking into account the theoretical justifications offered for it.

At the outset, we ask two questions: Why do we have a Senate constructed in this way? What purpose, if any, was equal state apportionment intended to perform? As we answer these questions, we use an approach developed by the new institutionalist movement in political science. This movement is foremost a rejection of structural-functionalist explanations of political institutions (see, for example, Almond 1960 and Easton 1965), which explained their structure by reference to their ability to serve certain ahistorical functions for political societies. Instead of looking to the functions political institutions now serve, scholars, including Stephen Skowronek (1982, 1993), Sarah Binder (1997), Richard Bensel (1990), Theda Skocpol (1992, 1995), and James March and Johan Olsen (1989), apply path dependence, an idea first developed in the field of evolutionary biology.

Traditional evolutionary biology is similar to the structural-functionalist approach to political institutions in that it emphasizes ahistorical explanations of the physical structures of organisms based on the uses those structures now serve. Explaining the function of an organism's particular physical structure, however, tells neither why that specific part is available to serve that function nor how it came to be so. This is a problem because many organisms have physical structures that are not optimally adapted to their functions. To address these issues, some evolutionary biologists turned to the history of those physical structures. They argue that an organism's present-day structures can be fully understood only by tracing the *path* of their development and that this path is *dependent* on any number of small, random events. This path dependence can explain what structural-functionalist explanations cannot: why physical structures in many organisms are not optimally adapted to their environments.

In *The Panda's Thumb,* for example, Stephen Jay Gould argues that the panda's thumb is best understood as a product of contingent historical development rather than of straightforward functional adaptation. Because pandas are descended from carnivorous bears, their original anatomical thumbs were suited to the limited motion needed for meat eating. Change in its environment required the panda to adapt to an herbivorous life that demanded more dexterity; but the panda's later adaptation was constrained by the available genetic pool, and it could not adapt altogether to optimally fit its new environment. Instead, the modern panda's thumb is really just an enlarged radial sesamoid bone of the wrist—"a clumsy, suboptimal structure" (Gould 1991, 61) that would "win no prize in an engineer's derby" (Gould 1980, 24). "Pathways of history," Gould writes, "impose such jury-rigged solutions upon all creatures" (1991, 61).

From the same perspective, political scientists and historians point to the inadequacy of functional explanations for understanding institutional structures, focusing instead on the "jury-rigged" character of political institutions (Bensel 1990; North 1990; Skocpol 1995; Skowronek 1982). Scholars writing within the new institutionalist framework begin by recognizing that all political institutions have histories. These histories differ, but they all share a certain broad outline. Political actors create institutions at particular moments in history and within particular social, political, and ideological contexts. They do so because existing institutions are not coping adequately with some pressing problem, and they often craft the new from the remains of the old. After the problem has been solved, or has just faded away, the once new political institution remains. In so doing, it comes "to define the framework within which politics takes place" (March and Olsen 1989, 18). The institution allocates power among political actors and establishes rules for appropriate behavior, thus shaping politics and later institutional developments. The many ways a political institution will affect subsequent events are largely unanticipated by its original creators. Understood in this way, institutions not only have histories, they make history.

Nevertheless, commentators and scholars continue to invoke functionalist interpretations of Senate apportionment. They speak of the framers' "purpose" in apportioning the Senate and maintain that the equal representation of states serves important functions in the American system of government. How useful are these functionalist approaches for understanding the origin and role of this unique characteristic of our national legislature? We explore these perspectives, then we advance a path-dependent interpretation of Senate apportionment, arguing that it is better understood as the result of a set of particular historical contingencies than as the institutional means to a functional end.

Functionalist Interpretations of Senate Apportionment

Defenders of the Senate often argue that its primary function is to serve as a more deliberative legislative body than the House. Although many institutional features of the Senate—such as its small size, its long terms of office, and its rules for debate—may help to create a more deliberative body, Senate apportionment bears no connection to this aim. Instead, functionalist explanations fall into two categories: those contending that Senate apportionment protects minority interests against majority tyranny and those that claim it expresses the federal nature of the American system of government. We explore these functionalist perspectives on Senate apportionment below and, after closer examination, reject them as unsatisfactory.

Protection of Minorities from Majority Tyranny

According to the first functionalist perspective, granting equal representation to states with unequal populations is an institutional mechanism designed to check majority tyranny (see, for example, Elazar 1987a, 57, 1987b, 91–107; Morley 1959, 226–40). For a legislative proposal to become law under this system, it must garner the support of both a majority of the representatives of a numerical majority (the House) and a majority of the representatives of states (the Senate). The proponents of this perspective contend that this arrangement makes majority tyranny less likely. As a contemporary example of this functionalist perspective on Senate apportionment, Steve Forbes argued in a 1995 editorial that Canada's governmental system is flawed because it grants too much weight to the most populous provinces, Ontario and Quebec. Forbes suggested that Canadians would be wise to adopt an upper house apportioned like the United States Senate, "where Wyoming, our least populous state, has the same number of votes as does California, our most populous state," so that Canadians residing in the less populous provinces would be better protected against redistributive "schemes hatched by Ontario and Quebec politicians" (Forbes 1995).

Advocates of this perspective on Senate apportionment do have circumstantial evidence in their favor. Those who praise equal state representation in the Senate as a check on majority tyranny can certainly begin from the undeniable premise that the framers had this goal in mind. The Senate in particular was integral to the framers' plan to check the institution they expected to be most susceptible to democratic excess: the House (Swift 1996). This prompts the following questions: Does the equal representation of states protect against majority tyranny? What minorities could Senate apportionment protect from what majorities?

The 1787 controversy over Senate apportionment is itself the only major political issue in American history that has ever created a sharp cleavage between states with large and small populations (Moffett 1895; Rogers 1926; Tocqueville 1990; Woody 1926). Madison, in fact, made this point many times at the Convention in opposing equal apportionment in the Senate. Equal state representation, he claimed, was unnecessary because there was no conflict of interest between the large and small states and thus no large-state threat to small states' interests in a chamber apportioned by population: "Look to the votes in Congress," he pleaded; "most of them stand divided by the geography of the country [i.e., between North and South], not according to the size of the states" (Farrand 1966, 1:476). If the interests of small states and large states are not opposed, how can enhancing the representation of small states protect against anything?

The idea that Senate apportionment protects minorities from majority oppression continues to find expression both on the Senate floor and among political observers. William White (1957) presents this argument in his classic book on the Senate of the 1950s, *Citadel*:

> The Senate, though the Senate of the United States, is in fact the Senate of the States, so that never here will the cloud of uniformism roll over the sun of the individual and the minority. . . .For the Institution protects and expresses that last, true heart of the democratic theory, the triumphant distinction and oneness of the individual and of the little State, the infinite variety in each of which is the juice of national life. (18)

Notwithstanding their rhetorical appeal, arguments like these turn on a "false psychological equation" that Robert Dahl describes: "Small states are equated with 'small interests' and small interests with 'small' or defenseless persons," so that "our humanitarian desires to protect relatively defenseless persons from aggression by more powerful individuals are thereby invoked on behalf of small states" (1956, 113).

There is no reason to assume that small states, simply by virtue of having small populations, embody easily trampled minority interests. Depending on how the borders of states are "drawn," states with small populations may disproportionately encompass interests that are already well represented nationally. Indeed, the equal representation of states may even enhance the representation of interests that are national majorities. To illustrate this point, it is useful to examine how Senate apportionment today affects the voting weight of racial and ethnic minorities in determining the composition of the Senate.

With regard to issues of race and ethnicity—which are some of the most profound and enduring in American political life—Senate apportionment works contrary to the purpose of protecting minorities. Although Madison was not thinking of racial and ethnic minorities when he pondered the need to protect minorities from majority tyranny, race has become so important in American politics that today the term "minority" is almost synonymous with racial and ethnic minorities. Instead of ensuring that these minorities receive additional representational weight, Senate apportionment has the ef-

Table 2.1 Percentage of Nation's Population in Selected Racial and Ethnic Groups Compared with the Percentages in the Median State, 1996

	National Population	In Median State
Black	12.5	7.1
Hispanic	10.0	2.8
Asian	3.4	1.3
American Indian, Eskimo, Aleut	0.8	0.4
White (non-Hispanic)	74.0	82.2
All minorities	26.8	18.1

fect (albeit unintentional) of diluting their influence (see also Baker and Dinkin 1997, 43–47).

One way of examining the influence of Senate apportionment on the representation of racial and ethnic minorities is to compare the diversity of the nation's total population on these dimensions with the diversity in the median state. Table 2.1 shows the percentages of the selected racial and ethnic groups for the national population and for the median state (the median Senate constituency).[1]

The data reveal that the median state is in every case less racially and ethnically diverse than the nation as a whole. For instance, although blacks account for 12.5 percent of the nation's total population, the median state has a population that is only 7.1 percent black. Similarly, although persons of Hispanic origin make up 10 percent of the nation's population as a whole, the median state is only 2.8 percent Hispanic. Asians also have a somewhat smaller presence in the median state (1.3 percent) than in the nation's population (3.4 percent). Whites, by contrast, constitute the only group that Senate apportionment advantages: the median state is 82.2 percent white, whereas the nation as a whole is only 74.0 percent white.

Senate apportionment also works contrary to the purpose of protecting racial and ethnic minorities because the states with smaller populations also tend to be less ethnically and racially diverse than the nation as a whole, whereas states with larger populations tend to be more diverse. This pattern is revealed in table 2.2, which shows the coefficients obtained by correlating the percentage of each state's population for various groups with the total state population.

A negative correlation coefficient means the group is advantaged by Senate representation compared with a population-based representation; a positive coefficient means it is disadvantaged. As shown here, whites are the only group strongly advantaged by Senate apportionment (correlation coefficient

Table 2.2 Are Less Populous States Less Diverse? Pearson Correlations of State Population and State Ethnic Diversity, 1996

State Population Correlated with the Percentage of the State's Population That Is	Correlation Coefficient
Black	.246
Hispanic	.479*
Asian	.033
American Indian, Eskimo, Aleut	−.252
White (non-Hispanic)	−.391*

*Correlation is significant at the .05 level or better.

$= -.391, p < .01$).[2] The ten least populous states are 89 percent white on average, but the ten most populous average only 72 percent white. Although the nation's population as a whole is not fully three-quarters white, fourteen states have populations that are more than 90 percent white, and every one of them is overrepresented in the Senate by a one person, one vote standard; in fact these fourteen states include six of the seven most overrepresented states (states with only one congressional district).[3]

Senate representation dramatically disadvantages Hispanics. The states with the largest percentages of Hispanic persons tend also to be more populous (correlation coefficient $= .479, p < .01$), meaning that the states where Hispanics have the largest presence in percentage terms are also underrepresented in the Senate by a one person, one vote standard. Approximately 75 percent of the country's entire Hispanic population lives in only five states: California, Texas, Florida, New York, and Illinois, all of which are highly underrepresented.

By this measure, blacks are somewhat less disadvantaged by Senate apportionment than Hispanics (correlation coefficient between state population and percentage black $= .246, p < .1$). Blacks tend to have their largest presence in percentage terms in the middle-sized southern states—states that experience little advantage or disadvantage from Senate apportionment compared with their standing if the Senate were apportioned by population. Even so, as a group the less populous states have substantially lower percentages of blacks than do the more populous states: in the thirty-one overrepresented states, blacks on average account for only 7.5 percent of the population; by contrast, in the fourteen underrepresented states blacks average 14.3 percent.

In sum, rather than protecting racial and ethnic minorities, Senate apportionment underrepresents these groups' presence in the nation as a whole. With all the controversy over racial gerrymandering in the House, it is surprising that the impact of Senate apportionment on the representation of minorities has drawn so little attention. This effect, it should be noted, is separate from the additional disadvantage (from the perspective of racial and ethnic minorities) that senators are elected at large, a method that generally produces fewer minority officeholders. Because Senate constituencies include even more whites than the nation as a whole, apportionment overrepresents the racial group that already constitutes a majority of the nation's population. With respect to race, arguably the most important and enduring political cleavage in American history, Senate apportionment undercuts the protection of political minorities.

Senate apportionment certainly affects interest representation, advantaging some political interests and disadvantaging others. There is, however, no reason to assume that the interests advantaged are minorities in need of protection from majority tyranny. When Dahl examined this matter in 1956, he found that Senate apportionment overrepresented farmers, and in particular producers of wool, cotton, and silver, while underrepresenting "Negroes, sharecroppers, migrant workers, wage earners and coal miners" (118). This led him to conclude that it exercised an "entirely arbitrary" effect on interest representation, one inconsistent with any particular theory of political representation (118). No doubt there is room for further research examining the effect of Senate apportionment on interest representation. Given what we already know about the demographics of the less populous states, however, it is safe to conclude that Senate apportionment does not function to protect political minorities per se. At most one can merely claim that Senate apportionment, like any other form of geographic districting, enhances the representation of some interests and diminishes that of others, without respect to majority or minority status.[4]

Senate Apportionment as a Symbol of Federalism

The second functionalist perspective contends that Senate apportionment is intended to express the federal nature of the American system. Many argue that the Senate's basis of apportionment was designed to institutionalize a place for the states in the national government, thus symbolizing an enduring commitment to federal principles (Anderson 1993; Elazar 1987a,b). "It is the Senate," one commentator writes, "which represents par excellence the federal basis of American government" (Morley 1959, 7).

This idea finds some support in the deliberations at the Constitutional Convention. Charles Pinckney of South Carolina, for example, argued early in the debate on the Senate that the composition of the Senate should express the "sovereignty" of the states (Sundquist 1986, 23). Madison provides some justification for this perspective when he writes in *Federalist* 62:

If indeed it be right that among a people thoroughly incorporated into one nation every district ought to have a proportional share in the government and that among independent and sovereign States, bound together by a simple league, the parties, however unequal in size ought to have an equal share in the common councils, it does not appear to be without some reason that in a compound republic, partaking both of the national and federal character, the government ought to be founded on a mixture of the principles of proportional and equal representation.

In a government characterized as both "national and federal," Madison argues, it only makes sense that the legislature represent both individuals and states. Senate apportionment thus gives institutional recognition to the "sovereignty remaining in the individual states" (Hamilton, Jay, and Madison 1987, 365). The record on this point remains ambiguous, however. The delegates chose to reject several measures that would have tied senators more closely to states—for example, they rejected proposals that senators be paid by state governments as well as that they be subject to recall by them. At minimum, it is clear from the Convention deliberations that the delegates intended and expected senators to be national legislators, not primarily representatives of state interests (Brant 1950; Malbin 1987; Rakove 1987; Swift 1996).

Even so, the "federalism" interpretation of Senate apportionment rests on more solid ground than the "minority protection" argument. Some of the delegates to the Constitutional Convention obviously subscribed to this view. The Supreme Court has given its imprimatur to this functionalist perspective, doing so in the same opinion requiring that all state legislatures be reapportioned according to a population-based standard (*Reynolds v. Sims,* 377 U.S. 533 [1964]). Because "political subdivisions of States—counties, cities, or whatever—never were and never have been considered sovereign entities," the Court argued, states may not employ apportionment schemes for their legislative chambers modeled on the federal Congress because they result "in the submergence of the equal population principle" (576). The Senate's basis of apportionment, by contrast, continues to symbolize "the heart of our constitutional system," at which "remains the concept of separate and distinct governmental entities which have delegated some, but not all, of their formerly held power to the single national government" (576).

Interpretations of Senate apportionment that emphasize its function in symbolizing the federal system, however, must be qualified by three complicating considerations. First, it is certainly not necessary that federal systems of government grant equal representation to each of the units represented in the federal chamber. The symbolic character of a legislative chamber that is designed to represent the members of the federation can be retained even when each member is not granted an equal share of representational power. Walter Bagehot (1873, 166) expressed this point clearly: "It is said that there must be in a federal government some institution, some authority, some body possessing a veto in which the separate States comprising the Confederation are all equal. I confess this doctrine has no self-evidence, and it is assumed, but not proved."

Most other countries with federal forms of government and bicameral legislatures do not grant full representational equality to the federal units in either chamber (Duchacek 1970, 244; Lijphart 1984, 174). Although it is common in federal systems worldwide for the less populous units to be over-represented in the federal chamber relative to their populations, no powerful legislature in the modern democratic world is as malapportioned by a population-based standard as the United States Senate (Lijphart 1984). The symbolic character of a federal chamber may be preserved at a lesser cost to the democratic value of "one person, one vote" by ensuring the representation of all the federal units but weighting their influence in the chamber, at least to some degree, according to their populations.

A second consideration qualifies this functionalist perspective on Senate apportionment. To contend, symbolically or otherwise, that states possess "residual sovereignty" as parties to an original federal compact is little more than a legal fiction. Beyond the original thirteen, most states never had any independent existence apart from the United States.[5] The territory out of which new states were formed was already claimed by the United States even before their formal organization as territories. Territories themselves were drawn by Congress, often with partisan and sectional goals in mind; territorial governors were appointed by Congress; and the laws passed by territorial assemblies were subject to revision by Congress. What "residual sovereignty" does Indiana, Arkansas, or Idaho have that must be represented in the United States Senate? Even the sovereignty of the original thirteen states before the ratification of the Constitution is open to dispute. The Supreme Court observed in U.S. v. Curtiss-Wright[6] that they always lacked one attribute of sovereignty—international standing in respect to foreign relations. The borders of the original thirteen states have even been changed since the adoption of the Constitution, with present-day Kentucky and West Virginia drawn out of the original Virginia and Maine carved from the original Massachusetts. In short, any functionalist perspective on Senate apportionment that emphasizes its role in expressing a fundamental truth about the nature of American federalism would be hard pressed to locate that truth in any real historical past. The federal nature of the American system is more muddled and less clear-cut than the proponents of this idea suggest.

Third, the Seventeenth Amendment creates additional complications for conceptualizing Senate apportionment as a federal symbol. The argument that the Senate expresses the federal nature of the American system must contend with the fact that since 1913 the Senate has represented the *people* of the states and not the states as states. Senators are no longer, in legal terms, representatives of the separate state *governments* within the federal framework. Direct election of senators instated a relationship of electoral accountability between senators and the people of the states, circumventing state governing institutions and thus obscuring much of the Senate's specifically *federal* character.

For these reasons, the Senate's symbolic value for expressing federal principles is lacking as a functionalist interpretation of its apportionment. Although Senate apportionment does give institutional expression to the federal character of the national government, these principles could theoretically be given symbolic life in the absence of the full representational equality of states, as in many federal systems elsewhere. In other words, the equal representation of states does symbolize the federal system, although it takes the symbolism further than the historical record warrants and is not a necessary means for accomplishing that end.

As we have shown, the two functionalist explanations examined here are inadequate to explain Senate apportionment. We now offer a path-dependent analysis that accounts for Senate apportionment as the outcome of a particular set of historical contingencies rather than of functional design.

Senate Apportionment as Panda's Thumb

A path-dependent analysis of political institutions begins by reconstructing the historical context of the political actors and reformers that shaped those institutions. In the case of Senate apportionment, we begin by recognizing that the delegates to the Constitutional Convention of 1787 did not deliberate in an institutional vacuum. To extend the analogy of the panda's thumb, equal apportionment was latent in the institutional "gene pool" from which they formed the Senate. First, bicameral institutions were the eighteenth-century norm, supported by a number of beliefs about their value and role. Second, the framers of the Constitution deliberated in the context of decisions they had already made at the Convention, decisions that made their eventual choice of equal Senate apportionment very likely. Third and most important, the broader preexisting institutional context—which dictated the voting rules at the Convention and demanded that the Constitution would eventually have to be ratified by the states—was biased in favor of equal state apportionment in the Senate.

Even a brief look back at the Convention deliberations calls into question the whole notion of the "purpose" of Senate apportionment. The records of these deliberations clearly reveal that the apportionment of the United States Senate did not result from the impartial application of any general principle—such as federalism or minority rights—but was instead the outcome of a clash between contending political interests within a particular institutional and ideological context. As Madison explains in *Federalist* 62, it was a product not of any theory of government but "of a spirit of amity and that mutual deference and concession which the peculiarity of our political situation rendered indispensable" (Hamilton, Jay, and Madison 1987, 365).

Bicameralism: the Institutional and Ideological Context

To say that Senate apportionment is the result of a "patchwork" of agreements and compromises (Roche 1961, 815), however, is not to say that the founders shared no common principles for constructing political institutions. The delegates to the Constitutional Convention held many similar beliefs concerning their hopes for a new national government and the proper structure of political institutions. These views influenced their eventual choice in favor of the equal apportionment of states in the Senate. The most important was their belief in the desirability of bicameral legislatures.

This consensus set the stage for the debate on Senate apportionment. The agreement on bicameralism was not the result of "splitting the difference" between two opposing camps, one favoring legislative apportionment based on population and the other in favor of state equality. Support for bicameralism came first, long before the debate over representation. As a general principle for constructing political institutions, bicameralism had as much appeal as the unanimously accepted notion of separation of powers (Banning 1995; Sundquist 1986). At the time of the Convention every state except Pennsylvania already had a bicameral legislature, and even Pennsylvania amended its constitution soon after 1787 to institute bicameralism. In short, the delegates did not deliberate in a theoretical vacuum: they met within an institutional and historical context where bicameral legislatures were the norm. The consensus was so broad that no debate was necessary before the Convention adopted the Virginia Plan's resolution that the "legislature ought to consist of two branches" (Bowen 1966, 48; Farrand 1966, 1:46; Main 1967; Wood 1969, 553).

The reason for the consensus was that the delegates to the Constitutional Convention were "educated in a culture that idealized the English constitution" (Banning 1995, 99; see also Swift 1996, 10–32; Wood 1969, 197–222). The political theory of the time taught the framers that the protection of liberty required that the interests of the few and the many be balanced. The English system of mixed government, with the interests of the many represented in the House of Commons and those of the few in the House of

Lords, was generally thought to be the best in the world. At the Convention, John Dickinson's frank desire to emulate the British model aroused no controversy: "In the formation of the Senate," he proposed, "we ought to carry it through such a refining process as will assimilate it as near as may be to the House of Lords in England" (Farrand 1966, 1:136).

Within the eighteenth-century logic of bicameralism, the primary purpose of the upper chamber was to serve as a check on the legislative excesses of the more democratic chamber. Whenever the delegates discussed the Senate, they would return to this logic. The most influential delegates to the Convention—including among others Madison, Dickinson, Randolph, Sherman, Wilson, General Pinckney, Morris, and Gerry—repeatedly affirmed this mixed-government view (Farrand 1966, 1:152, 136, 51, 234, 261, 137, 512, 155). The delegates did not see bicameralism, as we tend to do today, simply as a means of restraining legislative power generally, by slowing down the process and permitting a second chamber to review the work of the first. No one at the Convention, for example, praised the value of a House in auditing the work of a Senate. Madison stated this belief on June 7: "The use of the Senate is to consist in its proceedings with more coolness, with more system and with more wisdom than the popular branch" (1:152). Gouverneur Morris reiterated this position: the purpose of a second house, he stated, "was to check the precipitation, changeableness, and excesses of the first branch" (1:512).[7]

Why did the delegates fear that the House would be liable to "precipitation," "changeableness," and "excesses"? The simple answer is that they had in mind the troubling behavior of the popularly elected state legislatures. Shortly after independence, most of the state constitutions had been altered to strengthen the lower houses of the legislatures and to weaken the executives and the upper houses.[8] Constitutional changes like these "meant the absolute dominance of the legislature" in all of the states during the period of the Articles of Confederation, principally of the lower houses, where legislators were elected either annually or, in two states, every six months (Kramnick 1987, 22). As a result, during the financial crises that followed the end of the war, many of the state legislatures became dominated by debtor parties that produced a wide variety of redistributive legislation abrogating the rights of property, including inflationary paper money acts, stay laws deferring foreclosure on mortgages and other debts, and laws invalidating contracts and confiscating property (Banning 1995; Kramnick 1987, 16–31).

From a mixed-government perspective, these legislatures were representing "the many" instead of the whole. When Jefferson wrote that "173 despots would surely be as oppressive as one" he was referring to actions like these on the part of the state legislatures (Jefferson 1955, 120; cited in Kramnick

1987, 25). Echoing these concerns, Madison met with no dissent from other delegates when he stated at the Convention that the "interferences" with the "security of private rights, and the steady dispensation of Justice" that had been "practiced in the States . . . were evils which had more perhaps than any thing else produced this convention" (Farrand 1966, 1:134). The framers did not want to create a new national government that resembled these postrevolutionary state governments either in form or in practice. Because House members were to be popularly elected and to serve short terms of office, the framers feared that the House might engage in the same "schemes of injustice" prevalent in the states, as Madison called them in *Federalist* 10 (Hamilton, Jay, and Madison 1987, 128). In the Senate they hoped to create "a firm, wise and impartial body," less responsive to those short-term popular majorities that favored bold and unwise redistributive measures in response to economic crises—in other words, a check on "the many" represented in the House.

These ideological beliefs about bicameralism and the delegates' shared experiences with the state governments under the Articles provided common ground as they deliberated about the construction of the legislative branch.[9] Although the delegates disagreed about many details of the proposed national government—primarily about the scheme of representation in the national legislature—there was an existing consensus that the Senate should be a smaller, more distinguished, and less democratically responsive body than the House. This consensus structured all their deliberations concerning its construction.

Although these beliefs about bicameralism were not the immediate reason for their adoption of the Senate apportionment scheme, they were an important cause leading up to it. Proponents of equal state apportionment were able to use these beliefs to their advantage during the debate over the means of selecting senators, and this victory on Senate selection strengthened their hand in the debate over apportionment.

Selection of Senators

The method of selecting senators was a central problem for the delegates. The consensus vision of the Senate was as a small, independent body composed of wise, distinguished characters. The difficulty was how to create an institution that would embody this ideal. How could they ensure that people of this description would be selected to serve in the Senate? To whom, if anyone, would such legislators be accountable? The answer was by no means apparent. At times, as Rakove observes, the whole idea that "the Senate should embody wisdom and virtue and be above provincial concerns . . . risked ceasing to be a scheme of representation" (1987, 456). It was obvious to the delegates, however, that nothing approaching a replica of the House of Lords would be possible in the New World. "I revere the theory of the Brit. Govt. but we can't adopt it," observed Wilson, one of the most vocal of the many admirers of the British system of government at the Convention. Senators could not be selected as in the House of Lords because "we have no laws in favor of primogeniture—no distinction of families—the partition of Estates destroys the influence of the Few" (Farrand 1966, 1:159). There simply was no landed aristocracy to be represented in the Senate and serve as a counterweight to "the many" represented in the House.

The delegates seriously considered three alternatives for selecting senators: selection by state legislatures, selection by the House from persons nominated by the state legislatures, and direct election of senators in large, multistate districts. From the beginning, small-state delegates consistently preferred selection by state legislatures, because they perceived that this system would work to their advantage later in the debate over Senate apportionment. Madison, along with other large-state delegates, opposed this option and favored either of the other means.

Support for the selection of senators by state legislatures divided along the lines of state size because most delegates realized that an agreement to choose senators in this way would likely increase the representation of small states in the Senate. Why? If the state legislatures were to choose senators, it would be difficult to deny that every state must have at least one. Furthermore, if the principle of representation proportional to population was adhered to after allowing each state at least one senator, the Senate would need to be enlarged far beyond the size preferred by the delegates—who assumed that it needed to be small because a large body would tend to exhibit the kind of "passionate proceedings" they wanted to avoid (Farrand 1966, 1:51). Madison explained the problem on June 7:

> If the motion of Mr. Dickenson [in favor of selection by state legislatures] should be agreed to, we must either depart from the doctrine of proportional representation; or admit into the Senate a very large number of members. The first is inadmissible, being evidently unjust. The second is inexpedient. The use of the Senate is to consist in its proceeding with more coolness, with more system, & with more wisdom, than the popular branch. Enlarge their number and you communicate to them the vices which they are meant to correct. (1:151)

The average upper chamber in the states had only fifteen members and had historically served as an advisory body to the governors (Main 1967, 188). Clearly the delegates were thinking along these lines as they contemplated the composition of a national Senate. If they intended the Senate to be small, selection of senators by state legislatures was incompatible with the rule of representation proportional to population.[10]

The major problem for Madison, Wilson, and the other delegates opposing this method was that their proposals—selection by the House and direct election—did not fit well with the consensus vision of the Senate. It appears that Madison "knew better what he wanted to avoid than what he wanted to institute" (Rakove 1987, 456).

Randolph and Madison opened debate on Senate selection on May 31 by proposing in resolve 5 of the Virginia Plan that "the members of the second branch of the National Legislature ought to be elected by those of the first out of a proper number of persons nominated by the individual Legislatures" (Farrand 1966, 1:20). This proposal involved a "filtering" by which senators would be selected through the choices of two elite groups, state legislators and House members, thus ensuring the choice of wiser, more distinguished persons—or at minimum of persons respected by other political elites. This proposal became Madison's first major defeat at the Convention. Many delegates—not only delegates from the small states—rose to argue that this mode of selection would make senators "too dependent" on the first branch "and thereby destroy the end for which the Senate ought to be appointed" (1:59). This method appeared to contradict the theory behind bicameralism itself, for the Senate could not check the House if it was dependent on it.

After his first proposal went down to a swift 7–3 defeat, Madison's supporters were hard pressed to develop a persuasive argument that a second alternative, popular election of senators from large, multistate districts, would be in accordance with the consensus views about the proper role of the Senate. To no avail, Wilson called on Madison's "extended sphere" argument, contending that the larger electoral districts in the smaller Senate would themselves guarantee that senators would possess greater wisdom than House members. "There is no danger of improper election if made by large districts," argued Wilson, because "bad elections proceed from the smallness of the districts which give an opportunity to bad men to intrigue themselves into office" (Farrand 1966, 1:133). Again this method contradicted the consensus vision of the Senate, specifically that it should be less responsive to democratic majorities than the House. Taking advantage of this weakness, General Pinckney (a delegate who supported Madison on Senate apportionment) "differed from the gentlemen who thought that a choice by the people wd. be a better guard agst. bad measures, than by the Legislatures," by pointing out that "[a] majority of the people in S. Carolina were notoriously for paper money as a legal tender" (1:137).[11]

Madison's opponents, on the other hand, were much more successful in making a case on the commonly held principles of bicameralism that senators should be chosen by the state legislatures. After all, like the failed resolve 5 of the Virginia Plan, selection by state legislatures had the virtue, from a mixed-government perspective, of reserving the choice of senators to political elites without also making the Senate dependent on the House. Selection by state legislatures, they argued, would make the Senate independent of both the House and direct popular influence. In this spirit, even Elbridge Gerry of populous Massachusetts insisted that "the commercial & monied interest wd. be more secure in the hands of the State Legislatures than of the people at large" (Farrand 1966, 1:154).[12]

When the Convention returned to the issue for the last time on June 25, the delegates voted 9–2 (with only Virginia and Pennsylvania opposed) in favor of selection of senators by state legislatures.

This decision about Senate selection did, in fact, pave the way for the Convention to accept equal representation of states in the Senate, just as the small-state delegates had hoped and Madison and Wilson had feared. Madison was "deeply disappointed" by this decision (Banning 1995, 147), which he regarded as a turning point in the Convention.[13] After his defeat on Senate selection, Madison knew that the principle of representation according to population would likely be a casualty.

Senate Apportionment

The debate on representation was the most critical of the Convention, polarizing the delegates like no other issue (Birkby 1966, 127–28; Jillson 1988, 64–100). "The great difficulty lies in the affair of Representation," observed Madison, "and if this could be adjusted, all others would be surmountable" (Farrand 1966, 1:321). The controversy over representation, in turn, was fundamentally a debate over how to apportion the Senate. The clashes over the representation of slaves and House apportionment were minor, quickly resolved disputes compared with the six-week battle over Senate apportionment—the only issue that threatened to be fatal to the Convention.

From the outset Madison sought to do away with the scheme of representation used under the Articles of Confederation—the equal state vote—and to institute a population-based system of representation. To his mind the equal representation of states was "confessedly unjust," an egregious departure from fair principles, and should not be admitted into a new national government (Farrand 1966, 1:464). Hamilton articulated similar objections to equal state apportionment: "There can be no truer principle than this—that every individual of the community at large has an equal right to the protection of government. If therefore three states contain a majority of the inhabitants of America, ought they to be governed by a minority?" (1:473). Proponents of equal apportionment responded with legal arguments, maintaining that under the existing government states stood as sovereign equals and that any proposed union must continue to respect this fact (Storing 1981).

These principled legal and theoretical objections on either side of the debate were not, however, the real source of the controversy. The debate was not an abstract one over the best way to construct institutions to respect federal principles, democratic principles, or national unity. The dispute over representation became fierce and intractable because power interests were unambiguously in conflict, as is evident when we consider the principal figures in the debate. The leaders of the effort to abolish equal state representation and institute a population-based system were delegates from the two most populous states of Virginia and Pennsylvania, namely James Madison and James Wilson. Similarly, the leaders of the coalition favoring equal apportionment were all delegates from the smaller states of Connecticut, Delaware, and New Jersey, principally Roger Sherman, John Dickinson, and William Patterson. Nothing less than the distribution of power over the new government was at stake. Hamilton put the matter in stark terms:

> It has been said that if the smaller States renounce their *equality,* they renounce at the same time their *liberty.* The truth is that it is a contest for power, not for liberty. . . .The State of Delaware having 40,000 souls will *lose power,* if she has 1/10 only of the votes allowed to Pa. having 400,000: but will the people of Del. *be less free,* if each citizen [of Delaware] has an equal vote with each citizen of Pa.? (Farrand 1966, 1:466)

Even a proponent of equal state representation conceded that the small-state delegates were motivated by their own states' particular interests rather than by an adherence to principle: "Can it be expected that the small states will act from pure disinterestedness?" asked Bedford of Delaware during a particularly heated debate. "Are we to act with greater purity than the rest of mankind?" (Farrand 1966, 1:491).

The intensity of this conflict over Senate apportionment may seem surprising, given that no political issues united large states against the small states. Madison made this point repeatedly: It was "not necessary to secure the small States agst. the large ones," Madison argued, because the large states did not share a set of interests opposed to those of the less populous states.

> Was a combination of the large ones [states] dreaded? This must arise either from some interest common to Va., Mast., & Pa. & distinguishing them from the other states (or from the mere circumstance of similarity of size). Did any such common interest exist? . . . In point of manners, Religions and the other circumstances, which sometimes beget affection between different communities, they were not more

assimilated than the other states. In point of the staple productions they were as dissimilar as any three other States in the Union. The Staple of Masts. was *fish,* of Pa. *flower,* of Va. *Tobo.* Was a Combination to be apprehended from the mere circumstance of equality of size? Experience suggested no such danger. (Farrand 1966, 1:447)

The large states were different from one another in every important respect and were more likely to be rivals than to unite to oppress the small ones. In short, according to Madison and others, the small states had nothing to fear.

Nevertheless, the delegates from small states maintained consistently throughout the Convention that they would never consent to a new national government except on the condition of equal state representation in the Senate. What was their motive? Foremost, it is clear that they were simply resisting efforts to reduce their power and influence over the national government. The delegates from the small states were disinclined to relinquish the power their states already possessed under the existing government. Even so, the controversy over Senate representation drew some of its bitterness and intensity from a much older conflict among the states, the conflict over ownership of the western lands, which had been the subject of the single greatest contention in the Continental Congress. Ever since 1775, the "four-sided states" with their fixed boundaries had been intensely envious of the ever growing "three-sided states," with their increasing wealth and their claims of "indefinite rights of western expansion by reason of colonial charters" (Brant 1948, 89–103). During this period four-sided states, mainly Maryland, Delaware, and New Jersey, united against three-sided states—Virginia, in particular, which at that time claimed today's Virginia, West Virginia, and Kentucky and much of the Northwest Territory—by insisting that the unsettled lands be shared among all the states.[14]

These old battles over ownership of western lands were revived during the debate over Senate apportionment at the Constitutional Convention. The small states were hemmed in from future population and economic growth for as long as the economy continued to be principally agrarian, and they resented the populous states for their wide expanses of uninhabited land, whose sale could enrich state treasuries and attract new settlers. As soon as Patterson opened debate on Senate apportionment on June 9, Judge Brearly of New Jersey explained that he favored the equal apportionment of states in the Senate, even though "he would not say" that it was "fair . . . that Georgia should have an equal vote with Virginia." "What was the remedy?" he asked rhetorically; "only that a map of the U.S. be spread out, that all the existing boundaries be erased, and that a new partition of the whole be made into 13 equal parts" (Farrand 1966, 1:177). Read of Delaware made the matter even more explicit when he complained that "particular states" had appropriated the "common interest in the Western lands": "Let justice be done on this head," he demanded, and then "the smaller States who had been injured would listen then to those ideas of just representation" that the large states favored (1:405). Proposals like Read's and Brearly's illuminate the source of the small states' fears and jealousies that are so evident in these debates, even though, as delegates from the large states observed, they were utterly impractical and unrealistic as solutions to the problem of Senate representation.

Effect of Voting Procedure on Apportionment

Madison and the large-state delegates faced a distinct disadvantage as they sought to institute a population-based system of representation in both chambers of the new national legislature: votes at the Convention were taken by state. Despite the weakness of the Articles of Confederation for other national purposes, they did allocate power among the states in a particular way—equally. Voting at the Constitutional Convention followed the rule established in the Articles of Confederation and the precedent set in the Continental Congress. As a result, one basic political fact stood in the way of Madison's initiatives: only a minority of states would have benefited from population-based apportionment in both chambers. After all, a majority of the total population of the thirteen states in 1787 resided in just four states. The three most populous—Virginia, Massachusetts, and Pennsylvania— made up nearly 45 percent of the total population.[15] Observing this, Patterson warned Madison that ten of the thirteen states would be opposed to apportioning the Senate by population (Banning 1987, 116).

Madison recognized that the voting procedures at the Convention were biased against his proposals. Before delegates from a majority of states had arrived in Philadelphia, several delegates from Pennsylvania suggested that the Convention should institute a rule for voting that would be more favorable to proposals for population-based representation in both chambers of the national legislature. Gouverneur Morris, Robert Morris, and others submitted that "the large States should unite in firmly refusing to the small states an equal vote, as unreasonable, and as enabling the small States to negative every good system of Government, which must in the nature of things, be founded on a violation of that equality" (Farrand 1966, 1:11). Fearing that a confrontation over the rules just as the Convention was beginning its work "would beget fatal altercations between the large & small states," Madison persuaded the other large-state delegates not to take such a confrontational stance. Instead he proposed that "it would be easier to prevail" on the small states "to give up their equality for the sake of an effective government" during "the course of the deliberations" than to ask them "to throw themselves on the mercy of the large states" at the outset (1:11).

Why did Madison think he would be able to prevail on the representation issue during "the course of the deliberations," even given the voting rules at the Convention? The reason was that voting by state did not produce a natural majority on either side because two of the least populous states were not represented at the Convention. First, Rhode Island had not appointed any delegates and was never represented in its deliberations. Second, even though New Hampshire had appointed delegates, the state legislature had not yet appropriated the funds to send them to Philadelphia; they were very tardy, arriving a full week after the issue of Senate representation had been resolved.

Madison's strategy was to build majority support in favor of a population-based representation by uniting the delegates from the populous states with those from states that expected eventually to become populous. Like most people at the time, Madison believed the South and West would soon outstrip the North and the East in population growth. The conventional wisdom on this matter was, as Butler of South Carolina explained, that "the people & strength of America are evidently bearing Southwardly & S. westwdly" (Farrand 1966, 1:605). Using these expectations, Madison explained his strategy in a letter to George Washington: "To the northern states," an abolition of state equality "will be recommended by their present populousness; to the southern by their expected advantage in this respect. The lesser states must in every event yield to the predominant will" (cited in Brant 1950, 33).

To illustrate Madison's strategy, table 2.3 groups states according to whether they would have been better or worse off under a population-based apportionment in 1787 and whether they expected high or low population growth over time.[16]

This table reveals that Madison's best-case scenario was that he would win the support of delegates from six to eight states. He clearly expected to win all the states with high growth expectations, regardless of whether they would initially be better off under a population-based system—Virginia, Pennsylvania, Massachusetts, North Carolina, South Carolina, and Georgia. He may also have hoped to gain the votes of delegates from New York and Maryland, states that initially would have been marginally better off under a population-based system of representation even though the general assumption of the time was that they could not expect great population growth (Swift 1996).[17] Certainly, however, Madison had little reason to expect that he could gain the votes of three states represented at the Convention: Connecticut, New Jersey, and Delaware.

At first Madison's strategy looked as though it might succeed. He had little difficulty persuading the Convention to agree to a population-based apportionment in the House. Clearly the common belief that the House should represent "the many" played an important role here. Even in the debate over representation, a conflict much more about interests than about ideas, the consensus about the purpose of bicameralism structured the deliberations.

Table 2.3 State Interests with Respect to Senate Apportionment in 1787

	Better off under a Population-Based Apportionment	Better off under an Equal State Apportionment
High growth expectations	Virginia, Pennsylvania, Massachusetts	North Carolina, South Carolina, Georgia
Low growth expectations	New York, Maryland	Connecticut, New Jersey, Delaware New Hampshire,* Rhode Island **

* Not represented at the Convention for the debate on representation.
** Never represented at the Convention.

From the start there was little question that the Convention would agree to a population-based apportionment in the first branch of the legislature. Even the small-state delegates consistently affirmed that they would agree to the measure provided they retained an equal vote in the Senate. Madison's proposal early in the Convention (June 11) that representation in the House be based on an "equitable ratio" and "not according to the rule established in the articles of Confederation" garnered a strong 7–3 majority, with only New Jersey, Delaware, and New York opposed. Even the staunch small-state advocate Roger Sherman of Connecticut spoke in favor of the resolution to apportion the House based on population (Farrand 1966, 1:196).

Senate apportionment was a different matter. On the first vote taken at the Convention, Madison's proposal in favor of proportional representation in the Senate garnered six votes (the states expecting high population growth from table 2.3) against the small states' five (all of those expecting low population growth). Madison's narrow majority did not end the matter. The Convention's rules allowed the delegates to raise the same measure repeatedly, even after votes had been taken. A single vote yielding a margin of victory this narrow was not decisive enough to induce the small-state delegates to concede defeat, especially considering that they expected another vote in their favor once the appointed delegates from New Hampshire arrived. They immediately began to organize a counterstrategy.

The New Jersey Plan

Only four days after their narrow (6–5) defeat, a coalition of the delegates who had voted against Madison's proposal for a population-based representation in the Senate began a counteroffensive by introducing the New Jersey

Plan. The plan proposed retaining the unicameral Congress existing under the Articles, with its equal state apportionment, and only strengthening the national government modestly by adding a plural federal executive and a supreme court. Although some scholars have interpreted the New Jersey Plan as a "states rights" alternative to the Virginia Plan, it is clear that its quickly assembled proposals did not signal any sincere ideological opposition to Madison's centralizing goals (Banning 1987; Brant 1950; Kramnick 1987; Levy 1969; McDonald 1979; Roche 1961). With only a few exceptions, mainly Robert Yates and John Lansing of New York and Luther Martin of Maryland, the delegates were cohesive in favoring a strong national government. The New Jersey Plan's proposals "did not represent the real desires of any of their framers" (Banning 1987, 120); instead, they were a hodge-podge designed to construct a coalition out of the small minority of delegates who were opposed to a strong national government and the delegates from small states who favored a stronger national government while opposing any change in the apportionment of representatives under the Articles. As Charles Pinckney observed at the Convention: "Give New Jersey an equal vote and she will dismiss her scruples and concur in the national system" (cited in Kramnick 1987, 33).

In its broad outlines, the New Jersey Plan was little more than a revision of the existing Articles of Confederation. As such the plan contained a threat to Madison and the other large-state delegates: the small states would not support a substantial strengthening of the national government unless they were guaranteed an equal vote in the Senate. Most of the small-state delegates were favorably disposed toward Madison's centralizing initiatives and had supported the resolutions of his Virginia Plan. Confronting Madison, Dickinson explained the situation: "You see the consequence of pushing things too far," he admonished. "Some of the members from the small states . . . are friends to a good National Government; but we would sooner submit to a foreign power, than submit to be deprived of an equality of suffrage, in both branches of the legislature" (Farrand 1966, 1:242; cited in Rakove 1987, 439). The New Jersey Plan had the desired effect. Madison records that its introduction began "to produce serious anxiety for the result of the Convention" (1:242). It made the small-state delegates' intentions clear: the equal state vote in the Senate was their condition for supporting a new, stronger national government. They would not consent on any other terms. "Everything," Roger Sherman insisted, "depends on this" (1:201).

The Great Compromise

For nearly another month after the introduction of the New Jersey Plan, the delegates battled over Senate representation, accomplishing little. The Convention could not turn to other matters until this issue was settled. No one wanted to discuss what powers the new government would have until they had reached an agreement on who would control it. What happened to resolve this contentious issue? The name we give to the final agreement, "the Great Compromise," is a misnomer. Neither side truly compromised on the fundamental issue of Senate representation. No one ever doubted that the Convention would adopt population-based representation in the House; there was never even a close vote on the matter. The one compromise proposal that the small states offered to gain the large states' acceptance of equal apportionment in the Senate—that the House should originate all money bills, leaving the Senate with only the power to vote them up or down—was, in the eyes of the delegates from the populous states, no concession at all (Farrand 1:529, 544). When this "compromise" proposal came up for a vote, the delegates from the populous states voted against it (1:539).

The Convention agreed to grant states equal representation in the Senate because Madison's large-state bloc simply collapsed. In the end the small states won when two of the four delegates from Massachusetts, along with the North Carolina delegation, defected and joined the small states' side. They did so because they became convinced that the work of the Convention would otherwise fail. How did they come to this conclusion?

Over time, the debate on representation had become increasingly heated and bitter. None of the principal figures appeared willing to offer any concession, and leading delegates on both sides began threatening to walk out. Gunning Bedford of Delaware shocked the Convention by declaring that "the large states dared not dissolve the confederation" by establishing a new government without the small states' consent because "if they do, the small ones will find some foreign ally of more honor and good faith, who will take them by the hand and do them justice" (Farrand 1966, 1:492).

On their part, members of the large-state coalition threatened to do just what Bedford said they dared not do: go outside the Convention by agreeing to a new national government among themselves and then force the small states to go along with it. Madison explained that he saw two alternatives: "departing from justice in order to conciliate the smaller States" or "displeasing these [small states] by justly gratifying the larger states and the majority of the people" (Farrand 1966, 1:527–28). Given these alternatives, he "could not hesitate as to the option he ought to make": he would "pursue a plan . . . which would be espoused & supported by the enlightened and impartial part of America." In other words, he would unite the large states without the support of the small states. After all, he "had nothing to fear" from such a course because he did not believe that any of the small states "would brave the consequences of seeking her fortunes apart from the other States" (1:528). Eventually "all the other States would by degrees accede" to a "government founded on just principles" (1:529). Gouverneur Morris made Madison's threat even more explicit: "This Country must be united. If persuasion does not unite it, the sword will. . . .The stronger party will then make traytors of the weaker; and the Gallows & Halter will finish the work of the sword" (1 : 530).

These threats disturbed many delegates. All along, they knew that their proposals would eventually have to be ratified in the states. Rumors were already spreading across New England that "people were to be called on to take arms to impose the new government" (Brant 1950, 93). Although the procedure for ratification that the Convention would later adopt would not demand unanimity as was officially required to amend the Articles of Confederation, the delegates must have anticipated that the support of a super-majority of states would be necessary for a smooth and orderly transition to a new form of government. As a result, even if Madison was able to hold together his six-state coalition in favor of proportional representation in the Senate, the delegates could legitimately be skeptical that the Constitution would gain ratification by enough states to ensure its peaceful adoption (Roche 1961).

The Massachusetts delegates appeared particularly shaken by the threats to go outside the Convention. They had more to fear than most from a failure of the Constitutional Convention. The anxiety caused by Shay's Rebellion in the fall and winter of 1786 was, after all, one of the most important causes of the Constitutional Convention. Government had broken down in western Massachusetts in 1774, and ever since then the state had "lived under a series of mob-like committees and conventions" (Wood 1969, 327). As the Convention seemed on the verge of dissolution, the delegates from Massachusetts began to paint a grim picture of the consequences should it fail. During one of the many heated debates on Senate apportionment, Rufus King professed that "his feelings were more harrowed & his fears more agitated for his Country than he could express" because "he conceived this to be the last opportunity of providing for its liberty & happiness" (Farrand 1966, 1 : 489−90). "Something must be done" pleaded Elbridge Gerry, begging the delegates to consider "the State we should be thrown into by the failure of the Union" (1 : 515). In the end, Massachusetts delegates Gerry and Caleb Strong voted in favor of equal apportionment in the Senate, dividing the Massachusetts delegation against King and Gorham, who opposed it. Later, at the Massachusetts ratifying convention, Strong explained that he had voted in favor of the measure because "the Convention would have broke up if it had not been agreed to" (3 : 261−62).

North Carolina's defection is not surprising either. Even though they voted in favor of it until July 7, the delegates from North Carolina never seemed strongly committed to population-based representation in the Senate. Although they were optimistic about the prospects for their state's future population growth, the choice between an equal state vote and a Senate apportioned by population made little difference for their representation in the first Senate: in a Senate of twenty-six members, they would have received two senators either way.[18] Of the North Carolina delegates, only Hugh Williamson, the informal leader of the delegation, and Col. William Davie participated in the debate, and they did so rarely and with ambivalence. Davie expressed concern about proportional representation in the Senate as early as the end of June, arguing that it would mean a Senate that was too large because "it was impossible that so numerous a body could possess the activity and other qualities required in it" (Farrand 1966, 1:488). On July 5, Williamson let the large-state delegates know that he would not join them in any movement to take the matter of Senate apportionment outside the Convention.[19] Like the Massachusetts delegates, the North Carolina delegates became convinced that the small states "could not be reconciled any other way" and were unwilling to force the issue on them (3:341).[20]

The decisive vote on Senate apportionment was taken on July 16, the small-state coalition winning 5−4 with Massachusetts divided. The narrow margin makes the vote seem closer than it actually was. Yates and Lansing had just walked out of the Convention, but they would have cast New York's vote in favor of equal state apportionment had they been there.[21] In addition, had the vote been delayed just eight more days until the New Hampshire delegates arrived, the small-state margin would have been wider. Just before the final vote James Wilson, anticipating defeat, observed bitterly that the large states had been beaten by the voting rules at the Convention: "Our Constituents had they voted as their representatives did, would have stood as 2/3 agst. the equality, and 1/3 only in favor of it. This fact would ere long be known, and it will appear that this fundamental point has been carried by 1/3 agst. 2/3" (Farrand 1966, 2:4).

Conclusion

We have argued that the Constitutional Convention's adoption of equal apportionment for states in the Senate is best viewed as the result of several historical contingencies rather than as the product of functional design. We first evaluated the leading functionalist explanations of Senate apportionment: equal state representation as a protection for minorities against majority tyranny and as an expression of federal principles. Finding these functional interpretations inadequate, we turned to a examination of the Constitutional Convention to uncover the historical reasons for the adoption of equal state representation.

One key point to keep in mind from this historical presentation is that the equal representation of states was not central to the framers' vision of the Senate. Their guiding vision was of a small, elite body, relatively independent of popular majorities. The difficulty was that there was no consensus on how to put this vision into practice. This problem created an opportunity for the small-state delegates to press for equal state representation and thus to preserve the power their states had enjoyed under the Articles. After the delegates ruled out the large-state proposals—direct election of senators and selection by the House—only appointment by the state legislatures remained a viable option. That mode of selecting senators, however, implied that every state legislature would select at least one senator, which in turn conflicted with the requirement that the Senate be small. Once the delegates had agreed to selection of senators by the state legislatures, the large states were strongly disadvantaged in the matter of Senate apportionment.

Although equal representation of states was not central to the framers' shared vision of the Senate, it became the pivotal issue of the Convention. Given the background consensus on bicameralism—an important part of which was the idea that the House should be a democratically responsive body closely connected to the people—there was little question that the Convention would agree to a population-based apportionment in the first branch of the legislature. As a consequence, the small-state delegates were never able to put together a coalition large enough to pose a credible threat to population-based representation in the House. But when it came to the composition of the upper chamber, which was supposed to act as a check on the democratic lower chamber, the specific institutional and political context of the Constitutional Convention favored those contending for equality of state representation in the Senate. That states already had equal votes at the Convention, combined with the need for state-level ratification of the proposed Constitution, made it very unlikely that a population-based apportionment would prevail. In this sense the "apportionment" of votes at the Convention carried a procedural bias in favor of equal state representation.

The need for ratification in the states created an even greater bias against those favoring population-based representation in the Senate. The delegates' desire for peaceful acceptance of the Constitution meant they needed a supermajority of states to ratify it. Clearly the delegates from Massachusetts and North Carolina were unwilling to risk thwarting the strong and uncompromising preferences of the small-state delegates. Thus, despite the ability of Madison and others to call on principles of fairness in favor of population-based representation, both procedurally and politically they were at a distinct disadvantage.

Today Senate apportionment is best understood as the product of the collision of particular sets of political interests within a specific institutional and ideological context. The functionalist justifications offered for Senate apportionment are both flawed and ahistorical. They describe neither the functions that Senate apportionment currently performs in American government nor the reasons the framers adopted it at the Constitutional Convention. Equal state apportionment was accepted not because it was an integral part of the framers' shared vision for the body, but because it was the price of union.

Equal state apportionment persists not because it serves any current function, but as a path-dependent consequence of this initial agreement more than two hundred years ago. Over time the Senate has evolved away from the framers' vision of the body in many other ways. By founding era standards, the Senate has become a large legislative body. The Seventeenth Amendment made the institution more democratically responsive, directly accountable to the people just as the House is. Today the Senate is an outward-looking, active legislative body, very different from the small, elite, checking and advisory body that the framers envisioned (Swift 1996). One thing that has not changed, however, is its basis of apportionment. In this sense Senate apportionment is the "panda's thumb."

The underlying question for the rest of this book is, How far does the panda's thumb analogy apply? How does equal apportionment—which is all too often simply taken as a given—affect the institution more broadly, and are these effects, like the panda's thumb, less than optimal? Throughout our study we explore how Senate apportionment shapes the contemporary Senate as a legislative and representative institution—how it affects representational relationships, Senate elections, the strategic behavior of senators, and public policy. In the next chapter we begin by examining the way Senate apportionment shapes the most fundamental aspect of any representative institution—the linkages between representatives and their constituents.

3

The Representational Experience

In their wildest dreams the framers of the Constitution never imagined that the population of the United States would someday approach 300 million. Nor did they imagine that a single state—on the Pacific coast of the continent, no less—would have a population almost ten times that of the entire country at the first census. Virginia, the California of the colonial era, had fewer than 700,000 people, roughly equivalent to the population of Montana in 1990. The entire country in 1790 had roughly the same population as Connecticut today. Although these numbers now sound small to us, the "large" population of the republic created with the adoption of the Constitution was very controversial during the founding period. Conventional wisdom of the time held that it was impossible to represent such a large, heterogeneous population in one legislature.

The large numbers represented in the new federal Congress posed a difficult political challenge to the framers during the ratification debates. Their political opponents, the Anti-Federalists, argued time and again that the Constitution provided for too few legislators to represent the people of the United States. The prominent Anti-Federalist "Brutus," for example, argued that the scheme provided in the Constitution would not constitute a "true" representation, a legislature "like the people" (Brutus 124). Instead, Brutus concluded that "the natural aristocracy of the country will be elected. . . . The great body of the yeoman of the country cannot expect that any of their order in this assembly—the station will be too elevated for them to aspire to—the distance between the people and their representatives will be so very great" (125–26).

The Anti-Federalists forced the advocates of ratification to respond to criticisms like these concerning the "distance between the people and their representatives." So intense was the criticism of the large legislative districts the Constitution would establish that James Madison observed, "Scarce any article, indeed, in the whole Constitution seems to be rendered more worthy of attention by the . . . force of argument with which it has been assailed" (Hamilton, Jay, and Madison 1987, 335). Attempting to avert criticism of this kind, George Washington even intervened late in the Constitutional Convention in support of reducing from 40,000 to 30,000 the minimum number of constituents per representative in the House. During the ratification debates, Madison defended the representative scheme in the Constitution in several of his most famous *Federalist* essays, arguing in favor of "distance" between the people and their representatives (E. Lee 1997). Turning conventional wisdom on its head in *Federalist* 56, Madison even argued that a single individual could be sufficient to represent an entire state in the legislature.

The acceptance of Madison's new wisdom has been so complete that most people today give little thought to the distance that constituency size creates between representatives and their constituents. As the nation's population has grown, all House and Senate constituencies have, of course, grown as well. Because all House districts have roughly the same population, however, House members are all similarly situated as they engage in presentation of self and adopt various "home styles" to minimize the distance between themselves and their constituents (Fenno 1978). The problems senators face in overcoming this representational distance, on the other hand, are more varied. In chapter 1 we demonstrated how the equal representation of states has affected the Senate's representative character over time: Senate apportionment's deviation from the principle of one person, one vote has increased as the nation has grown, and it reached its all-time high after the 1990 census. States today vary more in population than ever before. This increased variation in Senate constituency size means that senators, unlike House members, are not similarly situated with respect to representational distance.

Although political scientists are attuned to many of the contextual factors that shape representational behavior, they have given little attention to the one that caused greatest concern during the founding era—constituency size. In *Home Style* (1978), the most prominent work on representational relationships, Richard Fenno demonstrated how differences among congressional districts—their heterogeneity, their compactness, their rural or urban character, among others—all affect the home styles House members adopt. In one sense, however, they all face the same constituency context: House districts are relatively equal in population. As a result, although Fenno's study of House members offers many important insights for comprehending representational relationships in the Senate and in other legislative institutions, it understandably cannot tell us about the effects of constituency size. Yet this may well be the most important contextual variable for understanding representational relationships.

Compared with our knowledge of representation in the House, we know much less about the linkages between senators and their constituents. We contend that one must take constituency size into account to understand these linkages. The political science literature on the Senate, however, offers little on constituency size and representation. Ironically, Senate constituencies are usually described in an undifferentiated way when compared with House districts. The conventional wisdom holds that senators have larger, more heterogeneous constituencies than House members and, accordingly, are not as close to their constituents. At minimum this generalization is overstated. It ignores the fact that many senators' constituencies are equal in size to a House district. Fourteen senators currently represent states with only a single House district. If House members have closer relationships with their constituents than senators because they represent smaller, more homogeneous populations, then senators who represent single-district states have closer relationships with their constituents than do senators from more populous states. More generally, the representational relationships of senators and their constituents should vary with state population.

In this chapter we examine the effect of state population on what we call the "representational experience" of senators and their constituents and discuss its implications for understanding the Senate as a representative institution. The representational experience refers to the complex interactions between senators and their constituents, including constituents' expectations and evaluations of senators, the quantity and quality of senator-constituent contact, and senators' accessibility to constituents and interest groups. In one sense, then, the concept is similar to Fenno's home style in that it focuses on variation in representatives' behavior. Like Fenno, we look to contextual differences in constituencies to account for this variation. In another sense, however, the concept is an extension and complement to home style because it takes into account the behavior of constituents as well as that of representatives. In operationalizing the representational experience, we look at the linkages between representatives and constituents from the point of view of both.

Organization of the Chapter

We hypothesize that much of the variation in the representational experiences of senators and their constituents can be explained by variation in constituency size. First we present evidence drawn from interviews and from the National Election Study (NES) Senate Election Study (Inter-University Consortium 1993) surveys that constituents' expectations of senators are shaped by constituency size. Our interviews reveal that senators from small-population states believe their constituents expect much more personal contact with them than do constituents in large-population states. We then analyze constituents' expectations about senators' behavior. Although constituency size does not affect the way constituents rank the importance of various activities that senators engage in, constituents' behavior in contacting their senators is affected by state population, in terms of both frequency and their reasons for doing so.

Second, we examine the quality and quantity of senators' contact with their constituents from the perspective of both. We find that the descriptions senators give of the quality of their interactions differ depending on state population. We also discover that constituents in less populous states report higher levels of contact with their senators than do those in larger states. In the least populous states, in fact, we find that they have more contact with their senators than with their House members.

Third, we assess the effect of constituency size on evaluations of senators. Constituents in less populous states evaluate their senators more favorably than those in larger states. Our interviews reveal that senators themselves are aware of the relationship between constituency size and constituents' evaluations and offer several explanations for it. In this context we examine constituency size as a constraint on fourteen particular senators, showing that it is a more important influence on their representational relationships than even their own individual preferences and representational styles.

Finally, we explore the effect of state representation on interest groups' access to senators. Lobbyists and other participants in the legislative process report that it is easier to obtain access to senators who represent less populous states and that lobbying contact with them is often more effective than contact with senators who represent larger states. In each of these four ways, then, we find that the representational experiences of senators and their constituents are fundamentally shaped by constituency size.

In evaluating the effect of constituency size on certain aspects of the representational experience, we consider two other variables that may be important: institutional context and the electoral cycle. The institutional differences between the House and Senate may have an effect. If institutional context is more important than constituency size for understanding representation, then the representational experiences of senators and their constituents should be similar regardless of population and, as a group, different from those of representatives and their constituents in the House. But if constituency size is more important than institutional context for understanding representation, the experiences of senators and their constituents in small-population states should be similar to those in the House and very different from those of senators and constituents in large-population states. The

Senate's staggered six-year election cycle may also exercise an independent effect. Taking this into account, we consider whether the proximity of the next election explains more about the character of the representational relationship than does constituency size.

Previous Research

As we noted above, political scientists have given little attention to variation in constituency size and its effect on Senate representation, and what information is available is indirect. Fenno's book on Sen. Mark Andrews (R–N.D.), for example, details how the small-state context conditioned Andrews's behavior, offering insight into the behavior of a senator who represented the same constituency in the Senate that he represented in the House (Fenno 1992). Because the book focuses on a single senator, however, we do not know whether Andrews is typical of small-state senators generally or whether Pete Domenici (R–N.M.)—another Fenno subject and in some ways Andrews's antithesis—better typifies the small-state senator (Fenno 1991). Studies of single senators, by definition, simply cannot tell us which is more important for understanding Senate representation—the personalities and preferences of individual senators or their constituency context.

Similarly, in *Senators on the Campaign Trail* Fenno deals with constituency context across states only elliptically, focusing instead on the cycles of election and governing for particular senators. He does, however, observe a pattern common to Sens. Claiborne Pell (D–R.I.) and David Pryor (D–Ark.), both of whom, throughout their political careers, emphasized authenticity, consistency, and good character in presenting themselves to their constituents (Fenno 1996, 324). Although he notes that Pell and Pryor represented small states, Fenno does not feel comfortable generalizing from these two cases. Nevertheless, his observations of individual senators from states of different sizes suggest that state population affects senator-constituency linkages.

The congressional elections literature pays some attention to the relationship between state population and Senate elections, focusing primarily on how population affects incumbency advantage (Abramowitz 1980; Abramowitz and Segal 1992; Hibbing and Brandes 1983; Krasno 1994). Analyses of the Senate Election Study surveys have shown that senator-constituent contact levels vary with state population (Hibbing and Alford 1990; Krasno 1994). But these studies have a different purpose than our inquiry does. Their concern is with the effect of senator-constituency contact on incumbents' reelection success. State size is of interest to them only in this narrow context.[1] We, on the other hand, view constituency size as central to understanding the representational experience as a whole. Although some of our analyses complement these earlier findings, representation—not reelection—is our focus.

In the end we are faced with a literature that only touches on constituency size and representation. In a political climate where national legislators are constantly criticized as being distant and "out of touch," the silence of political scientists on the matter is particularly striking. The framers and their political opponents were keenly aware of the connection between representative "distance" and constituency size. Were they right to be concerned? Does constituency size matter for representation? The unprecedented scale of variation in Senate constituency size today makes the answers to these questions all the more consequential.

Expectations of the Representational Experience

Constituents' expectations are a central component of the representational experience. These expectations, after all, define the kind of representational relationship senators must build in order to be successful. What do constituents expect from their senators? How do senators perceive these expectations? Are constituents' expectations and senators' perceptions of them conditioned by constituency size? We begin by considering what Fenno (1978) called "the perceptual question": How do senators themselves see the expectations constituents have of them? Do they believe that constituency size affects these expectations? To answer this question, we interviewed a number of senators and former senators, as well as other participants in the policy process including Senate staff persons and lobbyists. We asked senators broad questions about the choices they make in allocating their time, how they see their jobs in comparison with other senators, and the demands constituents place on them.

Senators' Perceptions

If constituency size does influence representational experiences in the ways we expect, then senators themselves, as well as those who have regular contact with them, should to some extent be aware of these effects. Our interviews reveal that senators do in fact perceive that constituency size shapes their constituents' expectations. Put simply, senators believe that constituents in less populous states expect to have closer and more frequent contact with their senators than do those in larger states. As one recently retired senator from a sparsely populated western state put it, "In [his state] they expect to see you. I guess they never see you in New York. If I'm not available, they say, 'That SOB's forgotten us!'" A former senator from the Midwest expressed the same sentiment when he contended there was more constituent demand "to see you in small states than in large ones. I see all the constituent groups who come to Washington. In large states they don't expect to see the senator." A third senator from a small-population state said, "You can get lost in a large state easier."

Some senators qualified their views. One former senator argued that senators from populous states have more staff and that their larger staffs effectively compensate for what the senator cannot do personally: "I looked at Javits. He had eighty people on his staff. Most of them were doing some aspect of casework. There were probably not more than ten people supporting his legislative effort." Similarly, another small-state senator argued that populous-state senators could still give personal attention despite the huge difference in the number of constituents: "If it's D'Amato or Moynihan, they might get the Dirksen Room for a meeting with two hundred constituents. With me I might meet with three people in my office. It's in the scale. . . . But Boxer or Pete Wilson do the same thing." A chief of staff to a former Senate leader agreed with this portrayal, saying that whether constituency service was done by the senator personally or by staff made no difference to the senator. She did note, however, that constituency size does make a difference to the constituents who seek personal attention from their senator.

What is clear from our interviews is that senators view representational relationships as being much more personal in small-population states. One senator compared his own experiences representing a small-population state with the relationships between California's senators and their constituents: There are "so many more people and organizations to pay attention to. You haven't got the person-to-person relationship." Another small-state senator claimed, "I read a good deal of my mail and answered some of it myself. In a small state you could do that." An aide to a long-retired small-state senator claimed that the senator "would get fifty letters a day from [his state]. And he'd dictate answers every day first thing." By contrast, several interviewees claimed that Barbara Boxer (D-Calif.) runs a round-the-clock operation to keep pace with the enormous flow of mail she receives from California. Although constituents in California still receive responses from their senator's office, they would have to be delusional to think those responses are personal. The difference constituency size makes was best summed up by a senator from a small-population state: "Pat Moynihan or Diane Feinstein or Boxer goes home for the weekend. Their constituents never see them. They never expect to see them. Here, if you miss the Warren Tomato Festival, you're suspect."

To sum up, senators recognize that state population affects the level of personal attention they can give to constituents and that they believe their constituents expect. Senators from less populous states are able to be more accessible and believe their constituents think they should be. In more populous states close contact is nearly impossible to achieve, even if the senator makes a substantial effort, and thus large-state senators do not think their constituents expect nearly as much as those in small states do.

Constituents' Expectations

Although senators themselves perceive that constituents expect different things from them depending on how many people they represent, it is difficult to determine from survey research what constituents actually do expect from their senators. Are senators correct about constituents' expectations? Do constituents in less populous states expect more frequent and more personal contact than those in larger states? The NES Senate Election Study, the best available data set for research on representational relationships between senators and constituents, did not ask respondents any questions about how frequently they expect their senators to contact them or about how accessible senators should be. The study did include an item asking respondents to assess the importance of three tasks that senators perform: "helping people in the state who have personal problems with government," "working in Congress on bills concerning national issues," and "making sure the state gets its fair share of government money and projects." Although these items do provide some information about constituents' expectations of senators' job performance, they are of limited use to us for two reasons: they do not bear directly on the matter that senators raised most often—constituents' expectations of personal contact in large and small states—and the question was asked differently in the 1988 and 1990 waves of the Senate study.[2]

In their analysis of the 1988 NES Senate Election Study, Hibbing and Alford (1990) hypothesized that respondents in more populous states prefer their senators to focus on issues of broad, national concern whereas respondents in smaller states want their senators to attend to particularized state needs and to the individual needs of constituents. They found a modest relation in the expected direction between state population and the percentage of respondents in each state who rated "making sure the state gets its fair share of money and projects" as "extremely important." They also found that constituents in larger states were slightly more likely to rate "working on national issues" as "extremely important" for their senators. They found no relationship, however, between state population and responses on the item rating the importance of "helping people in the state who have personal problems with the government." The importance of these findings, however, is called into question by the fact that there is very little variability across states in constituents' responses on any of these items. Nearly all constituents in every state rated all three of these activities as either "very important" or "extremely important."[3] State population accounts for only a very small percentage of the already small variation in constituents' responses to these items.

The 1990 question on senators' activities provided an opportunity to clarify the 1988 findings because respondents were required to rank the three activities listed in the 1988 question.[4] This question required constituents to set priorities in assessing their expectations of their senators' job performance. The percentage in each state selecting each of these activities as the "most important" part of a senator's job was regressed on state population. The results of our analysis of the 1990 data do not confirm even the modest findings of the 1988 data. In fact, the signs on the coefficients for state population were all opposite from the expected direction, and none were statistically significant.[5]

It would be a mistake, however, to conclude from the results on these survey items that constituency size has no effect on constituents' expectations of senators. Although the results lead us to conclude that constituents in more and less populous states do not have sharply different job expectations of their senators, the Senate Election Study did not include items to assess their expectations with respect to the full range of senators' representational activities or any direct measures of their expectations of personal contact with their senators. Constituents' behavior may, however, indirectly reveal more about their expectations than do their responses to these rather abstract survey questions. We now examine other items from the Senate Election Study that deal with more concrete forms of senator-constituent interaction.

The Quantity of Senator-Constituent Contact

The contact between senators and constituents is an integral part of the representational experience. It is no coincidence that one of the harshest criticisms that can be leveled at representatives is that they are "out of touch." If we think of representation as "acting in the interest of the represented in a manner responsive to them" (Pitkin 1967, 209), contact between representative and represented is a fundamental precondition of "responsiveness." Literally speaking, staying "in touch" means being in contact with constituents, being accessible to them, and maintaining strong ties in the constituency. To call representatives "out of touch," then, is to label them unresponsive and question their ability to be legitimate representatives at all. Large constituency size is an obvious barrier to being "in touch" in this literal sense. Senators who represent more populous states have a more difficult task as they seek to maintain close contact with their constituents.

The Senate Election Study asked a number of items about senator-constituent contact that allow us to examine its relationship to state population. How great a limitation does increasing population place on a senator's ability to stay in contact with constituents? Table 3.1 presents the results on a variety of contact items by constituency size (grouped by the number of congressional districts in the state). Two controls are included in this table. First, to control for the effects of the six-year Senate election cycle, constituents' responses regarding their contact with senators running for reelection

Table 3.1 Percentage of Respondents Reporting Contact with Senators (1988–92) and House Members (1988–90) by State Population

Item	Number of Congressional Districts in Respondent's State					
	1	2–3	4–8	9–19	>19	All
Met incumbent personally						
Senator running	32.6	26.8	19.2	13.3	8.0	19.6
Senator not up	26.7	21.3	15.5	11.8	8.6	16.6
Representative	21.1	21.7	22.2	21.3	16.2	21.1
Attended a meeting where incumbent spoke						
Senator running	28.9	25.9	21.3	14.9	12.7	20.5
Senator not up	25.9	22.9	17.9	15.3	12.2	18.8
Representative	19.4	21.1	22.4	21.7	20.0	21.4
Spoke with staff member						
Senator running	26.2	19.7	15.8	11.3	9.5	16.1
Senator not up	24.1	17.7	13.9	11.8	9.1	15.1
Representative	17.9	19.7	20.1	20.0	19.5	19.6
Received mail from incumbent						
Senator running	83.6	81.2	74.1	69.5	66.1	74.6
Senator not up	77.8	77.8	67.3	60.7	63.0	69.6
Representative	78.2	79.4	75.0	71.9	71.2	75.1
Respondent contacted incumbent						
Senator running	25.9	20.1	16.6	12.5	12.3	17.0
Senator not up	22.8	16.2	14.8	12.1	8.8	15.0
Representative	15.0	17.4	18.1	18.8	16.9	17.6

Source: NES Senate Election Study.

Note: The number of respondents for each state size falls within the following ranges (CD = congressional district):

	Senator Running	Senator Not Running	Representative
1 CD states	663–66	1,593–1,620	770–83
2–3 CD states	965–71	2,282–2,340	930–59
4–8 CD states	1,872–91	3,971–4,075	2,033–83
9–19 CD states	1,196–1,212	2,552–2,618	1,243–1,305
>19 CD states	629–36	1,222–56	615–53

are separated from those on contact with senators not up for reelection. Second, to account for institution-specific effects, the table also reports contact levels for House members.[6]

On all five items, reported levels of contact between senators and their constituents decrease stepwise as state population increases.[7] This pattern is evident for all senators, regardless of the proximity of their next election. Contact rates between senators and constituents are up to four times as great in the smallest states (one congressional district) as in the largest (more than nineteen). The effect of state population is most pronounced on the items asking if respondents had met the incumbent personally or had attended a meeting where the incumbent spoke.

These findings are hardly surprising. After all, senators are limited in how many constituents they can meet and how many meetings they can speak at. All else being equal, senators from more populous states cannot meet as great a proportion of their constituents as can senators from smaller states. A senator who represents California could personally meet fifty times as many constituents as one representing Wyoming yet have a lower rate of contact. Interestingly, state population even has an effect on reported contacts by mail. It is not clear that a senator's ability to reach constituents by mail is limited by constituency size, but that does appear to be the case.[8]

The regressions presented in table 3.2 provide more exact estimates of the relationship between contact levels and state population. This table shows the coefficients when the percentage of respondents in each state reporting contact was regressed on state population. For each item, the relationship between constituency size and the frequency of contact with senators is statistically significant at the .02 confidence level or better. The coefficient (B) ranges from -0.49 to -1.61, showing that state population has a sizable effect on the level of contact between senators and constituents. This means, for example, that for every one million additional constituents in the state the percentage of respondents reporting that they had personally met the senator declines by an estimated 1.2 percent. A coefficient of this size indicates that there is an estimated difference of thirty-three percentage points in reported constituent contact levels between senators representing the most and least populous states.[9]

These survey results are congruent with the perceptions that senators expressed during our interviews. They demonstrate that differences in constituency size create very different representational tasks for senators from more and less populous states. It is simply easier for senators representing smaller states to have contact with their constituents than for those from larger states. On this subject, one senator from a populous state drew a sharp contrast between his own more distant relationship with his constituents and that of two colleagues from small-population states, Joe Biden (D-Del.) and Pat Leahy (D-Vt.). He said: "Biden can't stop campaigning. He's seen every-

Table 3.2 Relationship between Percentage of Respondents in State Reporting
Contact and State Population (in Millions), 1988–92

Item	Coefficient (B)	Standard Error	Significance Level	R^2
Met incumbent personally				
Senator running	−1.20	0.20	.00	.44
Senators not up	−0.77	0.17	.00	.30
Representative	−0.39	0.17	.02	.10
Attended a meeting where incumbent spoke				
Senator running	−1.61	0.17	.00	.33
Senators not up	−0.66	0.14	.00	.31
Representative	−0.08	0.15	.57	.01
Talked with staff				
Senator running	−0.74	0.15	.00	.36
Senators not up	−0.56	0.12	.00	.33
Representative	−0.05	0.14	.74	.00
Received mail				
Senator running	−0.96	0.22	.00	.30
Senators not up	−0.49	0.21	.02	.10
Representative	−0.51	0.19	.01	.13
Contacted incumbent				
Senator running	−0.64	0.18	.00	.23
Senators not up	−0.55	0.11	.00	.33
Representative	−0.10	0.13	.46	.01

Source: NES Senate Election Study.

body in Delaware five hundred times. . . . There's probably not a living person in Vermont who hasn't met or seen [Leahy] if they wanted to. He's ubiquitous." No matter how hard they try, however, senators representing the most populous states can never make themselves nearly so "ubiquitous" to their constituents.

Institutional Context: House versus Senate

Although it is useful to see the magnitude of the contact differences between senators and constituents as state population varies, we doubt that legislative scholars are surprised that there is a relationship between state population and contact levels. We do expect, however, that it is something to which they may not have previously been sensitive. But just how "ubiquitous" small-state senators can be was the most striking finding in our analysis.

Small-state senators, in fact, have even more contact with their constituents than the House members in those states do. On all the contact items shown in table 3.1, senators representing states with three or fewer House districts have more contact with their constituents than House members.

This finding undermines the conventional wisdom that House members are closer to their constituents than senators are because they run for reelection every two years and in most cases represent smaller, more homogeneous constituencies. This conventional wisdom is correct when one examines respondents in the aggregate, as shown in the far right column of table 3.1: most of the respondents in the study reported more contact with their House members than with their senators.[10] It also is true when looked at only from the House member's perspective because most of them, given the way they are apportioned, represent districts in populous states. The conventional wisdom is not true, however, in the least populous states, those with three or fewer congressional districts. Respondents in these states report contact levels with senators that always equal or exceed contact with House members from those states. For example, 32.6 percent of respondents in states with only one congressional district report having met the incumbent senator who is running for reelection; by contrast, only 21.1 percent of these respondents report having met their House member. Given that more than one out of three senators represents a state with three or fewer congressional districts, the conventional wisdom stands in need of revision.

In short, these data reveal that constituency size is more important for contact between representatives and constituents than is institutional context. As a consequence, it is inaccurate to simply contrast representational relationships in the Senate and the House and conclude that senators on the whole have more distant relationships with their constituents than House members do. Senators as a group are not different from House members in the amount of contact they have with constituents. Instead, senators who represent constituencies that are similar in size to House districts have contact levels that mirror or exceed those of House members. At the same time, senators who represent large constituencies have more distant relationships with their constituents than do House members: in states with four or more congressional districts, House members consistently have more contact than the senators in those states. Constituency size, not institutional context, is the decisive factor determining contact between constituents and representatives.

The Electoral Cycle

Constituency size affects senator-constituent contact more than does the Senate electoral cycle itself. Political scientists usually place great emphasis on the electoral cycle in explaining senators' behavior. Certainly Fenno's work, for example, leads us to believe that the Senate's six-year term produces cycles of campaigning and governing for individual senators, cycles that are crucial to understanding the representational choices they make (Fenno 1978, 1982, 1991, 1992, 1996). His subject Mark Andrews, for example, perceived that the six-year term permitted him to be less attentive to his constituents than he had been in the House, where he faced reelection campaigns every two years. The data show, however, that constituency size is more important for predicting the amount of contact between senators and constituents than is the proximity of the next election.

To control for the effects of the electoral cycle on senator-constituent contact, in table 3.1 we separated constituents' responses to the contact items based on whether the senator was running for reelection at the time of the survey. The differences in contact between senators who are up for reelection and those who are not running are small compared with the differences caused by state population. Senators running for reelection have contact levels with their constituents that are rarely more than five or six percentage points greater than those of senators who are not running. The electoral cycle had the greatest effect on the item that asked constituents if they had received mail from their senator. In states with nine to nineteen congressional districts, 69.5 percent of respondents reported receiving mail from senators who were running for reelection, whereas 60.7 percent of respondents reported getting mail from senators who were not running for reelection. By contrast, on most of the items senators in the least populous states usually had contact levels at least twice as high as those of senators in the most populous states.

The effect of the electoral cycle on senators' attentiveness to their constituencies may be something to which senators, political scientists, and journalists are more sensitive than are constituents themselves. Our data suggest that constituents do not perceive a great difference in the attentiveness of senators in the last two years of their terms compared with their first four years in office. Instead, the data show that constituency size is a far more important influence on senator-constituent contact than the electoral cycle. This finding is surprising, given the attention scholars have devoted to the effects of the six-year cycle in conditioning the behavior of senators (Elling 1982; Fenno 1982; Thomas 1985; Wright and Berkman 1986) compared with that given to constituency size.

Constituent-Initiated Contact

The relation between senator-constituent contact and state population holds even for constituent-initiated contact. Constituency size not only is a constraint on senators as they seek to bridge the representational distance between themselves and their constituents, it is also a constraint on constituents when they consider whether to contact their national representatives. The effect of constituency size on constituents' choices about contacting their senators is not immediately obvious. After all, when constituents in populous states seek to reach a senator they do not face the physical and resource limitations that their senators face in trying to reach constituents. Constituency size, however, shapes the incentives of constituents both when they decide whether to contact a senator as well as whether to approach a senator or their House member.

When constituents make a decision about contacting an elected official for assistance with a problem or to request action on an issue, they consider three things: their chances of getting access, the official's clout or potential influence, and the likelihood that she will act on the request. These considerations lead constituents to reach different conclusions depending on the size of the constituency in which they reside.

When they consider which of their national elected officials to contact, constituents in populous states are likely to perceive that they have much better access to their House member than to a senator. House members in populous states simply have fewer constituent demands and requests to accommodate than the senators in those states. Constituents do not need a great deal of information to recognize this. One senator put it concisely: "The lines in large states are shorter to the congresswoman or congressman than to the senator." As a result, constituents in populous states have a greater expectation of access to their House members than to a senator. In addition, the House member is likely to have a nearby district office, to appear regularly at town meetings, to be a lifelong resident of the district, and perhaps to maintain a home there. Senators in populous states, by contrast, often come from entirely different parts of the state than do many of their constituents, visit the constituents' home areas infrequently, and may even speak with a noticeably different regional accent. Because the senator must deal with the demands of so many more people and meet the legislative needs of a large, diverse state, constituents may assume that their concerns will not receive high priority in the senator's office. Thus in populous states constituents perceive both that the likelihood of gaining access is greater for their House member than for their senator and that their House member is more likely to respond favorably to their request.

As state population decreases, however, House members and senators look increasingly similar in accessibility and responsiveness. As the perceived differences between House members and senators decrease, the rational actor will contact the more influential official. In the least populous states, in fact, constituents are likely to perceive that their House members and their senators will be equally responsive and accessible; as a result, constituents, as rational actors, become more likely to contact a senator than their House member.

Similarly, when constituents consider whether to contact a senator at all, those in more and less populous states will evaluate their chances of gaining access and favorable action differently. Constituents in more populous states are likely to perceive that their ability to gain access to their senators and achieve favorable action is limited by the large size of the constituency they live in. We would expect to find that constituents in populous states respond to these incentives by contacting their senators less frequently than those in smaller states.

An item in the Senate Election Study asking respondents if they or any member of their families had ever contacted a senator or a senator's office allows us to test our expectations.[11] The data for this item (shown at the bottom of table 3.1) reveal that state population does affect constituents' incentives. Respondents in states with a single congressional district were more than twice as likely to report contacting a senator than were those in states with more than nineteen districts. As shown in table 3.2, regressing the percentage of respondents in each state who reported having contacted a senator on state population yields a coefficient of -0.64 for an incumbent senator who was running for reelection and -0.55 for a senator who was not running, meaning that constituents in Wyoming reported having contacted their senator at estimated rates seventeen to twenty percentage points higher than respondents in California.

Constituents in more and less populous states also make different choices about which of their national representatives to contact. Those in all but the least populous states are more likely to contact their House member than a senator because they believe it is harder to gain access to and favorable action from a senator. And the data on constituent–initiated contact in table 3.1 strongly support this conclusion. Constituents in the most populous states do in fact show a marked preference for contacting House members over senators: respondents in states with nine to nineteen and more than nineteen congressional districts reported that they contacted their House member over 50 percent more frequently than a senator (as measured by an average of the contact reported with the incumbent running and the incumbent not up for reelection in table 3.1). The difference between the constituent-initiated contact rates of senators and House members is relatively small for states with four to eight congressional districts. Respondents in those states reported slightly more contact with their House members than with their senators. By the time we reach states with two or three districts, respondents reported more contact with their senators than with their House members. And as expected, constituents in the very least populous states are far more likely to contact a senator. In states with one congressional district, constituents contacted senators over 50 percent more frequently than they contacted their House member.

Constituency size thus affects the representational experience from both directions. Increasing constituency size constrains senators' ability to maintain close contact with their constituents, and it also shapes constituents' incentives as they consider whether to contact their senators. Constituents in more populous states are more likely to forgo contacting a senator than are those in less populous states—and when they do contact a national representative they tend to prefer their House member. Constituents in middle-sized states are more likely to contact their senators than those in the most populous states, and they report contacting House members and senators at similar rates. Constituents in the least populous states are those most likely to contact senators, and in fact they report doing so more often than contacting House members.

The Quality of Senator–Constituent Contact

That state population affects the quantity of contact between senators and constituents says one thing about the representational experience. But for understanding the experience as a whole it may be even more important to know whether the *quality* of senators' contact with their constituents differs in more and less populous states. First, to answer this question, we talked with senators at some length about the nature of their relationships with their constituents. We wanted to find out how they spoke about their constituents: Did they describe them in personal, individualized terms? How did they describe their contact—was it face-to-face or more impersonal? Second, we wanted to know how constituents themselves described contact with their senators. Why did they contact their senators? Did constituency size affect the types of demands they placed on them? Both our discussions with senators and constituents' responses to the Senate Election Study offer evidence that constituency size affects the quality of contact between senators and constituents as well as its quantity.

Senators' Perceptions of Contact with Constituents

Compared with their colleagues from populous states, senators from small states described their relationships with constituents in closer and more personal terms. We usually did not even have to ask small-state senators about the quality of these relationships before they began to speak of them with pleasure. To illustrate his closeness to the people in his state, for example, one Democratic senator from a small-population state retrieved a letter from his desk during our interview and read it aloud. The letter was from "a Republican banker in a very Republican small town" in his state. It began, "Dear [senator's first name]." The banker went on at length about how he had not talked with the senator in some time, then reminded him that he disagreed with him on most issues and had worked and voted for his opponents. He then thanked the senator for his work following a recent natural disaster in the state, explained how grateful everyone was, wished the senator the best in his future endeavors, and told him he would support him against future opponents. When the senator finished reading the letter he remarked that to him its most striking characteristic was that the writer used his first name throughout. He doubted that a small-town Republican banker in a populous state would feel comfortable and familiar enough to address his senator that way, especially if the senator was a Democrat. He then speculated that in a large state such a letter might never even make it past a staff person.

Senators from the less populous states give strong indications that they, like House members, nurture close representational relationships with constituents. A former White House lobbyist told a story about then Senate majority leader Robert Byrd (D-W.Va.) to illustrate how constituency size shapes the way senators deal with their constituents: "I was in the White House at the time, and Byrd was disabled in the hospital. I had to go up to see him, and there he is on the phone with a bunch of file cards with phone numbers calling people in West Virginia from five o'clock on, saying 'I want to congratulate you on your fiftieth wedding anniversary' and the like." Each of these anecdotes reinforces the point that not only are constituents in less populous states more likely to have contact with senators, but this contact is more likely to be personal.

A former Senate aide observed that his old boss, a long-retired small-state senator living in Washington, D.C., would still meet people from his home state and strike up conversations about where they were from and whom they knew. This aging senator would quickly make a personal connection this way, albeit often to the person's grandfather or great-aunt. A recently retired senator observed in an interview that in small states the first question you ask constituents is where they're from—as a way of making a connection. He said he was almost always able to find some personal link and thus to establish rapport right away.

Although our interviews offer evidence that senators in small-population states and those working with them perceive their relationships with constituents as closer and more personal than those of senators in more populous states, their perceptions may be selective and based on an incomplete picture. Senators may know why their own constituents contact them but not be well informed about the quality of contact between other senators and their constituents. The question remains whether constituency size affects the way constituents see the quality of their relationship with senators.

Constituents' Reasons for Contacting Senators

The Senate Election Study included an item that gives us some insight into how constituents in more and less populous states view the representational relationship with their senators. Respondents who reported contacting a senator or a staff member were asked whether they did so to express an opinion, get information, or seek help on a problem. This same item was asked in 1988 and 1990 about contacts with the respondent's House member. This "reason for contacting" question makes it possible to investigate whether state population affects the types of contacts constituents initiate with their senators and representatives.

The data in table 3.3 reveal a relationship between state size and the reasons respondents offer for contacting their senators. As state population increases, respondents are more likely to say they did so to "express an opinion" and less likely to say it was to "seek help with a problem." Respondents in states with three or fewer congressional districts are nearly twice as likely to say they sought help with a problem as are those in states with more than nineteen. Again the quality, not just the quantity, of contact is different. It may not be very difficult for constituents to contact a public official whom they have never met and never expect to meet simply to express their opinion on a particular issue. Asking for help with a problem, however, seems to require greater interpersonal comfort, just as people may be more reluctant to ask for help from someone they perceive as a stranger. This finding thus fits with the belief that constituents in smaller states have closer relationships with their senators.

The data in table 3.3 also allow us to compare respondents' reasons for contacting senators with the reasons they give for contacting their House members.[12] In small states (three or fewer House districts) the mix of reasons respondents give for contacting House members and senators are very similar. As state population increases, however, the reasons given begin to differ. In populous states constituents contact a senator mainly to express an opinion; they contact their House member when they need help with a problem. These data provide yet another indication that in the smaller states constituents' representational relationships with their senators are very similar to those with House members. For constituents in large states, by contrast, the data suggest that the relationships are quite different.

Again, the accepted generalizations about senators do not hold—the representational relationships of senators are not consistently different from those of House members. Constituents in small-population states appear to feel at least as close to their senators as to their House members, if not closer. Their senators are not distant figures whom a few of them contact on rare occasions to express an opinion on a public issue. Instead, their senators are as close to them as their House members are—and accordingly they expect the same things of both. It is as if constituents in these states have two extra House members, except that these "representatives" sit in a far smaller legislative body and accordingly have more influence.

Thus the data on reasons for contacting senators support the notion that

Table 3.3 Reasons Respondents Contacted Senators and House Members by State Population, 1988–92

Reason	Number of Congressional Districts in Respondent's State					
	1	2–3	4–8	9–19	>19	All
Senators						
To express an opinion	52.7%	51.7%	54.0%	55.5%	64.7%	54.3%
To seek information	38.7	35.6	32.0	34.7	27.7	34.3
To seek help with a problem	46.9	45.3	41.9	37.6	23.7	41.7
N	(520)	(536)	(858)	(447)	(173)	(2,534)
House members						
To express an opinion	57.5%	56.0%	45.9%	46.0%	48.5%	49.2%
To seek information	41.6	37.7	35.8	37.7	42.7	37.9
To seek help with a problem	40.7	43.4	55.2	48.1	44.7	48.7
N	(113)	(159)	(355)	(239)	(103)	(969)

Source: NES Senate Election Study.

constituency size affects constituents' expectations of their senators. Although, as discussed above, the job expectations they articulate do not demonstrate a consistent relationship to state population, the data on constituent-initiated contact show that both how frequently constituents contact their senators and their reasons are affected by constituency size. These findings in turn strongly suggest that constituents in more and less populous states view their representational relationships with their senators differently.

Constituents' Evaluations of Senators

Another important component of the representational experience of senators and constituents is simply how well constituents themselves are satisfied with it. If state population influences both the quantity and the quality of constituent-senator contact, it is also likely to affect constituents' evaluations of their senators. At minimum, people tend to view those with whom they have had personal contact more favorably than those with whom they have not, as psychologists have shown (Zajonc 1968). To determine the effect of constituency size on constituents' evaluations of their senators, we explore the perspectives of both survey respondents and senators.

An examination of three items from the Senate Election Study supports our initial expectation. As we can see in table 3.4, the smaller the state's population, the higher the constituents' evaluation of the senator.[13] Although the differences between respondents in the most and least populous states on the items measuring constituents' evaluations are not as great, or as uniformly stepwise, as for the contact items shown in table 3.1, they still represent an important effect on the representational experience. The 10 percent difference between the most and least populous states in constituents' thinking their senator will be very helpful and the 5–6 percent difference in approval ratings of job performance are hardly meaningless. In fact the trend in table 3.4 recalls the pattern found on the contact items. In the least populous states, constituents evaluated their senators who were running for reelection more favorably than their House members and their senators who were not running almost as favorably. Only constituents in more populous states evaluated their House members more favorably than their senators.

This interpretation is supported by the data shown in table 3.5, which presents the coefficients when the percentage of the respondents in each state who "strongly approve" is regressed on state population. For all the evaluation measures there is a statistically significant negative relationship between state population and the percentage evaluating the incumbent favorably. The relationship holds whether or not senators were running for reelection at the time of the survey. The regression coefficients shown here reveal that the effect of constituency size on constituents' evaluations of senators is considerable. The coefficient for the percentage of respondents who strongly approve of the incumbent's handling of the job, for example, is −0.75 for senators running for reelection, which translates into a job approval rating twenty percentage points lower for senators from California than for those from the smallest-population states. Similarly, the coefficient on the same item for senators not running for reelection, −0.61, would result in a rating eighteen percentage points lower in California than in the smallest states.[14]

Recent studies examining job performance ratings of senators as measured in Mason-Dixon polls conducted during the 1996 elections (Abramowitz and Segal 1997; Binder, Maltzman, and Sigelman 1998) support our finding of a strong relation between state population and senators' ratings. Binder et al. demonstrate that "for every increase of one million in a state's population, its senators' ratings fell by just over four-tenths of a point, so that, ceteris paribus, senators from a state like South Dakota, with a population of less than a million, would be rated 12 points higher than senators from California" (1998, 555). The effect they uncover is somewhat smaller than the one we found, but the authors use a different evaluation item and rely on responses during a single election year.[15]

These job evaluation items offer another perspective on how state population affects the representational experience. Constituents in small states not only are more likely to have contact with senators, they are also more likely

Table 3.4 Respondents' Evaluations of Senators and Representatives by State Population, 1988–92

Item	Number of Congressional Districts in Respondent's State					
	1	2–3	4–8	9–19	>19	All
Thinks incumbent would be very helpful if contacted						
Senator running	32.4%	33.9%	29.3%	22.2%	23.2%	28.2%
	(663)[a]	(964)	(1,862)	(1,996)	(628)	(5,313)
Senator not up	27.0	28.2	23.3	20.7	18.9	23.7
	(1,598)	(2,286)	(4,003)	(1,426)	(621)	(9,934)
Representative	29.5	30.9	33.9	30.4	30.4	31.6
	(773)	(935)	(2,056)	(1,278)	(635)	(5,677)
Recalls something incumbent did for state or district						
Senator running	29.5	32.9	25.2	20.2	22.4	25.7
	(661)	(967)	(1,867)	(1,199)	(629)	(5,323)
Senator not up	21.0	22.9	17.2	15.2	13.9	18.0
	(1,598)	(2,302)	(4,008)	(1,428)	(626)	(9,962)
Representative	19.9	21.6	21.8	21.6	19.2	21.1
	(774)	(939)	(2,059)	(1,279)	(637)	(5,688)
Strongly approves of incumbent's handling of job						
Senator running	47.9	51.6	49.8	39.8	42.9	46.9
	(572)	(830)	(1,594)	(982)	(499)	(4,477)
Senator not up	43.2	46.3	41.8	40.0	37.3	42.1
	(1,260)	(1,811)	(3,029)	(1,060)	(464)	(7,624)
Representative	45.7	46.2	50.2	48.0	52.2	48.6
	(624)	(770)	(1,626)	(993)	(439)	(4,452)

Source: NES Senate Election Study.
[a]*N*s in parentheses.

to perceive their senators as very helpful, to recall something they have done, and to give them high job approval ratings.

Senators' Perspectives on Constituents' Evaluations

In our interviews with senators we discovered they are aware that constituency size affects constituents' evaluations of their job performance. When we asked them about the higher evaluations that senators in less populous states receive, they offered three explanations: the different *trade-offs* that senators

Table 3.5 Relationship between Percentage of Respondents in State Giving Most Favorable Evaluation and State Population (in Millions), 1988–92

Item	Coefficient (B)	Standard Error	Significance Level	R^2
Thinks incumbent would be very helpful if contacted				
Senator running	−0.65	0.17	.00	.23
Senator not up	−0.55	0.14	.00	.23
Representative	−0.25	0.19	.20	.03
Recalls something incumbent did for state or district				
Senator running	−0.75	0.19	.00	.25
Senator not up	−0.39	0.16	.02	.10
Representative	−0.20	0.17	.25	.03
Strongly approves of incumbent's handling of job				
Senator running	−0.75	0.25	.00	.17
Senator not up	−0.61	0.21	.01	.15
Representative	−0.31	0.22	.16	.04
($N = 50$)				

Source: NES Senate Election Study.

in more and less populous states face when they return to their states to meet with constituents; the different needs of senators in more and less populous states to rely on the *media* to present themselves to their constituents; and the different degrees of political *heterogeneity* in more and less populous states.

First, senators from both large and small states spoke of the choices that senators from populous states must face when they are at home, compared with those who represent smaller states. They observed that senators in populous states must cope with difficult trade-offs when they decide which places and organizations they will visit during their trips home. Senators in smaller states, by contrast, can spread themselves across the state more effectively and thus face fewer of these difficult tradeoffs. One small-state Republican claimed that campaigning was easier in less populous states because "a small state like [state name] is manageable. You can go up and down and across the state in just a few hours." A Democrat from a less compact small state offered a similar perspective: "I get into every county in my state at least once a year. I get in my car and drive by myself, no staff, no schedule. When I drive into the typical town it takes only a half hour for the word to get out that I'm there. My visits are unannounced. They never know when I'm coming. . . . They'd never know in L.A. or San Francisco that you were there within a half hour. But if I'm in [lists three small towns in his state] they know I'm there."

Compared with the small-state senators above, senators from populous states describe campaigning as much more taxing. A senator from a large state who had previously served in the House said, "Representing a big state in the Senate is a very demanding job. The question is, How do you go to the state?" He then reminisced about serving in the House, recalling his visits to the main city in his two-county district, his ability to attend five to ten events a day in the district, and the rapport he had established with his constituents over his more than ten years of service in the House. He experienced more representational dilemmas and more difficult ones when in his constituency as a senator than he had encountered as a House member. Whereas he had previously found district visits relatively easy, as a senator he faced the per-plexing question, Where do you go? He also commented that after he was elected to the Senate, his constituents in his home congressional district complained that they no longer saw him enough.

Fenno (1996) describes Sen. Wyche Fowler (D-Ga.), also a former House member, expressing similar frustrations when comparing the tasks of cam-paigning in a single congressional district with campaigning across a whole state. On leaving a black church in Atlanta where the minister noted that they did not see Fowler as much now that he was a senator, Fowler admitted, "I didn't appreciate how much of a change it would be going from House to Senate, with 7 million people to represent. I can't get around to the churches as often as I used to. And when I go, I can't stay as long. I'm always hurrying to get somewhere else. . . . I have to get out of Atlanta so I can catch a plane to Waycross" (191). Fenno's analysis of Fowler's failed reelection campaign suggests that his constituents felt the loss of intimacy once he became a sena-tor, and that this was one reason for his defeat. The same difficulties do not confront small-state senators, even though many have made the transition from the House to the Senate. They are faced with institutional adjustments, but they represent an unchanged or only modestly larger constituency.

Contrast the Fowler dilemma with the behavior of the late Sen. Spark Matsunaga of Hawaii, who came to the Senate after serving seven terms in the House. Representing a small state, Matsunaga was still able to cultivate his constituents in much the same way he had as a House member. By the time of his death in 1990, Matsunaga's daily luncheons in the Senate din-ing room with constituents visiting Washington had become legendary in the Senate (Pearson 1990).[16] Several of our interviewees mentioned the "Matsunaga table" in illustrating the representational differences of senators from small and large states.

Second, senators observed that representation and campaigns in populous states mean relying more on the media to present themselves to constituents, whereas senators in smaller states can communicate effectively by meeting constituents face-to-face in interpersonal settings. Senators from larger states, they suggested, receive lower evaluations than senators from less populous ones because they must depend on others, especially the media, to reach their constituents. They were less able to communicate directly. One small-state senator made this connection: "You have more opportunity to develop personal, not media, relations [in a small-population state]. The media tend to report negative news and not the positive things. If you rely on television and newspapers to define yourself, you aren't going to be defined as favorably as will a person who goes out to meet with constituents." A former Democratic senator for a small state suggested a variant on this theme in comparing his situation with that of a senator from California: "[There are] so many more people, organizations to pay attention to . . . you haven't got the person-to-person relationship. You depend on others to a smaller degree in small states and aren't as subject to the pressures of an organization."

Third, senators argued that it is easier to attain high job evaluations in less populous states because these states are more politically homogeneous, both in the number of interests a senator must cope with and in the likelihood that these interests will conflict with one another. Speaking of the multitude of interests and demands facing senators representing populous states, one small-state senator observed, "I'm in awe of how they handle it. They get hammered every day." Another brought up this subject when discussing Senate election contests: "In those states [California, New York, New Jersey, and Pennsylvania were mentioned] you're always going to get someone angry with you regardless of how you vote." By contrast, this former small-state senator said, "I knew my state. I would meet with them and they knew what I'd do would be OK . . . with the great majority of them." Similarly, the staff director for a senator from a middle-sized state thought his boss "wouldn't want to represent New York or California in the Senate. . . . In New York there's upstate versus the city and in California, northern California and southern California. It's representationally harder."

A few of the individuals we interviewed suggested that there may be a countervailing advantage in that senators representing populous states can sometimes play off competing interests against one another. The "losing" interest in any one case might then "understand" that the senator had to choose between interests. Although this may give large-state senators some additional leeway, it does not mean the "losing" interests will be satisfied with losing. By contrast, in a small state senators are less likely to face splits in their constituencies in the first place; on many issues there may be no organized interest present at all. During an interview with a staffer for a populous-state senator who had previously worked for two senators from small states, the staffer recalled that in one of his earlier jobs "the mail was almost overwhelmingly—probably 50 percent of it—about dairy." Later he generalized about the difference: "It's a lot easier because you don't have conflicting constituencies. In New York there's an organized constituency against you on almost anything. . . . In small states it's more of a company town."

A small-state senator described the relationship between state diversity, state population, and the higher approval ratings of small-state senators in this way: "It's the diversity you'd have to represent in a large state. There's a commonality of interests in a small state. You can focus on three or four main issues." He then pointed out how in each of the four regions of his state there was a single dominant interest. In one area, he noted, "you can run for the U.S. Congress saying you are going to represent the ———— industry totally and not do anything else." When we shared with him the story above about the importance of dairy issues, he immediately drew a contrast with his own state. Although agriculture is a principal industry in his state also, he said, "I think that one-tenth of one percent of our mail would be about dairy."

The problem of developing "fit"—ideological or otherwise—with the constituency in a populous state is the major factor in Fenno's analysis of the failed Fowler campaign and of Fowler's inability to foster trust in Georgia. After noting that developing "constituent trust" is never easy for a first-term senator, Fenno (1996, 186) adds: "It is harder still in a state like Georgia where historic regional and racial divisions, coupled with contemporary population growth and demographic change, make it difficult for a politician to find a stable base to represent and from which to negotiate for trust." Large states are more likely to have such divisions and to experience the demographic changes that make a senator's task more difficult. Although small states have political cleavages just as large states do, the senators we interviewed observed that these tended to be fewer in number, narrower in scope, and thus easier to bridge.

In sum, more and closer contacts, person-to-person relationships, and more homogeneous constituencies allow small-state senators to achieve higher job approval ratings on average than their big-state colleagues. Although representing a small state is no guarantee that a senator will succeed in gaining constituents' trust—as Fenno's studies of House members and of Sen. Mark Andrews attest—it does make the task more achievable. For even the most successful populous-state senators, building trust may be so difficult that they may choose to spend their time in other ways.

Constraints on Individual Senators

Although it is clear that the representational experiences of senators and constituents in more and less populous states differ in general, we have not dealt directly with constituency size as a constraint on the experiences of *individual*

Table 3.6 Scores for Individual Senators on Contact and Evaluative Items, 1988–92

Item	Moynihan (N.Y.)	D'Amato (N.Y.)	Metzenbaum (Ohio)	Glenn (Ohio)	Reigle (Mich.)	Levin (Mich.)
Met the senator	3.4 (149)[a]	3.4 (145)	9.6 (167)	10.2 (166)	7.5 (201)	8.5 (200)
Attended meeting	8.2 (147)	6.9 (145)	15.0 (167)	15.7 (166)	8.5 (201)	9.0 (200)
Talked with staff	5.4 (147)	5.5 (145)	6.6 (167)	8.4 (166)	7.0 (201)	6.5 (200)
Received mail from senator	55.8 (147)	60.7 (145)	63.5 (167)	66.9 (166)	66.2 (201)	72.0 (200)
Contacted senator or office	6.8 (146)	7.5 (146)	13.1 (168)	14.3 (168)	9.5 (199)	8.5 (201)
Believe senator would be very helpful with problem	19.3 (145)	17.1 (146)	22.8 (167)	18.8 (165)	16.0 (200)	22.4 (201)
Recall something senator has done for the state	15.8 (146)	19.2 (146)	26.9 (167)	14.3 (168)	12.1 (199)	14.6 (198)
Does very good job keeping in touch	14.3 (147)	18.5 (147)	20.6 (165)	16.9 (166)	13.1 (199)	13.0 (200)
Approve strongly of job senator is doing	35.8 (106)	38.1 (105)	33.6 (143)	37.7 (138)	32.0 (147)	39.0 (159)

Source: NES Senate Election Study.
[a]*N*s in parentheses.

senators and their constituents. Are there senators from populous states who establish levels of contact similar to those of senators in small states? Are there senators from small states who have the low rates of contact characteristic of those from populous states? The reputations of some senators among attentive publics suggest that there are exceptions to the pattern described. In sum, how much variation is there among senators who represent states with similar populations compared with the variation between those who represent states with different populations?[17]

To investigate the constraints that state population places on the representational relationships between individual senators and their constituents, we examined the responses to the Senate Election Study items on contact and evaluation for senators from three large states (New York, Ohio, and Michigan) and senators from four small states (Delaware, New Mexico, West

Biden (Del.)	Roth (Del.)	Byrd (W.Va.)	Rockefeller (W.Va.)	Bingaman (N.Mex.)	Domenici (N.Mex.)	Wallop (Wyo.)	Simpson (Wyo.)
38.3	37.1	31.1	34.1	21.5	24.3	22.2	33.0
(196)	(194)	(211)	(211)	(181)	(182)	(198)	(203)
35.7	28.4	29.0	36.5	21.0	27.6	21.7	30.5
(196)	(194)	(210)	(211)	(181)	(182)	(198)	(203)
28.6	25.3	19.5	20.4	17.1	24.3	23.2	27.6
(196)	(194)	(210)	(211)	(181)	(182)	(198)	(203)
78.1	69.1	89.1	82.9	68.5	70.7	77.3	77.3
(196)	(194)	(211)	(211)	(181)	(182)	(198)	(203)
27.0	22.7	21.4	18.0	14.4	30.2	21.3	27.2
(196)	(194)	(210)	(211)	(180)	(182)	(197)	(202)
32.7	27.3	42.7	35.5	26.0	39.0	16.8	27.4
(196)	(194)	(211)	(211)	(181)	(183)	(196)	(197)
20.0	19.7	40.3	35.4	17.7	34.8	14.6	16.4
(195)	(193)	(211)	(212)	(181)	(183)	(198)	(201)
30.3	24.0	38.9	34.1	17.9	33.9	9.6	26.6
(195)	(192)	(211)	(211)	(181)	(183)	(197)	(203)
56.2	50.7	53.8	50.8	48.6	58.9	29.3	52.0
(162)	(144)	(197)	(179)	(136)	(157)	(167)	(171)

Virginia, and Wyoming). These states were selected to provide a sample of senators of different parties, from different regions, from states with different population densities, and with different reputations for attentiveness to constituency-oriented issues.[18] The constituent contact and evaluation data for these senators are presented in table 3.6.

The data shown in table 3.6 reveal few exceptions to the general pattern described throughout this chapter. Senators from the same states have similar levels of reported constituent contact even when they have very different reputations for attention to constituency-oriented matters. For example, although Moynihan and D'Amato had very different Senate reputations—the former is thought to be primarily concerned with national issues and the latter was thought of as akin to a ward heeler—there is little difference in the levels of contact they had with their constituents or the evaluations they received. For both, nearly the same percentage report meeting the senator, attending a meeting at which the senator spoke, talking with a member of the senator's staff, and contacting the senator. Even though a higher percentage of respondents recalled something D'Amato had done for the state—consistent with his reputation for "bringing home the bacon"—Moynihan scored higher than D'Amato on the item asking if respondents thought the senator would be "very helpful" with a problem.[19]

Providing a small-state comparison, West Virginia senators Byrd and Rockefeller offer us the same contrast in reputations as the New Yorkers while representing a state currently with only three congressional districts. Like the respondents in New York, those in West Virginia do not distinguish between their two senators in terms of constituent contact or in their evaluations of them. The responses on D'Amato do not look like those on Byrd, and those on Moynihan do not look like those on Rockefeller. The senators from West Virginia have closer contact with their constituents and receive higher evaluations than do the senators from New York. This is not to claim that Moynihan and D'Amato or Byrd and Rockefeller are not different kinds of senators, but these data do suggest that senators' relationships with their constituents are inescapably constrained by constituency size. Thus, even if D'Amato wanted to establish a reputation as an accessible, constituent-serving senator, the sheer magnitude of New York's population limited him. By contrast, the West Virginians are relatively unconstrained in this respect: they can maintain close constituent contact and receive higher evaluations even while pursuing very different career paths in the Senate.

Table 3.6 reveals little exception to the pattern of higher constituent evaluations in less populous states.[20] On ratings of helpfulness, keeping in touch, and overall job approval, respondents give the small-state senators higher scores. Only the results on the item asking constituents to recall something the senator did for the state are mixed.

One senator, Malcolm Wallop (R-Wyo.), is the notable exception on the evaluation items. Even though he represented the least populous state in the Union, his evaluations are the lowest, or among the lowest, on all four items. Wallop was nearly defeated for reelection in 1988 and (perhaps wisely) decided not to run in 1994. During our interviews several staffers and senators who examined this table made comments about Wallop's arrogance. More than one person we interviewed discussed the obvious tension between Wallop's California prep school, eastern collegiate education, and family link to the House of Lords and his claim to be a western populist. The numbers for Wallop suggest that it takes more than being a senator from a small-population state to establish a relationship of trust with constituents and to gain favorable evaluations from them. Presentation of self and identification with constituents (Fenno 1978, 1992, 1996) are still important, even for senators representing the least populous states.

There are no exceptions to the general rule among the six large-state senators, however. The more distant representational experience in populous states is a powerful constraint on their ability to achieve extremely high evaluations.[21] Of the senators Fenno has studied, the three who appear to have the strongest trust relationships with their constituents—Pell, Pryor, and Domenici—are all from small states.[22] When we brought Fenno's observations to the attention of a small-state senator and asked if he could think of any senators from populous states who had built comparable relationships of trust, he said they were very rare: "Javits probably came as close to it as any, but he lost his last race, but he was ill. . . .Phil Hart may have come close. Scoop Jackson. But they are few and far between." Even if we accept classifying Jackson as a senator from a populous state (Washington had only seven House seats during his years in the Senate), we are struck that our interviewee had listed senators who were "institutions" in the Senate, major players on issues of national concern, more than institutions at home. By contrast, Pell has become an institution in Rhode Island without being one in the Senate. Trust at home and clout in Washington may often be linked, but there are clear exceptions. For senators from populous states, even if they have the latter, the former may be impossible to achieve. For those from smaller states, trust at home may be a potential avenue for influence in the Senate, but it is no guarantee.

It may be useful to view the importance of constituency size within Fenno's "four constituencies" conceptual framework. The "primary constituency" is "something every congressman must have"; it is a legislator's "last line of electoral defense in a primary contest" (Fenno 1978, 18–24). To cultivate trust with members of this constituency, legislators must develop and maintain close, person-to-person relationships. Because personal relationships are essential to maintaining close ties, all legislators are limited in how many constituents they can cultivate this way. As a result, the primary constituencies of House members and small-state senators represent a larger proportion of their reelection and geographic constituencies than do those of large-state senators. In other words, House members and small-state senators are capable of building primary constituencies large enough to provide wide coverage throughout their geographic constituencies, but populous-state senators are not. As we shall see in chapter 5, this leads large-state senators to pursue different strategies than their small-state colleagues do in pursuing their goals in the Senate.

Senators, Interest Groups, and Constituency Size

An account of the representational experience of senators and their constituents would not be complete without considering the relationships senators have with organized interests. Constituency size is likely to affect these relationships in the same way as it affects those between senators and constituents. To gain insight into this matter we interviewed a number of prominent Washington lobbyists, asking them to describe their ease of access to senators from more and less populous states. In addition, we posed some of the same questions to former senators who are now lobbyists.

Lobbyists employ two broad types of strategies to influence legislators—"inside" and "outside" strategies (Wittenberg and Wittenberg 1989; Wolpe and Levine 1996). "Inside strategies" refer to lobbyists' efforts to build relationships with legislators in order to influence them directly. "Outside strategies" refer to their efforts to persuade lawmakers that their constituents favor a particular proposal or course of action. The size of the constituency a senator represents is likely to affect both strategies. First, it is likely to influence the access lobbyists have to senators, in the same way it does for constituents generally. As a result, lobbyists are likely to find that building the relationships necessary for inside strategies is more difficult with senators who represent populous states than with those from smaller states. Second, constituency size is likely to affect lobbyists' outside strategies as well. Lobbyists who seek to convince senators that their constituents favor a given proposal by using means other than public opinion polls—such as tapping "grass tops" in the constituency to make the case to the senator personally—are likely to face different tasks depending on constituency size.

Lobbyists' Access to Senators

Lobbyists must gain access to senators before they can even begin to build an inside strategy to influence the legislative process. The first step is for a lobbyist to convince a senator or the senator's staff to grant time for a meeting. Time is every legislator's "scarcest and most precious political resource" (Fenno 1978, 34). Even so, not all senators experience the same demands on their time. All else being equal, those who represent larger constituencies face a greater number and diversity of requests than those who represent smaller ones. In our interviews, we found that lobbyists perceived that the demands were greater on senators from populous states than on those from smaller ones, inhibiting their ability to build relationships with busier senators.

Even a small-state senator expressed astonishment at the number of constituent appointments a senator from a populous state had on his calendar: "I wanted to meet with D'Amato on something. He took a schedule out of his pocket to see when we could set up a meeting. And looking at his schedule, I couldn't believe it—every special interest group has a presence." Similarly, a lobbyist who had previously worked for a senator and a presidential administration described the difference constituency size makes for the number of interests making demands on senators:

In Utah, for example, Bennett (R–Utah) has cattle, oil, water, and in the last ten years, banking and credit . . . American Express, and some computers have moved there because of the workforce. Perhaps six industries or a dozen if you gave me some time to think about it. In Pennsylvania, it's five states. You've got industrial, welfare, coal . . . I could come up with thirty things. So there are thirty interests trying to see Specter (R–Pa.) and only five trying to see Bennett. Then you have the difference in the mail and the amount of pounding. . . . It's Pittsburgh versus Philadelphia. In Utah all you've got is Salt Lake.

As a result of pressures like these, lobbyists are likely to find that gaining access to senators who represent populous states is more difficult than reaching those from smaller states.

Many of the lobbyists we interviewed, in fact, reported that the number of constituents' demands on senators from more populous states made them less accessible.[23] One observed that senators from populous states "reflect constituencies that are microcosms of the nation." As a result, he argued, they "cannot neglect any detail, the competition for their time is greater. Their agendas are larger." "The small-state senator," by contrast, "can concentrate on a committee" because he or she has more "discretionary time." To illustrate his point, this lobbyist returned to his comparison of Senators Bennett and Specter: "Yesterday there was a lull in the Senate's consideration of the tax bill. Bennett had time to BS with me in the hall. Specter and he are both running for reelection," but Specter did not have time to talk. The greater time pressure on senators from populous states makes gaining access to them difficult for lobbyists, especially the casual access that permits personal relationships to develop.

One technique lobbyists commonly use to get a "foot in the door" is to contribute to the senator's reelection fund. As veteran lobbyists Ernest and Elisabeth Wittenberg observe, "If you haven't got any of these advantages [if you are not a constituent or a personal friend of the senator], your name should be known in the office as a contributor to the official's reelection fund" (1989, 23). Senators from the most populous states, however, need to raise far more money to fund a campaign than senators from the least populous states and, as we will discuss in more depth in the next chapter, must raise a much greater percentage of it from individual contributors. As a result, fund-raising events for senators who represent more populous states are likely to be larger and more frequent than for those from smaller states. This means that lobbyists who seek access to senators from populous states must raise or contribute more money to make a lasting impression. Even when a lobbyist does contribute to the reelection fund of a senator from a populous state, he or she will be just one name on a very long list of contributors and fund-raisers and therefore less likely to be remembered individually.

Our lobbyists described different experiences when attending fund-raising events for senators from more and less populous states. Several of them remarked that the likelihood of being remembered for attending a particular event depended on the number of people present—and they noted that they attended only smaller events. The greater financial need of senators from populous states simply means that they have to hold more large "cattle call" fund-raising events. Contrasting the fund-raising events for D'Amato (R-N.Y.) and Baucus (D-Mont.), one lobbyist claimed, "If I go to a D'Amato fund-raiser and give $1,000, I'm just one line on a four-hundred-line printout. And I'd have to give $1,000 even to merit that. On the other hand, he continued, "Baucus is more likely to call you personally and ask you to attend. And he might speak to you when you're there and remember you. . . . It's like the difference between going to a dinner party rather than a football game." At fund-raising events for populous-state senators, he concluded, "you're like an ant crawling on the body politic."

The Plant Manager Theory of Lobbying

Lobbyists are also affected by constituency size when they pursue outside strategies for influencing senators. One of the most important techniques lobbyists use to demonstrate constituents' support for a proposal is to ask important individuals within a senator's constituency to contact the senator on behalf of the issue. "A member of Congress would rather see one voter than 10 lobbyists," write Wittenberg and Wittenberg. "This is known as the Plant Manager Theory of Lobbying" (1989, 44). A lobbyist pursuing this strategy will need to find important constituents who have access to their senators and a stake in the relevant issue. Just as constituency size affects the ability of lobbyists themselves to reach senators, it affects their ability to find someone in a senator's constituency who has ready access and is prominent enough to carry some influence.

A lobbyist representing a major real estate developers' association (who had previously worked for an influential senator) talked to us about the difference constituency size makes for "grass tops" access. "We didn't have any of our members who knew Pete Wilson," he observed. "None of them ever shook hands with him!" Finding constituents who could influence their senators was no easier in New York: "Harry Helmsley, Donald Trump, and . . . didn't know their senators." "We did have one developer, ———, who was close to Moynihan," he noted, but because this developer was personal friends with him, "he wouldn't talk to Moynihan about business." Later in the interview he became vehement on the subject: "Who the hell would you call in New York to get to Moynihan?" "Everybody in this town dreads dealing with those big state senators," he related; "they have a hundred different pressures on them. It's hard just getting them to focus on your issue. . . . Even getting an appointment is [tough]." By contrast, he maintained that in small states it was easier to find "grass tops" who could reach their senators.

In discussing his access to various senators, one lobbyist talked about his ability to find prominent clients who could influence their senators. Because his television was tuned to C-SPAN2 with Byron Dorgan (D-N.D.) speaking on the Senate floor, we asked hypothetically whether it was easier for him to gain access to Dorgan than to Diane Feinstein (D-Calif.). He responded emphatically, "Absolutely!" Even though the industry he represented had relatively few employees in North Dakota but had "25,000 employees in San Francisco alone," he felt that Dorgan would be "more attentive to constituents and employees" but that "Feinstein will blow us off." It became clear as he continued that our question had hit a particularly sensitive nerve. He related how on one occasion he had accompanied three CEOs to Feinstein's office for a scheduled appointment: "To make an appointment with Feinstein, we had to make a written request and say everybody who would be there." Feinstein was late. When she returned to her office she never went to the meeting room where the three CEOs were waiting; meanwhile, the staff claimed she was tied up elsewhere. It was the worst kind of nightmare for the lobbyist. By comparison, he said, "Dorgan will be glad to see the lowest rep of one of our companies."

On the subject of bringing constituency pressure to bear on senators, we posed a hypothetical scenario to several lobbyists. We asked them to imagine that they represented the National Association of Automobile Dealers and that the Senate was considering an amendment to the Clean Air Act dealing with auto emissions. Given these circumstances, we asked whether state population would have any effect on their ability to find an automobile dealer who would be able to contact a senator directly. Each of the lobbyists argued that the association would find it easier to locate a dealer capable of reaching a senator who represents a less populous state. In response to this scenario, one lobbyist who earlier in his career had worked for Sen. Frank Moss (D-Utah) observed: "An auto dealer I know in Utah, ———, could call Moss regularly and get through." By comparison, he said, "if you take a dealer like Potamakin, which is the largest in New York and in Florida, I would doubt, although I don't know it for a fact, that they know their senators." From this he generalized, "It's easier for everyone in a small state. The head of the state chapter of Common Cause would find it easier to reach senators in the small states."

Lobbyists seeking to influence senators from populous states must find and employ very prominent or influential constituents with a stake in the legislation. In small states, however, lobbyists find that a large percentage of the constituents have relatively easy access to their senators. On this point one senator from a populous state remarked: "If Joe Smith calls from Peoria, that means something different than if Joe Smith calls from Bismark. You have immunity [in the populous state]." In other words, a senator who is representing a large state often will choose to duck a call from a relatively obscure constituent whereas a senator from a small state does not have quite the same choice.

On the subject of accessibility to "plant managers," one experienced lobbyist explained that senators who represent populous states were generally accessible only to members of his business association who had corporate headquarters in their states, not to those who only had employees there; by contrast, access to senators from small states was usually easy regardless of corporate connections. He said that reaching the senators from New York, for example, would be difficult because the association he represented had no corporate offices there. Reaching the senators representing Texas would be easier, because several member corporations were located in Dallas. He followed up with a second example based on his experience representing the cable television industry. Because this industry is not concentrated in any state other than Colorado, "it's all the same to senators" everywhere. Despite this, however, he found that cable representatives in less populous states were better able to gain access to their senators than those in larger states. Just because of their small populations, "cable TV is a more important industry in small states."

In fact, senators in less populous states will often know the "grass tops" in their states personally. One lobbyist told of taking an executive of a major company to see then Senate majority leader George Mitchell (D-Maine). During the meeting Mitchell telephoned a (name of the corporation) dealer in Maine and said, "I've got your boss here with me. Would you like to speak to him? And he puts the exec on the phone with the dealer. That doesn't happen in big states." In the smallest states, not only do the grass tops know the senator, the senator knows the grass tops.

In sum, because senators who represent populous states experience greater constituency demands on their time than those from smaller states, they must make more choices about whom they will grant access. This constraint affects lobbyists as they pursue both inside and outside strategies. They have greater difficulty building relationships with senators representing populous states than with those from smaller ones. It also means that lobbyists who want to convince large-state senators that their constituents favor a given proposal have more trouble engaging influential constituents than when they want to influence senators from less populous states. One senator from a state slightly larger than our smallest-state grouping conveyed this point clearly:

"The issue is one of access. I get people who just have plants in my state, not the company headquarters, coming in to see me, saying that they couldn't see the senator in the state where they're headquartered. Senators in the large states are so busy. There are so many CEOs."

Conclusion

We have shown how one contextual feature, constituency size, profoundly shapes the representational experiences of senators and their constituents: the larger the population represented, the greater the representational distance between senator and constituent. Constituency size affects every aspect of the representational experience—constituents' expectations and evaluations of senators, the quality and quantity of senator-constituent contact, and the accessibility of senators to constituents and interest groups.

Senators themselves perceive that constituents in more and less populous states expect different things from their senators. They believe that those in smaller states expect more frequent and more personal contact. Our analysis of the Senate Election Study contact items supports these perceptions. Respondents in small states report higher levels of contact with their senators than do respondents in large states on every contact item. Constituency size appears to shape even constituents' incentives to contact their senators. As state population increases, constituents become less likely to do so. Instead, those in large states choose to contact House members more frequently than senators. Because they perceive their senators to be just as accessible, however, constituents in the least populous states actually contact them more often than they do their House members.

The substance of senator-constituent contact, not just its frequency, is affected by constituency size. The reasons respondents give for contacting their senators vary with constituency size. As state population increases, they are more likely to say they wanted to express an opinion and less likely to say they sought help with a problem. In less populous states, constituents contact their senators for basically the same reasons as they contact their House members. And the senators we interviewed perceive qualitative differences in the character of senator-constituent contact in more and less populous states.

Constituency size affects how well constituents are satisfied with their senators, as measured by the job evaluations they give them. Senators from less populous states receive more positive evaluations than those from larger states. Our interviews reveal that senators are also aware of this effect of constituency size. They offer several explanations for it based on the difficulties that senators from populous states face in communicating with and responding to their greater numbers of constituents.

Finally, constituency size influences senators' relationships with the representatives of organized interests. Lobbyists find it easier to gain access to senators representing less populous states. Regardless of whether they seek to influence senators directly by building personal relationships with them or indirectly by employing influential constituents to make their case, lobbyists find that senators representing less populous states are typically more accessible than those from larger states.

Taken as a whole, these findings suggest that the constraints senators face in performing their role differ greatly depending on the population of the state they represent. Constituency size shapes a senator's representational tasks to an even greater extent than does the institutional context of the Senate itself. For the senator from a small-population state, developing a close representational relationship with constituents is very similar to the task faced by House members. As a result, in the seventeen states with three or fewer congressional districts, senators are much like two extra House members, except that they have more influence. As state population increases, however, senators become less able to build personal relationships with their constituents and gain their trust. They must communicate with them in larger, more impersonal, and less interactive settings. In short, senators from large states are inescapably more distant from their constituents. In turn, they must employ different strategies to achieve their goals and, with their weaker constituency attachments, have less flexibility in office (as we will discuss in depth in chapter 5) than small-state senators.

Although the subject has received little attention in the political science literature, the distance between representative and represented raises important broader questions for the study of representation. First, should the greater distance between senators and their constituents in large states concern us? The answer depends on what one expects from the representational experience. The evidence suggests that constituents in more populous states expect less close personal contact from their senators. Californians, New Yorkers, and Texans do not expect to have their senators visit every county in their states at least once a year, as one of the small-population state senators we interviewed claimed to do, or to meet personally with them when they visit, or even to address them by their first names. For these constituents it may be sufficient to see their senators on television, read about them in newspapers, or hear them speak as part of a large audience rather than in a more intimate setting.

However, constituents in large states are not wholly satisfied with these more distant relationships. They consistently evaluate their senators less favorably than do people in small states. Even though constituents in populous states have different expectations than their counterparts in smaller ones, the representational distance opened up by increasing constituency size creates special problems for senators from large states. Although representing a small state in the Senate may be no guarantee that a senator will develop a close representational relationship with her constituents, it does appear to be a necessary condition. Our data on individual senators suggest that those from more populous states are unable to build close relationships with constituents or to receive very high approval ratings regardless of the emphasis they place on constituency-oriented concerns.

Second, the great variation in Senate constituency size raises an issue of fairness. The smaller distance between constituents and senators in less populous states means that these constituents have greater access to elected national policymakers than do their counterparts in larger states. A constituent in a small state can often reach her two senators as easily as she can reach her House member. As constituency size increases, however, constituents have less access to their more distant senators, and thus their access to elected national policymakers is increasingly limited to their House members. One may ask whether these differences in access—and in representational distance—affect the way people feel about government. Do people in less populous states, for example, feel more efficacious in their dealings with government than people in larger states? Lower levels of perceived efficacy in larger states would then parallel the lower approval ratings that senators representing them receive.

The differences in representational experience and in distance between representative and represented also raise substantive questions about the Senate as an institution. Once one has established, as we have done, that constituency size affects representational distance, it seems only natural to ask, Is the distance between senators and constituents in the largest states too great? Is there any upper limit to constituency size beyond which the distance between representative and represented becomes too great? This last question also points to the changes that have occurred historically as state populations have increased over time. As state populations have grown, the distance between senators and their constituents has almost certainly increased as well, despite advances in communication technology.

In the context of these questions, it is interesting to recall the Federalist–Anti-Federalist debates over representational distance. The Anti-Federalists were concerned with the great numbers of constituents represented by a few men in the first Congress. The Federalists were less concerned, and some, including Madison, even saw potential benefits in these greater distances. Although it is beyond the scope of this book to resolve once and for all whether the cost of increasing representational distance outweighs its benefits, this chapter does point to the need for thought. Clearly, then, the effects of constituency size on the representational experience illustrated in this study of the Senate raise concerns that are not only for that institution or for this time.

In the next chapter we examine another consequence of the equal representation of states in the Senate, the effect of constituency size on Senate elections. It is only reasonable to suppose that if increasing constituency size affects senators' ability to maintain close relationships with their constituents, then that effect should be reflected in the character and outcomes of Senate elections as well.

4

Electoral Competitiveness, Campaign Fund-Raising, and Partisan Advantage

As in the general study of Congress, scholars of elections have devoted considerably more attention to the House than to the Senate. When political scientists have examined Senate elections, they have typically focused on the differences between House and Senate, thus obscuring the differences among Senate elections themselves (Fenno 1982; Herrnson 1998; Krasno 1994). Comparing the average House election with the average Senate election is useful up to a point, but given the great variation in state populations and thus in electoral contexts, it can take us only so far in understanding Senate elections (Gronke, n.d.). After all, running for a Senate seat in California is very different from running in Wyoming or North Dakota.

Recently political scientists have begun to recognize the ways this great variation among states affects Senate campaigns and elections (Abramowitz 1988; Abramowitz and Segal 1992; Fenno 1982, 20–25, 1986, 1996; Hibbing and Brandes 1983; Westlye 1991, 154–58). A number of studies, for example, have found a relationship between state population and incumbency advantage in Senate elections (Hibbing and Brandes 1983; Abramowitz 1988; Abramowitz and Segal 1992; Westlye 1991, 154–58). As we showed in the previous chapter, senators in small states are able to establish and maintain closer representational linkages with their constituents than those in more populous states, so it seems they should reap greater rewards from incumbency. Past studies have not, however, examined the effects of state population on the competitiveness of all Senate elections.

In this chapter we argue first that this focus on incumbency advantage has led researchers to miss the effect that state population has on the competitiveness of Senate elections, regardless of whether an incumbent is running for reelection. We find that it has an effect independent of the effects of incumbency—the larger the state, the more competitive the election, all else being equal. In fact, when we compare open-seat Senate elections and Senate elections with incumbents running, the effect is the same. The winners of Senate elections in small states, regardless of their incumbency status, tend to win by wider margins than the winners of Senate elections in large states. These findings raise some interesting questions about the connection between campaigning and governing, which we discuss below. Because they tend to win elections by wider margins, for example, do small-state senators enjoy greater flexibility in office? If a wider margin provides a stronger sense of constituent support—and our interviews suggest it does—these senators may also feel better able to take on tough issues in office.

Second, we turn to another important issue in Senate elections, campaign fund-raising. Observers have long recognized that Senate elections in larger states are more expensive than those in smaller states, and thus senators and candidates in larger states must raise more money. They have not considered, however, that state size might also affect the sources from which senators raise campaign funds. Elaborating a distinction formulated by Snyder (1993), we demonstrate that senators from small states can rely more heavily on "investors" (those who contribute to gain access and other private benefits) to fund their campaigns, while senators from more populous states must rely more on "consumers" (those who contribute to express their support for a candidate). The amount senators raise from investors does not vary with state population, so senators from larger states, who need more money to fund their campaigns, must work harder to raise it from consumers (individual contributors), whereas senators in the small states can raise much of what they need simply by tapping the investors (political action committees). In addition, senators from more populous states begin earlier in the election cycle and devote more time and resources to fund-raising, both because they need more money to conduct a campaign and because they must raise these additional funds from more labor-intensive sources. This means that large-state senators spend more time campaigning and thus have less time for governing than their colleagues from smaller states.

In the final part of the chapter we look at how apportionment has influenced the partisan composition of the Senate since the institution of popular elections in 1914. We find that throughout most of this century Senate apportionment has affected partisan composition by enabling the political party that does better than the other in small-state elections to hold Senate seats disproportionate to its share of the national vote. Apportionment has usually favored the minority party in the Senate, and thus equal representation of states has functioned in a countermajoritarian fashion for much of twentieth-century American history.

State Population and Electoral Competitiveness

The study of congressional elections is primarily the study of the causes of and constraints on competitiveness. Competitive elections are important for democratic government because lack of competition raises the specter of unaccountability. If representatives do not face viable challengers, at least periodically, they will be less concerned with the preferences and interests of their constituents. These beliefs lie at the root of the concern with measuring and explaining incumbency advantage (see Abramowitz 1991; Alford and Hibbing 1981; Collie 1981; Cover 1977; Cover and Mayhew 1977; Erikson 1971; Fiorina 1977; Jacobson 1987; McAdams and Johannes 1988), with the "misallocation of resources" in congressional campaigns (Fiorina 1981; Jacobson 1993; Jacobson and Kernell 1983), and with the differential resources available to incumbents and challengers (Herrnson 1997, 1998).

In this chapter we ask whether Senate apportionment has any influence on the competitiveness of Senate elections. Does the great variation in the size of Senate constituencies systematically affect electoral competitiveness? Are Senate elections in large states more competitive than those in small states? In the following sections we present and test two separate, nonexclusive hypotheses about the effect of state population on the competitiveness of Senate elections. The first hypothesis is that state population affects competitiveness because incumbency advantage is greater in less populous states than in more populous ones. The second is that smaller states are less politically diverse than larger ones and thus will have less competitive Senate elections regardless of incumbency status. We discuss each of these hypotheses below and specify the empirical results required in order to accept or reject them.

Two Hypotheses about the Effect of State Population

State Population and Incumbency Advantage

Incumbency advantage is defined as "the increment to the vote margin that a candidate gains by virtue of being the incumbent" (Erikson and Wright 1993, 100). As such, incumbency advantage is conceptually distinct from other factors that can make an incumbent electorally secure, such as characteristics of the state, especially its partisanship, and the tendency of incumbents to draw only weak challengers and to be strong candidates themselves. In short, then, incumbency advantage refers to the electoral returns on incumbent behavior—casework, use of the perquisites of office (staff, travel allowances, the frank) for advertising, position taking, and claiming credit for bringing home federal dollars to the state (Fiorina 1977; Mayhew

1974)—and to the systematic fund-raising advantages incumbents have over challengers.

State population size affects some, but not all, of these sources of incumbency advantage. As we discussed in the preceding chapter, constituents in less populous states are more likely to turn to their senators for help with a problem. Also, incumbent senators in smaller states are able to be more accessible to their constituents than incumbents in larger ones and thus to service a higher proportion of them. Therefore whatever advantages incumbents gain from being accessible to constituents and responsive to requests for casework should be greater in less populous states. Incumbents in small states are just as able as other senators to bring home particularized benefits for their states, but the smaller the state, the greater the per capita benefit for any given amount of federal funds. As we will discuss in the next chapter, small-state incumbents thus have even greater incentives than others to bring home particularized benefits and reap whatever electoral gains providing these benefits can afford.

In previous research, however, political scientists have been unable to demonstrate that casework and procuring particularized benefits for constituents improves incumbents' electoral success. Although members of Congress tend to believe that these activities matter for reelection (Davidson and Oleszek 1998, 125–18), studies have failed to uncover any relationship between constituency service and incumbent vote margin (Feldman and Jondrow 1984; Johannes 1984; Johannes and McAdams 1981; McAdams and Johannes 1988; Parker and Parker 1985; Stein and Bickers 1994a). Despite the lack of an established empirical link between constituency service and electoral success, it is safe to assume that if these behaviors do in fact affect success, then incumbents from small states are advantaged relative to their colleagues.

Another possible source of increased incumbency advantage for small-state senators lies in their closer representational relationships with their constituents. Because small-state senators maintain closer contact with their constituents—both qualitatively and quantitatively—they may have higher name recognition and be able to gain greater advantages from advertising, position taking, and credit claiming than senators from more populous states.

One must be cautious, however, not to overstate these advantages. Challengers to incumbent senators in less populous states are also able to develop closer contact with voters. As a result, the *differential* in voter contact between incumbents and challengers in small states may be little greater than that in populous states. Abramowitz and Segal (1992, 43–46) provide evidence for this in their study of Senate elections, showing that although voters in small states are more likely than voters in large states to recognize and to favorably evaluate their incumbent senators, they are also more likely to recognize and favorably evaluate challengers.

State population does not affect, or affects only marginally, some other sources of incumbency advantage. Incumbent senators in all states have advantages over their challengers in raising campaign funds.[1] There is no theoretical reason to suppose that challengers in small states will have systematically greater difficulty in raising funds to mount their campaigns than challengers elsewhere. Similarly, the frank and appropriate travel allowances are allocated to all senators, regardless of state population. Other perquisites of office, such as personal and committee staff, are granted in a way that reflects, albeit imperfectly, differences in the size of the constituencies senators represent. Although senators from more populous states receive larger staff allowances and more generous office accounts, the increments do not keep pace with state population, so small-state senators do have more staff per constituent.

Several political scientists have investigated the relationship between incumbency advantage and state population (Abramowitz 1988; Abramowitz and Segal 1992; Hibbing and Alford 1990; Hibbing and Brandes 1983). To test the hypothesis that incumbent senators become more electorally vulnerable as state population increases, Hibbing and Brandes regressed the average vote share received by incumbents in each state on the average number of congressional districts in the state for the period 1946–80, controlling for the average level of party competition in the state.[2] They found that incumbent senators could expect to receive 0.17 percent less of the two-party vote for each additional congressional district in the state, or a difference of nearly nine percentage points between senators running for reelection in the most and least populous states. Abramowitz and Segal (1992) found a smaller relationship between incumbent vote margin and state population in their analysis of Senate elections in the lower forty-eight states between 1974 and 1986: they reported that senators running for reelection in the least populous states could expect to receive 3 percent more of the vote than a senator running in California (111).

Recent research criticizes these findings. Krasno (1994) and Westlye (1991) observe that although regression analysis reveals that senators in less populous states tend to win reelection by wider margins, they are not more likely to be reelected than senators in larger states.[3] Thus, even if small-state senators are more likely to win by wide margins, they are not electorally advantaged in the most important respect—reelection success.

Another problem with these studies is that they do not consider that state population might affect all Senate elections, not just those in which incumbents are running. These studies all assume that state population affects only the ability of incumbents to win reelection: "The more constituents there are, the more difficult they are [for incumbents] to please" (Hibbing and Brandes 1983, 817). There is no reason, then, to expect population size to matter in open-seat elections. Abramowitz and Segal (1992), for example,

include state population as an explanatory variable in models predicting incumbents' vote percentage (109) but omit it from models predicting outcomes in open-seat elections (115). If state population affects the electoral
competitiveness of open-seat elections as well as of those in which incumbents are running, then these studies conflate an incumbency advantage effect with a broader state population effect.

The Diversity-Competitiveness Hypothesis

Our second hypothesis concerning the relation between state population and
the competitiveness of Senate elections is that small states are less politically
diverse and more homogeneous than large ones and thus should have less
competitive Senate elections. Unlike the incumbency advantage hypothesis,
this second hypothesis applies equally to all Senate elections, regardless of
whether an incumbent is running.

The idea that population size and diversity are closely connected is not
new. At the very beginning of political philosophy, Plato described his ideal
republic as being necessarily small because only a small city-state would be
homogeneous enough to possess a common good and avoid the dangers of
factional strife. Large states would be so heterogeneous that political conflict
would be inevitable. Modern political thinkers, including the American
framers, have been less concerned about the ill effects of political conflict,
tending to view it as both healthy and necessary. James Madison turned the
classical argument on its head in *Federalist* 10, arguing that large republics
were superior precisely because their greater diversity would make the formation of a majority faction less likely. The larger the republic, Madison
posited, the greater the variety of interests it would encompass and thus the
less likely it was that a single political majority could dominate (Hamilton,
Jay, and Madison 1987, 127). The politics of large republics would be more
pluralistic because majority coalitions would be difficult both to form and to
maintain.

Several empirical studies support the thesis that diversity is associated with
the size of the political unit (Eyestone and Eulau 1968; Lowery and Gray
1995, 1996). Lowery and Gray contend that there are "environmental constraints" on how many interest groups can survive in a state. The most important of these is population: smaller populations cannot sustain as many
interest groups as large ones, just as smaller ecosystems cannot sustain as many
species. Other research finds that diversity leads to more political conflict
(Black 1974; Dahl and Tufte 1973). In a comparative study of the smaller
European democracies, Dahl and Tufte concluded that both the diversity of
political parties and competition among them increase with the size of the

political unit (1973, 100). In a study of municipal elections in the United States, Black found that large cities tend to have competitive elections for city office more frequently than small cities (1974). Taken together, these studies support our contention that larger political units are more diverse and that diversity increases political competition.

We recognize that treating state population as a proxy for political diversity may provoke some criticism. Political scientists have typically viewed constituency size and diversity as conceptually distinct and thus have attempted to develop measures of diversity that are separate from constituency size (Bond 1983; Fiorina 1974; Gray and Lowery 1993; Hibbing and Alford 1990; Krasno 1994; Patterson and Caldeira 1984). These efforts to measure state political diversity without taking population into account, however, suffer from at least three difficulties.

First, one of the most striking things about existing measures of state diversity is the lack of variation they find across states. These measures—regardless of whether they are constructed using averaging techniques (Bond 1983; Fiorina 1974; Morgan and Wilson 1990; Patterson and Caldeira 1984), Herfindahl indexes (Lowery and Gray 1993), or standard deviations within states on responses to survey research items (Hibbing and Alford 1990; Krasno 1994)—typically vary little across states. The most commonly used measure, the Sullivan index of socioeconomic and cultural diversity (Bond 1983; Fiorina 1974), can theoretically range from 0 (least diverse) to 1 (most diverse). When applied to the fifty states in 1990, however, the states varied on this index only from 0.40 (Arkansas) to 0.55 (New York), with a tiny standard deviation of 0.04 (Morgan and Wilson 1990). Lowery and Gray's (1993) index of the diversity of state interest group systems—calculated using a Herfindahl index, which can theoretically range from a score of 1.0 for least diverse to 0.10 for most diverse—actually varies only from 0.1702 (for Pennsylvania, the least diverse state) to 0.1148 (for Kentucky, the most diverse state). Strangely enough, this measure classifies South Dakota (0.1157) as having a more diverse interest group system than California (0.1189). Diversity measures based on within-state standard deviations on survey research items also suffer from a lack of variation. Using this type of measure to assess ideological diversity, for example, Krasno reports that in the least ideologically diverse state (New Hampshire) the standard deviation on a Senate Election Study item asking respondents to place themselves on a seven-point ideology scale was 1.16, while in the most ideologically diverse state (Mississippi) the standard deviation was 1.72.[4] Clearly these measures are not adequately describing the rich variation among states.

Second, these measures often contradict what we think we know about state diversity. This is not to say that any indicator that does not conform precisely to our expectations is flawed, but when measures indicate that Mississippi is the most diverse state or that Pennsylvania is the least diverse, skepticism is justified. Similarly, any measure classifying South Dakota as more diverse than California is questionable to say the least.

Third, these measures of diversity have not served as useful explanatory variables in any of the models where they have been applied. Even though scholars have used different indicators, models, and dependent variables, they have found no statistically significant relationship between their measures of constituency diversity and their dependent variables of interest, including variables for electoral competitiveness and incumbency advantage (Bond 1983; Kenney and Rice 1985; Krasno 1994; Patterson and Caldeira 1984). Of course the lack of positive findings may simply mean that state diversity has no effect on incumbency advantage or electoral competition. On the other hand, it may also indicate that these existing measures are not capturing the kind of diversity that is likely to affect electoral politics.

State population may be superior to these other measures as an indicator of diversity for one important reason: it makes no assumptions about the kinds of constituent diversity that will be politically relevant at particular times. Socioeconomic diversity, for example, may not be a reliable or valid measure of *political* diversity in a constituency. Income, race, and other socioeconomic diversity certainly has the potential to create political cleavages, but over time none of these factors by itself will be a consistent predictor of political heterogeneity. Depending on the issues that are salient at any particular time, diversity along some dimensions will be politically relevant while diversity along others will not. Moreover, the sort of diversity that generates political conflict in one state will often fail to do so in another, depending on any number of factors, including how competing candidates frame the issues. Attempting to circumvent this problem by combining many kinds of variation into a single summary measure (like a Sullivan or Herfindahl index) tends to wash out differences across states. Using state population as a measure of diversity, however, requires only the Madisonian assumption that greater number of constituents alone means more political interests and thus more potential political cleavages.

Of course none of the states is as small as Plato's republic. Every state is large enough, potentially, to be politically heterogeneous. Large states, however, will encompass more political interests than small states, all other things being equal. In other words, constituency size and constituency diversity are not nearly so separate in reality as they are in theory. Although small population does not guarantee homogeneity, large population does result in heterogeneity. Population size is thus an imperfect measure of political diversity, but it is arguably superior to competing measures.

Testing the Two Hypotheses

There are four possible results from tests of these hypotheses: (1) If the first hypothesis (that state population affects incumbency advantage) holds but the second hypothesis (that state population affects the competitiveness of all Senate elections) does not, then our analysis of the margin of victory in Senate elections will show a statistically significant effect for the state population variable only for elections in which incumbents are running. (2) If the second hypothesis holds but the first does not, then state population will have the same effect on all Senate elections, regardless of whether an incumbent is running. (3) If both hypotheses hold, then state population will affect the competitiveness of all Senate elections, but there will be an additional, stronger effect for state population on elections in which incumbents are running. (4) Neither hypothesis may be supported.

Our hypotheses about the effect of constituency size on Senate elections are not confined to a particular historical period. Unlike previous studies that are limited, at best, to post–World War II Senate elections, we include all regular Senate elections since 1914, when the Seventeenth Amendment went into effect.[5] Using the longer time span is an advantage, given the many short-term factors that always influence Senate elections.

The dependent variable in our regression models is the margin of victory in Senate elections or, in the case of the model for elections with incumbents running, incumbent vote margin (meaning that margin of victory is negative when the incumbent loses).[6] The independent variable is the population of the state (in millions) at the most recent census.[7] In each of the models, we include a pair of dummy variables to control for the level of interparty competition in the state. Based on Ranney's regularly updated index of party competitiveness, states are classified as two-party competitive states, one-party states, or modified one-party states (Bibby et al. 1983, 1990; Ranney and Kendall 1954; Ranney 1965, 1971, 1976).[8] We include these controls to account for the unique historical factors that inhibited the growth of two-party competition in some regions of the country, particularly the South. For much of the period studied, southern states were both one-party dominant and middle-sized and thus will obscure the relationship between state population and the competitiveness of Senate elections unless appropriate controls—like the Ranney index—are included in the model (see Krasno 1994; Westlye 1991).[9]

In this study the unit of analysis is a Senate election in a particular state in a particular year. Employing this pooled time-series cross-sectional design has two advantages. First, it does not artificially reduce the amount of variation either in state population or in the dependent variable, margin of victory in Senate elections. Second, it accounts for the population growth that nearly all states have experienced over the period. If state population affects the competitiveness of elections, then population growth within states—not just differences in constituency size among states—should make Senate elections more competitive over time.[10]

Pooling time-series and cross-sectional data presents some problems for model specification. Although the relationship between state population and the competitiveness of Senate elections may be estimated by a straightforward ordinary least squares (OLS) model, as previous researchers have done, the assumptions of such a model may be too restrictive. The error term in a panel study is likely to be contaminated by systematic effects introduced by different cross-sectional units (states) and by different points in time (election years). These unmeasured state-specific and election-specific effects on the error term would not be disaggregated in a standard OLS model; there would be one error structure for the entire pool (Sayrs 1989).[11] As a result, the residuals in a standard OLS model may be contaminated by state- and election-specific effects. Therefore we employ fixed effects (or least squares, dummy variable) models to control for these otherwise unmeasured year-specific and state-specific factors (England et al. 1988). Dummy variables are included in the models for all election years and states in order to capture the effects associated with particular cross sections or election years. The estimates derived from the least squares dummy variables (LSDV) models will not be contaminated by the effects of unmeasured variables associated with the unique characteristics of particular states or election years (Sayrs 1989).

Findings

Table 4.1 shows the LSDV regression estimates for the effect of state population on the margin of victory in open-seat Senate races and on the incumbent's vote margin in races with incumbent senators running.[12] The results of these regressions reveal that state population has a significant effect on all Senate elections, not just on those in which incumbents are running. The coefficient for state population is negative for both models, meaning that as population increases, the margin of victory decreases, all other factors being held constant. In open-seat races, for each increase of one million in state population the margin of victory in the race declines by 1.07 percent ($p < .05$). In races with incumbents running, the effect of state population on incumbent vote margin is -1.65 percent ($p < .01$).

Results from standard OLS models mirror the pattern shown here, but the more appropriate LSDV models reveal a much larger effect of state population on Senate elections than has been found in any previous study.[13] The

Table 4.1 LSDV Estimates of the Effects of State Population on the Margin of Victory in Open-Seat Senate Races and on Incumbent Vote Margin in Races with Incumbent Senators Running, 1914–96

Variable	Open-Seat Races b (t-statistic)	Races with Incumbents Running b (t-statistic)
Population	−1.07*	−1.65**
	(−1.67)	(3.75)
One-party dominant	41.03**	34.08**
	(6.51)	(9.33)
Modified one-party dominant	2.18	5.36**
	(0.74)	(2.75)
F-statistic	13.01**	29.59**
Adj. $R^{2\,a}$	.75^a	.73^a
N	371	986
Mean	21.65	25.66

^{a} LSDV is a no-intercept regression model. As such, the value of the R^2 cannot be compared with the R^2 for models that include an intercept. (For this model, R^2 measures the proportion of variability in the ys about the origin explained by regression.)
**$p < .01$ level, one-tailed test; *$p < .05$ level, one-tailed test.

larger effect found with the fixed effects model over a standard OLS model suggests that failure to disaggregate the error term in the latter type of model leads to an understatement of the effect of state population on Senate electoral competitiveness.

As expected, the control variables in both models explain much of the variation in the dependent variable. The dummy variable for one-party states has the single greatest effect on the size of margin of victory—yielding coefficients of 41.03 ($p < .01$) in the model for open seats and of 34.08 ($p < .01$) in the model with incumbents running. An effect this large is not surprising given that during the heyday of one-partyism in the South margins of victory of more than ninety percentage points were not uncommon in Senate elections. The dummy variable for modified one-party states has a much smaller effect in both models, as one would expect, yielding a coefficient of 5.36 ($p < .01$) in the model for races with incumbents running and a not statistically significant coefficient in the open-seats model. These results also show that failing to control for regional one-partyism in some previous studies (Krasno 1994; Westlye 1991) yields an understatement of the relationship between state population and the competitiveness of Senate elections.

The results of these two regression models further reveal that state population is an important variable affecting all Senate elections. From these results, we reject the first possible outcome described above: state population does not simply enhance the incumbency advantage of senators from less populous states. Thus these findings demand that we revise conventional wisdom on *how* state population affects the competitiveness of Senate elections. State population structures the context for all Senate elections, not just races in which incumbents are running for reelection. In fact we must conduct some additional tests to determine whether state population affects incumbency advantage in Senate elections *at all*.

Given that state population affects the competitiveness of both kinds of Senate elections, we must determine whether the data support both our hypotheses (third possible outcome above) or only our second hypothesis (less populous states are less politically diverse than larger states and thus have less competitive Senate elections). To determine whether state population has the same effect on margin of victory in both open-seat Senate elections and elections with incumbents running, we began by conducting a Chow test to determine whether the regression coefficients in the models are different in the two subsets of Senate elections.[14] Results of this test show that we cannot reject the null hypothesis that the regression coefficients in the two equations are the same; thus we may estimate the relationship between state population and the competitiveness of Senate elections in a single regression model rather than in two separate models.

Does representing a less populous state increase a senator's incumbency advantage compared with that of senators from larger states? To answer this question fully we must separate the effect of state population on incumbency advantage both from its effect on the competitiveness of all Senate elections and from the advantage that all incumbents have. To do this, we add two new variables to the analysis, shown as model 1 in table 4.2. First, because Senate elections with incumbents running are generally less competitive than open-seat elections, we include a dummy variable indicating whether an incumbent is running. This variable will capture the incumbency advantage in Senate elections that is constant across all states. Second, to determine whether small-state senators benefit from any additional incumbency advantage, we include a variable interacting population and the dummy variable for whether an incumbent is running. If representing a less populous state enhances a senator's incumbency advantage, then the coefficient for this interaction term (population × incumbent running) will be negative.

The results of model 1 provide no support for the hypothesis that representing a less populous state increases a senator's incumbency advantage.

Table 4.2 LSDV Estimates of the Effect of State Population on the Margin of Victory in Senate Elections, 1914–96

Variable	Model 1 b (t-statistic)	Model 2 b (t-statistic)
Population	−1.73** (−4.28)	−1.49** (−4.42)
Incumbent runnning	2.26 (1.52)	3.34** (3.05)
State population × incumbent running	0.32 (1.08)	—
One-party dominant	35.06** (12.13)	35.01** (12.12)
Modified one-party dominant	3.54** (2.36)	3.53** (2.36)
F-statistic	46.22**	46.22**
Adj. R^2	.76 [a]	.76 [a]
N	1,357	1,357
Mean	24.56	24.56

[a] LSDV is a no-intercept regression model. As such, the value of the R^2 cannot be compared to the R^2 for models that include an intercept. (For this model, R^2 measures the proportion of variability in the ys about the origin explained by regression.)

**$p < .01$ level, one-tailed test; *$p < .05$ level, one-tailed test

The coefficient for the interaction term population × incumbent running is small, incorrectly signed, and not statistically significant. Although Senate elections in less populous states are generally less competitive than Senate elections in more populous ones, small-state senators gain no additional incumbency advantage from representing a small state.[15]

The best estimate of the effect of state population on the competitiveness of Senate elections is thus displayed as model 2 in table 4.2.[16] As shown here, for each increase in state population of one million, the margin of victory in Senate elections declines by 1.49 percent ($p < .01$). A coefficient of this size means that, all else being equal, Senate elections in more populous states tend to be decided by much closer margins than Senate elections in less populous states—predicting a difference of forty points in margin of victory between the least and most populous states. The coefficient for the variable indicating whether an incumbent is running shows that the presence of an incumbent in a Senate race tends to increase the winner's vote margin by 3.34 points

($p < .01$).[17] One-party and modified one-party dominance tend to increase the winner's vote margin by 35.01 ($p < .001$) and 3.53 ($p < .01$) points, respectively.

Discussion

These findings demonstrate that state population is an important contextual factor affecting the dynamics of all Senate elections. Although our results lend support to other scholars who have found that state population affects Senate elections, we establish that conventional wisdom about the relationship between state population and the competitiveness of Senate elections is flawed. Senators in less populous states do not win reelection by larger margins than senators in more populous states because they enjoy an enhanced level of incumbency advantage. Instead, state population shapes the outcomes of all Senate elections, regardless of whether an incumbent is running. As shown in our final regression model displayed in table 4.2, the effect of incumbency advantage is constant across all states, and the effect of state population is constant across both types of Senate elections—open-seat elections and elections with incumbents running.

These findings mean that incumbents in less populous states do not successfully exploit their status to rent their constituents' votes through constituency service to any greater extent than senators in other states. The closer representational relationships between senators and constituents in less populous states described in chapter 3 do not translate into additional electoral advantages. The most likely reason is that Senate challengers in less populous states compete with incumbents on the same contextual footing. In other words, although incumbents in small states can maintain closer contact with constituents than incumbents in large states, challengers in small states are also able to develop closer ties with voters. Furthermore, we cannot attribute the wider margins of victory in small-state Senate elections to the ability of incumbents in those states to service their constituents more effectively with casework and pork barrel projects, despite their significant advantages in this regard. Perhaps we should not be surprised at these findings, given that political scientists have been unable to establish any empirical link between variation in constituency service and incumbency advantage in congressional elections.

The wider margins of victory in small-state Senate elections simply mean that larger percentages of voters in small states tend to have endorsed the outcomes of their Senate elections. No doubt the higher approval ratings that small-state senators enjoy compared with large-state senators (discussed in chapter 3) reflect in part the wider margins by which they tend to be elected. Instead of attributing these wider margins of victory to an enhanced ability of incumbents in smaller states to "buy" the loyalty of voters through constituency service, we should recognize that the greater political homogeneity of less populous states makes it more likely that the winning candidate—whether an incumbent or not—will be able to appeal to a constituency significantly larger than a simple electoral majority. Accordingly, candidates in more populous states typically win by smaller margins because the greater diversity of those states makes it more difficult for any single candidate to appeal to a supermajority of voters.

Because representing a less populous state does not increase a senator's incumbency advantage, these findings do not raise troubling questions about electoral accountability in small states. Incumbent senators in small states do not appear to be less accountable to their constituents than those in large states. Our findings, unlike those of previous studies, fit with the established fact that reelection rates for incumbent senators are not higher in less populous states (Krasno 1994; Westlye 1991). Winners of Senate elections win by larger margins in less populous states because, all else being equal, these states are less politically diverse. If, as others had concluded, incumbency advantage were the source of the greater margins of victory in smaller states, then the fact that incumbent senators are reelected at similar rates regardless of state size would make much less sense. Our findings show that the effects of incumbency are constant across state population size, and similar reelection rates reflect this uniform effect.

The prominent recent defeats of small-state incumbent senators attest that small-state voters can hold their senators electorally accountable. The defeats of Sens. Larry Pressler (R-S.Dak.) in 1996, Chic Hecht (R-Nev.) in 1988, and James Abdnor (R-S.Dak.) and Mark Andrews (R-N.Dak.) in 1986 suggest that when small-state incumbents alienate important interests within their constituencies, they will pay the price at the ballot box, just as senators in larger states do. Small-state senators cannot use their constituent contact rates or their skills at constituency service to insulate themselves from electoral pressures to any greater extent than other senators.

Although these findings concerning the effect of state population on Senate elections do not prompt new concerns about electoral accountability, they do raise several issues about representation. First, these differences in margin of victory may affect the representational styles senators adopt. Fenno (1978) distinguishes between two stages in a representative's career, expansionist and protectionist. In the expansionist stage, a representative "is building a reliable reelection constituency" (172). She is reaching out to new voters and groups, getting involved in new issue areas, and experimenting with different home styles in order to first solidify a core of strong supporters and then broaden the reelection constituency. In the protectionist stage, however, a representative is "most concerned about keeping the electoral support already attained, about maintaining the primary-plus-reelection constituencies" (173). To do this he cultivates existing relationships with constituents, working to build stronger and deeper bonds of trust rather than forging new relationships. Our findings suggest that senators representing less populous states may be able to move from the expansionist to the protectionist stage of their careers more quickly than those from larger states. Even in their initial races, winners of Senate elections in small states tend to win by wider margins than winners in large states. Compared with senators representing populous states, then, senators from small states can afford to move to a protectionist strategy earlier in their careers, cultivating their existing supporters rather than seeking to enlist more. By contrast, senators representing more populous states win by narrower margins and will thus tend to feel more electorally vulnerable. This greater sense of vulnerability is likely to lead them to prolong the expansionist stage of their careers. Senators representing the most populous states—for whom close representational relationships with constituents are rarely if ever possible—may be forced to maintain an expansionist strategy continuously. (This may be another reason small-state senators do not enjoy higher levels of incumbency advantage.)

Second, if we draw a distinction between the activities of campaigning and governing, these findings suggest that senators from less populous states have more time for governing than do those from larger ones. The trade-off between maintaining constituent ties and achieving legislative success in Washington is intense for most members of Congress, who already face increased demands on both fronts and a legislative calendar extending nearly year-round (Fenno 1978). For senators in the most populous states—who must handle so many more demands on their time from interest groups and constituents—these tensions are even greater. When an incumbent wins by a slim margin, moreover, these tensions are compounded. Incumbents appear electorally vulnerable after winning very close races and thus encourage strong candidates to mount challenges against them (Jacobson 1992; Jacobson and Kernell 1983). As a result, an incumbent who recently survived a close race is likely to devote more time in office to cultivating constituents (Bickers and Stein 1996) and to amassing a campaign war chest to discourage strong challengers (Epstein and Zemsky 1995). In addition, campaigning in a hard-fought reelection race itself demands a great deal more from a senator in terms of personal time and energy than running a low-key campaign with only weak opposition (Westlye 1991).

The findings presented here mean that senators who represent more populous states can expect close races for reelection more frequently than senators from smaller states. Between 1946 and 1996, incumbents from the most populous states (twenty-seven or more congressional districts) faced close reelection races (defined as races won with less than 55 percent of the two-party vote) fully half the time. During the same period, senators from the least populous states (three or fewer congressional districts) faced close races for reelection only about one-third of the time. To the extent that these electoral experiences shape behavior in office, senators from large states experience greater pressures to devote time to campaigning.

Third, these findings suggest that senators who represent less populous states not only may have more *time* for governing than senators from larger states, they may also have more *flexibility*. Just as winning by a narrow margin can have representational costs for senators, winning by a wide margin can have representational benefits. Wide margins of victory often give legislators a sense of freedom or—to use Fenno's term—voting leeway (1978, 151). Because they tend to win with wider margins, senators who represent smaller states are more likely to have this leeway.

Wide margins of victory are valuable resources for members of Congress when they face difficult choices in office. One of the small-state senators we interviewed explained the connection between margin of victory and representational behavior in this way: "Margins of victory have effects on people. It gives encouragement to people to vote for a civil rights bill. It's given them a cushion to vote for things that were against interests in their home state. It's the cushion to vote for environmental issues that affect industries in your state. It gives you maneuvering room." A former chief of staff for another small-state senator explained the connection in similar terms: A wide margin of victory "gives them [senators] some comfort level. . . .Nancy Kassebaum wins with 85 percent and she doesn't have to be as concerned that she is not always voting in agreement with what her Kansans would want. . . .Winning by large margins usually gives a senator some wiggle room." This freedom is obviously never unlimited. The greater homogeneity of small states almost certainly means there are dominant interests in these states that their senators must not offend, regardless of the percentage of the vote they won in their last race. Even so, winning by a wide margin gives senators greater electoral security, and this sense of security can make a difference when they consider how to vote on a tough issue or whether to undertake an active role on a politically sensitive topic. The flexibility or "maneuvering room" obtained from winning by a wide margin may be particularly helpful to senators who seek leadership positions. We explore the advantages small-state senators have in terms of leadership in the next chapter.

State Population and Campaign Fund-Raising

Variation in constituency size affects Senate elections in a second important respect. It creates very different contexts as senators seek to raise campaign funds. Senators from large states face very different fund-raising tasks than those from small states, in terms of both the amount of funds they need and the sources from which they can raise them. Most political scientists who study campaign finance, however, are not sensitive to the way state population shapes the fund-raising needs and behavior of incumbent senators. Instead, they typically focus on comparisons between the fund-raising patterns of the average senator and the average House member (Goldenberg and Traugott 1984, 59–76; Herrnson 1998, 128–56; Jacobson 1989; Magleby and Nelson 1990, 48–71) or between those of the average Senate incumbent and the average Senate challenger (Abramowitz and Segal 1992, 123–43; Jacobson 1989; Magleby and Nelson 1990, 72–97). These analytic techniques obscure the great variation in fund-raising behavior among senators themselves. In this section we first examine how state population affects campaign fund-raising in the Senate and then suggest some reasons why this in turn influences representational behavior.

The most obvious way state population affects Senate reelection campaigns is simply that campaign costs are much higher in large states. Differences in constituency size result in great variation in the amount incumbent senators need to raise—far greater variation than among House incumbents. Media expenses account for about half of campaign expenditures in Senate races (Davidson and Oleszek 1998, 90). Beyond the initial fixed costs of producing television or radio advertisements, however, the cost of mass media increases with the number of people the candidate intends to reach.[18] Similarly, expenses for direct mail solicitations increase with the number of people targeted.

Senators representing small states may even choose to rely less on "wholesale" expensive mass media in their campaigns, preferring to meet voters at lower expense in face-to-face "retail" settings such as festivals, fairs, and factory gates (Fenno 1982, 20–25). Senators from large states, by contrast, have little choice in the matter. They simply must raise enough funds to mount a media-intensive campaign, the only way to communicate with so many people in the relatively short time available. As 1996 New Jersey Senate candidate Richard Zimmer explained, "In South Dakota, the Senate candidates can meet a very large percentage of the electorate just by going to one football game," but "in a state with eight million people and four million voters, regardless of how many people you can pack into a room, as a practical matter you are not reaching that large a percentage of the electorate" (MacFarquhar 1996). In light of this, Zimmer concluded that although "my preference is to knock on doors and to visit factory gates and talk to people one on one," these campaign techniques are "almost an indulgence given the realities of modern politics" (MacFarquhar 1996). Even, we might add, in a populous state as geographically compact as New Jersey. In short, senators running in less populous states need less money both because they have fewer voters to reach and because they may opt to rely more heavily on means that are less costly than mass media.

Less obviously, constituency size also affects the *sources* of campaign funds for senators. Building on the work of James Snyder, we distinguish between two types of contributors to Senate campaigns: investors and consumers. Investors, according to Snyder (1993, 219), contribute to Senate campaigns to attain "private benefits in return for their money." For many interest groups and corporations, the potential gains from investing in Senate campaigns are, as Snyder argues, private benefits—primarily access to a senator and a senator's support of government actions benefiting the investor, including the adoption of special tax exemptions, assistance with executive agencies, and procurement of government grants and contracts. We can, however, extend Snyder's definition of "investor" to include not just those who seek private benefits from government, but all those persons and organizations who contribute to a Senate campaign in order to influence the behavior of senators. Many investors contribute to senators not merely to obtain private benefits but to encourage them to participate in committee and on the floor on issues that these investors believe are in the broader public interest. Regardless of whether they want private benefits or the adoption of particular public policies, investors actively seek out Senate candidates to fund and thus to attempt to influence. Because they lose their "investment" should they support a candidate who fails to win the election, investors typically prefer to fund candidates who are very likely to win, thus favoring incumbents (Herrnson 1997; Jacobson 1989; Sabato 1984, 72–84).

Among incumbents, total investor contributions would differ across senators only when campaign investors as a group perceive some senators as being more powerful than others or otherwise better able to advance their goals. The Senate is highly individualistic, and its leaders have relatively few special powers, especially compared with leaders in the House. Thus the institutional power to advance investors' goals is broadly distributed in the Senate. For this reason total investor contributions will differ little among senators. In choosing which senators will receive their contributions, investors will take into account particular senators' voting records, the predominant economic interests in their constituencies, their committee assignments, their ideology, their partisanship, and any number of other factors (Grier and Munger 1993; Schiller 1997). In the aggregate, however, senators will acquire similar amounts of total investor contributions because they have relatively equal power in the institution. Accordingly, researchers have found that neither Senate leaders nor powerful committee members receive additional campaign contributions from investors generally (Grier and Munger 1993; Snyder 1993).

Because the power to advance investors' goals is not related to the size of a senator's constituency, state population should have no effect on the total amount of investor contributions that senators receive. As Snyder explains, "Total investor contributions will not depend on how close the race is, nor on the demographic or socioeconomic circumstances of the constituency in which the race is held, unless these circumstances directly affect the amount of favors the winning candidate can deliver" (1993, 220; see also Gerber 1998, 405). In other words, despite their greater need for funds, senators who represent large states are not more powerful than those from small states and thus will not be able to obtain more funds from investors.

"Consumers," by contrast, contribute to candidates less to influence their behavior once in office than simply to help them get elected. Compared with investors, this type of contributor donates funds to Senate campaigns for less instrumental and more expressive reasons. Consumers give funds to proclaim their support. They may do so because they share a candidate's partisan affiliation, ideology, ethnicity, or religious affiliation. Candidates themselves stimulate contributions from this type of contributor through direct mail and other solicitations. Consumers may even contribute simply "because they enjoy rubbing elbows with . . . political elites" (Herrnson 1997, 114). The important point about this type of contributor is that candidates who have more supporters will also have more consumer contributors. This simply means that, generally speaking, senators who represent more populous states will be able to raise more funds from this type of contributor than those who represent smaller states. A few will be exceptions to this pattern. Senators who attract large national constituencies because of their party leadership positions, strong ideological commitments, or celebrity status—Sens. Jesse Helms (R-N.C.) and Paul Wellstone (D-Minn.) are two obvious examples—have access to a broad base of consumer contributors beyond their geographic constituencies. For most senators, however, the bulk of their consumer contributors are drawn from within their geographic constituencies.[19]

According to this logic, we expect to find that state population affects the sources of campaign funds because senators from less populous states can rely more on investors to fund their campaigns while those from larger states must rely more on consumers. Because investors contribute relatively equally to senators—even though senators who represent large states need far more campaign funds—they supply a larger proportion of the total funds that small-state senators need. Only consumers respond to the greater funding needs of senators in populous states; as a result, senators from large states will have to draw proportionately more from consumers to fund their more expensive reelection campaigns. In the following section we test these hypotheses using Federal Election Commission data and find strong support for them.

Data and Findings

To assess the effect of state population on the fund-raising patterns of senators, we collected data on campaign contributions from the Federal Election Commission (FEC) for all incumbent senators running for reelection during the 1992–96 Senate election cycle ($N = 71$). We needed to classify the campaign contributions these senators received by source, that is, whether they were from investors or consumers. This is not an easy task because those who contribute to Senate campaigns do not report their motives, but the FEC provides some assistance by listing separately the contributions made by individuals and by political action committees (PACs).

We do know that PACs typically fit the definition of campaign investors. Most are created by corporations, labor unions, or interest groups for the express purpose of making campaign contributions to candidates running for office. As such, they are primarily campaign investors and contribute accordingly, demonstrating an overwhelming preference for incumbents. A small group of nonconnected PACs and leadership PACs, however, do not fit the definition of investors. These PACs act more like consumer contributors, supporting candidates who share their ideologies even when they are not likely to win elections. More of their money goes to challengers and little goes to candidates who are sure to win. But funds from these kinds of PACs account for only a very small portion of total PAC contributions.[20] The motives in the case of most PACs (and most PAC contributions), then, are clear: organizations establish PACs to advance their political interests by ensuring access to elected officials and encouraging favorable action from them.

The motives of individual contributors are less clear. Many are motivated by the same goals as PACs. Some are business owners or corporate executives who contribute to ensure that they have a sympathetic ear in the Senate. "Bundled contributions"—contributions that lobbyists, PACs, and other persons or organizations solicit from individuals and then present to candidates as bundles of checks—are classified as individual contributions under federal law but are little different from PAC contributions in terms of motivation. Thus many of the campaign contributions made by individuals are actually from investors. To the extent that individual contributors are investors, then, we would not expect senators who represent large states to receive more contributions from individuals than do senators from small states.

At the same time, many individuals contribute to Senate campaigns as consumers, to register their support for a particular candidate, often in response to a request for funds either in person or by direct mail. Contributions from consumers probably represent the bulk of individual contributions that most senators receive. Contributions of less than $200 constitute roughly one-third of the total campaign receipts of all House and Senate incumbents.[21] Certainly donors of amounts this small are unlikely to perceive them as "investments" in Senate access, although some of these smaller contributions will have been bundled by political entrepreneurs who in turn contribute them to senators as investments. Of the contributions over $200 that senators receive, only 20 percent are from out of state (Cantor 1997). No doubt many of the in-state contributions over $200 are made by consumers, who contribute because they are already political supporters of the senator, not because they seek to influence his behavior in office. Thus we may infer that a substantial proportion of individual contributions are made by consumers rather than investors. In practice, however, there is no straightforward way to disaggregate the individual contributions listed in FEC records.

Although not all individual contributors are consumers and not all PACs are investors, we know that, in percentage terms, more PAC contributors than individuals are investors, while more individual contributors than PAC contributors are consumers. As a result we may use the two groups—PACs and individual contributors—as rough proxies for investors and consumers in our analysis. If our expectations about investors and consumers hold, we will observe certain patterns in the FEC data on PAC contributions and non-PAC contributions, notwithstanding our difficulties in operationalizing these concepts.

First, because senators from more populous states are systematically neither more nor less able to advance the goals of investors than those from smaller states, state population should have no effect on the total contributions senators receive from PACs. Second, because consumer contributors increase with the number of a senator's supporters, greater state population should raise their number. As a result, the amount raised by senators from non-PAC sources should increase with state population, even though an unspecified number of individual contributors are actually investors, not consumers. Taken together, these two patterns should mean that senators from more populous states raise a larger proportion of the total funds they need from consumers, while those from smaller states raise a larger proportion from investors. Third, then, increases in state population should decrease the percentage of a senator's total reelection campaign funds raised from PACs.

To test these expectations, we regress the total amounts that senators received from PACs and from other sources on state population. We also include several control variables in the models. Because senators facing a close reelection race will typically raise more money than senators who expect to win by a wide margin, we included a dummy variable for the competitiveness of the race (1 means the race was decided by a margin of less than 10 percent). In addition, because senators with more seniority have had more time to develop long-standing relationships with individual campaign donors, they tend to raise less money from PACs and more from individuals.

Table 4.3 State Population and the Amount Incumbent Senators Raise for Their Campaigns, Controlling for Other Factors, 1992–96 Election Cycle

Variable	Amount from PACs	Amount from Non-PAC Sources	Percentage of Funds from PACs
Constant	$1,454,684 ***	$430,136	45.77 ***
	(9.74)	(0.64)	(12.33)
State population	18,343	410,919 ***	−1.40 ***
(in millions)	(1.44)	(7.09)	(−4.41)
Competitive race	159,154	1,850,265 ***	−2.73 *
(dummy)	(1.44)	(3.70)	(−1.83)
Seniority	−152,090 **	271,245	−2.73 *
	(−2.54)	(1.00)	(−1.83)
Does not accept PAC $	−1,297,256 ***	6,456,386 ***	−30.71 ***
	(−5.15)	(5.65)	(−4.90)
Adj. R^2	.34	.62	.44
F-statistic	9.3 ***	27.9 ***	13.85 ***
Mean of dependent variable	$1,271,049	$4,044,496	30.12%
N	71	71	71

Source: Compiled from Federal Election Commission data.

Note: t-statistics in parentheses.

$*p < .10$, two-tailed test; $**p < .05$, two-tailed test; $***p < .01$, two-tailed test.

For this reason we include a variable for incumbent's seniority, which is equal to 1 for freshmen, 2 for sophomores, and 3 for senators who have served three or more terms in office.[22] We also experimented with adding a variable for the senator's party, but it added no explanatory power to any of the models and thus is not shown here. Finally, we include a dummy variable for those few senators who do not accept contributions from PACs. The results of these regression equations are displayed in table 4.3.

The first column in the table reveals that, as expected, state population has no effect on the amount senators raise from PACs. The coefficient for state population in this model is positive, but it is small and not statistically significant. Similarly, the coefficient for the close race variable reveals that candidates facing a strong challenge—who tend to raise more in campaign funds generally (as shown in the second column in the table)—do not succeed in raising more from PACs. Senators with more seniority raise less from PACs than other senators, as we expected, though the effect is not dramatic.[23] Even though some senators need more campaign money than others, PACs do not provide additional funds in response to their needs.

PACs, like all campaign investors, contribute to candidates to advance their interests in the legislative process. Because senators have relatively equal power to advance the interests of investors generally, there is little variation in the total amount they are able to raise from PACs, especially considering the great variation in total campaign funds that different senators need. The average senator received $1,327,000 from PACs. Two-thirds of all the senators in our study raised between $775,000 and $1,767,000 from PACs, a difference of less than $1 million. And though a few senators refused to accept money from PACs or restricted the amount they would accept, no senator in our study raised more than $2.9 million from PACs. (Incidentally, Sen. Kent Conrad of North Dakota, one of the least populous states, raised this maximum amount.) This lack of variation, moreover, is not the result of the legal caps placed on the amount PACs can contribute to individual candidates, because PACs rarely give the maximum allowed under the law to any one candidate (Conway and Green 1995, 162; Sabato 1984, 84–86; Snyder 1993, 237). Senators raise similar amounts from PACs because, fundamentally, senators are not that different in what they can offer to PACs as a group. As one senator explained to us: "There's a simple reason for the fact that PACs give the same amount to all senators—all senators have the same number of votes."

The data on funds raised from non-PAC sources—the vast majority of which are from individual contributors—exhibit a pattern quite different from that of contributions from investors.[24] Senators who represent more populous states raise considerably more from non-PAC sources than those from smaller states. As shown in the second column in table 4.3, the coefficient for state population reveals that for each additional one million constituents, a senator raises $410,919 ($p < .01$) more in campaign funds from non-PAC sources.[25] Senators in close reelection races engage in more vigorous fund-raising efforts. Although they are not able to raise additional amounts from PACs, those who face competitive challenges do increase their campaign funds by more than $1.85 million ($p < .01$). Naturally those few senators who choose not to accept PAC funds make up for their refusal by raising additional funds from other sources, as shown by the large, positive coefficient for this variable. The overall regression model predicting the amount that senators raise from non-PAC sources is quite strong, yielding an adjusted R^2 of .62.

The fund-raising pattern that results is as follows: PACs (and theoretically all other investors as well) are not responsive to differences in senators' needs for campaign funds, whereas consumers as a group are. Figure 4.1 plots the

Figure 4.1. Predicted relation between state population and Senate incumbent campaign fund-raising, 1992–96 election cycle

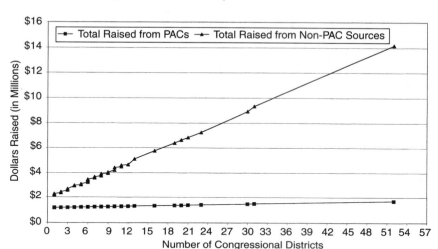

predicted relationship between state population and the amounts senators raise from PAC and non-PAC sources, holding all other variables constant at their means. As shown here, as state population increases there is a growing gap between the funds contributed by PACs and the amount contributed by other sources, principally individuals. As state population grows larger and thus senators' need for campaign funds increases, the line plotting the amount of PAC contributions is virtually flat. The regression line plotting the amount senators raise from non-PAC sources, however, ranges from $2.14 million in the states with one congressional district all the way to $14.18 million in a state with fifty-two. When senators need more campaign funds, whether because of competitive challenges or larger constituencies, they must look mainly to consumer contributors to make up the difference.[26]

Variation in state population thus affects the sources of senators' campaign contributions, not merely the amount they need. Between 1992 and 1996, the senators representing the least populous states (states with one congressional district) received on average fully 40.6 percent ($N = 11$) of their total reelection campaign funds from PACs. Interestingly, the average House incumbent running for reelection during the same period received almost exactly the same proportion from PACs, 41 percent ($N = 1,118$).[27] By contrast, senators representing the most populous states (states with more than twenty-five congressional districts) received on average only 14.4 percent of their funds from PACs ($N = 5$). Regression analysis confirms a consistent relationship between state population and the percentage of their total funds that Senate candidates raise from PACs. As shown in the third column of table 4.3, each increase of one million constituents decreases the percentage of their reelection campaign funds that incumbent senators receive from PACs by 1.40 percent ($p < .01$).

These findings that constituency size affects senators' fund-raising methods require us to modify accepted ideas on campaign finance patterns in Congress. Typically, political scientists observe that on average House members raise a considerably larger percentage of their funds from PACs than senators do, implying that senators are less dependent on PAC dollars for their reelection campaigns. Although our data confirm that between 1992 and 1996 the average House member raised 41 percent of his total campaign funds from PACs, while for the average senator it was only 30 percent, the use of averages obscures the considerable variation in senators' fund-raising patterns caused by Senate apportionment. Even though senators representing even the least populous states on average raised far more total campaign dollars ($2.99 million in states with one congressional district) than House members ($628,732), these senators raised their funds from precisely the same mix of sources. Senators representing states with only one congressional district strongly resemble House members in their fund-raising behavior, just as they resemble them in their representational relationships with their constituents. As constituency size increases, senators become increasingly different from House members. As a result, the difference between the two chambers in reliance on PAC dollars (the proportion of total funds received from PACs) is actually just a by-product of the variation in constituency size entailed in Senate apportionment and not a reflection of any inherent difference in the two institutions.

Fund-Raising and Representational Behavior

Having shown that state population affects both senators' need for campaign funds and the mix of sources they draw on, we now explore whether the fund-raising contexts created by differences in constituency size in turn shape senators' representational behavior. Jacobson contends that "incumbents can raise whatever they think they need" to run for reelection (Jacobson 1984, 57, cited in Davidson and Oleszek 1998, 70). Even if true, this does not mean that all incumbents devote similar amounts of their time in office to fund-raising. Senators generally perceive that fund-raising consumes time that would be better spent on legislative work. From a survey of House and Senate members and their staffs, the Center for Responsive Politics found that "52 percent of the senators surveyed thought the demand of fund-raising cut significantly into the time available for legislative work" and "another

12 percent believed fund-raising had some deleterious effect" (Magleby and Nelson 1990, 44).

Differences in constituency size in the Senate create great variation in senators' needs for campaign funds, a source of variation that has no counterpart in the House. Because campaign investors supply a relatively fixed amount to all senators and because senators in less populous states need fewer total campaign dollars, those who represent smaller states have a much greater proportion of their campaign funding needs met by investors than those from larger states. This prompts the question, Is campaign fund-raising less demanding, in terms of a senator's time and other limited resources, for small-state senators?

This question is difficult to answer directly. Obviously some individual senators are better managers of their time and staff or more efficient fund-raisers than others. In our interviews, moreover, senators themselves tended not to be very forthcoming about their fund-raising obligations. Questions on the subject of PACs elicited somewhat defensive responses like "I received only XX percent of my funds from PACs, a lot less than other senators." This is hardly an unlikely reaction from any politician in the context of ongoing campaign finance scandals involving both parties and continual calls for reforming the current system.

In this section, however, we offer two sets of reasons that senators representing less populous states can afford to devote less of their time in office to fund-raising than those from larger states. First, raising funds from campaign investors is easier than raising funds from consumers. That almost all senators accept money from PACs in the face of so much criticism about the influence of money in politics by itself suggests that they prefer not to raise it in other ways. Accepting PAC money is a ready-made campaign issue waiting for a challenger to exploit. As such, it constitutes an electoral risk that incumbents, already "inspired by worst case scenarios," probably would not undertake without reason (Jacobson 1992, 97).

The principal reason it is easier to raise money from investors than from consumers is that investors actively seek out opportunities to contribute. Investors organize PACs for the explicit purpose of giving campaign money to candidates. They donate funds to PACs and as individuals because they believe they derive important benefits from contributing to political campaigns. "Most PACs," after all, "are connected to organizations that lobby Congress for legislative favors on a regular basis" (Sabato 1984, 123). Because they feel they have something to gain from contributing, investors—whether or not they are organized PACs—have incentives to contribute to senators. Senators, in turn, are aware of this. As a result, they exert both tacit and overt pressure on investors to contribute. This pressure is often so palpable that representatives of PACs regularly complain, sometimes comparing it to extortion (see Sabato 1984, 112–14; Davidson and Oleszek 1998, 77–78). To wield this pressure, senators often need not make even an implicit threat. An experienced lobbyist hardly needs to be told that campaign contributions are very important for gaining access to members of Congress (Wittenberg and Wittenberg 1989, 23–29; Wolpe and Levine 1996, 48–68).

From the point of view of incumbent senators, PACs and other campaign investors are out there looking for senators to contribute to. Investors attend the Washington, D.C., fund-raisers to which senators invite them. They even sponsor fund-raisers on senators' behalf. Investors put pressure on others to contribute, and they raise bundled contributions for senators they want to impress. In short, they are a campaign finance resource just waiting to be tapped. As one senator said with emphasis, "PACs is the money you *know.*"

Contributions from consumers are not such a certain commodity. After all, consumers do not have the same incentives that investors have. Consumers are not afraid senators will make different, less beneficial choices in office should they fail to contribute to them. Therefore senators do not exert the same leverage over consumers as over investors. Senators who seek to tap consumers as a resource for campaign funds must actively court them, especially in an era of declining partisan affiliation. Many consumers will not contribute unless asked to do so. Direct mail solicitations generate small contributions from consumers, but these operations have very high costs and use up much of the money generated (Magelby and Nelson 1990, 53).

Consumers who have the resources to make large donations do not typically send them in response to a direct mail solicitation (Alexander 1992, 50). Raising substantial amounts from consumers thus means that senators themselves have to spend a lot of time on the telephone, at dinners, parties, and benefit concerts—in short, away from legislative work. In fact Senate leaders often complain of the difficulties they face in scheduling floor action on legislation at times that do not conflict with other senators' fund-raising calendars (Oleszek 1996, 198–203). To the extent that consumers are motivated to contribute by their egos and their desire to feel they are part of the political elite, senators must be willing to give their own time to maximize contributions.

Taken alone, the finding that senators who represent the least populous states raise more of their funds from PACs than other senators suggests that they spend less time fund-raising than those from larger states. In addition, an unknown proportion of individual contributions are donated by investors, who, like PACs, contribute in proportion to senators' power to advance their goals. Because power is distributed fairly equally in the Senate, we would expect that in the aggregate all investor contributions (whether or not they are from PACs) will, like PAC money, go to senators fairly equally, regardless of their need for funds. Depending on how many individual

Table 4.4 State Population and Fund-Raising Patterns of Incumbent Senators, 1992–96 Election Cycle

Number of Congressional Districts in the State	Percentage of Funds Raised in First Two Years in Office	Percentage of Funds Raised in Second Two Years in Office	Percentage of Funds Raised in Last Two Years in Office	N
1	5.36	9.21	85.43	10
2–3	6.20	9.12	84.68	12
4–6	5.12	11.93	82.95	15
7–10	6.92	10.36	82.72	13
11–20	12.61	10.51	76.88	8
20–25	9.29	19.89	70.82	3
26+	19.71	21.70	58.59	3
Total	7.54	11.76	80.70	64

Source: Compiled from Federal Commission data.

Note: Excludes incumbents who did not serve a full six-year term before running for reelection.

contributors are actually investors, then, the fund-raising task of small-state senators is made even easier.

FEC data on the fund-raising patterns of incumbent senators offer a second piece of evidence that senators from more populous states spend more of their time in office fund-raising than those from smaller states. We collected data from the 1992–96 election cycle on the percentages of their total campaign funds that senators running for reelection had raised in each two-year period during their six-year terms. Table 4.4 displays these percentages cross-tabulated with constituency size.

As shown here, senators who represent the most populous states raise larger percentages of their total campaign funds earlier in the election cycle. By the fourth year of their terms, senators representing the smallest states had raised on average less than 15 percent of the total they would eventually raise for their reelection campaigns. By that time senators representing the three most populous states had raised fully 41 percent of their (much larger) total.

These data strongly suggest that senators representing more populous states have to spread their larger fund-raising tasks over their entire terms in office rather than waiting until the last two years. Senators from smaller states, by contrast, can wait until their last two years in office, at which time they raise about 85 percent of their campaign funding totals. Interestingly, the relationship between state population and campaign fund-raising patterns is not monotonic. There is little difference in the patterns of all the senators representing median-sized and smaller than average states. These senators tend to raise just over 5 percent in their first two years, about 10 percent in their second two years, and about 85 percent of the total funds they need in their last two years. The percentage of funds that senators raise in their last two years of office begins a marked decline only with those representing the twelve states having more than ten congressional districts. Fund-raising thus remains a task that most senators—those representing middle-sized and small states—can manage to complete during their last two years in office. Of course one should note that the absolute dollar amounts senators raise at different points in the electoral cycle are larger in more populous states, even when their percentages of the total amount raised are not different. Thus, even when senators from median-sized states raise the same percentage of their total funds as small-state senators do at their second and fourth years in office, they have raised more total dollars. By this measure, however, about a quarter of the Senate appears to feel a fund-raising crunch caused by state population size, leading them to begin their fund-raising drives earlier in their terms. The effect is, as one would expect, most pronounced for senators representing the very largest states. For these senators, fund-raising is continuous.

Multivariate regression analysis confirms this pattern. In assessing the effect of state population on the timing of Senate campaign fund-raising, we include two control variables, one for seniority and a dummy variable for whether the senator experienced a challenge in the upcoming election. Because, as one Senate staffer explained to us, senior senators are more likely "to have their donor base already established," so that fund-raising is "a fairly systematic process," we expect that seniority in office increases the percentage a senator raises in the last two years and correspondingly decreases the percentage raised in the first four years. In addition, freshman senators often have campaign debts from their first election, prompting them to raise extra funds during their first two years in office. We also expect that anticipating a competitive race increases the percentage raised early in the cycle and decreases the percentage the senator waits to raise in the last two years.

Table 4.5 presents the coefficients obtained when we regress the percentage of funds that senators raised during each two-year period on state population. The dependent variables in the models shown in the first two columns are the percentages of campaign funds raised in the first and second two years of the Senate term. The coefficients for state population are positive and statistically significant ($p < .01$) for both models, meaning that increases in state population lead to increases in the percentage of total campaign funds that senators raise during their first four years in office. The dependent variable in the third model shown in this table is the percentage raised in the last two years. State population has a strongly negative effect on the percentage

Table 4.5 Relation between State Population and the Fund-Raising Patterns of Incumbent Senators, Controlling for Other Factors, 1992–96 Election Cycle

Variable	Percentage of Funds Raised in First Two Years in Office	Percentage of Funds Raised in Second Two Years in Office	Percentage of Funds Raised in Last Two Years in Office
Constant	7.71**	10.90**	83.16**
	(2.87)	(4.47)	(18.77)
State population	0.63**	0.53**	−1.13**
(in millions)	(2.83)	(2.63)	(−3.09)
Competitive race	0.57	0.93	−4.08
(dummy)	(0.30)	(0.54)	(−1.29)
Seniority	−1.52	−1.21	1.97
	(−1.45)	(−1.27)	(1.13)
Adj. R^2	.11	.10	.15
F-statistic	3.67**	3.23*	4.79**
N	64	64	64

Source: Compiled from Federal Election Commission data.
Note: t-statistics in parentheses.
$*p < .05; **p < .01.$

raised in the last two years, yielding a coefficient of −1.13 ($p < .01$). None of the coefficients for the control variables we included reached statistical significance, but all their signs are in the expected directions.

■ ■ ■

Taken together, our findings on the timing of and sources for campaign fund-raising strongly suggest that senators representing more populous states must devote more of their time in office to raising funds than those from smaller states. Because the demands on senators' time are already so great, time spent on fund-raising means less time spent doing other things. If senators typically had time left over after fulfilling their legislative obligations, that senators from large states must devote more time to fund-raising than other senators would cause less concern for representation. In today's legislative environment, however, senators must cope with expanded committee assignments, a broader interest group and policy universe, long workdays, and a Congress in session nearly year-round. Time pressures cause senators frequent scheduling conflicts, both for attending committee meetings and for floor activities (see Hall 1993). As Sinclair observes, "All senators, even those who were House members, complain of time pressure" (1989, 152). At the same time as the Senate's workload has expanded, moreover, the costs of campaigns overall have increased. The contribution limits enacted as part of the campaign finance reforms of 1974 required senators to expand their fund-raising efforts to draw on larger numbers of individuals and organizations. As inflation has in turn eroded the value of the maximum contributions allowed under law, fund-raising has become progressively more time consuming for all senators, increasing the pressures. A senator's expenditures of time thus occur in a zero-sum context. Time spent fund-raising is time that cannot be devoted to committee work, leadership duties, coalition building, policy briefings, meetings with activists and constituents, or any of a senator's other duties.

Our findings on Senate fund-raising behavior reveal, however, that these time pressures have not increased equally for all. Senators representing large states must raise more campaign funds than those from small states, and they must raise them from more labor-intensive sources. Our findings on the timing of fund-raising reinforce this point. Senators from the most populous states begin their fund-raising drives earlier, with those from the largest states raising more than a third of the total amount they need to run for reelection even before their fourth year in office. As Sen. Dianne Feinstein complained to reporter John Harwood (1994), "My people want me . . . to be on the phone [fund-raising] all the time." Similarly, a former senator who had represented one of the more populous states acknowledged to us that he typically began fund-raising "right away" after taking office and said, "During the last two years, I spent one-third of my time raising money." Senators from the average-sized and small states, however, can raise as much as 85 percent of the total they need in just the last two years of their terms. "The fund-raising for ———— takes less time than people think," remarked a member of a small-state senator's staff we interviewed, noting that fund-raising was "generally dormant for the first four years." Another small-state senator answered our inquiry about fund-raising emphatically: "I don't *ever* remember working hard at raising funds."

One former senator told us a story that epitomizes the fund-raising pressures on senators who represent the most populous states. On a recent visit to the Senate cloakroom, he saw Barbara Boxer (D-Calif.) "inquiring of the clerk about the schedule of votes that was upcoming," asking "whether it was true that there would be an hour of debate between votes." The reason for her inquiry, the senator observed, "was obvious . . . she would be going somewhere out of government buildings to make fund-raising calls, and she needed to be able to know how much time she would have. Evidently she would make calls for an hour, return and vote, then leave and make calls again." Concluding the story, the senator compared Boxer to a "squirrel on an exercise wheel in a cage." From his perspective, fund-raising on this scale both diverted the senator's time and attention from the "things she was sent there to do" and "detracted from the quality of the Senate as an institution."

Senate Apportionment and Partisan Bias

The equal representation of states affects a third aspect of Senate elections, the partisan composition of the Senate. Senate apportionment grants enormous weight to the partisan preferences of small-state voters relative to their proportion of the national population. Whenever small-state voters systematically differ from large-state voters in partisan terms, Senate apportionment will have important institutional consequences. Under these conditions, Senate apportionment confers added seats on the political party that does relatively better in small states. During the 1980s, for example, the Republican Party did particularly well in Senate races in the small states of the West. These Republican victories in small-state Senate elections, in fact, enabled Republicans to win and maintain control of the Senate from 1981 to 1987 even though Republican candidates did not win a majority of the total votes cast in Senate races (Oppenheimer 1989, 659–60).

Political scientists, however, have not explored the effects of Senate apportionment on the partisan composition of the Senate over time. This is surprising because so many studies have dealt with the ways electoral structures affect partisan representation in other contexts. Many scholars in the field of comparative politics, for example, have studied how various electoral systems influence the development and electoral success of political parties and their votes-to-seats ratios (Duverger 1984; Lijphart 1994; Lijphart and Grofman 1984; Rae 1967; Taagepera and Shugart 1989). Some students of American politics have even proposed instituting some form of proportional representation in the House to make the body more representative (Amy 1993; Lijphart 1998; Lind 1995; Zimmerman and Rule 1998). Despite the attention political scientists have paid to the consequences of electoral structures in these other contexts, the effect of Senate apportionment on partisan outcomes has largely escaped notice. This is yet another example of political scientists' taking Senate apportionment for granted.

How much and how often does Senate apportionment affect the partisan composition of the Senate? Which party, if either, is more advantaged by the system? To answer these questions, we developed a measure of the number of Senate seats that parties gain or lose as a consequence of Senate apportionment. We find that in nearly every election since 1914 Senate apportionment has had some effect on the partisan composition of the Senate, benefiting one of the political parties. Typically it has functioned to increase the Senate minority party's share of seats, and only rarely has it augmented the majority party's margin of Senate control. When the Senate is closely divided, moreover, Senate apportionment has occasionally been decisive for partisan control of the body. In short, apportionment has generally had a distinctly countermajoritarian effect on the partisan outcomes of Senate elections throughout the period since the adoption of the Seventeenth Amendment.

Measuring the Partisan Bias of Senate Apportionment

A measure of Senate apportionment bias cannot simply compare the percentage of the seats a party receives with its percentage of the national Senate vote. A simple seats-to-votes ratio of this kind is insufficient because it fails to take into account the effects of a system of plurality elections in single-member districts. A seats-to-votes ratio tells us the total deviation from proportional representation that occurs in Senate elections, but not all of this deviation is a result of Senate apportionment. As in House elections, the winning party in Senate elections receives a greater percentage of seats than its percentage of the national vote simply because of the winner-take-all system. Unlike the House, however, in the Senate the seats-to-votes deviates from proportional representation as a result of both the winner-take-all system and the equal representation of states with unequal populations. If we assume that the total partisan bias in Senate elections (the total deviation from proportional representation) is the sum of winner-take-all bias and the bias caused by Senate apportionment, then we can estimate the partisan bias of Senate apportionment from the difference between the total partisan bias in Senate elections and the bias caused by the winner-take-all system.

To measure the partisan bias of Senate apportionment, we begin by calculating the seats-to-votes ratio for the Democratic Party for each election year since 1914. This ratio simply sets the proportion of seats won by the Democratic Party in a Senate election over the proportion of the whole national vote cast for that party in all Senate races. Subtracting one from this ratio yields a measure of the total deviation from proportional representation in each Senate election.[28] When this measure is positive, the Democratic Party received a greater percentage of Senate seats than its percentage of the national vote in Senate races; when it is negative, the Democrats received a smaller percentage than their percentage of the national vote.

Next we isolate that part of the total deviation from proportional representation that can be attributed to the winner-take-all system for each Senate election year. To do this, we calculate another seats-to-votes ratio for each election year in which we weight the proportion of the vote cast for the Democratic Party in each state in order to simulate equal population across states. In other words, we calculate a hypothetical national Senate vote (to serve as the denominator in a seats-to-votes ratio) that weights all states equally. This measure is the seats-to-votes ratio that would have resulted in each election year if Senate seats were apportioned based on population in single-member, winner-take-all districts.[29] Subtracting one from this ratio yields the deviation from proportional representation caused by the winner-take-all system.

Assuming once again that the total deviation from proportional representation (PR) in Senate elections is equal to the sum of the deviations caused by apportionment and the winner-take-all system, the difference between the measure of total partisan bias and the measure of winner-take-all bias is equal to the partisan bias resulting from Senate apportionment.

$$\text{(Total deviation from PR)} - \text{(deviation from PR caused by} \\ \text{winner-take-all)} = \text{partisan bias of Senate apportionment}$$

This measure of the partisan bias of Senate apportionment indicates the percentage of seats the Democratic Party either gained or lost as a consequence of Senate apportionment. It is positive when the Democratic Party is advantaged and negative when the Republican Party is advantaged.

We should note that this measure of Senate apportionment bias is very conservative. It measures only the benefits that accrue to political parties as a consequence of the single fact that states are not equal in population. It does not take into account any issues of "gerrymandering"—whether the system of state lines itself may also involve partisan bias—even though we know that throughout the periods of national expansion in the nineteenth and early twentieth centuries, members of Congress did exploit the politics of state admission for partisan advantage, both when considering the timing of admitting new states and when drawing their territorial boundaries (F. Lee 1997; Stewart and Weingast 1992). In calculating winner-take-all bias, we assume that the two parties would have won the same vote percentages within each state even if the Senate were apportioned by population. This measure of Senate apportionment bias is thus only the advantage that a party gains by winning more small-state races than the other party.

Findings and Implications

We calculate the partisan bias of Senate apportionment for each Senate election from 1914 to 1996, then average it across each cycle of Senate elections. Figure 4.2 shows how many additional or fewer seats (in percentage terms) the Democratic Party would have won in each cycle if Senate apportionment had had no effect on the seats-to-votes ratio. In other words, this measure shows the average percentage of seats during each election cycle that the Democratic Party gained or lost as a result of Senate apportionment.

One of the most striking facts revealed here is that Senate apportionment almost always affects the partisan composition of the Senate. In the entire period since the adoption of the Seventeenth Amendment there were only

Figure 4.2. Effect of Senate apportionment on the Democratic Party's seats-to-votes ratio, moving averages across cycles of Senate elections, 1914–96

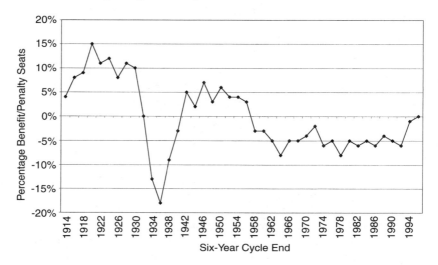

two Congresses—the 73d Congress (elected in the 1928–32 election cycle) and the 105th Congress (elected in the 1992–96 election cycle)—in which Senate apportionment had no effect on the seats-to-votes ratio. At different points over the period, each of the two major parties has benefited from Senate apportionment. It favored the Democratic party during two periods: from the 64th Congress (1915–16) until the 72d Congress (1931–32) and from the 78th Congress (1943–44) until the 85th Congress (1957–58), for a total of thirty-four years of Democratic gains from Senate apportionment. It also favored Republicans during two periods: during and after the New Deal realignment between the 74th (1935–36) and the 77th Congresses (1941–43) and for almost the entire period since the 86th Congress (1959–60), for a total of forty-six years of Republican gains from Senate apportionment. In the 105th Congress (elected in the 1992–96 election cycle), neither the Republican Party nor the Democratic Party fared better in small-state Senate races than in large-state races, and thus Senate apportionment did not result in an advantage for either party.

To determine how apportionment bias has affected the partisan control of the Senate over time, we compare the number of seats in the Senate that the Democratic Party actually held over the period with the estimated number of seats they would have held after factoring out the effects of Senate apportionment bias (shown in fig. 4.2). Table 4.6 shows these data for each Congress from 1915 to 1997, noting for each case whether Senate apportionment favored the majority or the minority party in the institution.

Table 4.6 Effect of Senate Apportionment on the Partisan Composition of the Senate, 1915–97

Congress	Actual Number of Dem. Seats	Estimated Number of Dem. Seats w/o Apportionment Bias	Which Party Benefits from Apportionment Bias?	Congress	Actual Number of Dem. Seats	Estimated Number of Dem. Seats w/o Apportionment Bias	Which Party Benefits from Apportionment Bias?
64th	56	52	majority	85th	49	46	majority*
65th	53	45	majority*	86th	65	68	minority
66th	47	38	minority	87th	65	68	minority
67th	37	23	minority	88th	67	72	minority
68th	43	32	minority	89th	68	76	minority
69th	39	27	minority	90th	64	69	minority
70th	46	38	minority	91st	57	62	minority
71st	39	28	minority	92d	54	58	minority
72d	47	37	minority	93d	56	58	minority
73d	60	60	neither	94th	60	66	minority
74th	69	81	minority	95th	61	66	minority
75th	76	93	minority	96th	58	66	minority
76th	69	78	minority	97th	46	51	majority*
77th	66	69	minority	98th	45	51	majority*
78th	58	53	majority	99th	47	51	majority*
79th	56	54	majority	100th	55	61	minority
80th	45	38	minority	101st	55	59	minority
81st	54	51	majority	102d	57	62	minority
82d	49	43	majority*	103d	56	62	minority
83d	47	43	minority	104th	47	48	minority
84th	48	44	majority*	105th	45	45	neither

* Indicates that Senate apportionment bias was decisive for partisan control of the body. It means that without Senate apportionment, the majority party would not have been the majority. In these cases, as in all the others in which the minority party benefited, Senate apportionment had a countermajoritarian effect.

The data shown here reveal a remarkably consistent pattern: Ever since popular election of senators was instituted, Senate apportionment has almost always functioned to augment the minority party's share of seats. This is very surprising because there is no theoretical reason to expect that it would consistently favor the minority party. Even so, the pattern is unmistakable. Out of the forty-two Senate elections between 1914 and 1996, Senate apportionment worked in favor of the minority party twenty-nine times. On seven additional occasions, Senate apportionment was decisive for partisan control of the body. In these seven cases the majority party would not have held a majority of seats in the Senate without the advantages it derived from Senate apportionment. In these cases as well, then, Senate apportionment worked in favor of the minority party by making it the majority party. Taken together, this means that in thirty-six of the forty-two Congresses since the institution of direct election of senators, or in 85 percent of those examined here, Senate apportionment worked in a countermajoritarian fashion.

The partisan effect of Senate apportionment has been more or less consistent regardless of which of the two major political parties is the minority party in the Senate at the time. During the Republican-dominated pre–New Deal era, the Democrats held more Senate seats than they would have under a system apportioned by population. This is due to the Democratic holdings in the South as well as in small, populist western states. In 1916, for example, Democrats won Senate races in all the states with one congressional district, enabling them to maintain a wider majority in the Senate than in the House during the 65th Congress. In elections when the Democrats ran poorly almost everywhere, as in 1920 and 1946, they still won Senate seats throughout the South.

On the other hand, Senate apportionment worked to the benefit of the Republican Party during the New Deal period, enabling it to hold on to more Senate seats than a system apportioned by population would have permitted. In the landslide Democratic Senate elections of 1932, for example, Republicans held on to seats in North Dakota, South Dakota, Oregon, and Vermont. In other words, during the New Deal period, Democrats would have dominated a Senate apportioned by population even more. Even during the 1946 and 1952 Senate elections, when Republicans took control of the Senate, Senate apportionment tended to work against majority rule, benefiting Democrats in both the 80th and 83d Congresses. In recent years—up until the 1996 elections—Senate apportionment has worked in favor of the Republicans, even accounting for their Senate majority between the 1980 and 1986 elections. Over this period the Republican Party won Senate seats in smaller states, especially in the West.

In the last election cycle (1992–96), however, neither party benefited from Senate apportionment. This suggests that the Republican Party has expanded its base of support outside the small-population states that had been crucial to its success in the 1980s. It was only in 1994, an election year in which Senate apportionment bias was not a factor in Republican success in the Senate, that Republicans took control of the House of Representatives as well the Senate. Because the most recent Republican gains are not dependent on apportionment, the current Republican control of the Senate may be more enduring than that of the 1980s.

These findings have important implications for the place of the Senate in the American system. As we discussed in chapter 2, the framers of the Constitution envisioned the Senate as a stabilizing institution in American government, one that would slow down the majoritarian impulses expressed by the House. This goal shaped many aspects of the Senate as an institution, including the length of terms, the body's small size, its staggered terms of office, and the appointment of senators by state legislatures. Ironically, the framers did not view the equal apportionment of states as central to the purpose of the Senate. As we also showed in chapter 2, the agreement on Senate apportionment was the product not of functional design but of the collision of a particular set of political interests in a specific institutional and ideological context, including the voting rules at the Constitutional Convention. Since the adoption of direct elections with the Seventeenth Amendment, however, Senate apportionment has had a consistently countermajoritarian influence on the partisan composition of the Senate. The framers clearly did not anticipate this outcome. They were not, after all, thinking about popular election of senators or political parties when they designed the Senate. Since the adoption of the Seventeenth Amendment, however, because of Senate apportionment the body has played a role in American government not unlike the one they envisioned.

Conclusion

The findings presented in this chapter demonstrate that the apportionment basis of the Senate, giving equal representation to all states, has important implications for Senate elections. Taken as a whole, these findings suggest that awareness of the effects of constituency size (and thus of electoral context) is crucial for understanding the Senate as a representative institution.

We first demonstrated that Senate apportionment affects all Senate elections, not just those in which incumbents are running. Generally speaking, the larger the state's population, the more competitive the election is likely to be, all else being equal. Although incumbent senators do enjoy some advantage over challengers, the size of that advantage is not altered by state population. Even though senators representing small states are able to establish and maintain closer relationships with their constituents than their colleagues from larger states, they do not gain a greater incumbency advantage. We suggest this is because challengers in small-population states may also be able to establish closer relationships with the incumbents' constituents than can those in large states, especially if an incumbent has alienated a sizable portion of his more homogeneous constituency. This helps to explain the finding that incumbent reelection rates are not greater in the smallest-population states.

That senators representing small-population states tend to win by wider margins than their larger-state colleagues suggests they may have more flexibility or leeway in the choices they make in office. Closely related to flexibility is the issue of time for governing. In the second part of the chapter we demonstrated that all senators raise similar amounts from PACs (all of those who take PAC contributions, of course). There appears to be a limit to how much senators can raise from this source of campaign funds. For senators from less populous states, this amount ($1.3 million on average in 1992–96) is often more than half of the total they will need for their reelection campaigns. Other senators, especially those from the largest states, must work harder to raise the bulk of their funds from other sources such as individual contributors. This means that in addition to facing more competitive elections, senators representing more populous states have to devote more time to fund-raising and less to governing.

We thus suggest that senators from large and small states have different incentives, and face different constraints, in the choices they make in the Senate because of their respective electoral contexts. Are these different incentives and constraints apparent in senators' Washington behavior? We explore this topic in the next chapter.

Finally, the findings presented here also have broader implications for understanding the place of the Senate in the American political system. In the third part of the chapter we demonstrated that apportionment has had a countermajoritarian effect on Senate elections for much of the twentieth century. Frequently one party has won a share of seats disproportionate to its national electoral support because of its success in smaller-population states. The countermajoritarian effect occurs because of the different weights given to the votes of those living in large- and small-population states. During certain periods this effect has been decisive in determining partisan control of the Senate. Even when it has not, the increased number of seats held by the minority party as a result of Senate apportionment is particularly meaningful in an institution in which the minority party, and each individual senator, enjoys a great deal of power.

The unequal weighting of votes owing to Senate apportionment, then, does affect the internal functioning of the Senate. In later chapters we take up this topic again, exploring the ways Senate apportionment affects the making of public policy, especially the distribution of federal funds to the states.

5

Senate Strategies

As a legislative body with a relatively small membership, unusual rules, and informal procedures, the Senate resists, even defies, generalization. It is much easier to generalize about the House of Representatives and the incentives that shape its members' behavior. For this reason political scientists have studied the House far more thoroughly than the Senate. The enormous range in its constituency size, in fact, is one of the reasons the Senate is so resistant to generalization. Any statement about the "average" senator immediately runs into trouble. Some senators represent constituencies the same size as a House district, while others represent states ten, twenty, and even sixty times that size. To generalize with any precision about the Senate, one must take into account the effects of this enormous variation in Senate constituency size.

In the previous two chapters we demonstrated that Senate apportionment has sizable and important effects on the representational experiences of senators and their constituents, on Senate elections, and on the partisan composition of the Senate. In this chapter and the two that follow, we turn to the effects of apportionment on the choices and behavior of senators within the Senate itself. Just as apportionment has important consequences for the Senate as an elective, representative body, there are equally good reasons to think it has important, previously unexamined consequences for the Senate as a legislative, policymaking institution. Reelection being the "proximate goal" of senators just as it is for House members (Fenno 1973, 139; Mayhew 1974, 16), senators will tailor their behavior in Washington to further this end. All House districts are approximately the same size, however, and thus constituency size is not an important variable in understanding the interaction of constituency and Washington behavior in the careers of House members.

Because Senate constituencies vary so much in size, we must take their size into account to understand how constituency factors shape senators' behavior in Washington.

We argue that constituency size influences senators' incentives in the following way. Senators from less populous states will have a greater incentive to pursue particularized benefits for their constituents than will those from larger states. Any given project in a small state will affect a greater proportion of the state's voters and will thus have greater "credit-claiming" value (Mayhew 1974, 52) than the same project in a large-population state. The same particularized benefit in a more populous state would affect a smaller proportion of the state's voters and thus would reflect less credit on the senator. A new bridge in San Diego has great credit-claiming value to the House member from that district but relatively little to a senator who represents all of California. A new bridge in Bismarck, North Dakota, or Montpelier, Vermont, on the other hand, has the same credit-claiming value for the senators as for the House members from these states. The "advertising" value (Mayhew 1974, 49) of particularized benefits similarly varies with state population. In small states there are relatively fewer stories competing for media coverage. To return to the example above, the new bridge in San Diego is unlikely to receive coverage in the Los Angeles or San Francisco media markets, but the Bismark bridge might well be reported across North Dakota.

Thus the credit-claiming and advertising value of relatively small particularized benefits ranges from its highest value in states like North Dakota and Vermont that have only one congressional district to its lowest value in California, with its fifty-two congressional districts (after the 1990 census). As one senator we interviewed said, "The smaller the state, the more important the projects."

Because similar particularized benefits are of greater value in small states, pursuing them is a more efficient strategy for small-state senators in advancing their goals, especially reelection, than for large-state senators. This is not to say that senators from populous states, even the most populous, will not spend time and resources seeking particularized benefits for their constituents. We assume that all senators will do so to at least some extent. Senators from more populous states, however, will need to pursue proportionately larger particularized benefits, either in scope or in number, to provide comparable benefits to their constituents and gain equal credit-claiming and advertising value for themselves. These larger benefits will be more difficult to secure, all else being equal, especially in times of budgetary constraint. Because of the greater difficulty of obtaining particularized benefits and their lower political value to senators in populous states, large-state senators will have fewer incentives to pursue them than their small-state colleagues. Instead, they are likely to devote their limited resources to other strategies.

Senators representing large states are more likely to turn to "position taking" (Mayhew 1974, 61) or, put somewhat less cynically, to a strategy of policy activism on a broad range of national issues to further their reelection goals. In this chapter we argue that activism on national issues is a means for these senators to attract the media attention they need to communicate with their larger, harder-to-reach constituencies. Just as small-state senators can use retail techniques when campaigning for reelection, senators' presentation of self in small states can be more face-to-face and rely less on mass media. Large-state senators, on the other hand, need the media to communicate with their constituents both when campaigning and in presenting themselves to their constituents generally. Sinclair (1990, 484–85) suggests that "knowing the futility of reaching a large proportion of their constituents through such retail contacts, senators from the largest states may actually deemphasize such activities and rely more heavily upon the media." As one former large-state senator we interviewed said, "When I campaign, it's all on television." We suspect that most of this senator's presentation of self was also "on television." Even when large-state senators do engage in "retail" political activities—meeting with voters individually or in small groups—their primary purpose, as one made clear to us, is to get television coverage and thus turn these retail activities into wholesale media events. Pursuing the policy activism strategy—sitting on policy committees, appearing on national television, developing policy expertise and a reputation among journalists and others for activism on national issues, in short, being a highly visible senator—is thus a more efficient use of large-state senators' limited time and resources than the particularized benefit strategy.

Once again, this is not to suggest that senators from small-population states will not (or cannot) use policy activism to advance their goals, including reelection. In fact, because of the more limited demands made on their time and resources both by constituents and by fund-raising, they may even have an advantage over their large-state colleagues in becoming active on a range of national policy issues. In addition, the relative homogeneity of their states means they represent fewer state-based interests and thus are likely to have fewer demands on their time and fewer constraints on their Washington behavior. If some small-state senators want to become active on foreign policy issues, for example, it may be possible for them to serve their constituencies, pursue particularized benefits for them, and still achieve national prominence for policy activism. The wider margins of victory that small-state senators win, compared with their large-state colleagues (discussed in chapter 4), also give them added flexibility and security to act on a broader range of issues—so long as they do not neglect or alienate their constituents.

We therefore expect great variation in the strategies senators adopt. We assume they all will adopt a hybrid strategy, made up of elements from both the strategies we outlined above. Still, the overall pattern should reflect the different incentives resulting from differences in constituency size. Because the demands on their time and resources are less, small-state senators can choose between emphasizing particularized benefits and stressing policy activism. There are good reasons to think, however, that many small-state senators will favor the former strategy because it is in significant ways safer. Claiming credit for particularized benefits secured for the district is less risky, all else being equal, than taking positions and proposing policy initiatives on a range of potentially divisive national issues. Those small-state senators who have personal interests in public policy, or presidential aspirations, or leadership ambitions within the Senate itself will pursue policy activism more vigorously. In many cases, however, they will do so to advance goals other than reelection.

Conversely, senators representing populous states may be able to pursue a particularized benefits strategy, but because that is more difficult in the large-state context, they will more often turn to policy activism as the more efficient use of their resources. If anything, large-state senators are more constrained in their choice of an effective strategy.[1]

One could say that we are adapting an existing idea about the differences between House members and senators by applying it to senators representing states with large and small populations. Mayhew (1974, 73), for example, observed that "within limits each member [of Congress] has freedom to build his own electoral coalition and hence freedom to choose the means of doing it. Yet there are broad patterns. For one thing senators, with their access to the media, seem to put more emphasis on position taking than House members; probably House members rely more heavily on particularized benefits." We expand on Mayhew's formulation by theorizing that the closer a state's population is to that of a House district, the greater the incentive for a senator to rely on particularized benefits. For senators from states with only one congressional district, the incentives are essentially the same as those of the House member.[2] In states with a large number of congressional districts, senators' incentives will differ greatly from those of House members. Senators from more populous states, accordingly, will have fewer incentives to pursue particularized benefits and more reason to adopt a media-based strategy.

In this chapter we examine whether constituency size affects senators' incentives as they develop their Washington strategies. First we analyze whether it influences their choice of committee assignments. Our theory predicts that senators from less populous states will tend to seek membership on constituency or "reelection" committees and that those from larger states will prefer policy committees. In the second section we investigate whether large-state senators receive more national media coverage than their small-state colleagues, controlling for other factors. If these senators are pursuing a policy activism strategy, then they should try harder to attract media attention than their small-state colleagues, and these greater efforts should translate into more national media coverage. Our analysis confirms our theory that constituency size affects senators' Washington strategies.

There are still other ways constituency size influences senators' Washington behavior. In the third section we ask whether small-state senators have an increased incentive to "hold out"—to withhold their support from legislation in order to obtain concessions or side payments in the form of particularized benefits in exchange for their support. The reasoning here is parallel to that in the first two sections: because small concessions or side payments have a relatively larger electoral payoff in a small state, small-state senators have a greater incentive to pursue them than do their large-state colleagues. Because holding out to extract concessions from coalition builders is a way of securing particularized benefits, we anticipate the small-state senators will be more likely to do so. In addition, because small-state senators' demands are likely to be less expensive to accommodate than those of large-state senators, coalition builders have incentives to seek out their support. Therefore small-state senators are more likely to be successful in holding out than large-state senators. Finally, we explore the greater constraints on large-state senators' choices, asking whether it is still possible for them to pursue leadership in the postreform Senate. Because of the time leadership positions take away from other activities, we argue that these positions may not be a viable option for large-state senators in the contemporary Senate.

Committee Assignments

For both House members and senators, the choice of committee assignments may be the most "well known and straightforward" linkage between constituency concerns and Washington behavior (Fenno 1978, 224–25). A House member whose constituents have an important or predominant interest that falls clearly within the jurisdiction of one of the standing committees has a strong incentive to seek assignment to that committee to further their interests and thus his own career goals. House members from farm districts, for example, typically seek assignment to the agriculture committees.

In this section we argue that state population size has a similar influence on senators' choice of committee assignments. The previous literature has not explored this question, primarily because it focuses on House committees. Because all House constituencies are roughly the same size, such studies understandably do not treat constituency size as an important variable. Even the scholars examining Senate committee assignments, however, have not considered that the great differences in constituency size may affect senators' choice of committee assignments (Endersby and McCurdy 1996; Fenno 1973; Smith and Deering 1990, 100–110).[3]

As we suggest in the introductory section, senators from large and small states are likely to adopt different strategies in Washington. Small-state senators will find that a particularized benefit strategy is an efficient use of their time and resources. Relatively modest particularized benefits in a small state affect a larger proportion of constituents than would the same benefits in a more populous state. Thus those Senate committees that enable their members to use this strategy—often referred to as "constituency" or "reelection" committees—will tend to attract small-state senators, because membership advances their reelection goals.[4]

Senators from more populous states, on the other hand, are unlikely to find that the particularized benefits strategy is such an efficient use of their time and resources. Because of the greater size and diversity of their constituencies, the benefits large-state senators might obtain from membership on constituency committees will appeal to smaller segments of their overall geographic constituencies. These populous-state senators would need to obtain larger benefits (or more of them) to get the same electoral return as the small-state senator receives from a relatively small benefit. Securing larger particularized benefits will be more difficult, all else being equal, and thus large-state senators are likely to adopt other strategies to advance their reelection goals.

Because of this incentive structure, large-state senators will find that a strategy of policy activism is a more efficient use of their limited time and resources. Activism on national issues is in this context a means of attracting media attention, which in turn enables them to communicate with their constituents and develop reputations as effective senators. Activism is also useful for reaching the broad base of campaign supporters (consumers) they need to fund their campaigns (discussed in chapter 4). Because policy committees receive more media attention than other Senate committees (Hess 1986, 34; Smith and Deering 1990, 100), they will be more attractive to senators from populous states than will constituency committees. For these reasons we believe those Senate committees that enable their members to pursue the policy activism strategy—the "policy" committees—will tend to attract senators from more populous states.[5]

Of course we are not claiming that constituency size is the only variable influencing senators' choices of committee assignments. Research on committee assignments, primarily in the House, has shown that variables such as personal preference, vacancies on committees, party loyalty, and regional balance, as well as reelection needs, all influence members' requests and assignments (Bullock 1976; Fenno 1973; Shepsle 1978; Smith and Deering 1990).

There is no reason to think these same variables do not similarly influence the requests and assignments of senators. We are not suggesting, for example, that small-state senators will never, or even rarely, seek assignment to policy committees. Those with public policy goals will seek membership on the relevant committees regardless of the population size of the state they represent. Despite these other variables, however, state size should still have an effect on assignments because of its effect on senators' incentives as they develop their reelection strategies.

To test our hypothesis that constituency size influences senators' choice of committee assignments, we first analyze the membership of three Senate committees—Appropriations, Finance, and Foreign Relations—for the 80th Congress through the 105th Congress (1947–98). We chose these committees for three reasons. First, these are the most highly preferred: senators request them rather than being assigned to them. Second, it is rare for a senator to serve on more than one of these committees simultaneously. Because they are so popular and influential, membership on one typically precludes membership on the other two. In the 104th and 105th Congresses, for example, sixty-six different senators filled the sixty-six slots on these three committees. We can assume that senators prefer the available committee they think will best help them advance their goals. Thus, choosing to serve on one of these is a statement of a senator's priorities.

Third, these three committees are useful to senators in advancing different goals. Smith and Deering (1990, 101) classify Appropriations as a constituency committee, Finance as a mixed constituency-policy committee, and Foreign Relations as a policy committee. By analyzing the membership composition of these committees, then, we can determine whether senators from large and small states have different incentives in choosing committee assignments. Our theory predicts that the states represented on Appropriations will tend to be smaller than those represented on the other two committees, that the states represented on Foreign Relations will tend to be larger than those represented on the other two, and that Finance, as a mixed committee, will fall somewhere between.

Table 5.1 presents the median state size (measured by the number of congressional districts) represented on each of these three committees for the period since 1946. We use the median as our measure of central tendency rather than the mean because the median is less sensitive to the presence of outliers. We then calculate the mean of the medians for each committee for the whole period, shown at the bottom of table 5.1.

The data support our hypothesis. The mean median state size represented during this period is 5.29 congressional districts on Appropriations, 6.35 on Finance, and 7.63 on Foreign Relations. This is precisely the pattern our theory predicts. The patterns summarized by the mean median measures in

Table 5.1 Median State Population (in Congressional Districts) Represented on Selected Senate Committees, Eightieth to 105th Congress

Congress	Appropriations	Finance	Foreign Relations
80th (1947−48)	5.0	9.0	10.0
81st (1949−50)	6.0	10.0	8.0
82d (1951−52)	6.0	8.0	8.5
83d (1953−54)	6.0	6.0	9.0
84th (1955−56)	8.0	6.0	8.5
85th (1957−58)	8.0	6.0	8.5
86th (1959−60)	6.0	8.0	8.0
87th (1961−62)	5.0	8.0	7.5
88th (1963−64)	5.0	8.0	6.5
89th (1965−66)	5.0	8.0	7.0
90th (1967−68)	4.5	7.0	6.5
91st (1969−70)	4.0	7.0	5.0
92d (1971−72)	2.5	6.0	4.5
93d (1973−74)	4.0	5.0	6.0
94th (1975−76)	4.5	5.5	7.0
95th (1977−78)	6.0	5.0	8.0
96th (1979−80)	4.0	7.0	8.0
97th (1981−82)	5.0	7.0	8.0
98th (1983−84)	5.0	5.0	8.0
99th (1985−86)	5.0	5.0	8.0
100th (1987−88)	5.0	5.0	8.0
101st (1989−90)	5.0	5.0	8.0
102d (1991−92)	5.5	5.0	7.0
103d (1993−94)	6.0	4.0	8.0
104th (1995−96)	5.5	5.5	8.5
105th (1997−98)	6.0	4.0	8.5
Mean	5.29	6.35	7.63

table 5.1 are also consistent throughout the period studied. In eighteen of the twenty-six Congresses studied, the Foreign Relations Committee had the largest median state size of the three, and Appropriations either had the smallest median state size or was tied with Finance for the smallest in twenty of the Congresses studied (in six Congresses, Appropriations was tied for smallest with Finance). Similarly, Foreign Relations never had the smallest median state size of the three committees during the period studied, and Appropriations never had the largest. Difference of means tests revealed that the differences in median state sizes among these committees are statistically significant ($p < .05$).[6]

These findings indicate that constituency size is a relevant variable in explaining senators' choice of assignments, at least for the three most requested

Table 5.2 Mean Median Numbers of Congressional Districts in the States Represented on Standing Senate Committees, 80th to 105th Congress, by Committee Type

Mean Median Number of Congressional Districts	Committee	Type
3.29	Energy and Natural Resources	Constituency
4.27	Environment and Public Works	Constituency
4.61	Veterans' Affairs	Constituency
5.29	Appropriations	Constituency
6.18	Commerce	Constituency
6.35	Finance	Mixed
6.42	Agriculture	Constituency
6.95	Judiciary	Policy
7.13	Governmental Affairs	Policy
7.23	Budget	Policy
7.25	Armed Services	Mixed
7.63	Foreign Relations	Policy
7.72	Small Business	Mixed
8.71	Labor	Policy
8.98	Banking	Mixed

Note: Committees are arranged from smallest to largest in terms of the mean median number of congressional disricts in the states represented on them

committees. Does the same relationship hold for other Senate committees? To determine this, we calculate the mean median number of congressional districts of the states represented on the other standing Senate committees for the same period (80th Congress through 105th Congress, 1947–98). These data are displayed in table 5.2.[7]

The first thing to notice in table 5.2 is that none of the eight committees with the largest mean median state size is a constituency committee, whereas the five with the smallest state size all are. The median state represented on the policy and mixed committees, moreover, is larger, on average, than the median state in the Senate. (For most of the period the median-sized state had six congressional districts. Before the admission of Alaska and Hawaii as states, it had 6.5.) By comparison, most of the states represented on the constituency committees are much smaller than the median state in the Senate.

The one qualification in the data is that the mean median state sizes represented on the policy and mixed committees are similar. Senators from populous states tend to seek assignment to both policy and mixed committees more often than senators from smaller states. In this context the "policy" aspect of these mixed committees appears to be more important than the "constituency" aspect. Thus, overall the data provide strong support for our argument that small-state senators tend to choose constituency committees whereas those from populous states choose more policy-oriented ones.

To test the strength and significance of the observed relationship between committee type and state size, we regress state size (as measured by mean median number of congressional districts represented on each committee during the period studied) on committee type, for which we used a dummy variable with a value of 1 for policy and mixed constituency-policy committees and a value of 0 for constituency committees ($N = 15$). The coefficient for this committee variable was 2.55, with a standard error of 0.52 ($p < .01$). The R^2 for this simple model was .62. During this period, then, the mean median state size represented on policy and mixed committees was on average 2.5 congressional districts larger than the mean median state size represented on constituency committees.

An additional observation is worth discussing. One constituency committee, Agriculture, had a mean median state size slightly larger than that of the Senate as a whole, and another, Commerce, was for all practical purposes representative of the Senate. Clearly, not all constituency committees are alike (for a House example, see Adler and Lapinski 1997). Agriculture attracts senators from some populous states because agricultural interests are important within their constituencies. More typical constituency committees, like Environment and Public Works and Appropriations, are useful to senators regardless of the particular interests concentrated in their states. Every state has an interest in the work of these committees because every state has roads and bridges, and every state receives funds at the discretion of Senate appropriators. But membership on these latter committees for reelection purposes is not equally useful to all senators. The predominance of small-state senators on these more typical constituency committees is not due to the concentration of interests in their states but is instead the result of the differing incentives of large- and small-state senators.

At times we found it difficult to explore the issue of committee assignments with our interview subjects. The senators, former senators, lobbyists, and staffers we talked with often discussed assignments in terms of the other variables that influence committee choice—personal preference, policy goals, or constituency-based reasons. Not surprisingly, a senator from a farm state felt constrained to serve on the Agriculture Committee even if that was not of great interest to him: "It was not a burning issue for me and I wanted to go on Finance. But I knew if I let a senator [from a neighboring state] have the seat on Agriculture, I'd never be forgiven." Similarly, we found that some senators choose policy committees because they have a special interest in a particular area of public policy. Another senator said, "I want to do things that will have an impact ten years down the road . . . instead of just getting a bridge or some project. . . .I wanted to be on committees that would allow me to look at the substance of issues." Then he went on to note that for this reason he had chosen to serve on Labor and Human Resources and on Foreign Relations rather than on Appropriations or Finance. He continued, "But it's policymaking that I'm really interested in. You see, on Labor, I'm a voice."

Other interview subjects, however, were sensitive to the way constituency size shapes senators' incentives as they choose committee assignments. When we asked a former staffer to a Senate leader, for example, if she had observed the effects of state size on senators' behavior in any areas we had not already discussed during the interview, she responded without hesitation, "Small-state senators just like to go places to get things, like Appropriations." In addition, a former small-state senator raised an interesting point that we had not previously considered as an incentive for small-state senators to serve on constituency committees. He argued that senators representing large states, with their larger number of House members, have more help from the other body in looking out for the state's interests than do senators representing small states: "It's more of a monkey on your back [in a small state] if the House member fails [because the senators have to protect the state's interests]. In a state with fifteen or twenty House members, or even five or ten, you're okay." In this context, he discussed a particularly important project in his state: "In the sixties and seventies we were able to ensure funding in the House. But in the eighties there wasn't money for it there. [The state's other senator] and I had to pull rabbits out of a hat to keep it funded." Pulling rabbits out of the hat was made possible in this case by the committee assignments of these two senators. In addition, it was something they could take credit for. They did not have to share or compete for it with House members as would usually be the case in more populous states.[8]

The evidence presented here supports our argument that small-state senators find a Washington strategy emphasizing particularized benefits for their constituents more useful for advancing their reelection interests than do senators from more populous states. Senators from large states tend to prefer policy-oriented committees. This bolsters our contention that senators from large states have a greater incentive to pursue a strategy of policy activism. Next we examine another aspect of large-state senators' strategies: their efforts to attract national media attention.

Media Coverage of Senators

We have just presented evidence that the membership of Senate committees reflects the different incentives of large- and small-state senators. Constituency committees are more attractive to small-state senators because membership is more useful in advancing their reelection goals. Large-state senators

find this strategy inefficient because it consumes more of their time and resources and has a relatively smaller electoral payoff than for their small-state
colleagues. Instead they have incentives to engage in a strategy of policy activism to advance their reelection goals. Thus populous-state senators prefer
membership on policy-oriented committees. These committees, after all,
"supply good platforms for position taking" (Mayhew 1974, 85).

We build on the same line of reasoning in this section as we investigate
the different incentives of large- and small-state senators to seek national media coverage. Membership on policy committees is more attractive to senators from more populous states in part because these committees receive
more media attention than constituency committees (Hess 1986, 34; Smith
and Deering 1990, 100). Large-state senators can use the increased media
coverage to reach their larger constituencies and thus to advance their reelection goals. Accordingly, Sinclair (1990) shows that national prominence as a
result of policy activism and media coverage does affect the visibility of senators in their constituencies. In addition, Schiller (1995) finds that senators
from larger states are active on more policy issues, as measured by their co-
sponsoring more bills than their small-state colleagues.

National prominence is not of equal value to all senators, however. Many
do not need national media coverage to achieve their goals. Hess (1986, 7)
writes that "those senators . . . who want little more than to serve their
constituents' local needs and to get re-elected . . . are of no interest to reporters for the national media." The converse of this statement is even more
true: the national media is of no interest to "those senators who want little
more than to serve their constituents' local needs." For the senator heavily
committed to a particularized benefits strategy, national media coverage may
even be undesirable. Who, after all, wants to be the subject of a "Fleecing of
America" story on the NBC Nightly News? Cook (1989, 85) and Schiller
(1998) both suggest that more constituency-oriented members of Congress
prefer local coverage of their activities to national coverage.[9]

For those senators who are less able to serve their constituents' local needs,
on the other hand, national media coverage and the resulting national prominence may be a necessary factor in getting reelected. Hess (1986, 85) quotes
from Sen. Alan Cranston's (D-Calif.) speech to freshmen senators in 1982: "I
think it's safe to assume that what senators—like most public figures—want
from the press is coverage. Lots of coverage." Cranston may not be speaking
for all senators, but he certainly was speaking for himself (he ranked second
in national media coverage on Hess's measures well before his involvement
in the Keating Five scandal) and for other senators who need the media to
communicate with their constituents or to advance their goals.

Another reason senators from larger states have more incentive to become active across a broad range of issues and to seek national prominence is their greater need to raise campaign funds from "consumer" contributors, discussed in chapter 4. To appeal to this group of campaign contributors, large-state senators must establish a record of activism on issues that are important to these consumers. This will be true regardless of whether a senator's consumer base is in state or national. Small-state senators, on the other hand, have less need to appeal to such contributors and accordingly have less incentive to engage in the sort of policy activism designed to appeal to them.

National media coverage is valuable to senators seeking to advance a number of goals, of course. Senators with presidential aspirations, for example, use the media in their attempts to build national constituencies, and others use the media to advance their public policy goals inside the Beltway. We are not suggesting that all the media attention senators receive is part of their reelection strategies (Sinclair 1989, 190). Similarly, not all the media coverage they receive is positive. There is no reason to think, however, that these other considerations affect large- and small-state senators differently. Senators from large and small states run for president. Senators from large and small states attempt to use the media to advance their policy goals. Senators from large and small states receive negative coverage from the national media. Despite all this, however, senators from more populous states get more national media coverage than those from smaller states, all else being equal, as we will demonstrate. This suggests that senators from larger states are seeking national media coverage, and the national prominence that comes with it, to further their reelection goals in addition to any other goals they have.

Much of the national media attention senators receive is the result of their own efforts to attract it (Hess 1986, 42; Sinclair 1990, 475). In order to make news, senators become involved in and develop expertise on the sorts of issues that draw media attention (choosing to serve on a policy committee is a part of this process; Hess 1986, 30), giving policy-related speeches, making themselves personally available to reporters, providing reporters with sound bites, and issuing press releases. Ornstein (1983, 201; cited in Hess 1986, 4) argues that since the 1970s "it [has become] possible for any member of Congress to get national coverage and become a nationally recognized figure." This is particularly true of senators, given their smaller number and much greater individual power in the institution.

Political scientists have studied the factors that influence the amount of media attention senators receive, typically concluding that their institutional position is the most important variable (Hess 1986; Sinclair 1989; Squire 1988; Weaver and Wilhoit 1974, 1980; Wilhoit and Sherrill 1968). A few previous studies—some examining media coverage of the Senate dating back to the 1950s—have also included state population in their multivariate analyses of the determinants of senators' media coverage, finding that senators from larger states tend to receive more coverage than those from smaller states (Squire 1988; Weaver and Wilhoit 1974, 1980; Wilhoit and Sherrill 1968). None of them, however, links this greater national media coverage with the different incentives of senators representing more and less populous states.[10] Weaver and Wilhoit (1980), for example, suggest that the reason for large-state senators' greater coverage is that they have larger staffs than senators from smaller states. Larger staffs, they argue, enable them to be more active on a greater range of issues than their small-state counterparts. They do not make the connection we make here between constituency size and choice of strategies. After all, having a larger staff is not by itself reason to be more active on policy issues—a large-state senator could use her staff to pursue particularized benefits for her state or to engage in other types of constituent tending. The electoral and representational contexts of large-state senators, on the other hand, enhance their incentives to seek national media attention and thus to increase their visibility and advance their reelection goals.

To determine whether large-state senators do receive more media attention than their small-state colleagues, we first gathered data on the number of times each senator serving in the 103d and 104th Congresses (1993–96) was mentioned or quoted on one of the national nightly news broadcasts (ABC, CBS, CNN, NBC). This information was obtained using the Vanderbilt Television News Archive Index. We used mentions on the news broadcasts rather than mentions in the *New York Times* or other such sources because television coverage, especially on the nightly news, is a better indicator of national prominence.[11] This study updates the previous work on media coverage of senators and uses an improved measure of media visibility.

Using the number of mentions of a senator on the nightly network news broadcasts (for each Congress) as our dependent variable, we employ multivariate OLS regression to test our hypothesis that state population affects the national media coverage of senators, controlling for other variables likely to affect the amount of coverage they receive. We include dummy variables in the regression for the Senate floor leaders, committee chairs, and ranking minority members. Every past study of the determinants of senators' national media coverage has found that leadership and committee positions are very important variables (Hess 1986; Sinclair 1989; Squire 1988; Weaver and Wilhoit 1980). We also include a dummy variable indicating whether a senator was running in the next election to capture the effects of campaign coverage, a dummy variable to control for senators running for president in the 1996 election (for the 104th Congress only) to control for presidential coverage, and a dummy variable indicating whether a senator was currently

Table 5.3 Effect of State Population on Senators' Network News Coverage, Controlling for Other Factors, 103d and 104th Congresses (1993–96)

Variables	103d Congress	104th Congress
Constant	8.57*	6.06*
	(2.67)	(1.95)
Number of congressional districts in state	1.00**	0.51*
	(4.75)	(2.55)
Party leader	183.95**	81.01**
	(13.09)	(7.17)
Committee chair	21.02**	12.53*
	(3.69)	(2.36)
Ranking minority member	11.89*	4.21
	(2.05)	(0.807)
Running in upcoming election	−0.155	5.25
	(−0.03)	(1.09)
Scandal	29.52*	—
	(2.09)	
Running for president in 1996	—	78.66**
		(7.97)
F-statistic	32.49**	29.49**
Adj. R^2	.66	.64
N	100	99[a]
Median number of news stories	17	11

Source: Vanderbilt Television News Archive Index.
Note: t-statistics in parentheses.
$*p < .05; **p < .01$.
[a] The missing case is the Oregon seat that Sen. Bob Packwood resigned in late 1995 and to which Sen. Ron Wyden was elected in early 1996.

involved in a major scandal to control for scandal coverage (103d Congress only).[12]

The regression results are displayed in table 5.3. In both the 103d and 104th Congresses, state population (measured in number of congressional districts) had the expected effect. For each additional congressional district in a state, senators received one additional mention on the network nightly news in the 103d Congress ($p < .01$), and approximately one-half a mention in the 104th Congress ($p < .05$), all else being equal. The smaller coefficient in the 104th Congress is explained in part by the lower total amount of national media coverage of the Senate at that time.[13]

The other variables in the model, for the most part, had the effects we expected. We find, as have previous studies, that holding a leadership position or serving as a committee chair makes a great difference in the amount of national media attention a senator receives. In the 103d and 104th Congresses, for example, no other senator received nearly as much media coverage as majority leader and presidential candidate Bob Dole (R-Kans.). The coefficient for ranking minority members was significant ($p < .05$) in the 103d Congress but not in the 104th. In the new Republican-controlled Senate, Democratic ranking minority members may have found it unusually difficult to attract national media attention.

The coefficients for scandal and for senators running for president were also significant and positive. Running for president is a very effective way for senators to get media coverage (and certainly provides a strong incentive to seek it) even if they do not get far in the presidential contest. Sen. Phil Gramm (R-Tex.), for example, always a visible and voluble senator, had 163 mentions in the 104th Congress, compared with 95 mentions in the 103d. Sen. Arlen Specter (R-Pa.) went from twenty-nine mentions in the 103d Congress to fifty-eight in the 104th, and Sen. Richard Lugar (R-Ind.) went from thirty-three to fifty. Senators caught up in scandals—like Sen. Bob Packwood (R-Oreg.), mentioned in eighty-one news stories in the 103d Congress—also receive a great deal of media coverage. (A complete listing of senators and the frequency of their mentions is given in appendix B.) The coefficients for senators running for reelection, however, were not significant in either Congress. It may well be that national news broadcasts do not devote much coverage to particular Senate races, with a few exceptions. These models explain a good deal of the variation in senators' national media coverage. The R^2 for the 103d Congress model is .66, and for the 104th Congress it is .64.

Along with the highly visible senators—Republican leader Dole, Democratic leaders George Mitchell (D-Maine) and Tom Daschle (D-S.Dak.), Gramm, Daniel Patrick Moynihan (D-N.Y.), and Edward Kennedy (D-Mass.), to name a few—there are several senators who receive virtually no national media coverage at all, and many of them come from small states. Sen. Daniel Akaka (D-Hawaii) stands out as the only senator serving in both the 103d and 104th Congresses not to receive a single mention on the network nightly news. Not coincidentally, Akaka serves almost solely on constituency committees: Energy and Natural Resources, Governmental Affairs, Indian Affairs, and Veterans' Affairs. Based on these committee assignments and his low media profile, Akaka certainly appears to favor a strategy of seeking particularized benefits. This is true of other small-state senators as well. In the 104th Congress Sen. Conrad Burns (R-Mont.) was mentioned in one story on the network nightly news—a story about the reintroduction of wolves into the national parks, an issue of great concern to his ranching constituents as well as to those who live near Yellowstone National Park. Burns also appears to have a constituency-oriented Washington strategy, serving on the Special Aging, Appropriations, Energy, Small Business, and Commerce committees. Another low-visibility small-state senator, Sen. Harry Reid (D-Nev.), received three mentions in the 104th Congress, one of which was a "Fleecing of America" story on a new $123 million visitors' center at Hoover Dam in 1995. Not surprisingly, Reid also has a distinctly constituency-oriented set of committee assignments, serving on Special Aging, Appropriations, Environment and Public Works, and Indian Affairs. For these less visible senators it is probably safe to assume that national media coverage is not part of their strategy to advance their goals, including reelection.

We have shown that constituency size is an important part of the context within which senators decide how to behave in Washington. In terms of reelection, small-state senators gain more from emphasizing particularized benefits while maintaining a low national profile. This is reflected in their choices of committee assignments and in their relatively low level of national media coverage. Large-state senators, by contrast, derive less electoral advantage from a particularized benefit strategy. They have greater difficulty communicating with their numerous constituents and thus need media coverage more than do small-state senators. For these reasons they gain greater electoral benefit from policy activism and national prominence. This strategy is reflected in their choices of committee assignments and in their higher level of national media coverage.

Again, as in chapters 3 and 4, our findings suggest that small-state senators behave more like House members than like other senators. There are strong incentives for both House members and small-state senators to seek assignment to constituency committees. This is not the case, however, for senators from more populous states. Constituency committees are not efficient "reelection" committees for them. Because they must reach more constituents than House members or small-state senators, policy committee assignments better serve their reelection goals.

Understanding the Washington behavior of senators, of course, requires that we take into account more than just constituency size. There is a great deal of variation in this behavior that is not explained by constituency size. Given that individual senators pursue their specific strategies for a variety of reasons—personal preference, ambition for higher office, ideology, and public policy goals, to name just a few—it is remarkable that constituency size explains so much of the variation in senators' behavior in Washington. This suggests that constituency size, as the context within which senators decide how to behave in Washington, is much more important than political scientists have previously recognized.

Holding Out

We have established that constituency size is important in shaping the strategies senators pursue in Washington. If its effects are apparent in these large-scale choices, such as committee assignments and the pursuit of national media attention, it may be that it also influences senators' incentives in making day-to-day legislative choices.

The argument we advance now is quite simple: Although all senators' votes are equal in the sense that no vote counts for more than any other in terms of passage, not all senators' votes are equally costly to the coalition builder (bill sponsor, president, lobbyist, or party leader) needing to pick up just a few more votes for passage of a particular piece of legislation.[14] A relatively small policy concession to benefit a small-state senator's constituents, or a relatively small side payment such as a special project for his state, may in some cases be enough to win support for a particular bill.[15] Winning the support of a senator from a more populous state, on the other hand, usually involves a larger policy concession or a larger side payment because small offerings will not have such great credit-claiming, advertising, or campaign benefit.

Coalition builders do not have unlimited resources and will choose to bargain for the support of the least expensive senator available. This has consequences for the strategic behavior of coalition builders and for senators generally. First, other things being equal, when looking for late deciders or even for senators who might switch their votes, coalition builders seeking out the least costly senators (in terms of policy concessions or side payments) will tend to turn to those from small states. Second, senators from large and small states will perceive the differences in the cost of their support and will act on this perception, at least in certain contexts. Senators from more populous states will often recognize that they are not likely to succeed in this behavior and thus will be more reluctant to engage in it. Small-state senators asking for small concessions, on the other hand, are apt to perceive that they have a better chance of success, at least in certain situations, and will thus be more likely to use the hold-out strategy.

In addition, if small-state senators have more voting leeway or flexibility than their colleagues from more populous states, as we argued in chapter 4, this will increase their ability to hold out. As we shall explain, holding out may involve some risks (costs), and small-state senators may be in a better position to minimize or absorb them.

For these reasons we argue that small-state senators will be more likely than their colleagues from more populous states to hold out on closely fought legislation and that coalition builders will be more apt to seek out their votes by making relatively small policy concessions or side payments. Note that senators can hold out without actually "renting" their votes: they may know from the start how they are going to vote but withhold support until coalition builders make an offer.

Of course the differences in the cost of senators' votes will not be an important consideration in all cases. Many bills are passed by large majorities, and thus coalition builders do not need to seek out votes in the manner we are discussing here. Even on closely fought bills, however, the issue of state size may not come up. Many senators, including those from small states, may have precommitted on the vote and thus find themselves unable to bargain (Fenno 1986, 7–8). Assuming that on closely fought bills there are always some senators who are either late deciders or open to persuasion, there may be other ways the coalition builders can gain their support. If a bill is an important part of the party's agenda, then appeals to partisan loyalty may suffice. Similarly, if a bill is important from the president's point of view and the senator is of the same party, then presidential lobbying may win her support. Some presidential lobbying involves promises of side payments, but other efforts may appeal to patriotism, party loyalty, or other values. In other cases party leaders or bill sponsors may be able to call in old favors, or make new promises, that have little or nothing to do with state size. In addition to small-state senators, ideological moderates may also be in a position to hold out, regardless of the size of their states, especially when the issues being considered are ideological. Thus state size is not the only variable affecting how (and when) senators decide to vote. It will matter in some cases, however, and it is those cases we are interested in exploring.

Before we advance to our research on this issue, a couple of caveats are in order. First, in looking for policy concessions or side payments made to small-state senators to secure their votes on the floor, we are not taking into account those they receive at earlier stages in the legislative process, for example, at the committee level. In fact, we expect that in their pursuit of particularized benefits, small-state senators will reap rewards from other obstructionist behavior. We occasionally came across anecdotal evidence that supports this extension. In discussing the hold-out behavior of small-state senators in the summer of 1995, one Washington lobbyist was quick to mention that "just today, Stevens and Murkowski are holding up the highway bill to get something for Alaska." After all, obtaining the support of small-state senators is less costly at other decision points as well. Further, we do not mean holding out is the only way small-state senators pursue benefits for their constituents. It is simply one more way that equal representation of states with greatly varying populations affects the Senate as a legislative institution.

Second, establishing that small-state senators receive policy concessions or side payments (especially the latter) is difficult in most cases. This is the sort of horse trading that senators themselves are often reluctant to discuss. In fact, in our interviews we never encountered a senator or former senator who would admit to engaging in this conduct, even those whom others perceived as master practitioners of the strategy. We found instead that senators and former senators would openly disparage their colleagues, past or present, who did so, but much of the time they did not want to name them. When we named certain senators with reputations for holding out for particularized benefits, they would grimace, raise their eyebrows, and even smile. One small-state senator, for example, went on at length about his abhorrence of vote trading on important national policy issues: "It's antithetical to me to trade a vote for a bridge or . . . a tunnel." Another interview subject—a former senator reputed to have often engaged in just such behavior—said, "I've heard that there have been some quid pro quos. Maybe that worked better with other members than it would have with me. If they'd offered me something for my vote, I would have told them to go shove it. There are others who ask, What's in it for me?"

Although our interviews suggest that senators do hold out, they try to do it covertly because of the disapproval of their colleagues and, potentially, their constituents. It may not be possible in every case, then, to point to the policy concession or side payment that was decisive in winning the support of a late decider or switcher. But if we can show that late deciders and switchers tend to be small-state senators—that small-state senators are over-represented among the senators engaging in these behaviors—then we have established a prima facie case for our hypothesis. If, in addition, we can point to policy concessions or side payments in at least some of the cases, then we have strengthened our case.

To test our hypothesis that small-state senators are more likely to hold out than their colleagues from more populous states, we examine close votes on important pieces of legislation. It is essential to look at close votes, of course, because only in those circumstances will withholding support work, with coalition builders having a strong incentive to make concessions or side payments.[16] We examine important votes because they are the only type for which there is likely to be sufficient reporting about late-deciding or switching senators. Starting with *Congressional Quarterly*'s Senate "key votes" from 1977 to 1997, we selected those votes on which a switch by four senators would have altered the outcome.[17] A total of ninety-eight key votes met this criterion. We then researched the politics surrounding these votes to determine which senators were holding out or being lobbied to switch by coalition builders.[18] In approximately forty cases there was either no reporting about late deciders or not enough coverage to tell which senators' votes were decisive. In approximately twenty cases we determined that the final outcome was not really as close as the final vote suggested.[19] In a handful of other cases the votes were so strictly along party or ideological lines that holding out could not be considered a viable option. In at least one case the vote occurred suddenly and thus there was no time for bargaining. (In some cases a vote could be eliminated for more than a single reason.) We were left with thirty-one key votes to analyze. They are listed in appendix C.

In sixteen of the thirty-one key votes in the sample (51.6 percent), the late deciders or switchers were primarily or exclusively from small-population states (defined here as states with four or fewer congressional districts). On the other hand, in only seven of the thirty-one key votes (22.6 percent) were the late deciders or switchers primarily or exclusively from medium-sized or large states, those with more than four congressional districts. In the eight remaining votes (22.6 percent) the late deciders or switchers were from both small and medium-sized or large states. Senators from states with four or fewer congressional districts make up less than 40 percent of the Senate throughout the period studied. (There were twenty such states in the 1970s, eighteen in the 1980s, and nineteen in the 1990s.) This means that senators from small states were holding out in a disproportionate percentage of the cases studied, compared with their presence in the Senate as a whole. Senators representing states with five or more congressional districts, by contrast, make up more than 60 percent of the Senate throughout the period studied but were the primary late deciders or switchers in only 22.6 percent of the cases. These findings support the hypothesis.

Although, as we mentioned above, it was not possible in very many of these cases to identify the "quid pro quos," there are a few in which the exchanges are relatively clear. In May 1985, for example, the first budget resolution passed the Senate 50–49, with Vice President George Bush casting the deciding vote. The Republican Senate leadership was forced to make several concessions to secure this narrow victory, sparing programs important to senators and their constituents to ensure passage of the budget: "Until hours before final action, Dole and Domenici were reworking sections of the package, adding back money here and there, reprieving programs targeted for extinction and revising assumptions, to bring as many Republican votes as possible—and Zorinsky—on board" (Wehr 1985, 872). Because budgetary constraints were intense, the most efficient way for Dole and Domenici to gain the needed votes was to make concessions on small programs to win the support of senators representing small states. Sen. Edward Zorinsky (D-Nebr.), the only Democrat to vote for the budget resolution, did so only after getting commitments on restoring certain farm loan guarantees and funds for agricultural export promotions, two programs important to his primarily agricultural constituency. Sen. James Abdnor (R-S.Dak.) voted for the resolution only after saving the Rural Electrification Administration from the budget ax. Sen. Mark Andrews (R-N.Dak.) also won concessions on agricultural programs. In addition, Abdnor and two other small-state senators, Ted Stevens (R-Alaska) and William Roth (R-Del.), won concessions on postal subsidies for small newspapers, and Sen. William Cohen (R-Maine) ensured funding for rural housing (Wehr 1985, 873–74).

In sharp contrast to these small-scale concessions made to small-state senators, two other senators from more populous states also forced changes in the 1985 budget resolution, but these concessions protected large-scale national entitlement programs dealing with health care and the handicapped from deeper budget cuts rather than securing particularized benefits. These concessions were generally more expensive than those made to the small-state senators, but in this case every vote counted and thus the coalition builders had to pay the higher price of these senators from more populous states. Dole and Domenici tried to make as few high-priced concessions as possible, thus losing the votes of some Republicans from large states. As Domenici said, commenting on the deals the leadership had made, "We didn't give away the kitchen sink" (Wehr 1985, 872).

The 1981 Senate vote on the resolution to disapprove President Reagan's proposed sale of AWACS planes to Saudi Arabia provides another example of small-state senators holding out. Fifty senators had cosponsored the resolution to cancel the sale. After extensive lobbying by the Reagan administration, the resolution, which had already passed the House, was defeated 48–52 in the Senate. The administration persuaded ten senators who had cosponsored the resolution to vote against it, and seven of the ten represented states with four or fewer congressional districts.[20] The last two switchers, Sen. William Cohen (R-Maine) and Sen. Edward Zorinsky (D-Nebr.), were from small states. In an article in the *Wall Street Journal,* Hunt (1981, 4) suggests that the White House had offered several senators deals to switch their votes. One senator we interviewed joked when asked about the AWACS vote, "We laughed about how many grain silos that cost." Interestingly, however, one of the late deciders in this case told Fenno (1986, 13) that "I got more flak from that vote by far than any I have ever cast in the Senate," but that "the Administration never thanked me for helping them on that vote, never gave me anything, never acknowledged that I helped them." Once again, this case shows the difficulty of establishing the existence of side payments.

The outcome of other close votes frequently hinged on the decisions of only one or two senators. In 1978 Sen. Paul Hatfield (D-Mont.) provided the crucial vote to ratify the Panama Canal Treaty. More recently, the outcomes of Senate votes on legislative issues of the highest significance were decided by the votes of small-state senators. The conference report on the 1993 Clinton economic package in the Senate passed when Sen. Bob Kerrey (D-Nebr.) provided the fiftieth vote, enabling Vice President Gore to cast the tie-breaker. When asked about the hold-out behavior of small-state senators, one of our interview subjects paused before responding: "Kerrey played that game all the time." Then he added rhetorically: "I wonder if they [Kerrey and Exon, also of Nebraska, another vote trader he mentioned] think their vote enables them to get pork from the White House." In 1994 the outcome of the Senate's vote on a balanced-budget constitutional amendment came down to the votes of North Dakota's senators.

There was at least one case in our sample of a small-state senator who unsuccessfully sought a side payment in exchange for his vote. In 1987 the administration lobbied Sen. Chic Hecht (R-Nev.) to vote to sustain Reagan's veto of the highway—mass transit bill. (Hecht had voted to override the veto the day before, in a vote in which the veto had been upheld.) One Hecht aide was quoted as saying, "Everybody but the pope called," including the president, vice president, and the president's chief of staff (Starobin 1987, 606). In exchange for his vote, however, Hecht wanted a guarantee that a proposed nuclear-waste dump would not be located in Nevada. The White House decided that such a guarantee in exchange for Hecht's vote would have been illegal (Hoffman and Cannon 1987). In the end Reagan's veto was overridden, and the nuclear-waste dump was located in Nevada (Davis 1987; see also Arnold 1990, 111–12).

Some of our interview subjects offered an additional explanation for how infrequently senators from medium and large states hold out. They suggested that in a larger state the political risks of holding out are greater. In close votes of national importance, late-deciding senators can find themselves in the national media spotlight. Although senators from larger states seek national media attention more actively than their small-state colleagues, there is a risk for senators who gain the attention associated with the hold-out strategy. In more populous states, senators are defined less by their face-to-face, person-to-person contacts with voters and more by the media. A senator who depends on the national media to communicate with his constituents does not want to be defined as a "horse trader" or as someone who "sells" his vote to the highest bidder. This risk may deter senators from larger states in many cases.

There are exceptions from time to time, however. In some of our interviews, our subjects mentioned the case of Republican senator Slade Gorton of Washington, a medium-sized state, casting the crucial vote in 1986 to confirm Daniel Manion, a conservative Reagan appointee to the federal bench, in exchange for freeing up the nomination of a Gorton political ally in Washington State. Gorton's role in Manion's confirmation made the national news. Gorton was up for reelection in 1986, and his Democratic opponent in the election used this coverage to cast him as a "craven vote-trader" (Duncan 1990, 1574). Gorton's narrow defeat in the 1986 election is credited in part to his vote trading on the Manion confirmation. We should note that it is not clear how much electoral benefit Gorton could have expected from the successful appointment of a political ally.[21]

There may be one other reason holding out is more costly for a large-state senator than for a colleague from a less populous state. Because small states contain a narrower range of political interests, there are more issues that are of little salience to voters and thus on which a small-state senator has considerable latitude. As one lobbyist we interviewed exclaimed, "Who gives a rat's ass about AWACS in Alaska?" Of course there are also a few issues about which the relatively homogeneous population of a small state cares a great deal, and on those a small-state senator has little flexibility. In these cases senators from small states—like two of the House members Fenno traveled with in *Home Style*—do what they have to on some issues so they are free to do what they want on others (1978, 153–57). Although senators from populous states, as a couple of our interview subjects observed, may gain some maneuvering room from having constituent interests on both sides of a particular issue—providing them with some cover when they take a position— a stand on these divisive issues will still involve electoral costs among dissatisfied constituents. By comparison, this dilemma will not often enter the calculus of small-state senators, who are free to choose their positions on matters of little concern to any important group within their states.

Holding out in exchange for particularized benefits large enough to make a difference in a populous state and thus offering some credit-claiming value without incurring undue costs, on the other hand, does occur in rare cases. In 1989 the Senate tabled an amendment by Sen. J. Bennett Johnston (D–La.) to the defense authorization bill to reduce Strategic Defense Initiative spending and to transfer funding from SDI to other weapons. Sen. Alphonse D'Amato (R–N.Y.) is credited with casting the crucial vote for the tabling motion. His support was tied to restoring funding for the F-14D fighter plane, which had been cut in the Senate bill. (The F-14D was built on Long Island.) In exchange for voting to table Johnston's amendment, the leadership reportedly promised D'Amato that the Senate conferees would be urged to accept the House's position authorizing funding for twelve more planes. This exchange made it possible for D'Amato to claim credit for saving the F-14D—and jobs on Long Island—even though the House's position on the plane might have been adopted in conference without his maneuvering (Fessler and Towell 1989). But the D'Amato case, like the Gorton vote on Manion, is an exception.

In a few of our interviews, our subjects suggested that the ability of ideo-logically committed senators to hold out is limited. As one lobbyist with long experience in both the Senate and the White House commented at first, "I know those cowboy senators are all conservative senators. There was not a question of how they were going to vote. Fannin and Goldwater and Hatch and Craig and back to Dominick. There wasn't any doubt about where they stood." This may be true in the case of ideological votes, but on many issues ideological moderation does not appear to matter. The senators engaging in hold-out behavior in the sample include western conservatives with Ameri-cans for Democratic Action scores less than 20—Hatch, Hecht, Murkowski, Stevens, and Symms—as well as liberal Democrats with ADA scores greater than 80—Biden, Bryan, Conrad, Dorgan, Kerrey, and Reid. Thus, holding out does not seem to be limited to ideological moderates. It is not limited to senators from small states either, but in our sample those holding out repre-sented primarily small states in more than half the cases (seventeen out of thirty-one). This suggests that small-state senators do have greater incentives to withhold their support on close votes than their colleagues from large states.

Although the empirical evidence for hold-out behavior is more limited than the data we presented on committee assignments and national media exposure, we believe the theory advanced here is sound. Constituency size affects both the political benefits senators can gain from engaging in this strategy and its potential risks. For coalition builders, moreover, the value of each senator's vote is unrelated to the population of the state he represents, whereas the cost of that vote will tend to increase with state population.[22] The link between hold-out behavior and constituency size is thus an example of how population influences senators' day-to-day behavior, not just their broad strategic choices such as committee assignments and pursuit of national media coverage. In this sense holding out illustrates but does not exhaust the ways constituency size influences the behavior of senators and their strategies for electoral success.

Leadership: Senate Apportionment as Constraint

The effects of constituency size on senators' Washington strategies as they choose committee assignments, pursue national media coverage, and engage in hold-out behavior are not new. Although our data on committee assign-ments extend back only to the 80th Congress, our theory of senators' incen-tives leads us to expect that large- and small-state senators have had different preferences in committee assignments for as long as they have been important to senators and their constituents. Similarly, our findings on national media coverage are supported by older studies finding that senators from large states received more national media attention than those from small states, at least back as far as the 1950s (Weaver and Wilhoit 1974, 1980; Wilhoit and Sherrill 1968). Even though our study of hold-out behavior examines only close votes occurring between the late 1970s and the late 1990s, there is no reason to believe that the relationship between holding out and constituency size is time bound. Small-state senators may well have used the hold-out strategy in the nineteenth century as, for example, they bargained over tariff schedules favorable to interests in their states.

Recent changes in the Senate, however, may have extended the influence of constituency size into another area of senators' Washington behavior, their inclination and ability to seek leadership roles. After all, the Senate experienced enormous change during the 1970s as its members responded to changes in the broader social and political environment. As the leading scholar of this transformation, Barbara Sinclair (1989, 70), argues, "An institution like the Senate will change when an appreciable number of its members find that its structure hinders rather than facilitates the pursuit of their goals." When this occurred during the 1970s, the Senate underwent great change. As "the result of senators' responses to the transformation of the Washington political community, senators changed their behavior and the institution to take advantage of the opportunities the new environment offered them" (Sinclair 1989, 70–71).

During and since this transformation, senators have faced an expanded political agenda (in terms of the number and complexity of issues), increased demands both from a growing interest group community in Washington and from constituents at home, greater media coverage of their activities, and a seemingly uncontrollable workload. The transformed Senate works from January to December (with regularly scheduled recesses to enable senators to tend to their constituents at home), not just for six to eight months. Not only are its committees more active, but the Senate floor has become an increasingly important venue for amending activity and for obstructionism (see also Smith 1989). The old norms of specialization and reciprocity have given way to an expectation that senators should be active across a greater range of issues and policies. Senators sit on more committees and subcommittees, have more staff, and offer more amendments. More of the Senate's work is done in the open and is visible, through the media, to constituents and organized interests. Compounding all this, reelection campaigns are more expensive in the contemporary Senate, requiring senators generally to devote more time to raising funds.

We propose that this transformation of the Senate did not affect all senators equally. First, the greater demands on their time mean that, all else being equal, senators from more populous states (particularly those from the largest ones) have *less time for governing*—less time for working within the Senate—

than those from smaller states. In previous chapters we have shown that large-state senators cannot maintain close representational relationships with their constituents. Because of the sheer size and diversity of their constituencies, moreover, the increase in the demands for time, access, and attention to issues in the transformed Senate has been greater for senators representing large states than for those from small states. In addition, the fund-raising pressures have become more intense for them than for their small-state colleagues: not only do large-state senators need more campaign funds, but they must raise them more constantly and from more labor-intensive sources. Senators representing more populous states also tend to face more competitive races for reelection. All these factors mean they face greater demands on their time than other senators, demands that are likely to constrain their ability to seek leadership in the institution.

Second, and equally important, is *flexibility in office*. If the number of interests in a constituency is in part a function of its size, as we argued above, then senators representing larger constituencies will have less voting leeway on more issues than their colleagues from smaller states. Small-state senators, in other words, are likely to have flexibility on more political issues than large-state senators because of the homogeneity of their states. A senator from South Dakota, for example, has little choice on agricultural issues but has considerably more on a whole range of other matters—defense, foreign policy, immigration, crime, education—than a senator from California. This reduced flexibility for large-state senators should translate into a greater constraint on their ability to serve as leaders. In addition, if winning election or reelection by a wide margin often gives a legislator a sense of freedom or "voting leeway" (Fenno 1978, 151), then the fact that senators representing the most populous states tend to win by narrower margins means they will have less leeway than their colleagues from smaller states.

These two considerations—time for governing and flexibility in office—are particularly important for senators interested in becoming leaders in the transformed Senate. In the folkways-driven Senate described by Matthews (1960), a floor leader did not have to worry about scheduling endless votes on controversial issues. By the 1970s all this had changed. The Senate was meeting year-round, dealing with a greater range of (controversial) issues, and facing a much greater volume of votes on amendments and more obstructionist tactics on the floor (Smith 1989). As one of our interview subjects, a former Republican senator, said (holding his arm at a forty-five-degree angle): "Chart the number of votes cast between 1950 and 1990 in the Senate. It's not impossible [to be a leader from a large state and manage the low number of votes cast in 1950] but . . . you cannot do that [manage the large number of votes in the 1970s and 1980s] and take care of your state [in a large state]." Serving as a leader in the contemporary Senate puts great demands on a senator's time, far greater demands than in the past. The responsibilities of a Senate floor leader—managing the party machinery, scheduling legislation, managing the flow of the Senate's business, contributing to policy innovation, and enhancing the electoral chances of other members of the party (Peabody 1981, 70)—could easily devour all of a senator's time, leaving little or none for other functions.

Similarly, being a leader often requires a senator to cast the tough vote, especially in the transformed Senate in which the number of floor amendments is nearly triple the 1950s levels (Smith 1989, 88). Party leaders in the Senate, moreover, typically vote with their party on party-unity votes considerably more often than the average senator (Davidson 1989, 296–300). To cast tough votes requires that a senator have flexibility or voting leeway. As it was explained to us by one large-state senator who had turned down an opportunity to seek party leadership: "Leaders have to worry where their troops are. I never wanted to worry about how to vote based on others' concerns." Referring to the former Democratic majority leader Sen. George Mitchell (Maine), he continued, "Mitchell once said to me, 'I had a much better voting record before I was leader.'" Senators who win elections by wide margins can more easily afford to take on difficult issues than senators who win by narrow margins. "You derive benefits from being secure in your district in terms of leadership," a small-state senator told us. "Everyone used to tell me that back when I was in the House, and it is basically true."

As a result of the new political environment of the Senate since the 1980s, we argue that senators representing populous states, particularly the most populous, face greater constraints in pursuing leadership positions than do senators from middle-sized and small states. The size of a senator's constituency, of course, will not itself have any effect on personal inclination to seek a leadership position in the Senate. The reasons particular senators aspire to institutional leadership are something of a mystery. That most leaders are ambitious for power in the institution or for higher office does not clearly differentiate them from their colleagues, many of whom are also ambitious in these ways but do not seek such posts. But given that some senators will want to be leaders, constituency size is likely to constrain their ability to do so. The position of majority or minority floor leader may no longer be a realistic goal for senators representing large states and may have become a career specialization for senators from smaller states.

Historically, however, Senate leaders have represented both large and small states. Table 5.4 shows the Democratic and Republican Senate floor leaders since 1911, when the election of majority and minority leaders was first established (Ripley 1969, 26). Until the 1960s, there was no clear relationship between state size and being party floor leader. Of the twenty-three floor leaders chosen before 1970, twelve represented states with ten or more

Table 5.4 Senate Floor Leaders, 1911–98

Democrats		Republicans	
Thomas S. Martin (Va.)	1911–13	Shelby M. Cullom (Ill.)	1911–13
John W. Kern (Ind.)	1913–17	Jacob H. Gallinger (N.H.)	1913–18
Thomas S. Martin (Va.)	1917–20	Henry Cabot Lodge (Mass.)	1918–24
Oscar N. Underwood (Ala.)	1920–23	Charles Curtis (Kans.)	1924–29
Joseph T. Robinson (Ark.)	1923–37	James E. Watson (Ind.)	1929–33
Alben W. Barkley (Ky.)	1937–49	Charles L. McNary (Oreg.)	1933–45
Scott W. Lucas (Ill.)	1949–51	Wallace H. White (Maine)	1945–49
Ernest W. McFarland (Ariz.)	1951–53	Kenneth S. Wherry (Nebr.)	1949–51
Lyndon B. Johnson (Tex.)	1953–61	Styles Bridges (N.H.)	1952–53
Mike Mansfield (Mont.)	1961–77	Robert A. Taft (Ohio)	1953–53
Robert C. Byrd (W.Va.)	1977–89	William R. Knowland (Calif.)	1953–59
George J. Mitchell (Maine)	1989–95	Everett McKinley Dirksen (Ill.)	1959–69
Tom Daschle (S.Dak.)	1995–	Hugh Scott (Pa.)	1969–77
		Howard H. Baker Jr. (Tenn.)	1977–85
		Bob Dole (Kans.)	1985–96
		Trent Lott (Miss.)	1996–

Source: Congressional Quarterly's Guide to Congress, 4th ed.

congressional districts (at the time of their selection), and six of these represented the most populous states. During the Eisenhower administration, when all the selected floor leaders—Johnson for the Democrats and Taft, Knowland, and Dirksen for the Republicans—were from very populous states and the posts kept their occupants in national prominence, it seems that representing a major state might even have been a requirement. This certainly appears to have changed, however, first in the Democratic Party and more recently in the Republican Party.

Although we recognize that we are dealing with far too few cases to draw statistical inferences, there does appear to be an interesting historical trend. Since 1961 all the Democratic floor leaders have come from small states. Sens. Mike Mansfield of Montana, Robert Byrd of West Virginia, George Mitchell of Maine, and Tom Daschle of South Dakota all represented states with four or fewer congressional districts. Of course one may assume that Mansfield's becoming majority leader was unrelated to his representing a small state because he moved into the leadership reluctantly and well before the transformation of the Senate discussed above.[23] But for Byrd, Mitchell, and Daschle, representing a small state may have been a prerequisite for successfully undertaking floor leadership.

In the part-time Senate of the 1950s, a large-state senator like Lyndon Johnson could lead the Senate and still tend to the needs of a large and diverse constituency. In Johnson's case, moreover, Texas was still dominated by one party, thus limiting his reelection concerns. By 1970—when leading the Senate had become a full-time job, most states had become two-party competitive, and campaign costs had risen significantly—a large-state senator could no longer aspire to be majority leader in most circumstances. When Byrd stepped down as the Democratic floor leader, two of the three candidates to succeed him, Sens. Daniel Inouye of Hawaii and George Mitchell, represented states with only two congressional districts. The third, Sen. J. Bennett Johnston of Louisiana, represented a median-sized state. With a very comfortable 86 percent of the vote in the 1984 election, however, Johnston may have felt he could make the time commitment. In fact he had briefly challenged Byrd in 1986. Neither of these efforts was successful, however. Interestingly, those forays may have contributed to what *Politics in America 1994* described as "renewed complaints that Johnston had 'Potomac fever'" as his 1990 reelection campaign began (Duncan 1994, 637). Even Mitchell, who succeeded Byrd, found the leader's workload such that he parceled out to other senators some of the duties Byrd had monopolized (Smith 1993, 272–73).

In 1995 the contest for Democratic floor leader came down to a choice between Sen. Tom Daschle of South Dakota, a small state, and Sen. Christopher Dodd of Connecticut, a median-sized state. Before the 1994 election, Sen. Jim Sasser of Tennessee, a state with nine congressional districts, was the front-runner to succeed Mitchell but was defeated in his bid for reelection. In a state the size of Tennessee, Sasser faced a competitive electoral environment in which an eighteen-year incumbent could quickly become vulnerable, especially one who seemed more attuned to the national political scene. Thus not only have all the Democratic leaders since 1961 represented small states, there have been no contenders from states with more than nine congressional districts. Sen. Alan Cranston of California, who had served in the far less demanding position of whip throughout Byrd's tenure as floor leader, never gave any indication of intending to move up the leadership ladder as Mansfield and Byrd had previously done.[24]

It is more difficult to make a persuasive case that state size affects the emergence of Republican floor leaders. When Sen. Hugh Scott retired in 1976, senators from the largest states had served as leader for twenty-four consecutive years, and only a single vote kept Sen. Robert Griffin of Michigan from extending that streak.[25] In this context, however, it is important that nearly all of this period is before the transformation of the Senate, and during this time Republicans were the minority party for all but the first two years. The workload is far less time consuming for the minority leader, who unlike the majority leader, is not responsible for managing a legislative program. With Howard Baker continuing as leader when the Republicans won control of the Senate in the 1980 elections, it was not until 1984 that the Republicans chose a new majority leader in the transformed Senate. Then four of the five candidates (Sens. Bob Dole, Ted Stevens, James McClure, and Pete Domenici) all represented smaller than median-sized states, with Dole of Kansas defeating Stevens of Alaska in the final vote.[26] When the leadership job conflicted with Dole's presidential campaign in 1996, no populous-state senator voiced interest or was mentioned as a possible replacement. Republicans chose between Trent Lott and Thad Cochran, both from Mississippi, a five-district state that is nearly as electorally safe for its Republican senators as it had been for their Democratic predecessors.

The limited number of cases, especially among Senate Republicans, hardly provides overwhelming evidence of a trend. Many of our interview subjects, however, strongly supported our perspective. A former Democratic senator from one of the more populous states observed that there is "a tremendous workload difference" between large- and small-state senators and that this explains the prevalence of small-state senators in the leadership. "The demands for fund-raising are up in the big states," he said. "Time gets chewed up, and it's harder to go into a leadership position. . . .[It] runs into the reelection cycle. You don't have the time and wouldn't want to do it." He added that "in large states people from the state take up time continuously." Similarly, a former lobbyist who had initially rejected as "happenstance" the idea that small-state senators had advantages in pursuing leadership quickly reconsidered: "Wait a minute. I speak too fast. The small states' senators have more time. More time."

When we asked a senior staffer to a former Republican leader whether there was a reason for small-state senators' holding leadership positions recently, she discussed these same constraints: "First, pulling Lott out of the list, most come through the ranks, and small-state members have more time available to focus on the leadership and the internal constituency of the Senate. . . .In New York or California there are so many challenges to a senator's time that they can't [do both]. Dole can manage the Senate and still have the time he needs to attend to constituents in Kansas. The scope of the issues is much narrower." This respondent then extended the reasoning and suggested that even Senate committee chairs from populous states faced some of the same problems because of the competing time demands of a large and diverse constituency: "Leadership in the Senate in any of the positions is an enormous commitment of time, and if you come from a constituency that consumes you, it's tough to manage." Recognizing that this was a relatively new trend for Republicans, this staffer observed that no one from a large state is currently moving up through the Republican Senate leadership ranks.

The difference in demands on the time of senators from large and small states that is reflected in our data and suggested in our interviews may make it almost impossible for large-state senators to seek leadership in the contemporary Senate. Note that we are not positing a linear relationship between state size and a senator's probability of becoming floor leader. There is probably some threshold, some state size, beyond which the probability of having the time, flexibility, and electoral security to pursue and win leadership approaches zero. For senators representing states smaller than this threshold, leadership is a possibility, depending on other relevant factors. We cannot specify that threshold with any precision, but we can get some idea by looking at the recent candidates for leadership positions. Among candidates for floor leader positions in the 1990s, Sasser of Tennessee represented the most populous state. Recent events, then, imply that the constituency-size threshold for a senator to seek leadership is a state with more than nine congressional districts. Even so, it is worth noting that in recent years only senators from relatively small states have been successful in their quests.[27] Because there are so many small states, many senators are relatively unconstrained by constituency size should they seek leadership. Senators representing states larger than Tennessee, after all, constitute slightly less than a third of the Senate.

Clearly, constituency size is not the only factor that affects senators' options to seek leadership. Many other factors are important, including electoral security, personal ambition, ideological compatibility with the party, personal relationships, and legislative skills. Given the small number of cases, especially since the transformation of the Senate in the 1970s, we simply cannot assess the relative weights of all these variables in statistical terms. Despite this, however, we maintain that the effects of constituency size in other areas—on senators' representational relationships with their constituents, on the number and diversity of constituent demands they face, on their electoral security, and on the time they need to devote to campaign fund-raising—in turn constrain the ability of large-state senators to achieve Senate leadership, especially in an era when it has become such a demanding task. In the context of the contemporary Senate, these factors taken together make it unlikely, if not impossible, for senators from the most populous states to become party leaders. In this sense our thesis in this section is the riskiest of political science endeavors—a prediction.

Conclusion

In this chapter we have shown that constituency size is an important contextual variable that shapes senators' behavior in Washington. Our findings indicate that it influences the strategies senators pursue there just as it affects the representational experiences of senators and their constituents (discussed in chapter 3) and Senate elections and fund-raising (discussed in chapter 4).

Constituency size is important in the Washington context because it affects the incentives of senators from large and small states differently.

From our analysis of committee membership and media coverage of senators, we find that senators from large and small states tend to pursue different Washington strategies. Senators from small states tend to seek assignment to committees that help them obtain particularized benefits for their constituents. This strategy is an efficient and effective one for small-state senators seeking to advance their reelection goals, much as it is for House members. But it is not as effective an option for senators from populous states for two reasons. First, in a small state the electoral benefits and credit-claiming value of relatively small particularized benefits are much greater than in a larger state. Second, closer representational relationships with their constituents and an ability to communicate with them in face-to-face, retail settings enable small-state senators to rely less on the media and to assume a lower national profile. Small-state senators, then, have greater incentives to emphasize particularized benefits for their constituents and low visibility in the national media.

Senators from larger states, on the other hand, tend to seek assignment to more policy-oriented committees. Because the particularized benefits strategy is a much less efficient use of their time and resources, they have greater incentives to use policy activism to advance their goals, including reelection. Large-state senators do not find constituency committees to be as effective vehicles for achieving their reelection goals as small-state senators and House members do. Instead they prefer a strategy of policy activism, including membership on policy committees and a higher national profile. Media attention is an important part of this strategy. Given the greater number of constituents they must reach and their inability to engage in the same retail politics as their small-state colleagues, senators from larger states will rely more heavily on the media to communicate with their constituents. As we demonstrated earlier, senators from more populous states receive more national media coverage than their colleagues, even after controlling for other factors. We argue that this is because they make a greater effort to attract national media attention.

We then looked at other ways that state size affects senators' incentives. In the third section we addressed the question whether small-state senators have a greater incentive than their large-state colleagues to withhold their support from important legislation in order to force concessions or side payments that will benefit their constituents. In the thirty-one close votes studied, we found that small-state senators engaged in this hold-out behavior in more cases than one would expect given their proportion in the Senate as a whole. In the fourth section we argued that the greater demands on large-state senators, compared with the demands on their colleagues from less populous states, constrain their ability to pursue leadership in the contemporary Senate. In all these ways, differences in constituency size as the result of Senate apportionment influence the strategies that senators pursue in Washington.

As we noted at the start of this chapter, political scientists have found it difficult to generalize about the Senate and about the behavior of senators, and our efforts to develop a systematic understanding of the Senate by assessing the effects of its apportionment scheme have had to confront two problems. One is an existing scholarly literature that has all but ignored the effects of Senate apportionment. The other is the reluctance of some of those we interviewed to accept that there are systemic underpinnings to the behavior of senators and to the operation of the Senate as an institution.

Many people we interviewed understand the Senate primarily in individualistic terms and questioned our efforts to generalize. This was particularly true of our generalizations on Senate strategies. One interview subject, a former staffer in the Senate leadership and the White House, expressed reservations about our approach. "You have to keep interpersonal relationships in mind," he said. "Some of these states do better because their guys are better senators. They have seniority and networks." He pointed to several examples of the importance of interpersonal relationships in the Senate, including a bipartisan prayer group of southern moderates and the ability of Kennedy, "the most effective senator," to develop friendships "with people like Hatch and others that you wouldn't believe." On this subject he also spoke of the relationship between Bob Dole and Sen. Daniel Inouye (D-Hawaii). He pointed out that Dole and Inouye had both been wounded in Italy in World War II at about the same time and that they met while recuperating in an army hospital. As a result of this personal relationship, Inouye told this subject, "Hawaii never suffered when Dole was majority leader."

Similarly, other interview subjects maintained that the recent dominance of small-state senators in floor leadership reflects nothing systemic about the Senate. The more vehement of those, a former small-state senator, said that the theory was "dead as a dodo." He compared it to the idea (once popular) that presidential candidates had to come from the East and vice presidential candidates from the West. Instead he felt that senators become leaders solely because of their personal characteristics and leadership abilities: "George Mitchell was just like cream rising to the top. Dole's the same way. It doesn't matter where they come from."

For these interview subjects, then, success in the Senate is achieved solely through skill in developing and understanding interpersonal relationships. In the world of a staffer or senator, this interpersonal perspective makes a lot of sense—it is the way they experience the Senate from day to day—and it is certainly a useful perspective in understanding the institution in all its richness and complexity. Each senator is, after all, a unique individual with his or her own qualities and circumstances, and the postreform Senate is particularly individualistic. But the problem with this perspective is that richness and complexity do not advance our search for generalizations. Despite the complexity of the Senate as an institution and the variation among senators as individuals, there are certain patterns in their behavior. By stepping back and looking at senators in their constituency-size contexts, we have been able to discern some of these patterns.

To put this in the language of social science, a number of variables help to explain the variation in senators' Washington behavior. Personal characteristics and interpersonal relationships are certainly important ones. These variables are difficult to measure and quantify, however, even for the Senate insider. Those who understand the Senate primarily in terms of these variables may find our approach in this chapter—focusing for the most part on senators' incentives in terms of their reelection goals—reductionistic. Senators have any number of goals: reelection, good public policy, power in the institution, higher office. All these goals play some role in their Washington behavior. We have not attempted, of course, to explain all of senators' Washington behavior with one variable. Instead we have focused on the effect of one variable, constituency size. This is important because constituency size is something scholars have tended to overlook even though it has always been there, a contextual constraint on individual senators and on the institution. We have argued that one must recognize state size as an important variable in any systematic effort to understand senators' Washington behavior.

In the next two chapters we turn to the effects of apportionment on the Senate as a policymaking institution, in terms of both federal outlays and its interactions with the House. We demonstrate that small-state senators' use of the particularized benefits strategy has important consequences for congressional policymaking.

6

The Small–State Advantage in the Distribution of Federal Dollars

I n 1926 political science professor Carroll Wooddy asked two rather simple and obvious questions: "Has equal representation in the Senate actually made any difference in the legislation of that body? If so, how much difference?" (Wooddy 1926, 219). Despite their importance, these fundamental questions remain unanswered today. Even though political scientists usually place great emphasis on the policy consequences of particular institutional arrangements, the "difference" that equal representation of states in the Senate makes continues to be neglected. Thus far in this book we have examined the effect of Senate apportionment on basic governmental processes — on the representational relationships between senators and constituents, on Senate elections, and on the strategic behavior of legislators. In this chapter we turn to its effect on public policy outcomes. Senate apportionment distributes power and influence across geographical areas differently than does the population-based apportionment of the House, enhancing the representational power of states with small populations. To the extent that political power influences who gets what from federal spending in the United States, then, the existing system should allocate funds differently than would a representative system based solely on population. Because the houses of Congress are coequal, the final allocation of federal funds must be acceptable to both chambers, presumably balancing their competing geographic priorities.

This chapter examines the current distribution of federal funds to states to see if it bears the imprint of Senate apportionment. We find that Senate apportionment affects the geographic distribution of federal funds in two ways. First, funds under domestic assistance programs are typically distributed so that a majority, often an overwhelming majority, of states benefit. Second, smaller states tend to receive more federal dollars per capita than

large states, controlling for differences in states' need for federal funds. Although this effect is not apparent in federal entitlement programs such as Aid
to Families with Dependent Children (AFDC) and Social Security (OASDI),
it is evident across a wide range of federal domestic spending programs, most
notably those where federal funds are allocated based on congressionally
mandated formulas.

Legislative Institutions and Public Policy

Americans have long believed that the formal arrangements of political institutions make a difference for public policy. Even the authors of *The Federalist
Papers* base much of their argument on the understanding that political institutions can be constructed to promote good government. Political scientists
in the United States have characteristically shared this concern. Congressional scholars in particular have devoted considerable attention to how
institutional structures influence the development and adoption of public
policy. Much work has been done, for example, detailing the policy effects
of the congressional division of labor into committees—from "iron tri-
angles" to "committee bias" to the pathologies of "subcommittee government" (Dodd and Schott 1986; Fiorina 1989; Hall 1993; Hall and Grofman
1990; Smith and Deering 1990). In a similar vein, political scientists have
produced a vast literature examining the institutional distribution of power
in Congress and its effects on the allocation of federal funds (Arnold 1979;
Ferejohn 1974; Fiorina 1989; Mayhew 1974; Rundquist and Griffith 1976;
Strom 1975; Wilson 1986). Despite their emphasis on the consequences that
institutional structures have for policymaking, political scientists have largely
neglected the effects of Senate apportionment.

This failure is even more surprising in light of the widespread scholarly
concern of the 1950s and 1960s with state legislative apportionment. During
the period before court-imposed reapportionment with *Baker v. Carr* and
Reynolds v. Simms, scholars of comparative state politics made many incon-
clusive attempts to correlate legislative malapportionment with patterns in
state policymaking.[1]

Only three studies have investigated the link between federal legislative
apportionment and public policy outcomes (Arnold 1981; Atlas et al. 1995;
McCubbins and Schwartz 1988). McCubbins and Schwartz (1988, 388) examine the effect of the changes in House apportionment following *Wesberry
v. Sanders.* They find that court-ordered redistricting created a large metropolitan majority in the House of Representatives that in turn reallocated
federal funds from rural to metropolitan citizens.

Atlas et al. (1995) test the proposition that "the unequal per capita representation in the U.S. Congress" has "predictable and significant effects on

states' shares of the federal net spending pie" (624). They find a positive and significant relation between a state's per capita representation in the Senate (the number of senators representing a state divided by the state's population) and its net receipts from federal expenditures (dollars received minus the federal taxes paid) (627).[2] Their study is undeveloped and rather preliminary, however. They examine only aggregate budgetary data on outlays to states; as a result, it does not include many important variables measuring states' need for particular federal programs. In addition, they fail to consider the politics surrounding different types of public policies and assume that the effects of Senate apportionment will be constant across all federal programs.

The final study that links Senate apportionment to public policy outcomes is Arnold's 1981 essay on geographic representation and its effect on federal domestic policy. Unlike most studies of distributive politics, this piece recognizes that Senate apportionment is likely to lead the Senate to prefer different distributions of federal funds than the House does because of the different geographic constituencies represented in the two chambers. Arnold's focus here, however, is on developing a theory to explain when geographic representation is most likely to influence federal policy, not on examining the effects of Senate apportionment. As a result, he provides no empirical test of his expectations.

In short, no systematic research has been conducted on the Senate's influence on distributive policymaking. Rather than analyzing aggregate budget data to estimate the effect of Senate apportionment on various public policies, we use a program-level data set. This research design enables us to take into account that obtaining geographic benefits will be more or less important to senators depending on the type of policy under consideration. This data set also allows us to conduct separate tests of our expectations for programs designed to serve different purposes in order to identify the policy areas in which the imprint of Senate apportionment is most apparent.

State Representation and Senate Policymaking

The reasons Senate apportionment is likely to affect the geographic distribution of federal funds lie in the already well established logic of the electoral connection. Constituents elect members of Congress to represent and serve their interests. Legislators understand their role in these terms and regard it as appropriate to seek to further those interests through favorable government action. The pursuit of reelection reinforces this connection, for it is in the self-interest of those who want to be reelected to please their constituents. Members of Congress are eager to provide benefits to their constituencies and reluctant to impose costs on them. Based on this understanding, then, one should expect the Senate to prefer distributions of federal funds that favor less populous states for two reasons: because the geographic constituencies represented in the Senate are weighted more heavily toward less populous states than those in the House and because Senate apportionment has an independent influence on the incentives of senators.

First, Senate apportionment grants more power to less populous states than would a legislative chamber that apportions representatives according to population. This is true not only because senators from small states have voting power equal to that of senators from large states but simply because there are so many small states. Table 6.1 presents a measure of state representation in the Senate. The index is a ratio of the state's actual population to one-fiftieth of the nation's population. When the ratio is equal to one, the state is neither over- nor underrepresented by reference to a one person, one vote standard; when it is less than one, the state is overrepresented; when it is greater than one, the state is underrepresented.[3]

From this table it is immediately apparent that there are far more overrepresented states (thirty-one) than underrepresented states (fourteen). In the extremely unlikely case of a coalition consisting of the twenty-eight senators from the fourteen underrepresented states, coalition leaders must seek out senators from overrepresented states just to build a minimum winning majority coalition. By contrast, the senators representing the overrepresented states form a sixty-two-vote majority on their own without including any other senators. In fact all that is needed to build a majority coalition are senators representing states with scores of 0.70 or less on the index.

Of course observers of American politics have never seen political conflict exhibit cleavages between large and small states. This very fact led early political scientists, such as Woodrow Wilson (1885), Carroll Wooddy (1926), and Lindsay Rogers (1926), to conclude that Senate apportionment had no important effect on Senate policymaking. If small states and large states do not differ on substantive policy grounds, why should we expect their equal representation to make a difference for public policy?

The reason Senate apportionment is important for distributive politics is that the pattern of constituency size in the Senate means Senate coalitions are likely to prefer to distribute funds in ways that disproportionately benefit constituents in less populous states *even in the absence of conflict between large and small states.* In fact one would expect small-state advantages in Senate policymaking to be strongly in evidence even in the case of universalistic coalitions (i.e., coalitions in which all states benefit from a program).

This point is best illustrated by a comparison with the House of Representatives. Hypothetically speaking, in the House a universalistic coalition based

Table 6.1 State Representation in the Senate, 1990

Overrepresented States (N = 31)		States Represented Approximately According to One Person, One Vote (N = 5)		Underrepresented States (N = 14)	
State	Index	State	Index	State	Index
Wyoming	0.09	Maryland	0.96	Indiana	1.11
Alaska	0.11	Washington	0.98	Massachusetts	1.21
Vermont	0.11	Tennessee	0.98	Virginia	1.24
North Dakota	0.13	Wisconsin	0.98	Georgia	1.30
Delaware	0.13	Missouri	1.03	North Carolina	1.33
South Dakota	0.14			New Jersey	1.55
Montana	0.16			Michigan	1.87
Rhode Island	0.20			Ohio	2.18
Idaho	0.20			Illinois	2.30
Hawaii	0.22			Pennsylvania	2.39
New Hampshire	0.22			Florida	2.60
Nevada	0.24			Texas	3.42
Maine	0.25			New York	3.62
New Mexico	0.30			California	5.98
Nebraska	0.32				
Utah	0.35				
West Virginia	0.36				
Arkansas	0.47				
Kansas	0.50				
Mississippi	0.52				
Iowa	0.56				
Oregon	0.57				
Oklahoma	0.63				
Connecticut	0.66				
Colorado	0.66				
South Carolina	0.70				
Arizona	0.74				
Kentucky	0.74				
Alabama	0.81				
Louisiana	0.85				
Minnesota	0.88				

Note: Mean = 0.99; median = 0.68; standard deviation = 1.07.

on an agreed-upon level of benefits allocated to every member would result in a roughly equal distribution of benefits to citizens in all areas of the nation because each member represents a roughly equal number of constituents. Because of its basis of apportionment, members of the House typically regard a fair distribution of federal funds as one based on population; senators, on the other hand, "prefer to think about the fundamental equality of states" (Arnold 1981, 269).

Senators think in these terms in great part because of the structure of the institution as a whole. At a fundamental level, every senator is the equal of every other. The Senate is an egalitarian institution—even Senate leaders have few powers beyond those possessed by every other senator. Senators regard one another in this way. Those from the largest states do not possess more influence or clout than those from the smallest states. Concerning senators from even the least populous states, one senator commented in an interview with us, "There's absolutely no difference in how you view them colleague to colleague." Other factors may affect a senator's clout in the institution, such as his margin of victory in his last election or others' perceptions of his legislative skills, but state population has no bearing on his prestige or influence in the institution. As a consequence, a "fair" distribution in the Senate is one that treats all senators "equitably," tending toward an equal allocation of funds across states.

Unlike the situation in the House, in the Senate an equal distribution of benefits means that constituents in less populous states receive far more per capita than those in large states. Because senators are not distributed to equal numbers of constituents, the equal representation of states means that even universalistic coalitions in the Senate are likely to result in distributions that disproportionately favor less populous states. Thus one would expect conflict between the House and Senate over the geographic allocation of federal funds even when there is little conflict within the chambers themselves and no conflict between the senators representing large and small states.

Richard Nathan (1993) describes in some depth an example of conflict between the branches in universalistic policymaking. The congressional negotiations over General Revenue Sharing exhibited clearly the two branches' different notions of equitable distribution. It is difficult to imagine a program more "universalistic" than General Revenue Sharing, which was enacted in 1972. During congressional deliberation over the program, the House and Senate adopted different formulas for distributing funds, the House formula favoring more populous states and the Senate formula favoring smaller ones. Under the House formula, the twenty-four smallest states would have received only 89 percent of the average per capita allocation to states; under the Senate formula these states would have received nearly 120 percent of the average per capita allocation (Fillipov 1996, 14). The compromise reached in conference simply expanded the program, distributing funds to each state according to the formula that was more favorable to it, producing a distribution that still disproportionately benefited small states.

A second set of reasons that Senate apportionment is likely to advantage less populous states lies at the level of individual incentives. To the extent that coalition builders can garner support for domestic assistance programs by expanding the number of states that benefit from them, they are likely to seek out senators from less populous states. As discussed in the chapter on Senate strategies, even though each senator's vote is of equal value to a coalition builder, they are not of equal "price." Program benefits can be included for less populous states at considerably less expense than for larger states. Thus a very modest award may be enough to persuade a small-state senator of a federal program's merits, but it would take a considerably more expensive allocation to gain the sympathetic ear of a senator from a populous state. A small-state senator's vote may be influenced at less cost to the program budget than that of a large-state senator. As a result, expanding the beneficiaries of the program to include small-population states will be less expensive for coalition builders, putting less pressure on budgets.

An example from the 104th Congress illustrates these coalition-building dynamics. As the new Republican majority in the Senate began to consider converting the welfare and Medicaid entitlement programs into block grants to states, a dispute developed over the formula used to allocate these funds (Katz 1995). The debate centered on whether the new funding formula would be based on the federal allocations to states under existing programs or on the number of poor children residing in them, the latter formula being more favorable to the quickly growing states in the Sun Belt. States in the Northeast, the Rust Belt, and the Pacific West, on the other hand, stood to lose substantially from a change in the formula. Senators Hutchison (R-Tex.), Gramm (R-Tex.), and Cochran (R-Miss.) led an initiative to modify the funding formula. Taking advantage of the dynamics of Senate apportionment, they proposed an alternative that guaranteed a minimum allocation to small states. Even though the justification for the alternative formula was based on the problems that high-growth states would face if block grant funds were held at current levels, the politics of building a coalition in the Senate led them to include small states not expected to experience high population growth. As a result thirty-six states—including all of the twenty most overrepresented states on the representation index—would have benefited from the proposed alternative formula.

Senate apportionment also affects senators' incentives to pursue particularistic benefits for their states because the same amount of money has different values to different-sized states. As discussed in chapter 5, senators who represent less populous states have greater incentives to actively pursue benefits for their constituents because "the per capita local benefit is higher for each dollar of net spending transferred to a state the smaller the state's population" (Atlas et al. 1995, 625). In other words, a particularized benefit in Wyoming has a greater impact on the state's economy and a senator's statewide visibility than the same benefit (in dollar terms) would have in California or even in Tennessee. Thus "bringing home the bacon" has more advertising and credit-claiming value to senators from small-population states, and it is easier for them to accomplish.[4]

In short, Senate apportionment is important because it affects the incentives of senators themselves, not only because it creates a set of geographic constituencies that are different from those in the House. In this sense it has an independent effect on congressional policymaking, one with no counterpart in the House. Rather than leading to conflict between senators from small and large states, Senate apportionment produces a dynamic whereby coalition leaders (regardless of the size of the state they represent) have incentives to seek out senators from less populous states to build winning coalitions at a relatively low cost to the program budget. Because of the vast differentials in state population, a coalition leader can even grant windfalls to the least populous states, helping to ensure the support of their senators, at a very low cost to the program. Senators from smaller states, moreover, have greater incentives to pursue particularized benefits for their constituents, making a coalition-building strategy that focuses benefits on their states even more likely to succeed.

Policy Type and the Small-State Advantage

The effects of Senate representation on the allocation of federal funds are not likely to be the same across all public policies. After all, as Arnold (1990) argues, geographic considerations themselves are not always primary in the minds of legislators. Political scientists, in fact, have often found that the politics surrounding various public policy types differ (Lowi 1964; Ripley and Franklin 1991).

Redistributive policies, by definition policies that "seek to reallocate valuable goods and symbols among different economic classes and racial groupings" (Ripley and Franklin 1991, 121), are characterized by high public salience and frequently intense ideological and partisan conflict. As such, geographic considerations are unlikely to be foremost among legislators' considerations when redistributive policies are at stake (Arnold 1990, 128).

In addition, many of the most important and expensive redistributive programs, such as Social Security and AFDC, are entitlements to individuals, thus diminishing the likelihood that Senate apportionment will affect the allocation of federal funds.

On the other hand, distributive policies are characterized by low levels of conflict and public salience. These policies often involve explicit decisions about which geographic areas will benefit, thus increasing the likelihood that small-state advantages in the Senate will come into play.[5]

There is good reason to further divide distributive policies into nondiscretionary and discretionary ones (Stein and Bickers 1995, 22–23). Nondiscretionary distributive policies are those that allocate funds according to a congressionally mandated formula, whereas discretionary distributive policies permit greater choice by executive agencies. When Congress makes explicit decisions about how recipients will be selected for inclusion in the program and how much they will receive (when it approves the formula), congressional control over geographic allocation of benefits is at its greatest level. Allocation formulas require Congress to define the areas eligible to receive benefits and to establish the criteria that determine the level of benefits for each eligible area. As a result, it is in nondiscretionary distributive policies that one would expect Senate apportionment to leave its deepest imprint (Arnold 1981).

This is not to say, however, that Senate apportionment will have no effect on discretionary distributive policies. Bureaucrats will not ignore the Senate as they work to ensure support for the programs they administer (Arnold 1979; Stein and Bickers 1995). As a result, for the same reasons that coalition building in the Senate is likely to offer some advantages to small states, the strategic behavior of bureaucrats in cultivating supportive coalitions in Congress will also work to their benefit.

Thus, to summarize: One would expect Senate apportionment to have its greatest effect on nondiscretionary distributive policies, a less pronounced effect on discretionary distributive policies, and no effect on redistributive policies.

In this chapter we investigate the effects of Senate apportionment on policymaking in three ways. First, we examine the number of states benefiting from federal domestic assistance programs: Are coalitions in support of federal programs built by ensuring that most Senate constituencies benefit from them? Second, we test the hypothesis that Senate politics will result in less populous states receiving more federal funds per capita for each of the three policy types: redistributive programs, nondiscretionary distributive programs, and discretionary distributive programs. To do this we employ multivariate regression techniques to control for differences in states' need for federal funds. Third, to detect the policy areas in which small-state advantages are most pronounced, we divide programs according to the functional policy goals they are designed to further.

Data and Operational Definitions

Program-by-program data on federal outlays to states are drawn from the *U.S. Domestic Assistance Programs Database* compiled by Bickers and Stein (1992) from the Federal Assistance Awards Data System maintained by the Bureau of the Census (Stein and Bickers 1995). This data set contains the annual federal outlays to congressional districts for federal domestic assistance programs for each fiscal year from 1983 through 1990. For our purposes these data have been aggregated to the state level so that the data set contains outlays to each state for each year. The programs in this data set account for 56 percent of the federal budget (Levitt and Snyder 1995). Examples of these programs include agricultural subsidies, transportation programs, community development and housing assistance grants, and Social Security payments as well as the many federal programs to support education and research.[6] Variables describing the programs are also included in the data set, including the types of recipients targeted, the policy goals of the programs, and whether funds are allocated by a congressionally mandated formula.[7]

The operational definitions of redistributive and distributive policies follow those employed by Stein and Bickers (1994a,b, 1995). The criterion for identifying redistributive policies is a variable that indicates whether the program includes income level or employment status in its eligibility requirements for program recipients (Stein and Bickers 1995, 18). In other words, this classification includes all domestic assistance programs that have, at least in part, the purpose of reallocating resources to needy persons and areas. Nondiscretionary distributive programs are distinguished from discretionary distributive programs by a dummy variable provided in the data set indicating whether funds are allocated by formula.

The Size of Coalitions in Senate Distributive Policymaking

Although rarely subjected to empirical evaluation, there is a widespread belief that legislators will construct oversized coalitions in distributive policymaking. In general it is thought that when legislators consider policies that confer geographically concentrated benefits and impose diffuse costs they will form coalitions larger than simple majorities (Collie 1988a; Mayhew 1974). The classic definition of universalism is "every member, regardless of party or seniority, has a right to his share of benefits" (Mayhew 1974, 88).[8] Formal models have identified uncertainty as the driving force behind universalistic coalition building: legislators' uncertainty about being included in the winning group leads them to form larger than minimum winning coalitions (Collie 1988a; Weingast 1979).

To the extent that the universalism thesis has been empirically tested at all, it has been tested with House data (Collie 1988b; Stein and Bickers 1994b, 1995). When Stein and Bickers evaluate the universalism thesis using data on the number of House districts benefiting from federal distributive programs, they find that "most individual programs are too limited in scope to sustain a winning legislative support coalition of any size, minimum or otherwise" (1995, 40). They report that universalism, understood as a condition where all or very nearly all congressional districts benefit from a federal distributive program, is extremely rare (Stein and Bickers 1994b, 306, 1995, 43).

There are good reasons to think the Senate will be more conducive to universalistic coalition building than the House. The rules of the Senate create a more individualistic policymaking process than prevails in the House, and the committee system in the Senate is less influential in determining policy outcomes (Oleszek 1996; Smith and Deering 1990). The Senate floor is an important arena of decision making where individual senators can wield influence on legislation regardless of committee membership (Sinclair 1989; Smith 1989). Because the decision rules in the Senate are more pluralistic and less majoritarian—allowing for broader participation in policymaking— the preferences of individual senators are generally more influential than those of individual House members. The Senate's individualism heightens the uncertainty that coalition builders face when they bring legislation to the floor, leading them to seek increasingly broad, even universalistic coalitions to ensure Senate passage.

The House, by contrast, seems more likely to form the type of coalitions posited by distributive politics hypotheses—for example, that the benefits accorded to seniority and committee membership would translate into targeted benefits to congressional districts (rather than benefits distributed to a universalistic majority of House districts). In building coalitions for policymaking in the Senate, it is more important to take into account the preferences of the whole chamber, including all intensely held minority and individual interests, than in the more majoritarian House, where committees are generally more autonomous and supermajorities are normally not needed to pass legislation. The rules of floor procedure in the House, moreover, permit coalition leaders greater control over the "decisional situation," diminishing uncertainty about legislative outcomes and thus their incentives to build universalistic coalitions (Bach and Smith 1988).

There are also House-based reasons why universalism might show up at the state level rather than across congressional districts. Representatives often have an incentive to work together to get funds for the whole state (Deckard

1972; Strom 1975). Many federal programs make funds directly available only to states as a whole. When states are the recipients of federal programs, then, the best way for a House member to help the district is to help the state. In addition, there are many programs where multiple congressional districts will benefit from a federal expenditure in only one district: a flood prevention expenditure upriver will benefit districts downriver. Enlarging the geographic unit of analysis (to the state level) to test the universalism thesis takes these considerations into account.

To the extent that legislative uncertainty about being included in the winning coalition creates incentives to form universalistic coalitions, they should be most likely when legislators themselves decide how funds are to be allocated. In other words, universalism will most likely occur when senators must approve the formulas for allocating funds under distributive programs. Conversely, universalistic coalitions should be less likely when Congress delegates allocational decisions to administrative agencies. Under these conditions, we expect that bureaucrats will work to ensure that their programs maintain majority backing in the Senate by making strategic awards to cultivate broad support, at least as far as program budgets will permit. Because bureaucrats are not subject to the uncertainty that drives legislators to construct universalistic coalitions, they do not have incentives to build supermajorities.

Table 6.2 displays the number of states receiving federal funds in discretionary distributive programs.[9] The median number benefiting from discretionary distributive programs for the whole period (1983–90) is twenty-five—not enough to garner a majority in the Senate solely on geographic considerations, but very nearly so. The broadest quarter of distributive programs benefit an overwhelming majority of states, always more than forty.

Of course half of all discretionary distributive programs do not benefit a majority of states. In fact the narrowest 25 percent are strikingly narrow, benefiting at most eight states (less than 20 percent of the Senate).

Despite these exceptions, the findings contrast sharply with those reported by Stein and Bickers in their research on universalism across congressional districts. Examining the number of districts that benefit from distributive programs, they find that the median program never benefits a majority of House districts; in fact it never benefits more than 20 percent. Even the narrowest 75 percent of programs never provide outlays to even a simple majority of congressional districts (Stein and Bickers 1995, 39). The universalism thesis finds much stronger support, then, from the Senate than from the House.

Table 6.2 also displays the number of states receiving federal funds in nondiscretionary distributive programs. Universalism across states is strongly in

Table 6.2 Number of States Receiving Federal Funds in Discretionary and Nondiscretionary Distributive Programs: Medians and First and Third Quartile Distances by Congress, 1983–90

Type of Program	Median Program	First Quartile	Third Quartile
Discretionary			
98th Congress ($n = 440$)	22	7	40
99th Congress ($n = 481$)	24	8	42
100th Congress ($n = 514$)	27	10	43
101st Congress ($n = 564$)	26	8	42
Whole period ($n = 1,999$)	25	8	42
Nondiscretionay			
98th Congress ($n = 71$)	48	28	50
99th Congress ($n = 78$)	47	31	50
100th Congress ($n = 87$)	49	39	50
101st Congress ($n = 89$)	50	39	50
Whole period ($n = 325$)	49	36	50

evidence when senators themselves write the formulas for allocating funds. The median number of states over the whole period that receive funds under nondiscretionary distributive programs is forty-nine. Even programs at and above the first quartile provide outlays to at least three-fifths of the states represented in the Senate—or, put differently, to filibuster-proof majorities of senators. The broadest 25 percent of programs allocate funds to all fifty states for every Congress examined here. In short, the overwhelming majority of nondiscretionary distributive programs benefit coalitions of states that are much larger than simple majorities.

These findings provide strong, albeit indirect, evidence that coalitions to distribute funds in the Senate are formed by expanding the number of states benefiting from programs so that majorities, frequently overwhelming majorities, of states receive funds.[10] Noting that the fourteen underrepresented states in the Senate (shown in table 6.1) alone account for 64 percent of the nation's population, it is easy to see how universalistic coalition building in the Senate is likely to benefit small-population states. In the House, "universalism" (the condition of all or nearly all congressional districts benefiting from a program) is frequently contrasted with "distributive politics," where funds are targeted to districts whose representatives have greater institutional power. In the Senate, universalism itself is likely to lead to allocations that target benefits to small states. Now that we have demonstrated that policies are frequently constructed to benefit majorities of states, it is appropriate to ask whether this leads to allocations that benefit the less populous states *disproportionately*.

Disproportionate Benefits

Our hypothesis is that overrepresented states receive a disproportionate share of federal funds after controlling for differences in states' need for federal dollars. To test this hypothesis, we employ a pooled cross-sectional time-series design. The dependent variables are per capita outlays to each state for each year from 1984 to 1990 for groups of domestic assistance programs.[11] Programs are grouped first according to the policy types identified above: redistributive, discretionary distributive, and nondiscretionary distributive, and then into twelve functional policy areas using the classifications provided by the *Catalog of Federal Domestic Assistance* (U.S. General Services Administration, 1996).[12]

The independent variable measuring Senate representation is the reciprocal of the representation index described above and shown in table 6.1 (1/representation index). The representation index is transformed in this way because it is an essentially nonlinear variable. Citizens in the least populous states are far more advantaged (in terms of one person, one vote) by comparison with the mean state than citizens in the largest states are disadvantaged. For example, Michigan and Idaho are approximately equal distances from the mean score on the index ($\pm$ 0.80); however, an individual citizen's vote in Idaho is worth five times as much as a vote in an average-sized state, while a vote in Michigan is worth only half as much. This nonlinear quality makes even more sense when one considers the hypothetical situation where one federal per capita dollar is redistributed from California to the least populous states. Obviously the small states would receive many more dollars per capita in exchange for the one dollar per capita lost by California. The reciprocal transformation allows the effect of Senate representation to be considerably greater at low values on the representation index (for small states) but for the slope of the line to flatten out at higher values. In other words, the relationship between the representation index and per capita outlays to states is expected to follow the Phillips curve. The transformation does not make it more difficult to interpret the results of the regression analyses: a value of 1 on the reciprocal transformation of the representation index indicates that a state is represented according to the rule of one person, one vote; a smaller value means the state is underrepresented by reference to this standard; and a larger value means it is overrepresented.

In each of the models, control variables are also included to account for variation in states' need for federal funds.[13] If small states receive more from the federal government because their needs in certain areas are greater, then this difference should not be understood as resulting from their representational advantages in the Senate. Measures of a state's relative economic standing, such as the median state income and unemployment rate, are good general gauges of its need for federal funds in many policy areas. Also, the percentage of a state's population receiving welfare or Social Security is a useful control measure for redistributive programs. When programs are grouped into functional policy areas, it becomes easier to identify the most important variables measuring states' need with respect to those policy areas. For example, the numbers of federal aid highway miles (both primary and interstate) are obviously important variables in estimating states' need for federal transportation dollars. Similarly, the values of farm acreage and farm marketings in a state are important variables in determining its need for federal agricultural subsidies. Following the guidance provided by other work in the field, we include appropriate control variables in each of the regression models.[14]

Pooling time-series and cross-sectional data presents some problems for model specification. The error term in these models is often contaminated by unit-specific autocorrelation, unit-specific heteroscedasticity, and contemporaneous correlation (Beck and Katz 1995; Hsiao 1986; Sayrs 1989; Stimson 1985). To control for the presence of a first-order autoregressive process, we included a lagged dependent variable on the right-hand side of the equation, as many authors have suggested (Beck and Katz 1995, 637; Sayrs 1989, 20–21). Including this variable is theoretically sound because one would expect federal outlays to states in particular policy areas to be relatively stable over time. In fact, previous work in the field has shown that outlays to a state in any particular year are a function of the outlays to that state in the previous year (Ray 1980). In addition, contemporaneous correlation is a problem for estimation: overall budgetary cutbacks or increases in particular fiscal years will affect all the outlays to states for those years. Dummy variables were included to capture the fixed effects of year-specific heteroscedasticity (Sayrs 1989; Stimson 1985). Even after we include these dummy variables for year, however, Lagrange multiplier tests for heteroscedasticity continue to show the presence of individual effects in all the regression models.[15] This problem with unit-specific heteroscedasticity was slightly more difficult to manage. Because the representation index varies very little over the seven-year period for which data are available, we could not include dummy variables for states to capture unit-specific heteroscedasticity—these variables would be perfectly collinear with the representation index (Judge et al. 1988, 490). To correct for these problems, we estimate the OLS results using panel-corrected standard errors (PCSEs) so that the errors provide accurate estimates of the variability of the OLS estimates (Beck and Katz 1995, 638).[16]

Findings

If the equal representation of states in the Senate translates into advantages for small states in procuring federal funds, then they will receive more federal dollars per capita than more populous states, all else being equal. Because low values on the reciprocal of the representation index mean a state is under-represented and high values mean it is overrepresented, we generally expect a positive relation between this measure and per capita outlays to states for most federal domestic assistance policies: as representation in the Senate increases, federal outlays to states increase.

The major exception to this expectation is in redistributive policies: because these involve entitlements to individuals and (in most cases) highly salient and controversial issues of national policymaking, concerns about geographic distribution are less important to senators when these programs are under consideration. Conversely, the relationship between representation and federal outlays to states should be most pronounced in nondiscretionary distributive policies. Because members of Congress must make explicit decisions about the geographic distribution of funds in writing these program authorizations, senators as a whole are likely to seek to ensure that their states receive a "fair share." Finally, the relationship between Senate representation and federal outlays should also be apparent, but less pronounced, in discretionary distributive programs. In these cases members of Congress make the decision to authorize a program, but they delegate to the bureaucracy authority to determine how and where these funds will be spent.

Table 6.3 reports the regression results for programs in each of the policy types examined—redistributive, nondiscretionary distributive, and discretionary distributive. The coefficient for the reciprocal of the representation index is positive and significant for nondiscretionary distributive programs ($p < .01$) and also, at a decreased level of confidence and a smaller magnitude ($p < .1$), for discretionary distributive programs. As expected, the effect of Senate representation on outlays in redistributive policies is not statistically different from zero.

The level of federal per capita outlays to states is more than a function of the need variables and the previous year's allocation: the representation of states in the Senate has an effect separate from those of these other variables. The overall fit of these regression models is quite good, suggesting that additional control variables would not change the results substantially: the

Table 6.3 Effects of State Representation in the Senate on per Capita Federal Outlays, 1984–90, Controlling for Policy Type and States' Need

Variable	Redistributive Policies b (t-value)[a]	Discretionary Distributive Policies b (t-value)[a]	Nondiscretionary Distributive Policies b (t-value)[a]
Reciprocal of the	1.22	1.21*	7.78***
representation index	(0.70)	(1.48)	(3.15)
Lag	0.96***	0.90***	0.64***
	(32.24)	(7.00)	(4.40)
Unemployment rate	2.60***	1.21	2.08**
	(2.68)	(0.55)	(1.77)
Percentage receiving AFDC	64.52	—	—
	(0.70)		
Percentage receiving OASDI	508.62***	—	—
	(2.78)		
Median income	−0.00001	−0.0001	0.0001
	(−0.68)	(−1.05)	(1.03)
1985 dummy	1.30	16.47***	−10.00***
	(0.43)	(4.26)	(−7.73)
1986 dummy	−39.70***	−8.08	−2.32***
	(−6.83)	(−0.86)	(−3.04)
1987 dummy	−15.84**	17.35*	−17.17***
	(−2.24)	(1.42)	(−7.97)
1988 dummy	33.59***	12.59	11.69***
	(3.34)	(0.69)	(6.93)
1989 dummy	60.37***	−61.00***	−28.37***
	(4.50)	(−2.73)	(−7.01)
1990 dummy	96.60***	−24.78*	10.37***
	(5.65)	(−1.58)	(5.49)
Constant	51.21***	25.51**	25.25**
	(3.49)	(1.84)	(1.88)
R^2	.98	.84	.79
N	350	350	350
Mean per capita	$1,507.23	$221.01	$149.39

[a] Computed using PCSEs.

***$p < .01$; **$p < .05$; *$p < .1$.

Figure 6.1. Effect of Senate apportionment on average per capita outlays, 1984–90

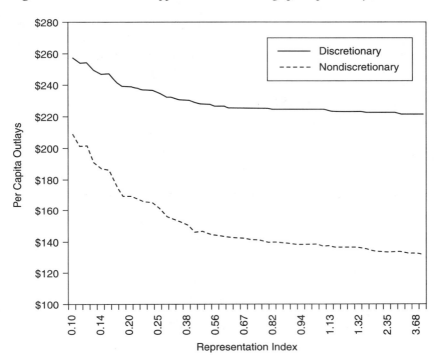

adjusted R^2 for the models predicting outlays in nondiscretionary and discretionary distributive programs is .79 and .84, respectively.

Because the relationship between state representation in the Senate and per capita federal outlays is not linear, figure 6.1 displays it in graphic form. This graph plots the predicted values for nondiscretionary and discretionary distributive policies for all state sizes when all other variables in the model are held at their means. In both models, the smallest states are remarkably advantaged over all other states in per capita terms. At the same time, however, the largest states are not as disadvantaged as the smallest states are advantaged. In fact the largest states are not dramatically disadvantaged relative to the middle-sized states, though the line always slopes downward. (Of course a difference of even a few dollars per capita between a middle-sized state and California is still a lot of money in absolute terms.) As expected, the effect of Senate representation is much greater on nondiscretionary distributive programs than on discretionary distributive programs.

The effect of Senate representation on per capita federal outlays in non-discretionary distributive programs is substantial. Holding all other variables constant at their means, the model predicts that a state as overrepresented on the representation index as Wyoming would receive an average of $209 per capita annually, whereas a state with California's score would receive only $132. By comparison, the model predicts that a state that is represented according to a one person, one vote standard (a state with a score of 1 on the representation index) would receive $139 per capita. Some examples help illustrate the effect this has on individual states. If Wyoming were represented according to the one person, one vote standard (if it had a score of 1 on the representation index), the model would predict that, given its actual scores on the control variables, it would have received $190 less per capita than it actually did on average over the period, a difference of approximately $44 million annually. If California had a score of 1 on the representation index, the model predicts that, given its actual scores on the control variables, it would have received $2.79 more for each citizen than it actually received, or $78 million more annually in nondiscretionary distributive funds. Similarly, the model estimates that Florida would have received $11.26 more per capita if it were represented in the Senate according to its population, or $135 million more.

State representation in the Senate also affects federal outlays in discretionary distributive programs, although its effect is not as pronounced as in nondiscretionary distributive programs. Again, holding all other variables at their means, the model predicts that a state with Wyoming's score on the representation index would receive $257 per capita in these programs, whereas a state with California's score would receive only $222. A state with a score of 1 on the representation index (and the mean scores on all other variables in the model) would receive $225 per capita. As an example of the impact this has on particular states, if Alaska had a score of 1 on the representation index (instead of 0.11), the model predicts that, given its actual scores on the control variables, it would have gotten $19 less per capita on average annually than it actually did, or nearly $10 million less in federal funds than it received on average over the period. Accordingly, the model predicts that, given its scores on the control variables, Texas would have gotten $17 more per capita than it actually received annually, or an increase of $284 million, if it were represented according to the one person, one vote rule.

Because of the difficulty of controlling for states' need when outlays for so many programs with so many different purposes are included together, twelve separate regression models were estimated for the twelve policy areas. Separating programs according to their purposes makes it easier to identify and control for the relevant need variables. Results of these regressions are displayed in table 6.4.

The coefficient for the reciprocal of the representation index is positive and significant ($p < .05$) in five of the twelve policy areas: disaster prevention and relief, community development, environmental quality, food and nutrition, and transportation. In other words, small states appear to have advantages in procuring federal funds in all these areas. Figure 6.2 displays in graphic form the results of the regressions in these policy areas.

As this figure shows, the effect of state representation on federal outlays to states is most pronounced in transportation policy. Even after controlling for the number of federal aid highway miles in each state, less populous states receive more per capita for transportation programs than larger states. When all other variables are held at their means, the model predicts that the smallest states will receive about $120 per capita while the largest states receive only $82. The benefits to small-population states are so pronounced in transportation policy in large part because of a high minimum outlay guaranteed to states by the funding formula for the highway planning and construction program. This one program accounts for 76 percent of the funds allocated for improving transportation; under its formula each state is guaranteed at least 0.5 percent of the $13.5 billion allocated on average annually by the program during the period.

Community development and environmental quality programs are also substantially affected by Senate apportionment. Holding all other variables at their means, the model predicts that the largest states will receive $49 per capita in community development funds while the smallest states will get $64; for environmental quality programs the model predicts that the largest states will receive $20 per capita while the smallest states will get $38. Again, minimum allocations to states under the programs are an important factor accounting for small-state advantages. One of the largest programs classified under both environmental quality and community development categories is the Construction Grants for Wastewater Treatment Works, accounting for 15 percent of all outlays for community development and 37 percent of those for environmental quality. Like the highway planning and construction formula grant, the wastewater treatment grant program requires that no state shall receive less than 0.5 percent of the total funds allocated by the program ($1.8 billion on average annually). Minimum guarantees like these are examined in more detail in chapter 7.

At a reduced level of confidence ($p < .1$), the coefficient on the representation measure is positive and significant for three additional policy areas: housing; education; and employment, labor, and training. Small states receive more in each of these programs than they would get simply based on need or the previous year's allocation.

State representation in the Senate is not estimated to have a significant effect on the geographic distribution of funds for health, income security, or

Table 6.4 Effects of State Representation in the Senate on per Capita Federal Outlays in Programs Grouped by Functional Policy Area, Controlling for States' Need, 1984–90

Variable	Agriculture b (t-value)[a]	Disaster Prevention and Relief b (t-value)[a]	Business and Commerce b (t-value)[a]
Reciprocal of the	1.90	0.54**	−0.32*
representation index	(1.18)	(1.66)	(−1.69)
Lag	0.83***	0.74***	0.59***
	(5.96)	(4.03)	(4.36)
Value of farms	−0.003**	−0.001***	—
(by acre)	(−1.85)	(−2.84)	
Farm marketings	0.012*	0.001*	—
(per capita)	(1.31)	(1.51)	
Failed businesses	—	—	−763.80
(per capita)			(−0.18)
New incorporations	—	—	24.01
(per capita)			(0.62)
1985 dummy	61.15***	5.27***	1.27***
	(18.98)	(19.58)	(4.38)
1986 dummy	33.42***	3.17***	0.83***
	(5.33)	(5.70)	(2.58)
1987 dummy	55.97***	1.27***	0.16
	(7.94)	(1.73)	(0.46)
1988 dummy	48.69***	2.67***	4.54***
	(4.50)	(4.73)	(11.51)
1989 dummy	−16.96*	10.84***	−6.26***
	(−1.27)	(16.29)	(−42.91)
1990 dummy	7.18	0.64	5.96***
	(1.09)	(0.29)	(5.86)
Constant	−23.70**	0.42	6.77***
	(−1.98)	(0.24)	(2.45)
R^2	.84	.60	.43
N	336[b]	336[b]	350
Mean per capita	$81.00	$16.00	$16.51

Table 6.4 (*continued*)

Variable	Food and Nutrition *b* (*t*-value) [a]	Transportation *b* (*t*-value) [a]	Environmental Quality *b* (*t*-value) [a]
Reciprocal of the representation index	0.49 ***	3.74 ***	1.77 ***
	(3.02)	(2.35)	(3.47)
Lag	0.70 ***	0.76 ***	0.50 ***
	(7.63)	(7.08)	(2.34)
Percentage in lunch program	67.42 ***	—	—
	(4.01)		
Percentage in poverty	0.08 **	—	—
	(1.97)		
Percentage receiving food stamps	223.15 ***	—	—
	(3.41)		
Primary highway miles	—	−0.002 ***	—
		(−2.68)	
Interstate miles	—	0.01 **	—
		(2.29)	
Vehicle registration (per capita)	—	2.43	—
		(.15)	
Hazardous waste sites	—	—	−22990.76
			(−0.19)
1985 dummy	−0.44 ***	−5.00 ***	−3.08 ***
	(−2.20)	(−6.72)	(−4.10)
1986 dummy	2.92 ***	−5.24 ***	−4.26 ***
	(10.67)	(−6.84)	(−2.40)
1987 dummy	−0.54 ***	−0.48	−5.24 ***
	(−9.92)	(−0.65)	(−2.07)
1988 dummy	5.11 ***	9.04 ***	8.46 ***
	(8.35)	(7.22)	(2.71)
1989 dummy	3.76 ***	−25.50 ***	−6.30 ***
	(4.83)	(−9.54)	(−12.80)
1990 dummy	15.17 ***	0.31 ***	4.07 ***
	(21.02)	(5.08)	(1.75)
Constant	−6.21 ***	15.05	7.21 ***
	(−3.56)	(0.83)	(1.32)
R^2	.94	.79	.48
N	350	350	350
Mean per capita	$75.05	$95.32	$1,527.51

[a] Computed using PCSEs

[b] Dollar values for farm marketings were not available for Alaska and Hawaii.

[c] Medicaid data for South Carolina were unavailabale.

***p < .01; **p < .05; *p < .1.

(continued

Table 6.4 (*continued*)

Variable	Community Development *b* (*t*-value) [a]	Employment Labor and Training *b* (*t*-value) [a]	Income Security *b* (*t*-value) [a]
Reciprocal of the representation index	1.51** (2.04)	0.49* (1.53)	−2.75 (−1.18)
Lag	0.64*** (5.28)	0.95*** (8.33)	0.54*** (4.80)
Median income	−0.00001 (−0.32)	—	−0.0001 (−4.00)
Unemployment rate	1.17** (1.79)	0.84** (2.11)	—
Percentage receiving AFDC	—	−19.79* (−1.47)	616.50** (1.70)
Percentage in poverty	−0.24*** (−3.15)	—	—
OASDI	—	—	3235.76*** (4.75)
1985 dummy	−21.23*** (−2.05)	−39.60*** (−9.48)	29.70*** (2.33)
1986 dummy	−6.37*** (−19.00)	−32.74*** (−9.03)	39.52** (2.07)
1987 dummy	−30.13*** (−41.13)	−32.81*** (−7.98)	59.57*** (2.42)
1988 dummy	−8.01*** (−2.23)	−32.22*** (−7.23)	119.52*** (3.59)
1989 dummy	−21.81*** (−7.05)	−31.51*** (−6.72)	172.27*** (4.13)
1990 dummy	−4.59 (−1.07)	−28.22*** (−5.90)	273.60*** (5.30)
Constant	21.73** (2.05)	31.60*** (19.84)	141.42** (2.33)
R^2	.68	.89	.91
N	350	350	350
Mean per capita	$53.71	$68.92	$1,527.51

Table 6.4 (*continued*)

Variable	Education b (t-value) [a]	Housing b (t-value) [a]	Health b (t-value) [a]
Reciprocal of the	0.86*	0.42*	0.88
representation index	(1.50)	(1.32)	(1.12)
Lag	0.97***	0.71***	0.79***
	(12.73)	(3.82)	(8.51)
Elementary enrollment	−6.33	—	—
(per capita)	(−0.97)		
Secondary enrollment	−42.76	—	—
(per capita)	(−0.38)		
Number of colleges	1817.67	—	—
(per capita)	(0.02)		
New housing starts	—	−266.70	—
(per capita)		(−0.94)	
Median home value	—	0.0001**	—
		(2.21)	
Percentage receiving	—	—	222.31**
Medicare			(1.99)
Percentage receiving	—	—	408.14***
Medicaid			(3.58)
Hospital beds	—	—	4004.21***
(per capita)			(3.61)
1985 dummy	13.48***	−1.25***	12.62***
	(55.24)	(−3.19)	(7.90)
1986 dummy	−7.05***	−0.41	0.66
	(−4.56)	(−0.46)	(0.15)
1987 dummy	3.51***	−0.55	5.84
	(2.98)	(−0.51)	(1.14)
1988 dummy	−0.25	45.63***	23.23***
	(−0.15)	(36.55)	(3.80)
1989 dummy	7.39***	20.51***	31.17***
	(4.13)	(2.80)	(3.64)
1990 dummy	0.69	24.00***	73.14***
	(0.27)	(2.77)	(6.87)
Constant	5.67	−1.62	−2.74***
	(0.77)	(−0.55)	(−0.35)
R^2	.89	.85	.90
N	350	350	343 [c]
Mean per capita	$68.71	$34.12	$381.46

Figure 6.2. Effects of Senate apportionment on average per capita outlays in selected policy areas, 1984–90

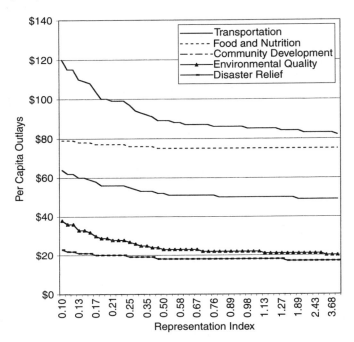

agriculture. Because the overwhelming majority of the funds allocated under the programs included in the health and income security policy areas are individual entitlements (Medicare and Medicaid in the case of health policies and AFDC and Social Security in the case of income security policies), one would not expect representation in the Senate to significantly affect per capita outlays in these policy areas. In addition, all the large agricultural stabilization programs, which constitute the vast majority of outlays for agriculture, are direct payments to farmers; thus one would not expect Senate apportionment to affect the geographic distribution of funds in this policy area.

On the other hand, it is somewhat surprising that state representation in the Senate has an effect on funds allocated under programs for food and nutrition, because programs in this category are generally redistributive in character. Overall, though, the effect of Senate representation in this policy area is the least substantial relative to the size (in dollar terms) of the programs in this category; the regression line is almost flat. Although small states are advantaged, it is only a very slight advantage.

The negative coefficient ($p < .1$) on representation for the model predicting federal outlays for business and commerce policies is anomalous: large states appear to have a slight advantage in procuring federal funds in this policy area; as in food and nutrition policies, however, the regression line is nearly flat.

Our analysis demonstrates that states with better per capita representation in the Senate tend to receive more per capita federal funds, all else being equal.[17] In eight of the ten policy areas where one would expect senators to be concerned about geographic distribution, small states receive more federal funds than would be predicted based on need alone. Putting aside the health and income security policy areas (which largely comprise individual entitlement programs), the areas affected by Senate apportionment include two of the largest in terms of actual federal outlays: community development and transportation. These two alone account for nearly 20 percent of the funds allocated for federal domestic assistance and over 40 percent of the funds allocated for all purposes other than health and income security. Even within the smaller functional policy areas, moreover, less populous states are measurably advantaged in six of the remaining eight. Generally speaking, then, the equal representation of states in the Senate leads to unequal per capita federal outlays to states.

Conclusion

The findings presented here reveal that the framers' institutional choice to grant equal representation to states in the Senate influences public policy-making in the United States today in two respects. First, we have shown that although previous research on the House has not supported the universalism thesis, federal programs tend to be constructed so that majorities of states benefit rather than majorities of congressional districts. This is especially true when senators themselves approve the formulas for allocating funds, as the universalism thesis would predict. In programs allocated by formula, overwhelming majorities of states tend to benefit. As a result it is apparent that the politics of coalition building in the Senate to support federal domestic assistance programs has some important effects on the geographic distribution of federal outlays. Second, we have shown that equal state representation in the Senate affects the per capita distribution of federal funds. As expected, small states are most advantaged in nondiscretionary distributive programs, but the effect is evident across most of the domestic policy areas examined here.

Studies of distributive policymaking have usually focused on the House; in fact such studies typically ignore the Senate altogether. Therefore this research fills an important void in the literature on congressional policymaking. After all, there is reason to expect that the incentives to seek federal funds for constituents may be even greater in the Senate than in the House. Stein and Bickers demonstrate that vulnerable House incumbents are more likely than other House members to seek federal grants for their districts (Stein and Bickers 1994a, 1995; Bickers and Stein 1996). Senate incumbents are more likely to face competitive races for reelection and are more vulnerable to electoral defeat than House incumbents (Abramowitz 1988). There is good reason, then, to expect that senators as a whole may be even more interested in procuring federal money for their constituencies than their House counterparts, despite the stereotype of the parochial pork-seeking House member. At minimum, however, the Senate should be recognized as an equal partner with the House in all aspects of distributive policymaking. The literature's neglect of the Senate has produced an incomplete picture of congressional policymaking. Our focus on the Senate is in this sense a corrective.

In addition, the effects of Senate apportionment on federal distributive policymaking are more pervasive and more substantial than the effects of distributive politics in the House. Despite the theoretical appeal of the distributive politics hypothesis—that powerful members of Congress typically use their influence to direct federal projects to their own districts—most studies have been unable to show much of an effect on aggregate federal outlays. Generally these studies focus narrowly on specific policy areas, and even then they usually find that the empirical effects of distributive politics are more limited than expected (see Arnold 1981, 13–18). The effect of Senate apportionment on public policy is greater than that of distributive politics in the House because the particular congressional districts that are advantaged by committee and party leadership in the House are not stable over time in the way small states in the Senate are. When new House districts become advantaged through changes in committee composition and party leadership positions, their representatives are limited in their ability to redirect funds both because previous federal investments elsewhere restrict them (Rundquist 1978) and because, in the case of formula programs, they are constrained by long-standing formulas that are very difficult to change (Arnold 1979, 217–18).

Small states, by contrast, have always had their two senators in the Senate and therefore have always been in a good position to reap extra benefits regardless of when Congress made decisions about how to distribute federal funds. Even the first formula grant, the Federal Aid to Roads Act of 1921, was highly beneficial to less populous states and provided a special minimum guarantee for them, ensuring that nearly one-quarter of the funds for highways would be distributed equally across states.[18] Congress changed this formula only once between 1921 and 1982 and never made it less favorable to small states (F. Lee 1997, 187). As a result of this constancy, the small-state advantage in federal distributive policymaking is more stable, prevalent, and substantial than the effects of distributive politics in the House.

Studying the effects of Senate apportionment on federal politics and policymaking is also important in light of the recent debates over devolving major federal programs to states in the form of block grants. As Congress converts federal entitlement programs, including welfare and Medicaid, into lump-sum grants to states, the politics surrounding these programs are likely to take on a more distributive, as opposed to a redistributive, character. When these programs become more distributive, the funding formulas are likely to show a more pronounced imprint of Senate apportionment.

In sum, Senate apportionment shapes public policy outcomes just as it shapes basic processes of American government—including representational relationships, Senate elections, and the strategic behavior of senators and those seeking to influence them. In the following chapter we examine patterns of House-Senate interactions in policymaking in order to establish that the Senate actually influences policymaking so as to produce the effects shown here. Rather than treating Congress as a black box, as many studies of distributive politics have done, we look at the politics of writing federal grants both within the Senate and between the two chambers to see if the effect of Senate apportionment is evident in the legislative process as well as in its final budgetary outputs.

7

Designing Policy: How the Senate
Makes Small States Winners

T he findings presented in the preceding chapter demonstrate that the
distributional patterns evident in federal outlays to states are consistent with Senate influence. Indeed, they strongly suggest that the Senate
acts to ensure that states get shares of federal dollars reflecting their equal
Senate representation. Across a wide range of federal programs, less populous states receive larger per capita shares of federal expenditures than larger
ones, even after controlling for state need. The small-state advantage is most
pronounced in formula grants (nondiscretionary grants), the type of federal
program for which Congress writes the formula determining the geographic
distribution of funds. Less populous states are also advantaged in programs
for which Congress delegates authority over the geographic distribution of
funds to federal agencies (discretionary or project grants), but their advantage
is not as great. The small-state advantage is evident in most substantive areas
of federal policy, including transportation, environmental quality, community development, and disaster prevention programs. The only exception to
this general trend is that small states are not advantaged in redistributive programs involving payments or reimbursements to individuals, such as Social
Security and Medicare.

To establish that the Senate is actually the source of this observed small-
state advantage, we now explore the politics of formula writing between the
House and Senate and within both chambers. Do the House and Senate
prefer different distributions of federal dollars among the states when authorizing domestic assistance programs? Does the Senate prefer distributions
that are more generous to less populous states than those preferred by the
House? If so, do Senate preferences win out in conference often enough to

account for the patterns in budgetary outlays observed in chapter 6? To answer these questions, we examine the politics of a sample of formula grants-in-aid to determine whether the House-passed and Senate-passed formulas differed in the expected ways and how often the Senate's preferences were enacted into law.

Why Study Formula Grants?

We chose to study the politics of formula grants for three reasons. First, formula grants are more important than project grants because they constitute the overwhelming majority of federal expenditures for domestic assistance. Although project grants substantially outnumber formula grants—446 to 133 in 1995—the bulk of all federal dollars for domestic assistance is allocated by statutory formula (Advisory Commission on Intergovernmental Relations 1995, 14). In fiscal year 1996, for example, nearly 90 percent of all federal dollars granted to states and local governments was allocated according to congressionally mandated formulas. Excluding Medicaid (the largest formula grant-in-aid, which alone accounts for about 40 percent of all expenditures for grants-in-aid), formula grants constituted 82.2 percent of all the funds allocated in FY 1996 under domestic assistance programs, while project grants accounted for only 17.8 percent.[1] In short, a better understanding of the congressional politics of writing formula grants goes a long way toward improving our understanding of federal domestic policymaking as a whole.

Formula grants have become increasingly important (in contrast to project grants) in light of the ongoing efforts since the 1980s to convert categorical grants (both formula-based and project-based) into block grants to states. The 1981 Omnibus Budget Reconciliation Act alone created nine new block grants, consolidating seventy-seven existing federal categorical grants (U.S. House, Committee on Economic and Educational Opportunities 1995, 46). Since 1981 three new block grants have been added, bringing the current total to fifteen. Both President Clinton and the recent Republican Congresses favor increased use of block grants because they are simpler for both states and the federal government to administer, as well as useful for imposing spending cuts (Advisory Commission on Intergovernmental Relations 1995, 19). Nearly all block grants allocate funds according to statutory formulas (U.S. House, Committee on Economic and Educational Opportunities 1995, 47). Any shift away from categorical grants toward block grants is also a shift toward formulas.

Second, formula grants are more important than project grants for understanding congressional policymaking because Congress exercises greater influence over them. In writing the formula, Congress establishes both a state's eligibility for program dollars and the level of funding each state will receive. As a result, executive agencies exert little influence over where money will be distributed, even if they retain considerable oversight of the expenditure of program funds. For this reason congressional influence over the geographic allocation of funds can be traced most clearly in formula grant programs. On the other hand, when Congress delegates authority to executive agencies to allocate program funds, congressional influence is indirect. It is very difficult to ascertain why a grant under a given discretionary program goes to one state rather than to another, especially in the absence of frank interviews with those administering the program. To know why a state received a discretionary (or project) grant, one would need to know which states had applied for program funds and the criteria by which the administrators chose the recipients. Was the state selected at the behest of a congressional committee or of a member of Congress? Was it selected to further the political aims of the bureaucratic agency administering the program? Or was the choice based on the agency's assessment of the state's merit or need? With formula grants, by contrast, a state or local government receives a certain level of funding simply because the formula written by Congress and adopted into law requires it.

Third, formula grants have been neglected by political scientists, who have instead focused on the political factors that influence the geographic distribution of project grants. The reason for this neglect is largely that the study of geographic allocation has been dominated by the "distributive politics model," especially popular in studies of the House (Arnold 1979; Ferejohn 1974; Ray 1980; Rundquist 1980; Stein and Bickers 1995; Strom 1975). This model posits that representational power within Congress (committee leadership, party leadership, etc.) yields advantages for states and districts in procuring federal dollars from bureaucrats administering project grants. Formula grants cannot be analyzed from this theoretical perspective, however, because the state's (or district's) representational power in Congress makes no difference after the formula is written. Every eligible state or locality receives the funds it is entitled to under the formula, regardless of the power or skill of its representatives. Formulas, moreover, are stable for long periods. If a formula (at the time of its writing) is designed to benefit certain members' districts, then it will in almost all cases persist long after they leave office. Formulas are also incompatible with the distributive politics model because they are typically very simple, containing only a few factors. Complex weighting schemes are rare, making it unlikely that most formulas are written to target particular members' districts or states.[2] The dominance of the distributive politics model has led political scientists to neglect the most important type of program in terms of understanding the bulk of all federal grants-in-aid.

The Politics of Writing Funding Formulas

Although the distributive politics model is not very useful for understanding congressional formula writing—and thus cannot account for the distribution of most federal funds—there is reason to think that the structure of Congress does influence the distribution of federal dollars. Even if formula-grant funds are not typically targeted to the states or districts of powerful members of Congress, political considerations can still be important in their geographic allocation. The different bases of apportionment in the House and Senate are likely to affect federal policymaking because the distributions of federal funds preferred by legislative majorities in the two chambers are apt to differ in significant ways and because senators are apt to have greater incentives than House members to insist on their preferred formulas during conference committee negotiations.

The different bases of legislative apportionment in the House and Senate are likely to influence the geographic distribution of federal funds for three reasons. First, the two chambers' bases of apportionment will produce different definitions of an "equitable" distribution for any given federal program. Second, as discussed briefly in the preceding chapters, the enormous variation in Senate constituency size affects senators' incentives in distributive policymaking, a consequence of legislative apportionment that has no counterpart in the House. Third, the Senate's preferences are likely to prevail in House-Senate conflict over funding formulas because these formulas affect Senate constituencies more directly, intensifying senators' preferences.

Notions of Equity in the House and Senate

One would expect that for the overwhelming majority of House members a consensus distribution—one regarded as equitable by a large majority of members—will be one based on population. This will be true regardless of whether the funds are distributed solely by population or based on some targeted population, such as the number who will be served by the program.[3] On the other hand, senators, especially those from the less populous states, are not likely to perceive a purely population-based distribution as "equitable." In theory, those senators whose states would do better under an equal distribution of federal funds among the states than under a purely population-based distribution should prefer an equal distribution. Given the tremendous variation in state population, however, it is obvious that an equal distribution would make no sense in terms of public policy and would be blatantly unfair to most states, especially the largest. Even so, many senators are likely to resist purely population-based distributions. Under these distributions, senators from less populous states would receive less than they feel is appropriate because they are likely to be "unpersuaded that New York and California deserve fifty or sixty times as much assistance as their great states" (Arnold 1981, 269). As a result, because of the equal representation of states the Senate will exhibit a greater tendency toward state equality in its distributions than the House.

Senators can produce less variable distributions of funds either by granting larger allocations to the smaller states or by including formula factors that serve an equalizing function.[4] An alternative method of creating a more equal distribution of funds is to cap the amount populous states can receive under a program, but this method is less preferred by coalition builders in the Senate. Because program caps create identifiable "losers," they invite conflict and opposition. Increasing the amount smaller states receive, on the other hand, will be uncontroversial in the Senate in most cases because it only increases the number of senators willing to support the program.[5]

In short, we expect that the House will typically prefer formulas that use measures of population as the primary criteria for distribution and that the Senate will seek to include equalizing provisions in respect of state equality. These provisions will tend to be floors below which no state can fall rather than ceilings that prohibit large states from receiving as much as they otherwise would based on the other factors in the formula. Thus, generally speaking, Senate funding formulas will be more generous to less populous states (and less generous to larger ones) than House funding formulas, and this difference will be a source of recurring conflict between the chambers.

Senators' Incentives

Although Senate apportionment taken alone is likely to lead the Senate to prefer distributions of federal funds that favor overrepresented states, two additional dynamics compound the advantages of less populous states. First, as discussed previously, great variation in Senate constituency size means that Senate coalition builders face a unique situation: although all senators' votes are worth the same to the coalition, not all have the same price. Thus it is less expensive in terms of program budgets for coalition leaders to ensure that senators from small states benefit from a program, giving them incentives to include disproportionate benefits for small-state senators in coalitions supporting federal grant programs.[6] As one staffer to a large-state senator explained, "There's no point in having big state buys. The small states are cheap dates." As a result, the staffer continued, small-state senators can simply "sit there and wait" for coalition builders to seek them out: "They just sit back and the money rolls in."

Second, small-state senators have greater incentives than other senators to insist on particularized benefits in the form of federal grants, projects, and funds for their states. As discussed in chapter 5, particularized benefits have greater advertising and credit-claiming value to senators representing small states because any given benefit will affect a greater percentage of their constituents. In addition, small-state senators are more likely to obtain particular benefits because even windfalls for small states will often be inexpensive in terms of overall program budgets. Much of the time a small-state minimum guarantee or floor—a formula provision ensuring that no state receives less than a certain amount of money or a percentage of the total program allocation—will be sufficient to accommodate the more intense preferences of small-state senators and enable coalition builders to substantially expand their margins of support in the Senate.

Many funding formulas do contain minimum guarantees. These minimums uniformly benefit less populous states, granting them more than they would receive based on other factors in the funding formula. As will be discussed below, the most common minimum guarantee requires that each state receive at least 0.5 percent of the total program allocation. In conjunction with a funding formula based on total state population (also common), this minimum means that the least populous states will receive as much as 178 percent more than they otherwise would. Thirteen states have populations that constitute less than 0.5 percent of the nation's population; therefore in the common case of a formula that apportions funds by state population, twenty-six senators represent states that would receive an additional amount under a minimum guarantee granting them at least 0.5 percent of the total program allocation.[7]

To illustrate what minimum guarantees of 0.5 percent mean, table 7.1 lists these states and the percentage increases they would receive above a population-based apportionment. It is clear from this table that a number of senators have a great deal to gain for their states by insisting on a minimum guarantee of this kind. With a program allocating $350 million each fiscal year (the median outlay for a formula grant program in the sample to be discussed below), for Wyoming a 0.5 percent minimum would mean an increase of $1.1 million over a population-based apportionment. The minimum would mean an increase of $630,000 for Montana and increases of more than $750,000 each for South Dakota, North Dakota, Delaware, Alaska, and Vermont. Recall that formulas tend to be stable over long periods, meaning that small states typically reap these additional funds year after year.

In the case of minimum guarantees, then, individual senators from the least populous states have particularly strong incentives to demand special consideration on funding formulas. In light of this, minimum guarantees should be viewed as a classic case of a program that confers a concentrated benefit by imposing a dispersed cost (Wilson 1973, 333). The small states

Table 7.1 Additional Percentages Received by Small-Population States in the Case of a Population-Based Funding Formula with a 0.5 Percent Minimum

State	State's Percentage of the Total U.S. Population (1990)	Percent (%) Increase over Population-Based Apportionment under the Minimum
Wyoming	0.18	178
Alaska	0.22	127
Vermont	0.23	127
North Dakota	0.26	92
Delaware	0.27	85
South Dakota	0.28	78
Montana	0.32	56
Rhode Island	0.40	25
Idaho	0.41	23
Hawaii	0.45	11
New Hampshire	0.45	11
Nevada	0.48	4
Maine	0.49	2

that qualify for additional funds under minimum guarantee provisions receive substantial windfalls, especially considering their small constituencies. At the same time, the cost of these minimum guarantees to the overall program budget is not very great. For a program allocating $350 million based on state population, a minimum guarantee of 0.5 percent would mean a redistribution of only 2.1 percent of the total program outlay, or $7.2 million. This cost would be distributed proportionately across all the other thirty-seven states.[8] As a consequence of this dynamic, senators from the "minimum guarantee" states have an incentive to insist on including these minimums in the Senate and retaining them in conference, but other senators and House members, even those from the most populous states, have little to gain from trying to remove them. Of these minimum guarantees, one Senate staffer remarked, "It's the price one has to pay in the Senate for the support of small-population states. It's a small price."

Interchamber Preference Asymmetry

Despite the expectation of recurring conflict between the House and Senate over formula distributions, we do not assume that the two chambers' preferences regarding formula distributions will be equal in intensity. The Senate is likely to care more about funding formulas than the House does because its geographic constituencies are in most cases more immediately affected by decisions about them. As a consequence of the special status of states in the federal system, most grants-in-aid are made to states rather than to local governments or to other organizations. As one small-state senator explained, comparing the tasks of senators and House members, "The Senate brings with it the responsibility to represent the state governments. You must represent the state's interests in the major formula programs, like Title 1, Chapter 1, Education, Medicaid, Transportation." "It is a special responsibility of senators," he continued. "They are there to give states an active policymaking role in federal policy. That is one of the purposes of the Senate envisioned from the very beginning."

In short, Senate constituencies (states) regularly receive formula grants-in-aid, but House constituencies per se do not. The only exceptions are those few House members who represent states with only one congressional district. In most cases House members representing constituencies in states with more than one congressional district will be uncertain whether and how much their constituency will benefit under any particular funding formula, even one highly favorable to their states. This uncertainty should increase with state population—the larger the state, the greater the uncertainty. Given that the median House member today comes from a state with thirteen congressional districts, most operate under a great deal of uncertainty. The connection between funding formulas and a House member's reelection interests, then, is tenuous in most cases.

By contrast, senators can be certain that their constituency will benefit under a favorable funding formula.[9] Therefore they are much more likely to perceive a connection between obtaining favorable formulas and their constituents' interests. Different levels of uncertainty thus will make senators more concerned with funding formulas than House members are.

When they take an interest in geographic distribution, House members will be more concerned with earmarking funds and procuring project grants that are certain to be located within their constituencies than with funding formulas that will not directly affect them. It is worth noting, in addition, that House members usually cannot claim credit for the benefits their districts receive from formula grants. As Arnold writes, they "could no more claim credit for the regular disbursement of checks for highway assistance, Medicaid, or revenue sharing than they could for Social Security checks" (1981, 75). When seeking to gain benefits for their constituencies or to claim credit for bringing federal dollars home, House members can more profitably spend their time procuring particular projects than working on funding formulas.[10]

An asymmetry of preference intensity will thus characterize conflicts between the House and Senate over funding formulas. Because the Senate usually cares more about them, it should be more likely to win when the House
and Senate go to conference over programs that distribute funds by formula.
Given this asymmetry, the House is likely to compromise or recede to the
Senate position on funding formulas in order to extract concessions on issues
of greater importance to it. For instance, if the House is more concerned
with special projects, then it would be willing to trade a concession on the
formula for a Senate guarantee that the special projects of concern will be
included in the final bill.

In addition, the rules of the Senate enhance House members' incentives
to concede during conference committee deliberations over funding formulas. Because Senate rules grant such broad powers to individual senators,
even a small minority of aggrieved senators can hold up or defeat important
legislation. Because of this, the strong preferences of a few senators must be
taken more seriously than the preferences of individual House members. After all, a single frustrated senator has the power to obstruct major legislation.
The common practice of including minimum guarantees in funding formulas, moreover, ensures that a substantial number of senators have very strong
incentives to demand that conferees maintain the Senate position. If the
House refused, for example, to include a Senate-passed small-state minimum
guarantee in the conference formula, representatives of the Senate position
could easily contend that the senators from the affected states would make
passage of the conference report difficult, if not impossible.

As a result, the asymmetry of House and Senate incentives is likely to
translate into Senate dominance over formula writing. House members have
fewer incentives than senators to take an interest because funding formulas
do not directly affect their constituents. In addition, some individual senators
are likely to have a substantial stake in insisting on Senate formulas in conference. The House thus seems to have more to lose than to gain from opposing the Senate.

Intrachamber Politics and Funding Formulas

Formula writing appears to be an inherently zero-sum game. Given a fixed
sum of money authorized for a program, the choice among different funding
formulas is a choice in which one state's gain is another state's loss.[11] Even so,
there are strong incentives for members of Congress to agree. The primary
alternative to formula distributions is to let the executive branch decide
where to spend program funds. Delegating responsibility over geographic
distribution to the executive branch is certainly not an attractive option,

because that entails greater uncertainty about how much particular legisla-tors' constituencies will receive. As Sen. Jennings Randolph (D–W.Va.) com-mented on the need for statutory formulas: "If there were ever the possibility for tremendous mischief, it would be in granting a large fund . . . to the Secretary to divide up as he saw fit" (*Congressional Record* 1978, 30568).[12]

Unless members of Congress can agree on a formula, then, no funds can be distributed. This provides a strong incentive for members of both chambers. Achieving agreement is less difficult in the House than in the Senate, how-ever, because House constituencies are roughly equal in population. This means that an equitable distribution readily presents itself in the House—simply sharing funds equally (or fairly equally) among constituencies. Ac-cordingly, one would not expect regular conflict over funding formulas in the House.

Conflict is more likely to occur in the Senate. Senators are apt to have more intense preferences about funding formulas than House members because their constituencies are more immediately affected by them, as dis-cussed above. Moreover, that Senate constituencies vary greatly in popula-tion is likely to produce differing notions of "equity" within the Senate as well as between the chambers. Senators from populous states are not likely to view an equal distribution across states as "equitable." In addition, Senate rules place fewer constraints on individual members than do the rules of the House. As a result, whereas a funding formula need only satisfy a majority of House members—a few dissatisfied members of the House can do little to cause trouble or controversy on the House floor—a few dissatisfied senators can delay even major legislation party.

Generally speaking, then, the politics of writing funding formulas is best understood as an interchamber matter. When intrachamber conflict occurs, however, it will probably occur in the Senate, where individual members (especially those representing less populous states) have more reason to care about funding formulas and greater power to insist on their preferences, even when they are in the minority party.

Sample and Methods

We now analyze a sample of formula grant programs to determine if the House and Senate act in the expected ways when they consider funding for-mulas. The universe of formula grants-in-aid funded in FY 1995 is provided in a 1995 report by the Advisory Commission on Intergovernmental Rela-tions (ACIR). This report lists all federal grants-in-aid (both project and for-mula grants).[13] In 1995 there were 133 grants that allocated funds by statutory formula.

In selecting the forty-two cases that make up the sample, we employed a representative sampling technique. Because the universe of formula grants is relatively small and very heterogeneous—in terms of program size, type, and purpose—we were concerned that a random sampling technique might not yield a sample representative of the population (Johnson and Joslyn 1991, 155; King, Keohane, and Verba 1994, 124–28). To obtain a representative sample of cases, we stratified the universe of formula-grant programs by the federal department or agency that administers the program.[14] Then we selected several programs from each group so that the proportion chosen from each department reflected their respective proportions in the total population. Within each department programs were generally selected at random, but occasionally we departed from randomness so as to include very large federal programs, such as the school lunch program and most of the block grants. It was important to include these programs because they exercise such a large effect on the overall character of federal outlays to states.[15] The sample of programs chosen through this procedure is substantial compared with the total population of formula grants funded in 1995.[16] It constitutes fully 31.6 percent of the total number of formula grants and accounts for 42.9 percent of all the dollars allocated under non–Medicaid formula grants in 1995.

For each program in the sample we asked several questions. When was the program formula originally written? On what occasions was it revised? When was the current formula established? Does the formula contain factors measuring state population? Does it contain a minimum for all states? Does the program contain a maximum allocation? Was there House–Senate conflict over the funding formula at any of these points? If so, what was it over and how was it resolved? Other facts about the programs were also compiled from the *Catalog of Federal Domestic Assistance* (U.S. General Services Administration 1996), such as the type of program (whether redistributive or distributive) and the dollar amount allocated in fiscal year 1995.

We found the answers to these questions in the following way. We located the section of the *United States Code* containing the program's funding formula. The *Code* references the occasions when the formula was amended, extending back to the program's initial authorization. We then compiled the public laws authorizing and reauthorizing the funding formula from the *Statutes at Large* and examined the House, Senate, and conference committee reports for each of these laws to detect the presence and nature of House–Senate differences and to determine which chamber's formula was adopted or whether a compromise formula was developed.[17] For each major authorization, we also referred to the entry in the appropriate year's *Congressional Quarterly Almanac* to find any additional information regarding controversy over the funding formula, as well as to get a broad perspective on the other issues at stake in developing the legislation. In addition, we examined the

Congressional Record to gain insight into the politics of any conflict over funding formulas and to determine whether they were amended on the floor in either chamber.

Interchamber Conflict over Funding Formulas

The influence of both chambers' notions of equity is apparent in the characteristics of the formulas sampled. Table 7.2 displays these characteristics.[18] As can be seen in the table, most of the programs in the sample are population based but, at the same time, accommodate the Senate's preferences.[19] Population is used as a factor in the overwhelming majority (76.2 percent), and most (71.4 percent) also contain some sort of small-state minimum. Most of the programs in the sample (59.5 percent), in fact, included both a population factor and a small-state minimum. Of the thirty-two formulas with a population factor, twenty-five also included a small-state minimum (78.3 percent). This suggests, even before we look at patterns of House-Senate conflict, that the House's preference for population-based formulas is being modified to accommodate the preferences of the Senate.

In theory, the incidence of House-Senate conflict over funding formulas should be related to both the type and the size of the program being considered. As we demonstrated in chapter 6, the effect of geographic representation is greater for some types of federal programs than for others. In the case of many redistributive programs, especially individual entitlements, for example, such issues are less important simply because the recipients of the funds are not states. It would not be surprising, then, to find little conflict over the geographic distribution of such programs.

The programs in the sample, however, are all formula grants in which states or local governments (or both) are the recipients of federal dollars. The individual entitlement programs included in the analysis in chapter 6 are not included in this data set. Members of Congress are thus likely to be interested in the geographic distribution of the sample programs regardless of whether

Table 7.2 Characteristics of Program Formulas in the Sample ($N = 42$)

Characteristic	%	N
Formulas with a small-state minimum	71.4	30
Formulas with a large-state maximum	4.8	2
Formulas with state population as a formula factor	33.3	14
Formulas with targeted state population as a factor	52.4	22
Formulas with a population factor	76.2	32
Formulas with a population factor and a small-state minimum	59.5	25

they are categorized as distributive or redistributive. Because all the programs examined are specifically grants-in-aid to geographic areas, conflict over geographic distribution in the redistributive programs in this sample will be more common than in the whole population of redistributive programs. But there is still reason to suspect that geographical considerations will play less of a role in redistributive than in distributive politics and that other considerations, such as ideology, will play a greater role. When ideological conflict occurs over redistributive programs, it is likely to overshadow issues of geographic distribution.

There is also reason to think that the size of the program will be related to the incidence of conflict between the chambers. The logic here is that there is little point in fighting to gain a bigger share of a very small pie. Members of Congress have greater incentives to press for a more favorable distribution of funds when there is more to gain from a change in the formula. The sample programs range in size from $2 million (the Elder Abuse Program under Special Programs for the Aging) to $4.9 billion (the National School Lunch Program), with a median program size of $350 million. All other things being equal, we expect to find more House-Senate conflict over large programs than over small ones.

Conflict between the House and Senate over funding formulas occurred on 64 percent of the programs examined here (twenty-seven out of forty-two).[20] Because the dependent variable in this case, House-Senate conflict, can take only two values (yes or no), OLS regression is not appropriate. Instead we employ a logit model to test the hypothesis that program type and program size are related to House-Senate conflict. Programs are coded as 1 if House-Senate conflict occurred over the program formula at some point in its history and 0 if it did not. Similarly, for the program type variable distributive programs are coded as 1, redistributive programs as 0, and for the program size variable large programs (>$350 million) are coded as 1, small programs (<$350 million) as 0.[21] The results of this logit model are displayed in table 7.3.

As can be seen in table 7.3, both the program type and the program size variables have a positive and significant effect on the incidence of House-Senate conflict. House-Senate conflict is more likely to occur over large programs than small ones and over distributive rather than redistributive programs. Also included in table 7.3 is the exponentiation of the coefficients, exp (B), which serves as "a single summary statistic for the partial effect of a given predictor on the odds" (Demaris 1992, 48). In this case exp (B) represents the increase in the odds that House-Senate conflict will occur if the program is distributive rather than redistributive (3.82) or large rather than small (5.79). In addition, table 7.3 includes a measure of fit, the proportion

Table 7.3 Logit Model of House-Senate Conflict over Program Formulas

Variable Name	B (SE)	exp (B)
Program type	1.34*	3.82
	(0.75)	
Program size	1.75**	5.79
	(0.76)	
Constant	−0.81	
−2 log likelihood	46.05	
Correctly predicted (%)	73.81	
N	42	

*$p < .1$; **$p < .05$.

of cases correctly predicted by the model, in this case 73.81 percent, suggesting that the model goes some way in explaining the incidence of House-Senate conflict.

Although table 7.3 shows that the expected relationships hold, it may be easier to assess them if the data used to obtain these estimates are also presented in tabular form. Table 7.4 displays this information, along with the chi-square tests for the cross-tabulations. The relationships between the variables shown in table 7.3 can be seen in table 7.4. House-Senate conflict, for example, occurred more often over the distributive programs in the sample (76.2 percent of the time) than over the redistributive programs (52.4 percent). Similarly, House-Senate conflict occurred considerably more often over the large programs (81.0 percent of the time) than over the small ones (47.6 percent). Within each size group, distributive programs were more conflictual: small distributive programs were considerably more contentious (63.6 percent) than small redistributive ones (27.8 percent); and large distributive programs (90 percent) were more conflictual than large redistributive ones (72.7 percent). As the controls included in table 7.4 show, most distributive programs in the sample were conflictual, regardless of size. Small redistributive programs tended not to cause House-Senate conflict; large redistributive programs, however, exhibited House-Senate conflict nearly three-quarters of the time. This suggests, as in table 7.3, that program size is a better predictor of House-Senate conflict than program type.

In sum, these findings reveal a pattern of House-Senate conflict over formula distributions, with disputes occurring in a majority of the cases examined. The presence of House-Senate conflict suggests that the findings in chapter 6 are not happenstance. Both chambers take an interest in formula

Table 7.4 House–Senate Conflict by Program Type and Program Size

Category	House–Senate Conflict	
	Yes	No
Distributive	76.2% $(16)^a$	23.8% (5)
Redistributive	52.4 (11)	47.6 (10)
Large (>\$350 million)	81.0 (17)	19.0 (4)
Small (<\$350 million)	47.6 (10)	52.4 (11)
Large distributive	90.0 (9)	10.0 (1)
Small distributive	63.6 (7)	36.4 (4)
Large redistributive	72.7 (8)	27.3 (3)
Small redistributive	27.8 (3)	72.2 (7)
x^2 for program type by House–Senate conflict	2.59	
x^2 for program size by House–Senate conflict	5.08**	
x^2 for program size, controlling for program type (distributive)	2.01	
x^2 for program size, controlling for program type (redistributive)	3.83*	
x^2 for program type, controlling for program size (large)	1.01	
x^2 for program type controlling for program size (small)	2.38	

^{a} N is given in parentheses.
*$p < .1$; **$p < .05$

distributions, especially when there is a large amount of money at stake. Although the politics of distributing federal funds is often characterized as consensual and based on logrolling within the House and Senate, these findings indicate that conflict between the chambers is more common than consensus.

The findings in chapter 6 suggest that House–Senate conflict will often reflect the differing apportionment bases of the two chambers and that much of the time the Senate will tilt the final distribution to advantage small states. We next address the substance and outcomes of these disputes to determine whether these expectations hold. Does House–Senate conflict occur over small-state minimums? Does it occur over the formula factors in ways that are consistent with the different bases of apportionment of the two chambers? If disputes do occur, are they frequently resolved in favor of the Senate? The answers to these questions will either support or call into question the empirical findings in chapter 6.

Substance of House-Senate Conflict

In this section we will explore the issues at stake in interchamber conflicts, who initiates disputes over existing program formulas, and most important, which chamber wins when House-Senate conflict occurs.[22] For the forty-two programs in the sample, there are fifty-five incidents of House-Senate conflict over funding formulas.[23] Table 7.5 classifies these incidents according to the formula characteristic at issue between the two chambers. As can be seen here, disputes were just as likely to be over formula factors (40 percent) as over minimum guarantees (41.8 percent). Disputes over maximum allocations were uncommon, but this is because maximums themselves are rare, appearing in only two of the forty-two sample formulas.

Conflict over Minimum Allocations

In twenty-two of the twenty-three cases in which a small-state minimum is the issue between the chambers, the Senate is in favor of the small-state minimum while the House opposes it.[24] This is true whether the Senate is trying to add a minimum to a program, increase the size of an existing minimum, or protect an existing minimum from the House's efforts to reduce or eliminate it. The House is on the other side of the issue, resisting the inclusion of minimums, opposing any increases in their size, and occasionally seeking to reduce or remove existing minimums.

A striking example of House-Senate conflict over a minimum allocation occurred in 1972 concerning the funding formula for state grants for area planning and social services under Title 3 of the Older Americans Act of 1965 (*Statutes at Large* 1965, 221). The original formula was, to say the least,

Table 7.5 Sources of House-Senate Conflict over Program Formulas

Source of Conflict	%	N
Conflict over minimum guarantee (only)	41.8	23
Conflict over other formula factors (only)	40.0	22
Conflict over both minimum and other formula factors	14.6	8
Conflict over a maximum (only)	3.6	2
All conflicts	100.0	55

very generous to small states. It included a 1 percent minimum for each state, thus distributing fully half of the total program funds equally among the states. Above this 1 percent floor, every state then received a share of the remainder based on its proportion of the nation's population aged sixty-five and older. Surprisingly, there was no House-Senate conflict over this formula in 1965, perhaps because the original authorization was small—only $5 million in 1966 (*Congressional Quarterly Almanac* 1965, 356).

As the program expanded twentyfold over the following six years (to $100 million by 1973), conflict over the minimum developed. In the 1972 reauthorization the House sought to reduce it to a floor of $250,000. Although this dollar amount was equal to about 0.25 percent of the total 1973 outlay, it would certainly decrease as a proportion of the program as it grew in subsequent years. The Senate bill in 1972 did not change the existing minimum of 1 percent, under which each state would have received more than $1 million in 1973 regardless of the size of its elderly population (at least $750,000 more per minimum allocation state per year than under the House formula).

In the conference compromise the two chambers agreed to reduce the small-state minimum from 1 percent to 0.5 percent, but this was not a simple matter of splitting the difference (U.S. House, Committee on Education and Labor 1972, 48). Instead, the conference compromise provided for two formulas to be used to distribute funds under this program, one for the first year of the authorization and another for subsequent years. Under the formula for the first year, every state would first receive the minimum allotment, 0.5 percent of the total, and then a proportion of the remainder based on its population sixty and older. (This was basically the old formula with the minimum reduced from 1 percent to 0.5 percent.) After the first year, however, the funds would be allotted to states solely based on population sixty and older, with the 0.5 percent minimum serving as a floor (no state could receive less than 0.5 percent of the total). This second formula was less generous to states with small populations in distributing the funds solely by population aged sixty or older rather than equally among the states at first. The amount allotted to each state under the formula in the first year, however, served as a "hold-harmless" provision under the conference compromise, meaning that no state could receive less in any year than it had received in that year. This "hold-harmless" provision protected the minimum allocation states that would have lost funds under the new formula.

Defending the conference report on the House floor, Representative Albert Quie (R-Minn.), the ranking minority member on the House Committee on Education and Labor, made it clear that the dispute over the minimum was rooted in the different apportionment bases of the two chambers and their differing notions of an "equitable" distribution.

Another major bone of contention was the difference between the distribution formulas for program grants to the states under Title III. . . . the Senate bill would have distributed a full 1 percent of the appropriations to each state . . . before anything was allotted on the basis of the number of persons to be served. Thus the Senate version proved very unfair to all of the medium-sized and large population states, particularly those having higher concentrations of elderly citizens. While it could be argued that the House version might not give enough to the smallest states to permit them to mount an effective effort. . . . The final compromise was to use for the initial year a formula which gives the smaller states a little bit more than under Title VII, and then revert to the Title VII formula in succeeding years but using the first year allotment as a minimum amount. . . . So it appears the result will be fair to all states, at least after the first 2 fiscal years. (*Congressional Record* 1972, 36400)

The conflict over the formula, and especially the minimum, as described by Quie, was between the House position, representing the interests of "medium-sized and large population states" and the Senate's 1 percent minimum, rooted in that chamber's concern for "the smallest states." Note Quie's skepticism about the Senate's claim that the House version, with its $250,000 floor, was unfair to the small states. This skepticism is reflected in his qualified concession that "it could be argued that the House version might not give enough to the smallest states to permit them to mount an effective effort." Skeptical of the Senate conferees' interpretations of "fairness" or not, Quie and the House had to accept them to get the program approved and thus to secure any benefits at all for their constituents.

This case is atypical, however, in that the House rarely attempts to reduce or eliminate a small-state minimum. Conflict between the chambers over minimum allocations usually occurs when the Senate adds a new minimum guarantee to a program or seeks to increase the existing one. After a new minimum is successfully added by the Senate in conference, the House does not typically revisit the issue. Rarely does the House have enough at stake to challenge minimum allocations. It appears that only a formula like this example, one with such an expensive minimum, provides enough incentive for the House to seek reductions in the minimum, and then only after the program has grown large enough to make it worthwhile.

There are at least two reasons to think the 0.5 percent minimum reflects a sort of interchamber modus vivendi. First, this is the most common type of minimum. In the sample, 70 percent of the small-state minimums are percentage minimums (twenty-one out of thirty), guaranteeing every state a percentage of the total allotment to all states, and 80 percent of these percentage minimums are 0.5 percent floors (seventeen out of twenty-one). In short, a majority of the minimums in the sample (seventeen out of thirty) are 0.5 percent minimums (56.7 percent).

Second, there are instances in the public record of senators' stating that the 0.5 percent minimum is the most they can generally expect the House to agree to in conference. In a 1984 debate over the Interstate Repair Program (referred to as the 4-R program, CFDA 20.205), for example, several senators expressed this view in response to an amendment that would have raised the minimum from 0.5 percent to 1 percent. Sen. Arlen Specter (R-Pa.) offered this amendment in an effort to induce the Senate to adopt the House's population-friendly formula for the program.[25] The Senate committee bill contained another formula, more favorable to less populous states, but with only a 0.5 percent minimum. Arguing against the Specter amendment, Sen. Steven Symms (R-Idaho) said:

> Mr. President, the formula change offered today by the Senator from Pennsylvania concerns me greatly. In its current form, this formula even benefits slightly my own State of Idaho. However, we think all Senators should note that the only reason it does so is because it contains the 1 percent minimum.
>
> Now, my colleagues . . . who have been on these conferences longer than this Senator, can tell you if the Senate went to conference with the other body, we would find it virtually impossible to come back with a 1-percent minimum allocation. We have done very well to have a half-percent minimum allocation. So all those who may think your State is getting more from Specter, after conference you will probably not be doing so well.
>
> There has been a long tradition of minimum allocations to ensure that each State has a viable highway program, and I do support that concept. But I think it is unrealistic to believe that a 1-percent minimum can be maintained for the 4-R formula when the House has no minimum, and current law is one-half of 1 percent. (*Congressional Record* 1984, 29807)

Symms considers the Senate fortunate to have maintained the 0.5 percent minimum against previous House opposition and warns his colleagues that seeking a higher minimum would be "unrealistic," because it would never survive conference negotiations. Symms's point is reinforced by several other senators. Speaking next, Sen. Randolph (D-W.Va.) commented that he did "not believe that it [the 1 percent minimum] could be retained in a conference with the House of Representatives" (*Congressional Record* 1984, 29808). The chair of the Environment and Public Works Committee, Sen. Robert Stafford (R-Vt.), said this:

According to the Specter formula my own state of Vermont would get twice as much as it currently does. This is certainly a great temptation. However, this increase is due entirely to the change from the current formula's one-half of 1 percent minimum to a 1-percent minimum. Because of my long association with the Federal-Aid Highway Program and the tremendous effort it has taken to maintain one-half of 1 percent minimums for this program, I know that 1 percent is wishful thinking. The interstate 4-R formula in the House bill has no minimum at all. I assure my colleagues that I will do everything I can to maintain the current one-half of 1 percent minimum. If that is not possible, I believe transportation legislation this year is very doubtful. I urge my colleagues who represent one-half of 1 percent States not to vote for this formula, however, on the basis of unrealistic increases. (*Congressional Record* 1984, 29812)

Stafford is clear, based on his "long association" with the program, that "tremendous effort" has been required to maintain the 0.5 percent minimum and that the "1 percent [minimum] is wishful thinking." He goes so far to say that if he and his fellow conferees cannot maintain the current 0.5 percent minimum then "transportation legislation this year is very doubtful." In other words, the passage of the program itself in the Senate depends on the inclusion of the 0.5 percent minimum.

These comments suggest the following situation. Although senators, especially those from small states, might want to increase the small-state minimum, they know that the House would reject such an increase in conference. The House, on the other hand, would prefer to remove small-state minimums—at least from large programs like the 4-R program—but if these senators are to be believed, removing or decreasing small-state minimums would in many cases jeopardize the passage of the final bill. The 0.5 percent minimum in this case (as well as in the case of Special Programs for the Aging discussed above and likely in many others) represents an equilibrium point above which the House will not go and below which the Senate will not accept the legislation. Whatever the type or amount of the minimum, however, this observed pattern of Senate proclivity toward minimum allocations and House resistance to them clearly demonstrates that the differences in the apportionment bases of the two chambers lie at the root of their different preferences.

Conflict over Formula Factors

Preference for minimum allocations is obviously related to the Senate's basis of apportionment. It is somewhat more difficult to demonstrate unambiguously that conflicts over other formula factors result from the different apportionment bases of the two chambers because doing so requires more data than are usually available. To make this case one must have data showing the funds states would receive under the alternative formulas. Many times these data are unavailable: members of Congress do not usually introduce this information into the *Congressional Record,* and it is rarely included as part of any committee or agency report. The conflict over the Substance Abuse block grant, however, provides strong indication that House-Senate conflicts over formula factors are also the result of the two chambers' different bases of apportionment.

In 1988 and 1992 there was House-Senate conflict, as well as a great deal of controversy within the Senate between senators from large and small states, over the funding formula for the Block Grants for Prevention and Treatment of Substance Abuse (CFDA 93.959), a large federal grant program that allocated more than $1.2 billion to states in 1995. During committee consideration of the bill in 1988, Sen. Edward Kennedy (D-Mass.) sought to rework the formula to weight it toward urban youth, those thought most likely to need treatment for substance abuse. The Senate-passed version of the bill contained a formula factor for urban population, weighted at 20 percent. But the House took advantage of Kennedy's initiative to direct funds to urban areas by pressing for even greater increases in the urban population factor weight.

Bills reauthorizing the program had passed both chambers late in the One Hundredth Congress, and members were under pressure to complete the legislation before adjourning. Because of this time constraint there was no official conference—differences were worked out during informal meetings and a "leadership summit" (*Congressional Quarterly Almanac* 1988). When the final version of the bill emerged from this "quasi-conference," the program contained a new funding formula weighted twice as heavily toward urban areas as that passed by the Senate (a 40 percent weight for the urban population factor). The compromise bill with the heavy urban weight passed the Senate at 3:00 A.M. on October 22, the last action taken by the One Hundredth Congress. Many senators felt they had been "blindsided" by the surprise change in the formula (Dumas 1991a, 1590).

Even before the program came up for reauthorization in 1992, many senators were pressing for a change in the formula to reduce the weight on urban population. In 1990 Sen. Tom Harkin (D-Iowa) introduced legislation (S. 2256) that would have eliminated the urban factor in the formula. Changing the formula was one of Sen. Dale Bumper's (D-Ark.) announced top priorities for 1991 (Dumas 1991a, 1590). Other senators tried to amend the funding formula before reauthorization through the appropriations process (Dumas 1991a). Responding to this pressure, the Senate passed a change in the funding formula in 1992, under the leadership of Kennedy once again, to revise the urban population factor downward, despite the expectation of a "battle with the House" over the issue (Dumas 1991b, 1990).

The 1992 House bill did maintain the existing formula favoring urban areas. As one might expect, there was no conflict in the House between 1988 and 1992 comparable to the uproar in the Senate. The House bill did make one minor concession to rural areas: a proposal for a new Office of Rural Mental Health under the National Institute of Mental Health to conduct research and administer project grants to provide more mental health services in rural areas. By doing this, the House sought to accommodate complaints from rural areas in a way (project grants) that was more consistent with its apportionment base than a shift away from urban areas in the national funding formula. This proposal, however, did not go far enough toward rural areas and small states to satisfy the Senate.[26]

The 1992 conference "essentially adopted the Senate formula" (U.S. House, Committee on Energy and Commerce 1992, 135), which substantially reduced the weight on the urban population factor. The House conceded to the Senate on this issue to gain something more important to it—a reorganization of the program to make states more accountable to Congress, a measure opposed by Republicans in the Senate as well as by the administration (*Congressional Quarterly Almanac* 1992, 423). When the conference report was considered on the House floor, a number of members from populous states criticized the legislation. The Florida delegation was particularly exercised. The statement of Rep. Porter Goss (R-Fla.) is characteristic of the criticisms raised:

> I would like to be able to rise in support of S. 1306 because it has a lot of good material in it that is going to do a lot of good for needs that we have in our Nation that have been well-identified. Unfortunately, it also has a fatal flaw of unfairness in it. It has retroactively taken away from our fourth most populous State, which has many, many well-documented needs in this area, funds which are critical for us to do our job down there, to the point it has alerted the Governor and the whole delegation. (*Congressional Record* 1992, 3388)

Despite such complaints, the conference report passed the House (358–60). Sen. Bob Graham (D-Fla.) objected to taking up the conference report in the Senate and forced a number of delaying measures, but the Senate invoked cloture (84–9) and then approved the conference report as well (86–8). As one might expect, senators from populous states were willing to approve the conference report because sustained opposition would not have gained more for their states and might have prevented any funds from being authorized at all, given the preferences of the Senate as a whole.

The conflicts over the formula factors for apportioning the Substance

Abuse block grants clearly derived from the different apportionment bases of the two chambers. The measure increasing funds for urban areas and populous states was uncontroversial in the House in 1988 and thereafter. The Senate's hasty agreement to it at the end of the One Hundredth Congress, however, caused three years of ongoing controversy, with senators from small states pressing for a change in the formula. In fact subsequent events might lead one to conclude that the 1988 change never would have occurred had the Senate had more time to consider it. The formula was changed again by the Senate in 1992, despite the House's opposition. The conflict over this block grant is a clear example of the ways the different bases of apportionment influence preferences for formula factors in the House and Senate. In the following section we examine whether the differences between the two chambers over formula distributions are greater than the differences among their respective members.

Intrachamber Conflict in the House and Senate

The dispute between urban and rural states within the Senate over the Substance Abuse block grant (discussed above) illustrates how conflict over formulas occurs more frequently in the Senate than in the House. Only two floor fights over funding formulas occurred in the House (among the programs examined in the sample). These took place during consideration of the two Community Development block grant programs in 1974 and 1978 (CFDA 14.218 and 14.228).[27] In the Senate, by contrast, there were floor fights over five separate programs: the Substance Abuse block grant program (CFDA 93.959); the Low-Income Home Energy Assistance program, or LIHEAP (CFDA 93.568); the Interstate Construction program (CFDA 20.205); the Minimum Allocation highway aid program (CFDA 20.205); and the Vocational Rehabilitation Services program (CFDA 84.126). Differences in state population size were at the root of all but one of these internal conflicts over distribution.[28] The one exception was the floor fight over LIHEAP, which pitted states with warm climates against states with cold climates in a battle over home energy subsidies. In the rest of this section we will discuss the 1978 Senate floor fights over the Vocational Rehabilitation Services program, which clearly illustrate the different notions of equity in distribution held by senators from more and less populous states.

Although the Vocational Rehabilitation Services program is one of the oldest grants-in-aid, dating back to the Smith-Fess Act of 1920, the funding formula at issue in the 1978 floor fight had been established in 1954. The conflict was not over the minimum, which had been raised in 1973 to $2 million or 0.25 percent of the total authorization, whichever was greater, but over the formula factors. In fact, small-state minimum guarantees were not the subject of any of the Senate floor fights in the sample. Because in most cases minimum guarantees account for a very small proportion of the funds distributed to states, they are not likely to cause much controversy in the Senate. Formula factors, on the other hand, have the potential to impose far greater costs on the larger states. This is the problem with the Vocational Rehabilitation Services formula, which placed heavy weight on state per capita income, thus weighting the distribution toward poorer, less populous states.[29]

In 1978 the Senate Committee on Labor and Human Resources, under the leadership of Sens. Edward M. Kennedy (D-Mass.), Jacob Javits (R-N.Y.), and Harrison Williams (D-N.J.), reported out the reauthorization bill containing a revised formula for the program. Under this formula, program funds up to the fiscal year 1978 level ($760 million) would have been allotted under the old formula, but funds over that level would have been allotted solely by state population. The reason offered for this change in the committee report was that "the effect of the [existing] formula has been to increase the disparity of funding among the States. By fiscal year 1973, for example, the 25 States receiving the lowest per capita allotments for vocational rehabilitation services contained virtually 75 percent of the Nation's population" (U.S. Senate, Committee on Labor and Human Resources 1978, 6).

When this committee bill was brought up for consideration on the Senate floor, this new formula was immediately challenged by an amendment, offered by Sen. Dale Bumpers (D-Ark.), that retained the 1954 formula unchanged. Introducing his amendment, Bumpers argued: "What the new funding formula does is strike a mortal blow to States such as mine, the State of West Virginia, and other States similarly situated. What we are going to do under this bill is betray the American ethic. We will not just help those people who need help, but we will help those people who happen to have the most people in their state" (*Congressional Record* 1978, 30560). It is clear from this statement that Bumpers's resistance to the new formula was due to the funds his state would lose to the more populous states if even some of the program funds were distributed solely by population. Bumpers continued this line of attack, framing the formula change in zero-sum terms:

Let me give an example. New York is going to enjoy an increase of more than $2 million in 1979, with corresponding increases of $4.2 and $4 million during the next two years. California's share is going to increase by $3.3 million in 1979, $5.1 million in 1980, and $4.9 million in 1981.

What we are doing here is changing the way we have been dividing up the Federal pie. We will not pay attention to need any more. We will just use a head count.

I know the distinguished Senator from New York who is here in the Chamber says that his State deserves an additional $1 million in 1979 alone. But I wonder if he realizes that the $3 million increase for his State in 1979 is more than the total grant received by 9 States in 1978. That increase to New York under the amount of money being appropriated is being given to them at the expense of the poorest people in the country. (*Congressional Record* 1978, 30560)

Bumpers's argument is that New York's gain is a loss for "the poorest people in the country," so long as those poorest people reside in relatively small states. The senators opposing the new formula on the floor tended to be, like Bumpers, from smaller than average states that did not benefit from the small-state minimum. The minimum allocation states would not have been adversely affected by the new formula; in fact the committee bill included an increase in the minimum from $2 million or 0.25 percent of the total, whichever was greater, to $3 million or 0.33 percent. Interestingly, Bumpers observes in this context that the additional $3 million provided for New York under the proposed alternative formula was more than nine other (small) states received in total funds under the program. His comment reveals the disadvantage senators from populous states face in bargaining over distributive programs in the Senate. Large states are very expensive compared with small ones; increasing benefits to them is similarly more expensive. By contrast, providing additional funds to small states is inexpensive, making it much easier for Senate coalition builders to accommodate the preferences of small-state senators.

In response to the Bumpers amendment, Javits offered a perfecting amendment that would have reduced the formula's weight on per capita income. Javits's statement evinces frustration with formula politics in the Senate:

Mr. President, I am going to belabor this issue. It is high time that it was belabored, because, Mr. President, there are few things more unfair in this country than the formulas, encrusted with age and injustice, under which funds like these have been distributed. Handicapped people who need to be rehabilitated are just as handicapped and deserving if they live in New York or California or Illinois or Michigan as they are if they live in Arkansas. What is being attempted here by this amendment on the part of Governor Bumpers is to perpetuate a deep injustice, which, at long last, we are trying a little bit to undo, but which, the argument is made, should not be undone, notwithstanding that every reason why this was incorporated in the law, this formula, exists to show that it should now be undone.

Now, Mr. President, the usual stops are pulled out. I have heard them so many times. I hope that Members of the Senate are listening on their little speakers to this debate, because it ought to be decided on its merits, and on its merits the committee position itself ought to be sustained, even though, because I am a realist, I have just put in an amendment which very materially modifies the committee position.

These unjust formulas, which have been very harmful to highly populous States, have been perpetuated here—and "perpetuated" is exactly the right word. This one is 24 years old and is made completely obsolete by the fact that the income situation in Arkansas and every other State has changed. . . .

Second, we are now appropriating 34 times what we appropriated for this purpose when this formula was written: 34 times more. . . .

Now, what arguments are used to try to perpetuate this outworn, completely unjust formula? The usual ones. I have heard them in this Chamber for 20 years: get New York. . . .

Second, he [Bumpers] said, "Look at your chart and you'll see you get a little more dough."

This is the same argument. People rush in to vote and look at the chart. If they get a little more money, they vote that way. (*Congressional Record* 1978, 30563)

The conflict in this case is clearly between two notions of equity. Javits's idea is that similar numbers of people needing rehabilitation services should receive equal amounts per capita. Weighting the formula to deviate from a purely population-based distribution is unjust: "Handicapped people . . . are just as handicapped and deserving" regardless of the population of the state they reside in. The senators from smaller states saw things in a different light, however. As Sen. Strom Thurmond (R-S.C.) pithily summed up this position: "Are we going to ignore the small States and the rural States and give to the big rich States many more billions of dollars?" (*Congressional Record* 1978, 30565).

Interestingly, Javits's statement suggests that the problem (from his point of view) was greater than just this one program: "There are few things more unfair in this country than the formulas, encrusted with age and injustice, under which funds like these have been distributed." He even makes the connection between this greater problem and the Senate's apportionment base. Senators "will not listen and pay attention to the equity argument," he argues, because "they rush to consider the chart" (*Congressional Record* 1978, 30564) and then vote for the formula that gives them "a little more dough." Because the most populous states are outnumbered—as well as so expensive to program budgets—they tend to lose out under "unfair" funding formulas that favor smaller states. The Senate often prefers, in Javits's words, to "get New York" in formula politics because New York is where the money is and where Senate votes are not.[30]

The outcome of this floor fight suggests one reason such disputes over funding formulas are rare, even in the Senate: the formulas in Javits's amendment and the committee bill were both voted down on the Senate floor. A compromise, put together hastily during a quorum call, sent the matter to conference for resolution (*Congressional Record* 1978, 30568). The conference version, passed into law in 1978, distributed funds up to the fiscal year 1978 level based on the 1954 formula. Half of the funds beyond the fiscal year 1978 amount were then to be distributed by the 1954 formula with a reduced weight on per capita income, and the other half solely according to state population (U.S. House, Committee on Education and Labor 1978, 2–3). In the end Javits and his colleagues from the more populous states were able to increase their states' shares, but not nearly so much as they wanted. The more populous states just do not have the votes in the Senate to win floor fights over formula factors. Bumpers put the matter in stark terms: "If we are going to get into the city boy–country boy fight, we can stack this body up against New York City, and New York City will get about eight votes" (*Congressional Record* 1978, 30565).

Given the distribution of constituency size in the Senate, the notion of equity held by senators from the less populous states can be expected to win out when conflict between large and small states occurs in the Senate. The notion put forth by Javits, on the other hand, holds greater sway in the House. In fact these two notions of equity were not an issue in the two floor fights over funding formulas in the House. These conflicts were regional in nature, pitting Sun Belt against Rust Belt. There is no evidence of conflict between large and small states in House floor fights, because the House typically writes formulas that distribute funds by population without controversy. In other words, House members from populous states, even though they are a majority in the body, do not typically press for formulas that would distribute more to their states than they would receive based on population. But what is not controversial in the House is in some cases controversial in the Senate, and—given the distribution of votes in the Senate—the Senate is very unlikely to approve a formula favorable to populous states. Thus these competing notions of equity often lead to House-Senate conflicts.

Outcomes of House-Senate Conflict

When there is conflict between the House and Senate over funding formulas, which chamber wins? A number of previous studies have dealt with this question in its broadest form—asking which chamber is more influential in conference committees—but not specifically with reference to House-Senate dispute over funding formulas (Longley and Oleszek 1989; Steiner 1951; Van Beek 1995; Vogler 1971). Many studies of conference committees, in fact, have focused solely on appropriations and tax policy (Fenno 1966; Ferejohn 1975; Manley 1970; Pressman 1966). Here we ask which chamber typically wins in formula writing, a question that has not been the subject of any previous work. To avoid some of the difficulties caused by the sequential nature of the process, a chamber is counted as "winning" a House-Senate conflict only when its preferred formula emerges from conference *unchanged;* any other outcome is regarded as a compromise.[31]

We explore next the relation of program size, program type, and the specific issue at stake to the outcome of House-Senate conflict. To summarize the findings presented below, program size has little effect on which chamber wins; program type, on the other hand, makes a difference, with the Senate winning a majority of the battles over distributive programs and compromise occurring most often on redistributive programs; and finally, when conflict is over a small-state minimum in the program formula, the Senate wins an overwhelming majority of the time.

Table 7.6 displays data on the outcome of House-Senate conflict cross-tabulated with program type and program size. For all programs, a Senate victory is the most common outcome, occurring in almost half of the cases in the sample (47.3 percent). House-Senate compromise is the second most common outcome, occurring about a third of the time (34.5 percent). The House rarely wins outright; in the sample, the House wins in fewer than one-fifth of the conflicts (18.2 percent).

Program size does not appear to have much effect on the outcome of House-Senate conflict. For both large and small programs, a Senate victory is most common. The only difference between large and small programs in the pattern of outcomes is that compromise is more common for large programs, occurring over 40 percent of the time on large programs but less than 20 percent on small ones. It makes intuitive sense that compromise would occur more often over large programs, when more money is at stake. The finding that, overall, program size does not have much effect is somewhat surprising given that program size is important for predicting the incidence of House-Senate conflict (see table 7.2). Once conflict occurs, however, program size has little effect on which chamber wins except that compromise is more likely over large programs.

Program type, on the other hand, is more important than program size for understanding the outcome of House-Senate conflict. Although a Senate victory is the most common outcome for distributive programs (57.9 percent), compromise is the most common for redistributive programs (47.1 percent), with the Senate winning less than a quarter of the time

Table 7.6 Outcome of House-Senate Conflict by Program Type and Program Size

Category	Outcome of Conflict		
	Senate Wins	House Wins	Compromise
All programs	47.3%	18.2%	34.5%
	(26) [a]	(10)	(19)
Distributive	57.9	13.2	28.9
	(22)	(5)	(11)
Redistributive	23.5	29.4	47.1
	(4)	(5)	(8)
Large	43.6	15.4	41.0
	(17)	(6)	(16)
Small	56.3	25.0	18.8
	(9)	(4)	(3)
Large distributive	51.9	7.4	40.7
	(14)	(2)	(11)
Large redistributive	25.0	33.3	41.7
	(3)	(4)	(3)
Small distributive	72.7	27.3	0.0
	(8)	(3)	(0)
Small redistributive	20.0	20.0	60.0
	(1)	(1)	(3)
x^2 for program type by outcome	5.76 *		
x^2 for program size by outcome	2.59		
x^2 for program type, controlling for program size (large)	5.01 *		
x^2 for program type, controlling for program size (small)	8.37 **		
x^2 for program size, controlling for program type (redistributive)	0.50		
x^2 for program size, controlling for program type (distributive)	7.41 **		

[a] N is given in parentheses.
* $p < .1$; ** $p < .05$.

(23.5 percent). The Senate's success in House-Senate conflict over funding formulas, then, is due principally to its edge in distributive programs. Because conflict is more common over distributive programs, as shown in table 7.3, the Senate does better than the House for all program conflicts. This competitive edge in distributive programs is what one would expect given the small-state advantage in such programs found in chapter 6.

The control tables suggest that for distributive programs, program size does influence which chamber wins. Although a Senate victory is the most common outcome for both large and small distributive programs, the Senate wins in almost three-quarters of the conflicts over small distributive programs (72.7 percent), but only in about half of the disputes over large distributive programs. Compromise is fairly common over large distributive programs (40.7 percent), but it never occurred in a conflict over a small distributive program in the study. This is the same pattern observed above in the discussion of program size, with compromise being more common over large programs. These findings suggest that if either chamber has a strong preference about the formula for a small distributive program, then that chamber will win if there is conflict. For large distributive programs, in which more money is at stake, it is more likely that both chambers will care about the outcome, making compromise much more likely. For small distributive programs, on the other hand, House members are less likely to have a strong preference because the program money will be spread so thin that they will expect little benefit. Because states are the recipients of these program funds, senators will have a greater stake even in small distributive programs. This will be especially true of senators from less populous states because "the per capita local benefit is higher for each dollar of net spending transferred to a state the smaller the state's population" (Atlas et al. 1995, 625). There is evidence that at least some senators think this way. Sen. Strom Thurmond (R-S.C.), for example, said in the context of a debate over one program formula:

> If we fail to amend section 105(b) by 1983, almost one-third of vocational rehabilitation funds will be allotted to the States strictly on the basis of population. In South Carolina, . . . the money lost in the formula change would not impress persons from the more populous areas of the country. South Carolina will lose approximately $4.6 million. However, to the people of my State, particularly to those handicapped individuals who seek these services, you can be certain that it means a great deal. (*Congressional Record* 1978, 30565)

Although the amount of money at stake in this program may not be enough to "impress" senators from more populous states, it is enough to concern Thurmond and other senators, especially those from states with populations even smaller than South Carolina's.

These findings suggest that the hypothesized asymmetry of House and Senate incentives does exist. The Senate does appear to be more concerned with funding formulas (for both large and small distributive programs) than the House. Although no direct measurement of the intensity of chamber

Table 7.7 Outcome of House-Senate Conflict by Issue

Issue	Outcome of Conflict		
	Senate Wins	House Wins	Compromise
Minimum only	73.9%	8.7%	17.4%
	(17)[a]	(2)	(4)
Factors only	31.8	27.2	40.9
	(7)	(6)	(9)
Both minimum and other factors	25.0	0.0	75.0
	(2)	(0)	(6)
All[b]	49.1	15.1	35.8
	(26)	(8)	(19)

[a] N is given in parentheses.
[b] The two conflicts over maximum allocations are excluded.
$x^2 = 17.39**$ (.002); $**p < .01$.

preferences is possible here, that the two chambers are formally equal in power, coupled with the finding that the Senate tends to win so much more often in such conflicts, points to a difference in the intensity of the chambers' preferences. That the same pattern does not hold for redistributive programs—compromise is the most likely outcome of House-Senate conflict for both large and small redistributive programs—suggests that the Senate's preferences in redistributive programs are similar to the House's in intensity, making compromise more likely. This difference in preferences may stem from the smaller role geographic considerations play in redistributive policymaking.

The issue in the conflict—whether it is over the minimum, the formula factors, or both—also affects the outcome in a way that supports the findings in chapter 6. Table 7.7 displays the cross-tabulation of outcomes with the issue in the conflict. As can be seen in the table, the Senate wins outright almost three-quarters of the time (73.9 percent) when the conflict is over the small-state minimum. As we argued above, the House will not in most cases resist including small-state minimums in formulas because these provisions represent a concentrated benefit for some senators paid for by a highly dispersed cost distributed over the majority of House districts. When there is conflict over the minimum—for example, when the Senate bill includes a small-state minimum and the House bill does not—the theory and the data agree that in most cases the House will concede. The 0.5 percent minimum appears usually to be acceptable to the House. In short, the prevalence of small-state minimum guarantees is best explained in the words of one large-state senator we interviewed: "It's a compromise because of the nature of the Senate."

When conflict is over the formula factors, on the other hand, the Senate is much less likely to win (31.8 percent). Compromise is the most likely outcome when conflict is over the formula factors (40.9 percent). The House wins less than a third of the time in such cases (27.2).

Note that six of the eight House wins in the sample occurred when the dispute was over the formula factors alone. Four of these House wins took place during the 1974 and 1977 conflicts over the formula for the Community Development block grant programs (CFDA 14.218 and 14.228). These two programs are the only ones in the sample in which the recipients of the funds are not states. Instead, the Community Development block grants go to metropolitan areas, small cities, and local governments,[32] decreasing House members' uncertainty over what their districts will receive. This reduced uncertainty is clear from the numerous tables that House members circulated during consideration of the program, showing how much different cities would receive under alternative formulas (*Congressional Quarterly Almanac* 1974, 1977). Congressional districts, then, were analogous to states in most other formula situations, and the preferences of House members for a particular formula were similar to the preferences of senators under normal conditions. More generally, it may be that the preferences of the House as a whole for a particular formula will increase in intensity as the uncertainty of particular House members decreases.

These few House wins—occurring when unusual circumstances intensified House preferences—are the exception rather than the rule. Overall, the Senate wins almost half of the time when there is House-Senate conflict (49.1 percent), especially over a small-state minimum. In most cases when the Senate does not win outright, there is compromise (35.8 percent of all cases). Together these two outcomes account for 84.9 percent of all House-Senate conflicts. Most of the time, then, the distribution formula preferred by the House is altered toward the Senate position, either in part or in full. This is especially important because movement toward the Senate position is almost always movement away from a population-based distribution. In bargaining with the Senate, the House does not typically "bid up" its preferences by producing formulas that are skewed toward populous states. Instead, it typically sets a population-based distribution as its benchmark before negotiations with the Senate. As a result, even when compromise between the chambers does occur, it is also typically a "win" for the Senate. The pattern shown here suggests that the small-state advantage observed in chapter 6—especially in nondiscretionary distributive policies but across most of the substantive policy areas as well—can be credited to the Senate's influence.

Chapter 6 Revisited

The data presented here go a long way toward confirming that the small-state advantage observed in chapter 6 is the consequence of Senate apportionment and not simply the result of accident or even of House influence. This chapter has also established that one of the primary mechanisms by which the Senate influences funding formulas to advantage small states is minimum guarantees. Disagreements over these small-state minimums account for much of the observed House-Senate conflict. More important, the Senate usually wins these disputes (almost three-quarters of the time), securing the inclusion of a small-state minimum in the funding formula over House opposition.

Small-state minimums, however, may be even more common than House-Senate conflict. In the sample, conflict occurred at some point in the authorization of over 64 percent of the programs, but small-state minimums were included in more than 70 percent of the formulas. There is not always House-Senate conflict over a small-state minimum. Minimum guarantees can be included in any number of consensual ways. When writing the formula for a new program, for example, the House and Senate may adopt the formula from an existing program, and thus its minimum, without conflict (this occurred twice in the sample). In addition, the House members may anticipate Senate objections and include a small-state minimum in the House bill to avoid unnecessary disagreements. Further research might demonstrate that members of both chambers take the inclusion of small-state minimums for granted owing to the asymmetry of House and Senate preferences for them.

Is the imprint of these small-state minimums visible in the aggregate data on per capita outlays to states presented in chapter 6? Under a common formula based on state population with a 0.5 percent minimum, states with less than 0.5 percent of the United States population will get additional funds as a result of the minimum. Therefore these states will receive a windfall, but all others will receive equal per capita outlays. Recall the shape of the curves presented in figures 6.1 and 6.2. All these curves reveal a pronounced advantage in per capita outlays (controlling for state need) for states with the lowest scores on the representation index, with each curve flattening out over the higher values on the index.

Figure 7.1 reproduces the curve for average per capita outlays under nondiscretionary distributive programs from figure 3.1 (after holding all the control variables in the model constant at their means), with a vertical line added at 0.25 on the representation index, the equivalent of 0.5 percent of the total United States population.[33] The states on the left of this line receive additional funds as a result of 0.5 percent minimums under the typical formula

Figure 7.1. Effects of Senate apportionment on average per capita outlays for nondiscretionary programs, 1984–90; vertical line indicates states with less than 0.5 percent of the nation's population

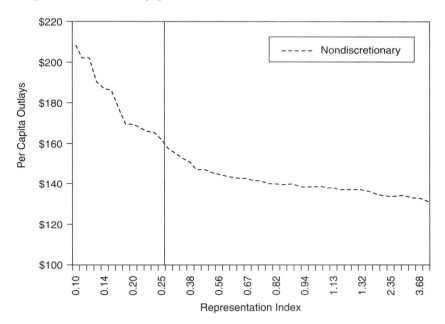

and thus higher per capita outlays. The states on the right side, however, receive funds based solely on their populations. Although the curve to the right of this line is not flat (as it would be under a purely population-based distribution), it is much flatter than the curve on the left. There is more than a $40 per capita difference between the least populous state (Wyoming, 0.10 on the representation index) and the state on the 0.5 percent vertical line (Maine, 0.25). The difference in per capita outlays between the 0.5 percent line (Maine) and the most populous state (California, 5.98), a much greater range on the representation index, is only about $30.

The same pattern holds for the curves in figure 6.2 for per capita outlays in programs grouped by policy area. Some of the programs in all of these policy areas are formula grants. In fact, minimum guarantees in these formula grants probably account for much of the shape of these curves, biasing the distribution toward small states.

Figure 7.1 suggests that the presence of 0.5 percent minimums explains a considerable proportion, but not all, of the variation in per capita outlays under federal programs. The rest of the variation seen in figures 6.1 and 6.2

stems from three other causes. First, some of the variation not explained by the 0.5 percent minimums is undoubtedly due to formula factors—such as state per capita income in the case of Vocational Rehabilitation Services—that advantage less populous states, although the effect of these is more difficult to gauge. Second, in the case of the project grants-in-aid represented by the curve for discretionary distributive programs in figure 6.1 and included in the substantive policy areas displayed in figure 6.2, the observed small-state advantage is in part attributable to the tendency of small-state senators to seek assignment to constituency committees, as discussed in chapter 5. Small-state senators' overrepresentation on constituency committees gives their states an additional advantage in procuring discretionary funds. Third, the strategic behavior of bureaucrats in cultivating Senate coalitions to support the programs they administer compounds the small-state advantage. In particular, adding small-population states as beneficiaries helps bureaucrats build support for their programs because these states cost less. Even so, it is clear that the pervasive small-state minimums—which the Senate so often adds over House opposition—are one of the most important causes of the small-state advantage in federal per capita outlays to states.

Conclusion

The politics of formula writing in Congress can be summarized in the following way. The typical funding formula is—as one would expect given the apportionment bases of the two chambers—a modified population-based distribution. Senate preferences require the modifications of the population-based distributions preferred by the House. As one senator commented in a debate over a formula, "Any time we put something on a population base, we do not have to be 'broke out with brilliance' to know who is going to benefit from it. Everyone knows where the most people are in this country" (Sen. Jennings Randolph [D-W.Va.], in *Congressional Record* 1978, 30566).

Senate modification of the population-based distribution takes the form of a minimum guarantee or of formula factors favoring smaller states. In most cases a minimum guarantee is used, because representatives of populous states in both House and Senate will object to formula factors that distribute too much to the small states or too little to the large ones. In this context it is interesting that the Senate usually does not win outright when there is disagreement over formula factors, as it does when the dispute is over a minimum. When conflict over funding formulas occurs within the Senate, it typically centers on formula factors that senators from more populous states regard as unjustly biasing distributions. A minimum, by contrast, is a concentrated benefit with a dispersed cost and thus will not generate the same intensity of opposition as a biased formula that imposes greater costs on more populous states.

Thus differences in their bases of apportionment shape the distributional preferences of the two chambers, leading to conflict between them. Equal representation of states in the Senate causes that chamber to prefer distributing federal funds more equally across states than does the House. Senate preferences, especially regarding small-state minimums, tend to predominate in the writing of funding formulas, producing a small-state advantage in per capita distribution.

The most interesting aspect of the findings presented here is that they have for so long escaped scholarly and political attention. This lack of attention is especially odd given the intense feelings that issues of representation—ethnic, racial, or gender—often evoke. The reason is clear: Americans, and political scientists who study American politics, tend to take the Senate, and its effects on American democracy, for granted. We hope these findings will enable us once again to view the Senate for what it is—an institutional choice with enduring consequences, both anticipated and unanticipated.

Madison certainly did not take the Senate for granted. In *Federalist* 62, an essay defending the Senate, he wrote:

> No law or resolution can now be passed without the concurrence, first, of a majority of the people, and then, of a majority of the States. It must be acknowledged that this complicated check on legislation may in some instances be injurious as well as beneficial; and that the peculiar defense which it involves in favor of the smaller States would be more rational, if any interests common to them, and distinct from those of the other States, would otherwise be exposed to danger. (365)

He was well aware that "this complicated check" would be, "in some instances . . . injurious as well as beneficial" and that this "peculiar defense . . . in favor of the smaller States" was somewhat less than perfectly "rational." Logic, after all, did not dictate the Senate—politics did.

From a path-dependent perspective, the effects of Senate apportionment on federal distributive policy today can be described as the unanticipated consequences of an institutional choice made in the late eighteenth century. Even though they deliberated at length about Senate apportionment, Madison and the other founding fathers certainly did not foresee the extent of the federal government's present role in administering and distributing funds for domestic programs. This new federal role meant that a preexisting institution, Senate apportionment, came to influence American politics in a new way. The overrepresentation of the citizens of the least populous states means that they receive more program funds per capita from the federal government than the citizens of the most populous states. One unanticipated consequence of the Great Compromise, then, is that it now creates a situation in which citizens are treated differently based on where they happen to reside.

As we argued above, this inequality built into the system is not counterbalanced by the House of Representatives. Madison maintained that the House's role in initiating revenue bills would prevent the equal representation of states in the Senate from having much of an effect: "The larger States will always be able, by their power over supplies, to defeat unreasonable exertions of this prerogative of the lesser States" (366). This has not proved true because the incentives of the two chambers regarding distribution formulas are not the same. Because they can never be certain how much their constituents will actually receive, most House members have less incentive to pursue funding formulas favorable to their constituencies than do senators, who operate under much less uncertainty. In addition, House members cannot plausibly take credit for benefits accruing to their states from a funding formula. This imbalance of incentives is especially important given that the bulk of domestic assistance funds are distributed by statutory formula.

This is an interesting finding because most of the congressional literature has implicitly assumed that the House is more concerned with particularistic benefits than is the Senate. It is true that House members are likely to pursue project grants, which they can be certain their constituencies will receive. Senators, on the other hand, are more concerned with funding formulas. If project grants are the pork barrel of the House, formula grants are the pork barrel of the Senate. As Sen. Robert S. Kerr (D-Okla.) said about the reason formulas are favored by the Senate:

> In the absence of a formula, the Senator from New Hampshire might go back home and tell the people of his State about the great highway bill we passed, and the many billions of dollars which are to be spent on the development of an Interstate System, and then have the unhappy experience of seeing two years go by and not a dollar spent either in New Hampshire or in Oklahoma—which would be a matter, I am sure, of as grave concern to the Senator from New Hampshire as it would be to the Senator from Oklahoma. (*Congressional Record* 1956, 9082)

Senators prefer formulas to other means of distribution because they can be certain their states will receive funds under a favorable formula. This enables them, Kerr argues, to claim credit for the funds allocated to their states. This is the sort of credit claiming usually associated with project grants in the House, but the money at stake in the typical formula grant is much greater than that in the typical project grant. In other words, senators can pursue much larger particularistic benefits for their constituents, and then claim credit for them, because of the central place of states in the federal system. As they do so, the Senate's unique basis of apportionment comes to shape the way those federal funds are distributed, creating a pronounced and pervasive small-state advantage.

8

The Undemocratic Senate?

E qual representation of states in the Senate was the price paid for political union in 1787. The Great Compromise settled the most divisive issue at the Constitutional Convention and paved the way for the eventual ratification of the United States Constitution. When the framers made Senate apportionment the most untouchable part of the Constitution, however, they could not have anticipated all its future effects. Many of its consequences were completely outside their experience. The idea that Senate apportionment would influence the geographic distribution of federal funds, for example, certainly could not have occurred to them. They were not designing a modern welfare state. The national government they envisioned was one of very limited scope. Even if they had anticipated the federal government's current size and role, they would probably have assumed, as many people do today, that any effects of Senate apportionment would be counterbalanced by the population-based House, as Madison suggested in *Federalist* 62.

Similarly, the framers could not have anticipated how Senate apportionment would later shape the representational relationships of senators and their constituents. They could not have envisioned the immense size of the largest states today. Remember that at its founding the United States had a population of only about three million people. In other words, its entire population in 1790 was approximately equal to that of Connecticut today. Even at the time of the Louisiana Purchase, Jefferson—perhaps the most visionary member of his generation—estimated it would take one hundred generations to populate the new territory. It took only five (Duncan and Burns 1997, 225). The problems of representing California, Texas, or New

York could not have presented themselves to men considering the government of what is, by today's standards, a tiny population.

In addition, the framers did not conceive of senators in the "representative" role they play today. The responsive, "outward-looking" (Sinclair 1989, 2) character of the contemporary Senate is a later development (see Swift 1996). In fact Madison argued for the Senate in *Federalist* 63—his most detailed discussion of the Senate's role in the proposed government—on the grounds that it would "be sometimes necessary as a defense to the people against their own temporary errors and delusions" (370–71). The Senate was expected to play this role because of its greater distance from the people, and individual senators would gain this distance through their long terms of office and their indirect mode of selection. Until the ratification of the Seventeenth Amendment, senators were not popularly elected but selected by the state legislatures. As a result, the framers could not have foreseen the effects of apportionment on Senate elections in terms of either competitiveness or, more recently, campaign fund-raising.

The subsequent development of political institutions has caused Senate apportionment to have other effects that the framers could not have anticipated. They drafted the Constitution before the invention of the modern political party and thus could not have foreseen the effects of apportionment on partisan control of the Senate. The same obviously applies to the ways Senate apportionment shapes the strategic behavior of senators. The framers could hardly have expected that it would influence senators' choices of committee assignments, their level of national media coverage, or their ability to pursue party leadership. None of these institutions—the congressional committee system, national news media, or institutionalized party leadership—existed in 1787.

The contemporary consequences of the Great Compromise for the Senate as a representative and legislative institution are in large part the result of changes in the Senate and its political environment over the past two centuries, changes outside the framers' knowledge or imagination when they agreed to it. Equal representation of states continues to shape the Senate's politics and policymaking in fundamental ways. We have established that Senate apportionment affects four central aspects of the institution: representation, election, strategic behavior, and policymaking. This is true even though the fears of the small-state delegates at the Constitutional Convention have proved unfounded—the most populous states have never joined together to tyrannize the smaller ones. In this sense Senate apportionment protected the small states against a myth. Nevertheless, it continues to have these effects even though the original reason for its adoption, political union among the states, is no longer at issue.

The Senate's basis of apportionment leaves no aspect of the institution untouched. It conditions the representative relationships of senators and their constituents, the cornerstone of democratic government. It influences the competitiveness of elections, the financing and conduct of campaigns, and the partisan control of the Senate. It affects senators' behavior in performing their governing duties as well as the behavior of those trying to influence them. State population size influences the choices senators make regarding their time and resources, the strategies they pursue, and their opportunities for influence within the Senate. Most important, apportionment shapes the way the Senate designs public policy and distributes federal funds to states— the who gets what, when, where, and how that are the basic building blocks of politics. The assumption that the House acts to counterbalance the Senate simply does not hold in distributive policymaking because House members have different incentives than senators.

That Senate apportionment has all these important effects raises several normative issues. Most obviously, equal representation of states violates the principle of one person, one vote. This is important because that principle is the only tenable standard for apportioning legislative chambers in democratic theory today. As political theorist Charles Beitz (1989, 141) has written, "The meaning of quantitative fairness has become a settled matter: it requires adherence to the precept 'one person, one vote.'" Given that the Senate markedly deviates from this "settled matter," it raises issues of "quantitative fairness" indeed. Remember that the Senate is the only legislative body in the United States to which the courts have not applied the one person, one vote standard. Deviation from that standard, however, has not been the focus of our research. Instead we focus on the great variation in the population sizes of the constituencies represented in the Senate. It is these great differences— differences of millions of residents and voters—and not simply the deviation from some mathematical ratio, even one as "settled" as one person, one vote, that affects the Senate as a representative and legislative institution.

Because we focus on the absolute differences in population sizes, this book raises normative issues that go beyond the narrow one person, one vote concerns of others (Eskridge 1995; Geoghegan 1994; Lind 1998). In chapter 3, for example, we demonstrated that people living in states of different population size have markedly different levels of potential access to their congressional representatives. A person in a state with only one congressional district has an equal probability of access to three members of Congress— one House member and two senators. A person in a state with many congressional districts, on the other hand, has access to her House member equal to the small-state resident's but a much lower probability of access to her state's two senators. Moreover, because senators have much greater institutional power than House members, all else being equal, residents of the smallest states reap a bonus in terms of congressional representation.

Intuitively, this bonus presents a normative problem. There is simply no good reason for residents in small states to have significantly greater access to their members of Congress than do residents in large states, and this raises a question of fairness. The issue here, however, is one of equality of access—or at least equality of potential access—not simply one person, one vote, although the two concerns are of course closely linked. This disparity is a problem for the access of both individuals and interest groups to influence in Congress. Democratic theory, in fact, seems to require equality of access to political power because "only under such a system can governmental structure be considered as allowing all significant groups a potentially equal degree of accessibility to the decision-making process" (Baker 1955a, 110). As a result of Senate apportionment, however, individuals and interest groups in small states have representational advantages in the form of greater access to their senators than those in large states. This applies to minority racial and ethnic groups, which tend to be concentrated in large states, and to other interests as well.

The effects of Senate apportionment on partisan control of the Senate also raise issues of fairness. In chapter 4 we showed that equal representation of states often means that one political party wins Senate seats disproportionate to its share of the national popular vote, owing to its success in small-state elections. In an institution that often requires supermajorities to function, the effects on the partisan composition of the Senate need not be great enough to shift control from one party to the other in order to have important consequences. A few seats won or lost can make a great difference in the final shape of public policy. Because of the immense variation in state population, Senate apportionment grants disproportionate weight to small-state voters in determining the composition of the Senate.

Small-state senators are also advantaged by Senate apportionment in a number of ways. In elections, senators from less populous states tend to win by larger margins than their colleagues from larger states. For some, wider margins of victory translate into greater voting leeway. Similarly, campaigning for reelection costs much less in a small state. Small-state senators, then, spend less time raising funds, and they can also raise a higher percentage of what they need from "investors," which, as we suggest in chapter 4, is easier than raising funds from "consumers." Senators from larger states have to spend more time raising campaign funds, start earlier, and raise proportionately more from "consumers." Again, small-state senators have greater flexibility—both in voting leeway and in the allocation of their resources—than their large-state colleagues.

These flexibility advantages raise normative concerns insofar as they result in unfair treatment of those being represented. The greater incentives of small-state senators to pursue a particularized benefits strategy raise similar concerns. Our findings in various areas—committee assignments, hold-out behavior, and the distribution of federal funds—all point to the inequalities that result from the equal representation of states of very different sizes. Similarly, if we are correct about the link between state population and senators' ability to pursue floor leadership in the contemporary Senate, then this would further bias the patterns of influence. Even in an institution characterized by considerable member equality and individual prerogatives, Senate floor leaders still possess power, influence, and resources not available to their colleagues.

Of all our findings, however, those concerning the effects of Senate apportionment on distributive policymaking raise the most important normative issues. Here we are faced with one of the oldest questions in moral theory—distributive justice. Since Aristotle, distributive justice has meant giving everyone his or her due, treating equals equally and treating unequals unequally in proportion to their inequality (see Aristotle 1985, 122–24; Yack 1993, 34). The chief problem for moral theory has always been determining the relevant criteria for equality and thus the appropriate distribution of the goods in question. In public policy this problem is simpler, because the criteria for distributing funds are closely related to the goal of the policy being considered. Funds would then be distributed to states, and thus to the people who live in those states, based on a formula that determines need, the relevant criteria in this case. Equals in terms of need would then be treated equally and unequals in terms of need unequally in proportion to their needs.

This is not what happens in actual policymaking, of course. As we demonstrated in chapter 6, even after controlling for need, people living in the small states receive more per capita than those in the large states. Those similar in all respects other than their place of residence are treated differently. This problem too is more than just one of deviation from the one person, one vote principle: the distribution of federal funds is affected greatly by the vast differences in population among the states. Similarly, our findings that senators from large and small states tend to pursue different strategies in seeking to advance their goals, including reelection, compound the problems for distributive justice raised by Senate apportionment. To some extent the small-state advantage in terms of federal outlays also results from small-state senators' increased incentives to pursue a particularized benefits strategy. This manifests itself in their concern over formulas (chapter 7) as well as in their choice of committee assignments (chapter 5). Senate apportionment creates different incentives for senators representing large and small states, so that people are treated differently based solely on place of residence.

The common theme of all the normative issues raised by this book is that Senate apportionment works to the advantage of residents and senators from the small states and to the disadvantage of those from the larger states. If its effects were random—with small states and their residents advantaged in some cases and large states and their residents advantaged in others—then equal representation might not raise normative concerns. But that is clearly not the case. In almost every instance, advantages accrue to the small states, their residents, and their senators. These unfair advantages in greater voting power, access, and the distribution of federal funds are the direct result of the equal representation of states that vary greatly in population.

We recognize that any apportionment scheme would have biases (see Dixon 1968), just as rules and procedures generally are never neutral. Even when rules are fair—in that they treat everyone equally—they still advantage some players over others. Accordingly, apportioning legislative seats by the one person, one vote standard—as in the House of Representatives—is not neutral among interests, as the recent debates over majority-minority districts attest. Unlike most sets of rules and procedures, however, Senate apportionment fails to meet the standard of fairness. In a democratic system with geographic representation, a population-based apportionment is the only theoretically defensible option, as suggested above. Only such a system can provide for equal access to decision makers, equal influence in the outcome of elections and the makeup of government, equal chances for senators to become leaders within the institution, and relatively fair distributions of federal funds. Senate apportionment, by comparison, clearly violates all these norms, and more important, the discrepancy between the ideal and reality is in this case large and growing.

It is customary in a work like this to conclude with suggestions for reform. After documenting the effects of Senate apportionment and discussing their normative implications, it only makes sense to examine the prospects for dealing with the issues raised. The prospects for reform of Senate apportionment, however, are particularly dim, notwithstanding Senator Moynihan's (1995, xxi) prediction that "change will come." As we noted earlier, Senate apportionment is for all practical purposes a permanent feature of the United States Constitution.

Moynihan's interest in the effects of Senate apportionment is motivated by his conviction—confirmed in this book—that his constituents are unfairly disadvantaged by it. Other elite political actors may take an interest in the effects of Senate apportionment on the distribution of federal dollars when they become more generally known. Because of the ways Senate apportionment affects the incentives of political actors, however, senators from large states may not care much about its reform or devote their resources to this goal. The reason is that the costs of Senate apportionment in distributive policy are widely dispersed among residents in the populous states, whereas the benefits are concentrated in the small states. Thus small-state senators have much greater incentives to protect Senate apportionment than large-state senators have to change it. Similarly, House members from more populous states have very little incentive to try to reform Senate apportionment. It is not clear what benefit individual House members could expect from activism on this issue. Even if they were more incensed about Senate apportionment than they currently are, however, senators from the most populous states would have to argue for reform in a body in which a majority of the membership represents a minority of the population. To alter Senate apportionment, populous-state senators would have to win the support of those the current scheme advantages.

Some might appraise the prospects of reform more favorably by looking to the adoption of the Seventeenth Amendment as a precedent. After all, when the Senate of the Sixty-second Congress finally agreed to propose the amendment to the states for ratification—after the Senate had obstructed and rejected similar proposals for nearly twenty years—senators risked their own reelection interests. Similarly, when three-quarters of the state legislatures agreed to the proposed amendment, they relinquished control over the selection of senators, one of their sources of influence in federal policymaking. In this sense the Seventeenth Amendment presents an example of constitutional reform that ran counter to the narrow self-interest of those who proposed and ratified it (Hoebeke 1995, 23).

Despite some similarity, however, there are at least three critical differences between the Seventeenth Amendment and any reform of Senate apportionment. First, as discussed in chapter 1, the Constitution seems to demand that all states approve any constitutional change in the basis of Senate apportionment instead of its passing by the three-quarters majority that the normal amending process requires. Second, political pressure from their constituents during the Progressive Era encouraged both senators and state legislatures to agree to the Seventeenth Amendment (Crook and Hibbing 1997, 845; Haynes 1938, 96–106; King and Ellis 1996, 72–74). By contrast, it is difficult to imagine that constituents in small states would ever favor a change in apportionment that would reduce their influence. Because most states are overrepresented in the Senate by the one person, one vote standard, one would not expect majorities within most states to support a change even if a national majority favored it.

Third, the general public's lack of interest in the topic presents yet another obstacle to any reform. It is safe to say that Senate apportionment—unlike popular election of senators during the Progressive Era—is not one of the burning issues of our time. In part this is because most of the people disadvantaged by it are unaware that they are disadvantaged. One reason for this lack of awareness is that the effects of Senate apportionment have never before been systematically studied, and thus information on the topic has not been available. Still, can Senate apportionment really be "unjust" if no injustice is felt? Most Americans are not even conscious of the vast differences in state population. We were surprised while working on this project to discover just how few people, including senators themselves, know how many small states there are. Once again, Senate apportionment often produces a concentrated benefit with a widely dispersed cost, and thus it is not surprising that most of those paying the cost are not aware of it.

Furthermore, the issue is unlikely to generate much public feeling because Americans tend to be very conservative when it comes to their political institutions, even when they are very dissatisfied with their present performance (Hibbing and Theiss-Morse 1995, 42–46). As long ago as 1902, for example, political scientist John Burgess speculated that a constitutional amendment requiring direct election of senators would eventually spur a movement to reapportion the Senate to better "accord with the principle of distribution according to numbers" (1902, 659). Burgess's prediction proved incorrect. Americans seem particularly committed to the theory of federalism embodied in the equal representation of states. At an earlier point in American history, many were even willing to extend that theory to lower levels of government. During the height of the movement for legislative apportionment reform at the state level, voters in many states rejected referenda to reapportion their state legislatures on a population-based standard in favor of retaining their "little federal" systems (Dixon 1968). In the end, reapportionment occurred only through the intervention of the Supreme Court—if the matter had been left up to the voters in the states, many state legislatures would still be malapportioned today.

In light of its apparent permanence, understanding Senate apportionment's effects—not arguing for its reform—has been our main concern. Even if we believed it would be wise to rethink the apportionment scheme, such a campaign would very likely be futile. There is nothing to be gained from tilting at windmills. Rather than being a reason to ignore it, however, the enduring nature of Senate apportionment makes it an even more important topic of study. Because the equal representation of states is going to be with us for the indefinite future, it is essential that we develop a better understanding of its effects.

Studying the Senate

In addition to the normative issues raised by our findings, this research also has major implications for political scientists who study the Senate. Throughout this book we have argued that recognizing the effects of equal representation of states is necessary for a complete understanding of the Senate as a representative and legislative institution. By this point we hope to have persuaded our readers that this is indeed the case. We are confident that students of the Senate will conclude that any analysis that does not take its apportionment scheme into account is incomplete.

In addition, and perhaps more important, this book should change the way scholars develop generalizations about the Senate. Political scientists studying Congress have typically followed two approaches to the study of the Senate, and our findings have implications for both. The first approach, often taken by those who specialize in studying the House of Representatives, contrasts the Senate with the House. This often means contrasting the "average" senator with the "average" House member. As we have discussed above, there is no such thing as the "average" senator when one takes into account the great variation in Senate constituency size. Many of our ideas about the Senate and senators must be reconsidered in light of our findings. The common generalization that senators represent larger and more heterogeneous constituencies than House members do, for example, must be revised to acknowledge that fourteen senators represent constituencies that are identical to House districts and appear to behave more like House members than like their Senate colleagues from more populous states. Similarly, the idea that House members are more parochial in outlook and concern than senators must be balanced against our findings that many senators from small states pursue particularized benefits for their constituents as vigorously as any House member.

In short, this first approach to the study of the Senate obscures the great variation that exists among senators themselves because political scientists often just attempt to apply what they know about the House to the Senate. The Senate, however, is not another House—it is in many ways unique. As such, the Senate presents its own set of questions.

Those political scientists employing a second, opposite approach focus on the Senate's many unique features. There is a considerable literature, for example, detailing its unusual rules and procedures, especially the filibuster and the strategically important cloture rule (Binder and Smith 1997; Sinclair 1989; Smith 1989). Similarly, Senate elections raise many issues that political scientists are just beginning to explore. Scholars have become increasingly sensitive to the importance of the staggered, six-year terms of senators, as evinced by the recently completed NES Senate Election Study. The dual nature of Senate representation—that each state has two senators—also presents interesting issues for research, although this area has until recently been largely ignored (see Schiller 1995). Yet despite scholarly interest in the unique features of the Senate, political scientists, even those specializing in it, have taken for granted what Matthews (1960, 6) called the Senate's "almost incredible" basis of apportionment.

It is high time for political scientists studying Congress to add Senate apportionment to the list of unique features that warrant study. Apportionment is perhaps more deserving than the Senate's other features because it has so many consequences. As we have documented, the equal representation of states varying greatly in population affects every aspect of the Senate as a representative and legislative institution. In the following section we suggest some avenues for future research.

Future Research

Although we have demonstrated that apportionment affects the Senate in numerous interrelated ways, we have not exhausted the research potential of this topic. While working on this book we uncovered more than a few research questions related to Senate apportionment that were outside the scope of our study. We alluded to some of these earlier; here we will elaborate on some potential topics for future research.

In chapter 3 we touched on how Senate apportionment affects interest representation, a topic that arose during our interviews. Many of our subjects commented that interest groups find small-state senators much easier to reach than senators representing larger states. This finding raises several questions. Do interest groups pursue different strategies in the Senate than in other legislative institutions? Are interest groups sensitive to the different incentives of senators from small and large states as they construct coalitions? Does state size affect the grassroots and media campaigns that interest groups develop to influence Senate decisions? Are decisions regarding independent expenditures by interest groups in Senate elections influenced by state size? Finally, how does the Senate's over- and underrepresentation of particular interests shape public policy?

Throughout the book we demonstrate that state size influences the strategic behavior of senators. One topic we have not examined is the possible effect of state size on the emergence of Senate candidates. Although candidate emergence has received considerable scholarly attention in recent years, research has focused exclusively on House candidates (Fowler 1993; Fowler and McClure 1989; Kazee 1994; Maisel, Stone, and Meastas 1997). State population clearly structures the opportunities of politically ambitious individuals in one way: a person has a much greater chance of being elected to the Senate in a small state than in a large one. State size may also affect the emergence and recruitment of Senate candidates in other ways as well. Do Senate candidates in small states have different political backgrounds than those in large states? Are different skills, resources, and attributes important in running for the Senate in small and large states? Are small-state candidates more likely to possess the skills of retail politicians than large-state candidates? Do the costs of running for the Senate—which we know increase with state population—affect candidate emergence differently in small and large states?

In chapter 5 we examined four areas in which constituency size affects senators' strategic Washington behavior, but its effects may not be limited to these areas. Senators from different-sized states, for example, may allocate their staff differently, in terms of both location (Washington or the home state) and the kinds of tasks assigned to them. Similarly, state size may influence senators' allocation of other resources. As Richard Hall (1993) has shown, there is great variation in legislators' attendance and participation on committees as they make choices about how to allocate their scarcest resource, their time. We have demonstrated, for example, that small-state senators are more likely to serve on constituency committees than those from larger states. This incentive structure should have implications for participation on committees as well. One possible hypothesis for future research is that senators from small states are more likely than their large-state colleagues to actively participate on constituency-oriented committees.

Finally, Senate apportionment may affect public policy in several ways that we have not addressed. We examined the effects of Senate apportionment on the geographic distribution of program funds, but there is reason to believe that it affects the substance of policy as well. Similarly, pork barrel politics in the Senate is an understudied topic. As discussed in chapters 6 and 7, scholars interested in distributive politics have focused almost exclusively on the House. This attention has been misplaced, at least in that the funding formula decisions that so deeply concern senators involve far greater sums than do the special projects that typically interest House members.

Our findings also raise questions about the effects of Senate apportionment on the distribution of discretionary program funds. Does Senate apportionment affect the relationship of the federal bureaucracy to Congress? Are bureaucrats sensitive to its effects as they build coalitions to support their programs in the Senate? Last, have less populous states become more dependent on the federal government than larger states because of their advantages in procuring federal dollars? Are the tax burdens of small-state residents affected by these advantages? Although this may not be a topic that legislative scholars wish to investigate, it should have considerable appeal to students of state politics and intergovernmental relations.

■ ■ ■

The study of the Senate's unique apportionment scheme is much richer than we imagined when we began working on this book. What is strange is that political scientists have ignored the subject for so long. Senate apportionment and its effects have always been there, waiting to be studied. These effects increased in importance as the nation's population grew and the role of the federal government expanded, yet they still remained unexamined. We may be able to suggest a reason. In our conversations about this project, we often found that our interlocutors initially thought Senate apportionment uninteresting. Everyone knows that each state has two senators, after all, and many have assumed that was all there was to know. This book is our answer to this incurious attitude. There is a lot more to know about Senate apportionment than most people—political scientists included—have suspected. We hope, in the end, that our readers are convinced of the importance of this until now ignored facet of American government.

Appendixes

Appendix A

The Schubert-Press Measure of Legislative Malapportionment

The Dauer-Kelsay measure of malapportionment discussed in chapter 1 has certain limitations. Although it does tell us something useful about Senate representativeness—"the difference between the mean of the population of representatives and the mean of the general population" (Schubert and Press 1964, 305)—it does not describe the shape of the overall distribution of state sizes. Schubert and Press (1964) developed a more sophisticated measure, the apportionment score, to assess the extent and kind of malapportionment.

Assuming that the underrepresentation of the many citizens residing in the largest states is a more serious form of malapportionment than the overrepresentation of the few living in the smallest states, the apportionment score (combined with measures of skewness and kurtosis) is designed to better determine the shape of the distribution. The apportionment score ranges from 0 to 1, with 1 indicating a perfect population-based apportionment and lower values indicating degrees of malapportionment. If the distribution of state sizes described by the apportionment score is positively skewed and if states are ranged on a distribution from smallest to largest, the mode will be to the left of the mean, with a small amount of variance to the left of the mean and considerable variation to the right. In other words, malapportionment is more severe in that most people reside in a few underrepresented states, some of them seriously underrepresented, while comparatively few people live in the many states to the left of the mean. The index of kurtosis shows the peakedness of the distribution, telling how many states are of similar size. When the distribution is skewed, a high level of positive kurtosis reveals that units are concentrated in the left tail, meaning that the modal state is small. Thus "the negative ideal would be characterized by maximal variance" (a low apportionment score), "extreme positive skewness" (greater than $+1.0$), and "extreme positive kurtosis" (greater than 3.0).

Table A.1 shows the apportionment scores for Senates at ten-year intervals as well as the measures of skewness and kurtosis. Using this more sophisticated measure, contemporary Senate apportionment appears in an even worse light than with the

Table A.1 Senate Scores on Apportionment Indexes of Central Tendency, Dispersion, Variation, Skewness and Kurtosis, 1790–1990

Year	Mean State Population	Standard Deviation	Apportionment Score	Skewness	Kurtosis
1790	262.00	179.34	.59	.94	1.00
1800	313.19	215.64	.59	.92	.18
1810	372.94	274.11	.60	1.04	.20
1820	408.35	338.84	.55	1.42	1.92
1830	523.21	437.41	.54	1.75	3.54
1840	641.38	535.85	.54	1.96	4.36
1850	748.97	665.65	.53	2.04	4.92
1860	937.61	810.21	.54	2.05	5.19
1870	1037.16	944.39	.52	1.91	4.22
1880	1309.24	1099.79	.54	1.74	3.64
1890	1417.59	1303.57	.52	1.75	3.74
1900	1664.47	1562.90	.52	1.82	4.00
1910	1942.85	1843.14	.51	2.12	5.56
1920	2192.19	2117.04	.51	2.09	5.26
1930	2485.21	2528.58	.50	2.15	5.41
1940	2729.29	2690.55	.50	2.05	5.08
1950	3117.06	3098.80	.50	1.94	4.05
1960	3678.56	3788.63	.49	1.86	3.53
1970	4050.86	4334.65	.48	2.05	4.53
1980	4518.22	4715.03	.49	2.14	5.37
1990	4962.04	5459.78	.48	2.54	8.28

Dauer-Kelsay measure. Just as shown in figure 1.1, the Schubert-Press measure reveals that the Senate has become steadily more malapportioned over time. Senate apportionment scores have declined from a high of 0.60 in 1810 to a low of 0.48 in 1990. There are only four points in the period at which the previous decade's apportionment score was lower, and these are momentary bumps upward in an overall downward trend.

The data on Senate apportionment presented here reveal the contemporary Senate to be even more malapportioned than shown in figure 1.1 because the measures of skewness and kurtosis on the distributions of state sizes demonstrate increasingly serious malapportionment, especially in recent decades. In fact, combining the apportionment score with the measures of skewness and kurtosis shows that the 1990 Senate is more malapportioned than any other in the nation's history. The 1990 score ties with the lowest score (1970), but the distribution is more seriously skewed than in 1970, revealing that the largest states have become even larger; additionally, the kurtosis score is higher, showing that the distribution is even more highly peaked to the left of the mean, signifying that there are more overrepresented states.

Appendix B

Senators' Mentions on National Nightly News Broadcast, 103d and 104th Congresses

Senator	State	TV Mentions 103d Congress	TV Mentions 104th Congress
Abraham	MI	—	4
Akaka	HI	0	0
Ashcroft	MO	—	2
Baucus	MT	18	6
Bennet	UT	0	2
Biden	DE	52	14
Bingaman	NM	3	1
Bond	MO	15	4
Boren	OK	52	—
Boxer	CA	26	16
Bradley	NJ	32	28
Breaux	LA	70	18
Brown	CO	9	5
Bryan	NV	17	7
Bumpers	AR	8	5
Burns	MT	3	1
Byrd	WV	37	22
Campbell	CO	2	8
Chafee	RI	53	17
Coats	IN	2	14
Cochran	MS	8	7
Cohen	ME	30	34
Conrad	ND	9	12
Coverdell	GA	1	1
Craig	ID	1	11
D'Amato	NY	69	105

Senator	State	TV Mentions 103d Congress	TV Mentions 104th Congress
Danforth	MO	14	—
Daschle	SD	22	79
Deconcini	AZ	50	—
Dewine	OH	—	5
Dodd	CT	31	46
Dole	KS	200	200
Domenici	NM	26	49
Dorgan	ND	17	14
Durenberger	MN	20	—
Exon	NE	16	19
Faircloth	NC	5	12
Feingold	WI	2	9
Feinstein	CA	66	21
Ford	KY	2	3
Frist	TN	—	7
Glenn	OH	42	18
Gorton	WA	2	2
Graham	FL	25	2
Gramm	TX	95	163
Grams	MN	—	3
Grassley	IA	9	22
Gregg	NH	3	10
Harkin	IA	17	6
Hatch	UT	46	38
Hatfield	OR	5	18
Heflin	AL	7	3
Helms	NC	32	35
Hollings	SC	20	6
Hutchinson	TX	31	16
Inhofe	OK	—	3
Inouye	HI	10	2
Jeffords	VT	1	4
Johnston	LA	15	7
Kassebaum	KS	22	30
Kempthorne	ID	2	3
Kennedy	MA	57	31
Kerrey	NE	45	26
Kerry	MA	29	29
Kohl	WI	7	6
Kyl	AZ	—	5
Lautenberg	NJ	21	11
Leahy	VT	33	15
Levin	MI	12	2
Lieberman	CT	0	8

Senator	State	TV Mentions 103d Congress	TV Mentions 104th Congress
Lott	MS	19	66
Lugar	IN	33	50
Mack	FL	15	17
Mathews	TN	0	—
McCain	AZ	71	87
McConnell	KY	7	17
Metzenbaum	OH	31	—
Mikulski	MD	18	8
Mitchell	ME	191	—
Moseley-Braun	IL	14	4
Moynihan	NY	90	22
Murkowski	AK	3	9
Murray	WA	9	1
Nickles	OK	15	25
Nunn	GA	108	45
Packwood	OR	81	—
Pell	RI	1	2
Pressler	SD	8	10
Pryor	AR	20	5
Reid	NV	7	3
Riegle	MI	20	—
Robb	VA	26	5
Rockefeller	WV	35	2
Roth	DE	6	15
Santorum	PA	—	4
Sarbanes	MD	8	7
Sasser	TN	15	—
Shelby	AL	14	14
Simon	IL	37	20
Simpson	WY	27	26
Smith	NH	4	10
Snowe	ME	—	11
Specter	PA	29	58
Stevens	AK	3	6
Thomas	WY	—	2
Thompson	TN	—	14
Thurmond	SC	9	18
Wallop	WY	7	—
Warner	VA	24	19
Wellstone	MN	17	13
Wofford	PA	8	—

Source: Vanderbilt Television News Archive Index.
Note: Number of mentions on the ABC, CBS, CNN, and NBC national nightly news broadcasts.

Appendix C

Key Votes Included in the Analysis of Hold-Out Behavior in Chapter 5

Date of Vote	Subject of Roll Call	Vote	Population of State(s) of Crucial Senator(s)
March 16, 1978	Panama Canal treaties ratification—adoption	68–32	*Small* Hatfield (Mont).
May 3, 1978	Waterway user fees—Domenici amendment to phase in fees	43–47	*Small* Byrd (W. Va.), Dole (Kans.), Case (N.J.), Gravel (Alaska), McGovern (S. Dak.), Hansen (Wyo.)
September 26, 1980	State, Justice, Commerce, Judiciary appropriations—reconsider vote on Pressler amendment	43–39	*Small* Chafee (R.I.), Schmitt (N. Mex.), Stafford (Vt.)
October 28, 1981	Saudi AWACS—adoption of resolution of disapproval	48–52	*Small* Cohen (Maine), Zorinsky (Nebr.)
July 14, 1982	Tobacco program revisions—tabling Eagleton amendment to end permanent authorization	49–47	*Not small* Bentsen (Tex.)
July 22, 1982	Budget reconciliation—passage	50–47	*Not small* Helms (N.C.), D'Amato (N.Y.), Armstrong (Colo.)

Date of Vote	Subject of Roll Call	Vote	Population of State(s) of Crucial Senator(s)
September 10, 1982	Supplemental appropri-ations—veto override	60–30	*Small* Murkowski (Alaska), Stevens (Alaska)
June 13, 1984	Defense authorization—table Percy's amendment to cut SDI funding	47–45	*Mixed* Cohen (Maine), Nunn (Ga.)
September 17, 1985	Immigration reform bill	51–44	*Not small* Lugar (Ind.), Quayle (Ind.), Specter (Pa.), Riegle (Mich.), Rudman (N.H.)
May 9, 1985	First budget resolution—Dole perfecting amendment	50–49	*Small* Abdnor (S. Dak.), Andrews (N. Dak.), Stevens (Alaska), Roth (Del.), Cohen (Maine), Zorisky (Nebr.), Durenberger (Minn.), Weicker (Conn.)
March 25, 1986	Balanced budget constitu-tional amendment—passage	66–34	*Small* Burdick (N. Dak.), Byrd (W. Va.), Stafford (Vt.), Hatfield (Oreg.), Pell (R.I.), Ford (Ky.)
June 5, 1986	Saudi arms sale—Veto override vote of resolu-tion to block	66–34	*Small* Exon (Nebr.)
July 30, 1986	Manion nomination—confirmation	48–46	*Not small* Gorton (Wash.)
August 5, 1986	Department of Defense authorization—motion to table Johnson amend-ment to limit funds for SDI	50–49	*Small* Hatch (Utah)
August 7, 1986	Department of Defense authorization—Pryor amendment to delete funds for "Bigeye" chemical bomb	50–51	*Small* Roth (Del.)
April 2, 1987	Omnibus highway re-authorization—veto override	67–33	*Mixed* Hecht (Nev.), Symms (Idaho), Sanford (N.C.)

Date of Vote	Subject of Roll Call	Vote	Population of State(s) of Crucial Senator(s)
May 11, 1988	Department of Defense authorization—recon-sider tabling of Johnston amendment to use SDI funds for space shuttle	48–50	*Not small* Glenn (Ohio), Garn (Utah), Heflin (Ala.), Dixon (Ill.), Gore (Tenn.), Wirth (Colo.)
July 27, 1989	Department of Defense authorization—tabling of Johnston amendment to reduce SDI funding	50–47	*Not small* D'Amato (N.Y.)
March 29, 1990	Clean Air Act reauthoriza-tion—Byrd amendment for benefits to coal minors losing jobs	49–50	*Mixed* Biden (Del.), Symms (Idaho), D'Amato (N.Y.)
January 12, 1991	Use of force against Iraq—passage of resolution	52–47	*Small* Reid (Nev.), Bryan (Nev.)
September 24, 1992	Family and medical leave—veto override	68–31	*Mixed* Stevens (Alaska), Boren (Okla.)
June 25, 1993	Budget reconciliation—passage	50–49	*Small* Kerrey (Nebr.)
September 9, 1993	Defense authorization—Sasser amendment to cut funding for ballistic mis-siles defense program	50–48	*Not small* Feinstein (Calif.)
March 1, 1994	Balanced budget constitu-tional amendment	63–37	*Mixed* Pell (R.I.), Pryor (Ark.), Stevens (Alaska), John-ston (La.), Harkin (Idaho)
June 29, 1994	Product liability reform—cloture	57–41	*Mixed* Feinstein (Calif.), Conrad (N. Dak.), Dorgan (N. Dak.), Specter (Pa.), Thurmond (S.C.), Reigle (Mich.), Pressler (S. Dak.)
July 1, 1994	Department of Defense authorization—amend-ment to end Bosnia arms embargo	50–50	*Small* Bryan (Nev.)
March 2, 1995	Balanced budget constitu-tional amendment	65–35	*Small* Dorgan (N. Dak.), Conrad (N. Dak.)

Date of Vote	Subject of Roll Call	Vote	Population of State(s) of Crucial Senator(s)
June 21, 1995	Foster surgeon general nomination—cloture vote	58–40	*Mixed* Hatfield (Oreg.), Stevens (Alaska), Roth (Del.), Warner (Va.), Thompson (Tenn.)
October 28, 1995	Budget reconciliation— passage	52–47	*Small* Chafee (R.I.), Jeffords (Vt.), Kassebaum (Kans.), Snowe (Maine), Specter (Pa.)
December 22, 1995	Shareholders lawsuits— veto override	68–30	*Small* Exon (Nev.)
March 4, 1997	Balanced budget constitutional amendment	66–34	*Mixed* Torricelli (N.J.), Johnson (S. Dak.), Landrieu (La.)

Appendix D

Programs Studied in Chapter 7

Program Name	Appropriations (FY 1995) ($)	CFDA Number
Payments to Agricultural Experiment Stations (Hatch Act)	162,648,431	10.203
Animal Health and Disease Research	5,200,000	10.207
National School Lunch Program	4,587,634,772	10.555
Child and Adult Care Food Program	1,446,862,400	10.558
WIC Farmer's Market Nutrition Program	7,300,000	10.572
Community Development Block Grants:		
Entitlement Grants	3,139,000,000	14.218
Nonentitlement Grants	1,830,000,000	14.228
Wildlife Restoration (P-R Program)	218,082,000	15.611
Federal Employment Service	838,912,000	17.207
Job Training Partnership Act, Title 2A	996,813,000	17.250
Summer Youth Employment and Training Program (Title 2B)	867,000,000	17.250
Federal-Aid Highway Program: [a]	20,114,373,000	
Surface Transportation Program		20.205
National Highway System		20.205
Minimum Allocation		20.205
Interstate Construction		20.205
Interstate 4–R		20.205
Promotion of the Humanities: State Programs	28,014,000	45.129
Air Pollution Control Program	181,000,000	66.001
State Public Water Systems Supervision	70,000,000	66.432
State Underground Water Source Protection	9,900,000	66.433

Program Name	Appropriations (FY 1995) ($)	CFDA Number
Adult Education: State Administered Programs	252,800,000	84.002
Special Education Grants to States	2,467,000,000	84.027
Public Library Services	81,562,000	84.034
Vocational Education: Basic Grants to States	979,000,000	84.048
Rehabilitation Services—Vocational Rehabilitation Grants to States	2,054,000,000	84.126
Rehabilitation Services—Client Assistance Programs	9,800,000	84.161
Drug-Free Schools and Communities: State Grants	434,000,000	84.186
Rehabilitation Services—Supported Employment for Individuals with Severe Disabilities	36,536,000	84.187
Special Programs for the Aging:		
Elder Abuse Prevention	4,732,000	93.041
Ombudsman Services	4,449,000	93.402
Disease Prevention	16,982,000	93.403
Supportive Services	306,711,000	93.404
Nutrition Services	469,874,000	93.405
In-Home Services for Frail Older Individuals	9,263,000	93.406
Vulnerable Elder Rights Protection Programs	1,976,000	93.409
Projects in Assistance in Transition from Homelessness (PATH)	28,870,000	93.150
Low-Income Home Energy Assistance Program	999,800,000	93.568
Community Services	396,600,000	93.569
Emergency Community Services for the Homeless	N/A	93.572
Child Welfare Services	292,000,000	93.645
Social Services Block Grant	2,800,000,000	93.667
Substance Abuse Prevention and Treatment Block Grant	1,234,107,000	93.950
Number of programs in sample	42	
Total amount allocated in sample programs	$47,999,300,000	
Total amount allocated under all formula grants		
Including Medicaid	$201,507,269,000	
Excluding Medicaid	$111,857,678,000	

[a] The dollar amounts for the highway aid programs are not listed separately in the 1996 *Catalog of Federal Domestic Assistance*. The reason is that after 1991 the funds for all these programs were allocated to the states as two *large* block grants, even though the distribution apportionments under the preexisting categorical grants listed here were retained.

Appendix E

Data on the Sample of Formula Grants-in-Aid

Appendix E (continued)

CFDA Number	Type	Size (million $)	Population	Minimim	Type of Minimum	Number of H-S Conflicts	Number of Formula Changes	Year Created
10.203	Distributive	162.6	No	Yes	3	0	0	1955
10.207	Distributive	5.2	No	No	*	0	0	1977
10.555	Redistributive	4,900.0	No	No	*	1	3	1946
10.558	Redistributive	1,445.0	No	No	*	0	3	1975
10.572	Redistributive	7.3	Yes	Yes	2	1	1	1992
14.218	Redistributive	3,139.0	Yes	No	*	2	1	1974
14.228	Redistributive	1,830.0	Yes	No	*	2	1	1974
15.611	Distributive	218.0	No	Yes	1	1	1	1937
17.201	Distributive	838.9	Yes	Yes	1	1	0	1982
17.250	Redistributive	996.8	Yes	Yes	1	1	0	1982
17.250[a]	Redistributive	867.0	Yes	Yes	1	1	0	1982
20.205[b]	Distributive	4,000.0	No	Yes	1	1	0	1990
20.205[b]	Distributive	4,000.0	No	No	8	2	1	1982
20.205[b]	Distributive	4,000.0	No	No	*	5	1	1978
20.205[b]	Distributive	4,000.0	No	Yes	1	1	0	1991
20.205[b]	Distributive	4,000.0	No	Yes	1	9	1	1956
45.129	Distributive	28.0	Yes	Yes	3	0	0	1976
66.001	Distributive	181.0	Yes	Yes	1	3	2	1963
66.432	Distributive	70.0	Yes	Yes	1	1	0	1974
66.433	Distributive	9.9	Yes	No	*	0	0	1974
84.002	Distributive	252.8	Yes	Yes	1	2	2	1964
84.027	Distributive	2,467.0	Yes	No	*	2	2	1970
84.034	Distributive	81.6	Yes	Yes	3	1	2	1956

Appendix E (*continued*)

CFDA Number	Type	Size (million $)	Population	Minimim	Type of Minimum	Number of H-S Conflicts	Number of Formula Changes	Year Created
84.048	Redistributive	979.0	Yes	Yes	1	3	2	1963
84.126	Distributive	2,054.4	Yes	Yes	4	1	1	1973
84.161	Distributive	9.8	Yes	Yes	2	2	2	1984
84.186	Distributive	434.0	Yes	Yes	1	0	0	1986
84.187	Distributive	36.5	Yes	Yes	2	1	0	1992
93.041	Redistributive	4.7	Yes	Yes	1	0	0	1987
93.042	Redistributive	4.5	Yes	Yes	1	0	0	1987
93.043	Redistributive	17.0	Yes	Yes	1	0	0	1987
93.044	Redistributive	306.7	Yes	Yes	1	2	1	1965
93.045	Redistributive	470.0	Yes	Yes	1	0	0	1972
93.046	Redistributive	9.3	Yes	Yes	1	0	0	1987
93.049	Redistributive	2.0	Yes	Yes	1	0	0	1992
93.150	Redistributive	28.9	Yes	Yes	2	2	1	1987
93.568	Redistributive	1,400.0	No	Yes	1	2	2	1979
93.569	Redistributive	396.6	No	Yes	1	2	1	1981
93.572	Redistributive	19.7	Yes	Yes	1	0	0	1987
93.645	Redistributive	292.0	Yes	No	*	0	1	1935
93.667	Redistributive	2,800.0	Yes	No	*	0	0	1981
93.959	Distributive	1,234.1	Yes	No	*	3	3	1981

Note: "CFDA Number" is the number assigned to the program by the *Catalog of Federal Domestic Assistance.*

"Type" indicates whether the program is distributive or redistributive, using the same criteria employed in chapter 6.

"Size" indicates the amount (in millions of dollars) allocated under the program in FY 1995, according to the 1996 CFDA.

Appendix E (*continued*)

"Population" indicates whether the program's formula contains a factor measuring either the number of people in the states or the number to be served by the program ("targeted population").

"Minimum" indicates whether the program contains a minimum allocation to small states.

"Type of Minimum" indicates the type of minimum guarantee in the formula: 1 denotes a minimum that guarantees every state a given percentage of the total amount authorized; 2 denotes a specific dollar amount; 3 denotes a floor, meaning that every state receives a certain percentage of the total and then an additional amount based on formula factors; 4 denotes an "either/or" minimum, meaning that a state receives either a percentage of the total allotment or a specific dollar amount, whichever is greater.

"Number of H–S Conflicts" is the number of times the House-passed and Senate-passed authorizations or reauthorizations of the program differed on the formula distribution.

"Number of Formula Changes" is the number of times the formula was changed after the program's initial authorization.

"Year Created" lists the year when each program was authorized.

[a] These are separate programs in the *Catalog of Federal Domestic Assistance*, even though they have the same CFDA number. The first program is the Adult and Youth Program; the second is the Summer Youth Program.

[b] Each of these probrams is listed as a separate program in the CFDA, even though they are all assigned the same CFDA number. The first program listed is the Surface Transportation Program; the second is the Minimum Allocation Program; the third is the Interstate 4–R Program; the fourth is the National Highway System; and the fifth is the Interstate Construction Program. The 1996 CFDA gives only one dollar amount for these programs ($20.1 billion), which I have coded as $4 billion for each separate program.

Appendix F

House–Senate Conflict
over the Programs Sampled

CFDA Number	Year	Winner	Conflict over Minimum?	Conflict over Factors?
10.555	1972	Compromise	No	Yes
10.572	1994	Senate	Yes	No
14.218	1974	House	No	Yes
14.218	1977	House	No	Yes
14.228	1974	House	No	Yes
14.228	1977	House	No	Yes
15.611	1946	House	Yes	No
17.207	1982	Compromise	Yes	Yes
17.250	1982	Compromise	Yes	Yes
17.250	1982	Compromise	Yes	Yes
20.205	1990	Senate	Yes	Yes
20.205	1982	Compromise	No	Yes
20.205	1991	House	No	Yes
20.205	1978	Senate	No	Yes
20.205	1981	Senate	No	Yes
20.205	1982	Compromise	No	Yes
20.205	1987	Senate	No	Yes
20.205	1991	Senate	No	Yes
20.205	1991	Senate	Yes	No
20.205	1956	Compromise	Yes	Yes
20.205	1970	Senate	Yes	No
20.205	1973	Senate	Yes	No
20.205	1976	Senate	Yes	No
20.205	1978	Senate	Yes	No

CFDA Number	Year	Winner	Conflict over Minimum?	Conflict over Factors?
20.205	1981	Senate	Yes	No
20.205	1987	Senate	Yes	No
20.205	1991	Senate	Yes	No
20.205	1982	Senate	Yes	No
66.001	1963	Senate	No	No
66.001	1970	House	No	No
66.001	1977	Senate	No	Yes
66.432	1974	Senate	Yes	No
84.002	1970	Senate	Yes	No
84.002	1984	Senate	Yes	No
84.027	1974	Compromise	No	Yes
84.027	1975	Compromise	No	Yes
84.034	1970	Senate	Yes	No
84.048	1963	Senate	No	Yes
84.048	1984	Senate	Yes	No
84.048	1990	Compromise	Yes	No
84.126	1978	Compromise	No	Yes
84.161	1986	Senate	Yes	No
84.161	1992	House	Yes	No
84.187	1992	Senate	Yes	No
93.044	1972	Compromise	Yes	No
93.044	1978	House	No	Yes
93.150	1987	Compromise	Yes	Yes
93.150	1990	Compromise	Yes	Yes
93.568	1980	Senate	Yes	Yes
93.568	1984	Compromise	No	Yes
93.569	1981	Compromise	Yes	No
93.569	1990	Compromise	Yes	No
93.959	1984	House	No	Yes
93.959	1988	Compromise	No	Yes
93.959	1992	Compromise	No	Yes

Notes

Chapter One

1. Of course we recognize that senators in the smaller-population states had a higher probability of being chosen as their states' delegates just by chance. (There was, in fact, a tendency to select the dean of a state's delegation.)

2. Even in federal chambers elsewhere, it is not common to grant equal representation to all federal units, regardless of the size of their populations (Duchacek 1970, 244).

3. *Wesberry v. Sanders,* 376 U.S. 1 (1964), applied the principle of one person, one vote to congressional districts; *Reynolds v. Sims,* 377 U.S. 533 (1964), applied the principle to both houses of all state legislatures; *Avery v. Midland County,* 390 U.S. 474 (1968), and *Hadley v. Junior College District of Metropolitan Kansas City, Missouri,* 397 U.S. 50 (1970), extended the rule to all local units "exercising governmental powers" and then to all local government elections.

4. There is an extensive literature on districting and minority representation. For studies of the effects of at-large districting see Austin 1998; and Bullock 1994; Bullock and MacManus 1987; Cottrell and Fleischman 1979; Davidson 1984; Davidson and Korbel 1981; Engstrom and McDonald 1986; MacManus 1979; and Welch 1990. Studies of the effects of congressional redistricting include Cameron, Epstein, and O'Halloran 1996; Gerber, Morton, and Rietz 1998; Grofman, Handley, and Niemi 1992; Lublin 1997; Overby and Cosgrove 1996; Peacock 1997; Peterson 1995; and Whitby 1997. On the state legislative level see Gormley 1994; Persons 1997; and Scarrow 1983. And for additional material on city councils and school districts see Robinson and Dye 1978; Stewart, England, and Meier 1989; Taebel 1978; and Welch and Karnig 1978. This is not an exhaustive list,but it does illustrate our point that there is no lack of scholarly interest in the effects of districting schemes.

5. Excluding Nevada and Arizona (two small-population states with population growth rates far above the mean) state population size is positively correlated (.28) with population growth rates for the decade 1980 to 1990.

Chapter Two

1. Population statistics are drawn from the 1997 *Statistical Abstract of the United States.*

2. By this second measure, Senate apportionment gives some advantage to American Indians, Eskimos, and Aleuts, taken as a group (correlation coefficient = −.252, $p < .1$). The less populous states tend to have larger percentages of persons in this ethnic group than do the more populous states. Even so, by the first measure used in the chapter, Senate apportionment does not appear to favor the representation of this group: although American Indians, Eskimos, and Aleuts together make up 0.8 percent of the nation's population as a whole, they are only 0.4 percent of the population of the median state.

3. The states with populations that are more than 90 percent white are Utah, Wisconsin, South Dakota, Wyoming, Idaho, Montana, Nebraska, Kentucky, Minnesota, North Dakota, Iowa, New Hampshire, Maine, and Vermont.

4. The converse may even be true: Senate apportionment may result in the underrepresentation of political minorities *as a general rule.* If large states are more politically diverse than small states—containing more interests and organizations that are not present in small states—then Senate apportionment underrepresents more political minorities than it protects.

5. California and Texas had declared themselves "republics" before being admitted as states. Hawaii had been a monarchy before being annexed as a territory.

6. *U.S. v. Curtiss-Wright,* 299 U.S. 304 (1936).

7. There is no evidence in Farrand's *Records of the Federal Convention* that any delegate ever questioned the notion that the Senate should be constructed so it would be more likely to exhibit caution and wisdom than would the House.

8. In Pennsylvania, reformers had even gone so far as to abolish both the governor and the upper house (Wood 1969, 137–38).

9. These "mixed-government" theories favoring bicameralism would be obscured during the ratification period. To counter Anti-Federalist criticisms that the Federalists were establishing an aristocracy, the Federalists typically emphasized the role of the Senate in checking political power generally rather than checking specifically popular political power. But the Convention debates—which were not made public until 1840—reveal the predominance of the earlier "mixed-government" theories in conceptualizing the role of the Senate. On the subject of the Federalists' redefinition of bicameralism for public consumption, see Gordon Wood's treatment in *The Creation of the American Republic, 1776–1787* (1969, 553–64).

10. On this point Rufus King (of Massachusetts) observed that "the choice of the second branch . . . by the state legislatures would be impracticable, unless it was to be very numerous, or the idea of proportion among the states was to be disregarded. According to this idea [proportional representation], there must be 80 or 100 members to entitle Delaware to the choice of one of them" (Farrand 1966, 1:52). C. C. Pinckney (of South Carolina) made the same connection: "If the small states should be allowed one Senator only, the number will be too great, there will be 80 at least" (Farrand 1966, 1:150).

11. Roger Sherman of Connecticut made the same point: "Elections by the people in districts . . . [are] not likely to produce such fit men as elections by the State Legislatures" (Farrand 1966, 1:154).

12. Dickinson appealed to the delegates' support of the British constitutional system on this point, arguing that selection of senators by state legislatures was superior to other methods because it was "like the British house of lords and commons, whose powers flow from different sources, are mutual checks on each other and will thus promote the real happiness and security of the country" (Farrand 1966, 1:156–57).

13. In a footnote to his record of the vote in favor of Senate selection by state legislatures, Madison recognized that his efforts to preserve a population-based representation in the Senate had been seriously jeopardized: "It must be kept in view that the largest States, particularly Pennsylvania & Virginia always considered the choice of the second branch by the State Legislatures as opposed to a proportional Representation to which they were attached as a fundamental principle of just Government" (Farrand 1966, 1:408).

14. Originally the four-sided states were Maryland, Delaware, New Jersey, New Hampshire, Pennsylvania, Rhode Island, and South Carolina; the three-sided states were Virginia, North Carolina, Georgia, New York, Massachusetts, and Connecticut (Brant 1948, 89). By the time of the Convention, Connecticut had ceded its claims to western lands, with the exception of the tract known as the Connecticut Reserve, and had no great hopes of future population growth. Virginia, New York, and Massachusetts had also ceded their competing claims north of the Ohio to the nation. The states of the Deep South were continuing to press their claims westward (Brant 1950, 62).

15. Population figures are drawn from C. C. Pinckney's estimates, which according to him were "the most accurate accounts we could obtain" (Farrand 1966, 3:253).

16. Data on state population in 1787 are from Farrand (1966, 3:253). Data on state growth expectations are drawn from Swift (1996, 33) and McDonald (1985, 218–19).

17. Maryland and New York had populations only slightly larger than the average state in 1787. In a Senate of twenty-six members apportioned by population, each would have received two senators, the same number they would receive under an equal apportionment.

18. Calculations were made using C. C. Pinckney's population estimates (Farrand 1966, 3:253).

19. After Madison's and Morris's threats to unite without the small states, Williamson distanced himself from the large-state delegates, saying that he "did not conceive that (Mr. Govr. Morris) meant that the sword ought to be drawn agst. the smaller states" and that he hoped expressions like these by some "individuals would not be taken for the sense of their colleagues" (Farrand 1966, 1:532).

20. Davie explained his perception of the situation to the North Carolina ratifying convention on July 28, 1788: "Although it militates against every idea of just proportion that the little state of Rhode Island should have the same suffrage with Virginia, or the great commonwealth of Massachusetts, yet the small states would not

consent to confederate without an equal voice. . . .This difficulty could not be got over. It arose from the unalterable nature of things. Every man was convinced of the inflexibility of the little states in this point" (Farrand 1966, 3:348).

21. New York had voted in favor of equal state apportionment in the Senate on every occasion when a vote had been taken.

Chapter Three

1. These studies are also limited because they rely primarily on data from the 1988 wave of the Senate Election Study rather than using all three waves that are now available. This means that their data are drawn from only one of the three points in the Senate election cycle. The sample size is also constrained when subsamples are used to address certain questions, especially when states or groups of respondents from different-sized states become the units of analysis.

2. In 1988 respondents were asked to rate each activity separately on its level of importance: extremely important, somewhat important, not very important, or not at all important. In 1990 respondents were asked to rank order the importance of the three activities.

3. Constituents were asked to rate each of the three activities as "not at all important" (coded as 0), "not very important" (coded as 1), "somewhat important" (coded as 2) or "extremely important" (coded as 3). The mean response rating the importance of working on national issues was 2.7, with a range across states of only 0.3. The mean response rating the importance of helping people with the government was 2.4, with a range of 0.6. The mean response rating the importance of generating benefits was 2.7, with a range of 0.4.

4. There were problems with the 1988 wave of the Senate Election Study that raised some questions about these findings. Sample size in each state for the 1988 wave averages only about sixty-three respondents on these items. It is likely that there is considerable sampling error within states. States were at different points in the Senate election cycle, with one-third not involved with a Senate campaign in 1988. In addition, the items' wording allowed respondents to treat the activities equally. On all three activities a large percentage of respondents rated them as "extremely important."

5. For the regression of percentage of respondents in the state that selected "working on national issues as the "most important" for the senator, the slope was -0.295, standard error $= 0.21$, and $R^2 = .04$. "Getting government money and projects for the state" had a slope of 0.095, standard error $= 0.19$, and $R^2 = .01$. And the "helping people" response had a slope of 0.009, standard error $= 0.16$, and $R^2 = .00$. Efforts to account for these unanticipated findings were largely unsuccessful. For example, respondents may have answered differently in states having Senate elections in 1990. However, conducting the analysis for only those states with Senate contests produced regression coefficients that were for all practical purposes equal to zero.

6. The contact items were asked only with reference to House members in the 1988 and 1990 waves of the survey.

7. The contact levels reported in table 3.1 almost certainly exaggerate actual

senator-constituent contact. One has only to multiply the percentages in table 3.1 by the populations of the states to see that some of the reported contact rates are physically impossible for senators to achieve. Even though respondents overreport, however, there is no reason to suppose that overreporting systematically occurs more often in less populous than in more populous states.

8. Krasno (1994) finds that even in terms of media contacts more respondents in small-population states report these forms of contact than in populous states. We have chosen not to analyze the media contacts because of their highly impersonal nature.

9. Some scholars have suggested to us that part of the negative relationship between state population and constituent-senator contact may be a result of different levels of seniority. And several of the senators and lobbyists we interviewed also speculated that senators from small-population states may build up more seniority than those from more populous states. An examination of senators' seniority levels in 1988, the time when the first wave of the Senate Election Study was conducted, does not support these concerns about seniority differences. First, the differences in the mean seniority of senators in the five groupings of state population that we employ in table 3.1 (1, 2–3, 4–8, 9–19, and >19 congressional districts) are small. Seniority ranged from a mean of 10.4 years to a mean of 12.8. Second, there was not a steplike relationship across the five population groupings. Third, and perhaps most important, the levels of seniority were fairly high for all the state population groupings. Given that respondents are more likely to recall recent contacts with senators (as opposed to distant ones), it is unlikely that there will be much of an increase in respondents' recall of contacts once a senator's seniority goes beyond a certain level.

10. The difference is probably understated as a result of the sampling method for the Senate Election Study. Because there was an effort to include an equal number of respondents in each state, respondents come disproportionately from small states. And in smaller states respondents report contact levels with senators that are even higher than those with representatives. If respondents were weighted for state population, the contact rate differences of senators and representatives would be greater than those shown in table 3.1. The disproportionate sampling of small-state respondents is one of the reasons states are used as the unit of analysis in the regressions reported in this book.

11. Respondents were asked each of these contact items for each senator separately.

12. This item about contacts made with the respondent's House member was only asked in 1988 and 1990.

13. These findings conflict with those of Levy and Squire (1994, 9). Their analysis shows that there is "at best, weak support for the hypothesis that senators from smaller population states are better able to gain their constituents' favor." But their analysis is based only on responses for the 1988 and 1990 waves, is limited to incumbents up for reelection, and uses only three groupings of state size (single district, two to three districts, and four or more districts).

14. The data in table 3.4 suggest that the differences in approval ratings across the states when grouped by population are considerably smaller than the OLS regression estimates. One needs, however, to keep in mind that the category of states with more than nineteen congressional districts has a very large range within it, stretching from

Illinois with twenty districts to California with fifty-two. The OLS equation would predict only about a 7 percent lower approval rating for a senator from that state than for a senator from states with a single congressional district. That figure is more in line with the difference in table 3.4.

15. Another reason Binder et al. uncover a smaller effect of constituency size on job approval is that they employ some variables in their multivariate model—such as the senator's ideological "fit" with the state, state ideological polarization, and the incumbent senator's vote percentage in the prior election—that may not be independent of state population.

16. During the Senate eulogies for Matsunaga many senators specifically referred to the luncheons. Sen. Rudy Boschwitz told of a conversation he had with Matsunaga when Boschwitz was chair of the Republican Senatorial Campaign Committee: "I told him one day—I happened to be going out to the Far East, to Thailand. I said, 'I am going to come back by way of Hawaii, Sparky, and I want to recruit somebody to run against you, and I am going to talk to some people.' He said, 'Who are you going to talk to?' I said, 'If you would give me a list of those people you have not taken out to lunch in the Senate dining room, I will start with them'" (*Congressional Record,* April 19, 1990, S4463–64).

Matsunaga's attentiveness evidently was as well known in Hawaii as in Washington. One lobbyist related the story of playing in a golf tournament in Hawaii with some bankers. He asked one what he thought of his senators. The banker was most effusive in his praise of Matsunaga, bragging that Spark had taken him to lunch in the Senate dining room. One suspects that the lobbyist was not the first to hear the story, nor was the banker the only one telling it.

17. This question is stated as an analysis of variance problem for which a multiple regression approach may be appropriate. However, there are some problems in doing this. In each wave of the Senate Election Study the contact and evaluation items were asked only about incumbent senators who were running for reelection or who were not up for reelection in that year. Only seventy-one senators were asked about in all three waves. In addition, because the data are organized by respondent and each respondent is asked about two senators (and in different order in each wave of the survey), gathering the contact and evaluation item responses for each senator was a task we did not undertake. Instead we decided to present a sampling of senators to illustrate that variance across state population appeared far greater than among senators within the same-sized states. The results are obviously less exact than would be obtained from regressing the response percentage for the senators on state population and other relevant independent variables such as seniority.

18. A state's senators were included only if both senators were asked about in all three waves of the survey. This ensures that respondents were included from the three points in each senator's electoral cycle. In addition, it allowed us to maximize the number of respondents. Even so, the number of respondents for each senator generally fell in the 150–200 range. Because the number of respondents who contacted a given senator is quite small, we did not analyze the reasons for contacting them.

19. By 1996 D'Amato's ratings had suffered relative to Moynihan's. Binder, Maltzman, and Sigelman (1998) find that D'Amato receives the lowest job approval rating in the Senate. It is likely that his controversial handling of the Senate Banking

Committee hearings on Whitewater, among other things, may have contributed to his low ratings. We speculate that senators in populous states are less likely to retain diffuse support that insulates them from sharp declines in approval than are senators in less populous states.

20. The favorable job ratings for small-population state senators shown in table 3.6 are not a function of a lack of party competition in small-population states. In Delaware Biden and Roth, and in New Mexico Domenici and Bingaman, receive high job ratings despite being of different parties.

21. The situation may be somewhat analogous to the generally higher evaluations students give professors teaching seminars compared with the evaluations they give in very large lecture classes.

22. Pell was able to achieve a high level of trust in Rhode Island without developing close person-to-person relationships with his constituents. In Pell's case much of his success came from the reputation he was able to establish for "integrity, character, ethics, and honesty" (Fenno 1996, 277). But a personal link based on those attributes could more easily be fostered in a small-population state where the senator has the ability to define himself rather than being defined by others.

23. Not every lobbyist we interviewed complained about the difficulty of gaining access to senators from populous states. Four of them had experience working in the congressional relations office of presidential administrations and thus had good access to most senators regardless of state size. One of them, trying not to sound arrogant, said, "I'm not the right person to ask. I can get to see Kennedy as easily as I can get to see Dorgan." Generally speaking, however, he thought that lobbyists would typically find it more difficult to reach senators who represent populous states than those who represent smaller states.

Chapter Four

1. We will discuss the effects of state population on incumbent fund-raising in the next section. Because incumbents all raise enough to mount a credible campaign and those facing highly competitive campaigns spend more than other incumbents, incumbent spending is actually inversely correlated with reelection success. For this reason, even if incumbents in less populous states are able to raise the money they need more easily, this should not substantively alter their advantages over challengers.

2. It is unclear why Hibbing and Brandes (1983) used means over the period rather than individual cases. This technique artificially reduces the amount of variation in both the independent and dependent variables as well as increasing the margin of error in their estimates for predicted incumbent vote share. Averaging the number of congressional districts over time also creates problems because this number is not a stable measure of population throughout the period; states that grew over the period can have averages similar to those of states that have held relatively constant in population. As a result, number of congressional districts in the state is more a measure of average relative size than an average of actual state size.

3. Krasno (1994) and Westlye (1991) also argue that regression analysis of the relationship between incumbency advantage and state size is misleading because it is not monotonic. Very populous states are the most competitive, but middle-sized

states, not small ones, consistently have the least competitive Senate elections. From this they conclude that state population affects incumbency advantage only in the very largest states. There is a serious problem with this conclusion, for they do not control for the noncompetitive character of elections in the South for most of the postwar period. Southern states tend to be middle-sized states; thus, including them in the analysis without controls greatly inflates the average margin of victory for states in their size group. Controls for the overall partisan competitiveness of states are necessary to assess the relationship between state population and incumbency advantage.

4. These scores mean that two-thirds of respondents in New Hampshire classify themselves within 2.3 points on a seven-point scale, while two-thirds of respondents in Mississippi classify themselves within 3.4 points on a seven-point scale, a difference of just slightly more than one point.

5. The core of the data for this study is derived from the Inter-University Consortium for Political and Social Research data set titled *Candidate and Constituency Statistics of Elections in the United States, 1788–1990* (1990). This data set contains the margin of victory in all Senate elections until 1988. We confine our study to regular, not special, Senate elections. We have coded other variables into this data set. Official election results from the 1990 and 1992 Senate elections were compiled from *America Votes* (Governmental Affairs Institute 1992). Results for the 1994 and 1996 Senate elections were compiled from the election issues of *Congressional Quarterly Weekly Report*. Data on state population for each census were drawn from the *Statistical Abstract of the United States*. We also coded the variable indicating when an incumbent is running in the election.

6. This is simply the percentage of the vote received by the winner minus the percentage received by the runner-up. Using this variable avoids the problems caused by using "winner's vote share" as the dependent variable. Unlike winner's vote share, margin of victory is not affected by the number of candidates running.

7. Using the number of congressional districts in a state as a population measure is problematic with time-series data. Because the number of House seats has remained constant, congressional districts have increased in population as the total United States population has grown. For example, the largest state with one congressional district since the 1990 apportionment is Montana, which has a population of 799,000. In 1910, however, Colorado also had a population of 799,000 and had four congressional districts. For this reason state population, rather than relative population, is our independent variable.

8. Ranney classifies the level of interparty competitiveness of states according to an index. This index is an average of four percentages: the average percentage of the popular vote won by Democratic gubernatorial candidates; the average percentage of the seats in the state senate held by Democrats; the average percentage of the seats in the state house held by Democrats; and the percentage of all terms for governor, state senate, and state house in which Democrats had control. Following Ranney, we classify states as one-party, modified one-party, and two-party competitive based on their raw scores on the index. States receiving scores of .9000 or greater or less than .0999 are considered to be one-party states. States receiving scores between .7000 and .8999 and between .1000 and .2999 are considered to be modified one-party

states. We could not employ the raw scores in the regression analysis because the raw Ranney scores for states before 1946 were unavailable, but we do have his classifications for this period, which are scored in the same way.

Because these are averages over limited periods, this index is, as Ranney terms it, "a snapshot of an object moving in time." Fortunately for this study, this index has been recalculated seven times, so the classifications are dynamic to reflect that all states are becoming two-party competitive. For example, for the period 1946–54 there are sixteen states classified as one-party states. In the period since 1981, only one is classified as a one-party state.

9. Although one-party states are not randomly distributed with respect to state population (southern states tend to be middle-sized and one-party), there is only a very weak linear relationship between population and one-party states. Correlating the two variables yields a correlation coefficient of −.05.

10. Our examination of Senate elections over time in selected high-growth states lends support to our contention that actual, not relative, state population is the appropriate independent variable. For example, California Senate elections appear to have become more competitive as that state's population has increased, although other factors like incumbency and national partisan swings in given elections affect that relationship. A time-series analysis of Senate elections in each of the states would be necessary to isolate the effect that population growth taken alone has had on competitiveness. This study tests for the effects of both population growth over time and cross-sectional differences in population across states.

11. The error term in a pooled time-series, cross-sectional study is composed of three components: an error associated with unique effects produced by nonconstant variance across pooled points in time, an error associated with unique characteristics of states, and a purely random error.

National partisan swings in particular election years are likely to increase the margin of victory for candidates of one party across all states regardless of state population. This would mean that in an OLS model the year of the election—an omitted variable, thus subsumed in the error term—would be correlated with the dependent variable, margin of victory, biasing slope estimates.

The nature of the Senate as an institution also has certain effects. Unlike House elections—in which every seat is contested each election year—Senate seats are contested in three separate classes, each class being composed of seats distributed across thirty-three or thirty-four states. Thus the dependent variable will be affected both by national party trends and by factors specific to the seats being contested in that year.

Similarly, each state has its own distinctive characteristics, characteristics that are stable over time and that, in an OLS model, would be subsumed in the error term. If these state-specific effects are correlated with the margin of victory, slope estimates will be biased.

12. Controlling for fixed state-specific and year-specific effects reveals a relationship between population and margin of victory in Senate elections that is as much as 3.8 times as large as estimates obtained for the simple OLS model. Below are the results from standard OLS regression models.

For open seat races:

Margin of victory = 16.23 + (−0.701 × Population) + (52.72 × One party-dominant) + (6.70 × Modified one-party dominant). All variables except modified one-party dominance are significant at $p < .01$; $R^2 = .53$.

For races with incumbents running:

Incumbent vote margin = 17.39 + (−0.473 × Population) + (51.14 × one-party dominant) + (5.95 × modified one-party dominant). All variables are significant at $p < .01$; $R^2 = .44$.

13. The coefficients on the dummy variables for years and states included in the LSDV model are not shown here because they do not provide useful information about the relation between state population and competitiveness in Senate elections. These coefficients are difficult to interpret in part because they do not identify the variables that might cause the regression line to shift over time and across states. As Maddala (1977) noted, these coefficients merely represent "specific ignorance" rather than the general ignorance subsumed in the error term. In short, the LSDV model is a good way to resolve the problems for OLS assumptions caused by pooling time-series data, but it is not helpful in understanding the dynamics of Senate elections in particular states or election years.

14. We obtained an F-statistic for this test of 0.72, which is less than the critical value for 5 percent significance, 1.00. The test is described in Greene (1993, 211–12).

15. The interaction term adds no explanatory power to the equation. Conducting an F-test to compare the restricted and unrestricted regression models, we obtained a test statistic of 1.15, which is less than the critical value for 5 percent significance, 3.84. Thus we cannot reject the null hypothesis that the coefficient for the omitted interaction term is zero.

16. Below are the results from the standard OLS regression model:

Margin of victory = 14.79 + (−0.488 × Population) + (3.11 × Incumbent running) + (51.64 × One-party dominant) + (5.04 × Modified one-party dominant). All variables are significant at $p < .01$; $R^2 = .47$.

17. Reestimating the model only for the postwar period reveals that incumbency advantage is greater in the recent period. The coefficient on this variable for postwar Senate elections is 5.51, although the other variables are relatively unchanged.

18. Fragmentation of media markets can also increase costs for congressional candidates (Campbell, Alford, and Henry 1984; Stewart and Reynolds 1990).

19. A Congressional Research Service report on out-of-state money in the congressional elections of 1992, 1994, and 1996 concluded that individual contributions from out of state "constitute a small share of total funding."

20. Herrnson reports that nonconnected and ideological PACs contributed only 10 percent of total PAC funds in the 1996 congressional elections (1998, 116).

21. The Federal Elections Commission Act does not require the disclosure and itemization of the source of contributions of $200 or less, so there is no way to know for certain whether these small contributions come from within the state.

22. Our analysis shows that serving more than three terms does not lead to ad-

ditional increases in either the amount or the percentage of funds that a senator raises from non-PAC sources.

23. The coefficient for seniority is −152,090 ($p < .05$), meaning that senators who have served three or more terms in office raise $304,000 less from PACs than senators who have served only one term, a 23 percent decrease in PAC funds compared with that for the average senator.

24. Individual contributions constitute, on average, 85 percent of all the campaign funds that Senate incumbents raise from sources other than PACs. The other 15 percent comes from other sources, including party contributions, loans, and contributions from the candidates themselves.

25. The per capita amounts that senators raise for their campaigns, however, are not constant across state size. Small-state senators raise considerably more per capita than large-state senators from both PAC and non-PAC sources. In states with only one congressional district, the average senator in the 1992–96 election cycle raised $2.60 per capita from non-PAC sources and $1.90 per capita from PACs, for a total of $4.50 per capita. Senators representing states with twenty-six or more congressional districts, by contrast, raised only $0.56 per capita from non-PAC sources and $0.09 per capita from PACs, for a total of $0.65 per capita. Regression analysis shows that these findings are not an artifact of grouping. As state population increases, the per capita amount raised by senators from all sources decreases at a declining rate, a relation best modeled by using the reciprocal of state population as the independent variable. For total amount raised:

Total per capita amount raised = .49 + (2.39 × reciprocal of state population) + (.36 × close race). Coefficients for variables are significant at $p < .01$; $R^2 = .65$.

Results from regression analyses of per capita funds raised from PAC and non-PAC sources reveal the same pattern. Unless there are very substantial economies of scale in conducting Senate campaigns, these data mean that Senate races in small states are overfunded relative to Senate races in large states. At any rate, it is worth noting that the average senator representing a state with eight or fewer congressional districts raised more than a dollar per constituent for her Senate race during the 1992–96 election cycle, more than Michael Huffington used in his celebrated 1994 Senate race, when he spent about one dollar per constituent in California.

26. The political parties' national and senatorial committees can contribute little to assist needy candidates. The amount political parties can contribute directly is fixed at $17,500 per election cycle for all Senate candidates, regardless of state population. However, parties may also assist Senate candidates by spending as much as $0.02 for every person of voting age in the state in coordinated expenditures. This enables parties to provide a limited amount of additional assistance to their candidates in populous states, permitting them to spend at most $1.3 million in coordinated expenditures in California, compared with a maximum of $58,600 in the smallest states. These coordinated expenditures are not reflected in the FEC data on campaign contributions that we examine here, and given the cost of campaigns today, they do little to alleviate the fund-raising pressures on individual candidates (Davidson and Oleszek 1998, 74).

27. Data on House incumbents were compiled from Ornstein, Mann, and Malbin 1998.

28. The formula is as follows:

$$\text{Ratio } A - 1 = \text{total deviation from proportional representation}$$

$$\text{where ratio } A = \frac{C}{\Sigma (PSV)_i \ldots * (SV/TV)}$$

where C = Proportion of seats won by the Democratic Party in Senate elections

$(PSV)_i$ = proportion of votes won by the Democratic Party in a state

SV = total number of votes cast in the Senate election in a state

TV = total number of votes cast in Senate elections nationwide

29. The formula is as follows:

$$\text{Ratio } B - 1 = \text{deviation from } PR \text{ caused by plurality elections}$$

$$\text{where ratio } B = \frac{C}{\Sigma (PSV)_i \ldots * (TV_w)}$$

where C = proportion of seats won by the Democratic Party in Senate elections

$(PSV)_i$ = proportion of votes won by the Democratic Party in a state

TV_w = total number of votes cast in Senate elections nationwide weighted for equal state size.

Chapter Five

1. Large-state senators who pursue a particularized benefit strategy may do so for one of two reasons. First, they may have a more limited political repertoire. This might be true of politicians who have extensive experience serving a small constituency before coming to the Senate or who lack skill in presenting themselves on television. Second, they may do so in error, expecting political payoffs beyond what actually exist.

2. We recognize that other institutional differences, such as length of term, may also affect senators' incentives.

3. Although Fenno devotes a chapter of his *Congressmen in Committees* to "Senate Comparisons," he does not explicitly discuss state population size as a variable affecting senators' goals in choosing committee assignments. He observes that "Senators hold the same range of personal goals as Representatives—re-election, good public policy, influence in the chamber, and career ambition beyond the chamber. Like House members, they perceive committees to be differentially useful in the pursuit of these goals" (1973, 139). In fact he quotes a legislative assistant of a senator representing a populous state as saying, "No Senator with a broad constituency could fail to see the re-election benefits of Appropriations membership" (143). We provide evidence below that calls into question the assessment of this legislative assistant. Similarly, Stephen Horn is not sensitive to the way constituency size shapes senators' incentives to serve on the Senate Appropriations Committee, concluding from a flawed test that on Appropriations "representation was fairly evenly divided among states with differing levels of population (1970, 30).

4. We advance this hypothesis even though we realize that committee assignments are less important to senators than to House members. In part, owing to its smaller size, the Senate is less dependent on committees for the conduct of its busi-

ness. In addition, the Senate floor is more permeable to the legislative input of those who are not committee members than is the House floor. Thus, unlike a House member, a senator does not have to rely on committee membership as a pathway to influence in a given policy area, especially in the contemporary Senate (Sinclair 1989). Even so, we expect that the different incentives of senators from large and small states will have an effect on committee assignment patterns in the Senate.

5. Some might argue that large-state senators have increased incentives to seek assignment to policy committees because constituents in populous states expect their senators to be more active on national policy issues than do constituents in smaller states (see Hibbing and Alford 1990, 589–91). We examined the Senate Election Studies data on constituent expectations of senators in chapter 3 of this book and found little evidence that constituents in more and less populous states have different expectations in this regard.

6. For the Foreign Relations–Appropriations and for the Foreign Relations–Finance pair, the t-statistic was significant at the .01 level. For the Finance–Appropriations pair, the t-statistic was significant at the .05 level.

7. We analyze membership only on standing Senate committees that existed as of the 105th Congress. Thus the District of Columbia Committee, the Post Office and Civil Service Committee, and the Space Committee, which were all abolished in the mid-1970s, are not included.

8. Periodically the effort of small-state senators to obtain particularized benefits for their states draws national attention. In early 1998, for example, the national media covered the successful effort of Senator Patrick Leahy of Vermont to have Lake Champlain classified as one of the Great Lakes so that researchers at Vermont colleges and universities studying Lake Champlain could qualify for a share of the $56 million Sea Grant program (Kamen 1998; Seelye 1998). National media coverage—which, we later argue, a small-state senator may prefer to avoid—was critical of Leahy's undertaking, as demonstrated by an editorial in the *New York Times* (March 4, 1998). But in Vermont Leahy received substantial positive coverage in news stories and comment in newspapers, especially in Burlington and Rutland (Bloomer 1998; Seiler 1998). We could not imagine populous state senators having the incentive to seek such a small benefit for their states. (Lake Champlain is part of the border between Vermont and New York. Senators Moynihan and D'Amato demonstrated no interest in its inclusion in the Sea Grant program. In fact, those applying for grants to study Lake Champlain would compete with those in New York studying Lakes Erie and Ontario.) But the Lake Champlain story was big news in Vermont and one for which Leahy could reap credit.

9. A number of political scientists have pointed out that most senators can expect to receive very little national media attention, and therefore most focus their efforts on local news outlets (Hess 1987; Schiller 1998; Sinclair 1989). This does not mean, however, that efforts at gaining national media coverage do not have important effects at the local level. Cook (1989) suggests that national media attention has a "trickle-down" effect on local media: local media outlets often cover national media stories about members of Congress, and thus stories in the national media can increase their local visibility. Similarly, Sinclair (1990) argues that national media attention and national prominence translate into greater visibility among a senators' constituents.

10. Squire (1988, 143) suggests that "politicians from large states have an easier

time becoming national figures than those from smaller states." It is not at all clear why this should be the case, and Squire offers no reasons or evidence for this contention.

11. Because few constituents read national newspapers, it is more likely that any given senators' constituents will watch the nightly news than that they will read the *New York Times*. In addition, using newspaper coverage raises the problem of "hometown" bias—the New York senators, for example, receive an inordinate amount of coverage in the *New York Times,* and this creates difficulty for model specification (Sinclair 1989, 190–91).

Despite these problems, we estimate the effect of state population on the number of *New York Times* stories mentioning senators in 1985 using data provided by Barbara Sinclair. The regression results are similar to our findings for network news coverage of senators: Number of stories in 1985 = 4.14 + (0.24 × number of congressional districts in the state) + (64.79 × leader dummy) + (9.28 × committee chair dummy) + (4.64 × ranking minority dummy). All variables were statistically significant at $p < .05$ or better; $R^2 = .44$.

12. This variable was coded to capture the effects of scandals involving two senators during the 103d Congress: Sen. Bob Packwood (R-Oreg.) and Sen. Dave Durenberger (R-Minn.).

13. In the 103d Congress, for example, there were 2,606 mentions of senators on the network nightly news broadcasts; in the 104th there were only 1,947, and many of these were devoted to the senators running for president. Similarly, in the 103d Congress the median number of mentions of a senator was 17; in the 104th, it was only 11. The reason for this falloff in media coverage is that in the 104th Congress the Republican takeover of the House and the House's leading role for most of the Congress overshadowed the Senate, leading to less coverage for senators in general.

14. Of course there may be instances when the vote of a particular senator is more valuable than that of other senators, especially if that senator is strategically important or serves as a cue for others. But that was more likely to have been the case in the Senate of the 1950s and 1960s, when senators were seen as "insiders" and "outsiders" or "whales" and "minnows" (Matthews 1960; McPherson 1972, 48–50) than in the Senate of recent decades, when individualism has been a far more accurate description. There is no reason to suppose that senators' influence in the Senate as cue givers or power brokers has ever been related to the population of the state they represent.

15. We would be remiss if we did not give appropriate credit to the stimulus for the hold-out idea. In reading Fenno's *When Incumbency Fails* (1992), we took note of Sen. Mark Andrews's (R-N.Dak.) devotion to securing particularized benefits for his state. It seems that Andrews took advantage of every opportunity in which he knew his vote would be needed. In addition, Fenno (1992, 120) observes that Andrews's predecessor, Sen. Milton Young, and his North Dakota colleague Sen. Quentin Burdick fit the same mold and were in part responding to the expectations of North Dakota voters.

Of equal interest to us were the costs of the projects Andrews worked for— $4 million for an air-traffic control training facility at the University of North Dakota,

$2.2 million for atmospheric research, $1.75 million for a pedestrian walkway demonstration project, $15 million for a bridge over the Missouri River, $500,000 for local rail service assistance (Fenno 1992, 91–95). All of these projects were large enough, at least in North Dakota, for Andrews to claim credit for them. But if any of these projects were the price in bargaining for Andrews's vote, it was a cheap one.

Contrast these small projects with Andrews's actions as chair of the Transportation Subcommittee of the Appropriations Committee. When Charles Percy (R-Ill.) voted to sustain President Reagan's veto of a supplemental appropriations bill, Andrews punished Percy by cutting nearly $100 million from a Chicago project. At the same time, Andrews was able to protect some programs from cuts, and even to increase others, simply by concentrating the dollar-amount cuts on a single project—a large project in a large state. In doing so he was able to receive credit from other members of the subcommittee for protecting their programs.

16. There are times when coalition builders will have an incentive to gather votes beyond the minimum number needed to win. The larger margin of victory attained may advantage conferees in sustaining a position in conference bargaining with the other house's version of the legislation, for example, or demonstrate that there is sufficient support to override a presidential veto.

17. Originally we planned to extend back farther in time, but we found that the amount of detail in the coverage of roll-call votes decreases as one goes back.

18. This information was gathered primarily from *Congressional Quarterly Weekly Report* and the *Washington Post,* but in a few cases we consulted other news sources and secondary sources.

19. In these cases the news coverage suggested that the outcome was not in doubt, that the losing side had already gained all the votes it was going to get, or that party or coalition leaders were not exerting pressure to gain additional votes. Those who switched at the end or decided late in these cases had been free from pressure and could do as they pleased.

20. The AWACS vote is coincidentally also the example that Richard Fenno used in his American Political Science Association presidential address (1986). He examines the context and sequence of decision making of six senators—two early deciders, two active players, and two late deciders—whom Fenno identifies as Senators A and B, C and D, and E and F, respectively. One familiar with Fenno's work might well guess the identities of each of these senators. In a conversation with us, Fenno confirms that Senators A, C, and D represented states with more than ten congressional districts. Senator B was from a state in the four-to-six congressional district group. Interestingly, Senator B does say that he was invited "to the White House for a chat" about the vote (1986, 9). As our hypothesis would predict, Senators E and F, the late deciders, represented states with one and two congressional districts.

21. The ability to deliver on a federal judgeship nomination may be quite important to the professional legal community and to other political activists in a senator's state or in that segment of a larger state the nominee comes from. In this case the advertising and credit-claiming benefits are with those who are politically active.

22. It has been suggested that coalition builders may find it more helpful to gain the support of a populous state's senator because those senators may also assist in gaining support in the House, where the populous state has greater representation.

However, House members in populous states may have very different constituency concerns than do that state's senators.

23. But it is also clear that coming from a small state related in an auxiliary way to Mansfield's selection first as whip and then as leader (Peabody 1976, 340). Because he came from a small, nonsouthern state, he was relatively free from constituent pressure about civil rights, the issue that was splitting the Democratic Party in the Senate. Another southerner in the leadership would be unacceptable to northern Democrats. And a northerner from a populous state would be under substantial constituency pressure to be aggressive on civil rights legislation. A small-state northerner was the ideal and perhaps the only option. Nevertheless, Mansfield's selection is more idiosyncratic than part of a small-state pattern.

24. But Cranston, unlike Byrd, was not an active whip. Even if he had wanted to be more committed to leadership duties, that may not have been a viable option for a California senator. The constraints of a demanding and highly competitive constituency and the need to raise money for increasingly expensive reelection campaigns required too much of his attention. Not surprisingly, Cranston was never considered as a challenger to or a replacement for Byrd. Instead the outlet for this populous-state senator's political ambitions led him to seek his party's presidential nomination in 1984. Note that Cranston was seventy-four years old when Byrd stepped down as floor leader in 1988.

25. Subsequent to losing the floor leadership contest, Griffin's 1978 reelection bid was unsuccessful. In a populous state like Michigan, Griffin's electoral margins had never been secure. After being appointed to fill the seat when Pat McNamara died, Griffin won with 56 percent of the vote in 1966 and just over 52 percent in 1972, both of which were good years for Republicans nationally.

26. These four senators all represented states with five or fewer congressional districts. The fifth contender for the position was Sen. Richard Lugar of Indiana, a state with ten congressional districts. After Dole's selection, the Republican Conference chose Wyoming's Alan Simpson as whip and Rhode Island's John Chafee as conference chair. They represented states with one and two congressional districts, respectively.

27. Senators from larger than median-sized states who have sought leadership positions in recent years—Sens. J. Bennett Johnston, Richard Lugar, and Jim Sasser—have been notably unsuccessful. In some cases perhaps their colleagues perceived that the senators from smaller states seeking the leadership position have more time to devote to running the Senate and more electoral security. Beyond the failure of senators from middle-sized states to win floor leader contests, we have no hard evidence to support this speculation.

Chapter Six

1. The preponderance of the pre-reapportionment studies concluded that malapportionment has little impact on state spending patterns (Dye 1966; Erikson 1973; Frye and Winters 1970; Jacob 1964; White and Thomas 1964). Of those studies that uncovered some policy effects of state malapportionment (Pulsipher and Weatherby 1968; Sharkansky 1966), the effects tended to be more limited than those hypothe-

sized. Later studies comparing state policymaking before and after reapportionment discovered some policy changes attributable to legislative reapportionment (Becker 1983; Frederickson and Cho 1974; Hanson and Crew 1973). But the jury is still out on the issue, because the three most ambitious and comprehensive of these studies (Frederickson and Cho, Pulsipher and Weatherby, and Hanson and Crew) suffer from multicollinearity problems that invalidate their findings (Newcomer and Hardy 1980).

2. Their findings are called into question by Levitt and Snyder (1995) in an article about the influence of political parties in targeting federal spending to congressional districts. Levitt and Snyder report that congressional districts in populous states receive slightly greater, not smaller, amounts of federal funds (968). It is possible that the cause of these contrary findings lies in the different methods and data employed in each. Atlas et al. employ aggregate budget data that do not allow them to assess the impact of Senate representation on different federal programs and policy types. The program-by-program data set used by Levitt and Snyder permits greater precision in measurement, but their primary focus is on accounting for federal funds allocated to congressional districts; for this reason they cannot draw persuasive conclusions about federal outlays at another level of analysis (i.e., states) from their findings.

3. Figures for state population were obtained from the 1992 *Statistical Abstract of the United States*.

4. In addition, senators from less populous states are allocated greater resources to engage in pork barrel politics: they have more staffers per capita than senators from states with larger populations (Fenno 1973). Not only is access to senators for help with casework easier for constituents in small states, these senators have greater per capita resources to assist their constituents in procuring federal assistance.

5. The third policy type usually identified by political scientists is the regulatory policy. Regulatory policies cannot be measured effectively by expenditure because "the policy output of a regulatory program need not be a direct or indirect expenditure, but rather is typically an authoritative action intended to obtain compliant behavior" (Stein and Bickers 1995, 17). Because of the difficulty of measuring geographic benefits in this policy area, we do not examine the effects of Senate apportionment on regulatory policies.

6. Three types of domestic programs are excluded from the data set: programs designed to address one-time only problems of named entities or persons (such as the Chrysler bailout); domestic programs administered by quasi-governmental corporations (such as the U.S. Postal Service); and contingent liability programs including insurance and direct or guaranteed loans (Stein and Bickers 1995). The funds that the federal government requires to pay its employees or its own procurement expenses are also not included here. Defense spending is not classified among domestic assistance programs.

7. These data are compiled by Bickers and Stein from the *Catalog of Federal Domestic Assistance,* a publication produced by the General Services Administration.

8. The definition of universalism employed here is distinct from the usage of Collie (1988b, 865), who defines universalism as roll-call votes that reflect "a high degree of consensus among the voting membership." This study defines "universalism" in the more traditional way, referring to those legislative coalitions for distribu-

tive programs that are built by ensuring that an overwhelming majority of legislators' constituencies benefit.

9. A state is coded as benefiting from a program when the outlays to the state under that program are greater than zero.

10. Of course the nature of many programs limits legislators' ability to expand the number of geographic constituencies that benefit from them. A program designed to provide earthquake relief obviously cannot provide benefits to a majority of states. The striking finding here is that so many programs are constructed to provide benefits to at least a majority of states.

11. The dollar outlays to states under federal policies are divided by state population. Because per capita indexes are nonlinear transformations of the data, methodologists warn against using per capita measures without adequate theoretical justification. Uslaner (1976) regards the use of per capita data as appropriate when "the theoretical concern of the research involves explicit comparisons among cases, involving the 'relative deprivation' of one group of people contrasted to that of another population" (131–32). The question explored in this chapter explicitly involves such a comparison; thus per capita data are appropriate.

12. The twelve functional policy areas examined in this chapter are not exhaustive of all the policy areas identified by the General Services Administration. These twelve policy areas do, however, constitute in dollar terms the most important policy areas in the federal domestic assistance budget (Bickers and Stein 1991, 8).

13. The data for the control variables were compiled from the *Statistical Abstracts of the United States* for 1985, 1986, 1987, 1988, 1989, 1990, 1991, and 1992. Because several of these control variables, such as number of business failures in a state, are partly a function of state population, they have been transformed into per capita figures.

14. A great deal of help in selecting appropriate control variables was provided by Rundquist, Lee, and Luor (1995), appendix 2.

15. The test is described in Judge et al. (1988, 486–87).

16. Beck and Katz (1995, 638) provide the formula for panel-corrected standard errors. This technique does not affect the OLS coefficients.

17. One possible objection to the argument being made here is that less populous states will necessarily receive higher per capita outlays in federal dollars simply because sparsely populated areas face certain fixed costs of capital investments in buildings and other facilities even though fewer people will be served by them. This economy of scale objection has certain problems, however. First, a number of states with small populations, such as Rhode Island, Hawaii, and Delaware, are compact in size and largely urban; as a result, they have the same advantages in terms of scale as do urban states with large overall populations. The small-population states, moreover, do not have a monopoly on sparsely populated areas in the United States. Extremely sparsely populated areas are often in states with large overall populations. The 13th, 17th, and 23d congressional districts in the northwest and southwest expanses of Texas are certainly sparsely populated areas likely to face problems with economies of scale. The list could go on: downstate Illinois, Michigan's upper peninsula, upstate New York, and northern California all contain sparsely populated areas that are as likely as small-population states to be subject to such problems. In short, because a

number of states with overall large populations have problems with economy of scale in some areas whereas some states with small populations overall are not subject to these difficulties, this objection is not persuasive.

18. The formula apportioned funds one-third in the ratio that the area of each state bears to the total area of all the states, one-third in the ratio of the population of each state to the total national population, and one-third in the ratio of the mileage of rural delivery routes in each state to the total national mileage of rural delivery routes. The formula further provides that no state would receive less than 0.5 percent of each year's total allocation for the program (Statutes at Large 1921, 202).

Chapter Seven

1. These statistics are calculated from information in a report by the Advisory Commission on Intergovernmental Relations (1995) and the 1996 *Catalog of Federal Domestic Assistance* (U.S. General Services Administration 1996).

2. The availability of personal computers has made it easier for staff and members of Congress to devise funding formulas to target particular states (see Nathan 1993). Even so, most funding formulas in existence in the late 1990s are still quite simple, reflecting little targeting. For this reason Arnold's skepticism about congressional targeting of formula grants is still warranted: "In theory it is possible for Congress to write a formula that seemingly allocates benefits according to objective criteria (e.g., per capita income) but that actually allocates them according to political criteria. In practice it is very difficult. Congress would first have to select objective criteria that were good surrogates for all the political criteria, and then would have to devise a complicated weighting scheme capable of differentiating between states on the basis of their congressional representation" (1979, 217).

3. House members do, however, resist factors that are designed to target funds narrowly. Factors distributing funds according to total population are more common than factors distributing funds to narrowly defined groups based on need (see, for example, Arnold 1981).

4. Factors that serve this purpose are generally measures of state characteristics, as opposed to measures of numbers of people in different populations. For example, a heavy weight on a factor measuring state per capita income will bias funds away from populous states toward poor states, and especially toward small poor states. A heavy weight on a factor measuring the number of highway miles in the state will bias funds away from populous states toward states with a lot of highway miles.

5. This is not to say that the Senate will never seek to impose caps on large-state allocations, only that caps are more painful and thus less attractive.

6. Senate politics surrounding the 1991 reauthorization of federal transportation programs provide an excellent illustration (see F. Lee 1997, 201–5). Sen. Daniel Patrick Moynihan (D-N.Y.) succeeded in building a majority coalition to distribute federal transportation dollars by providing funds generously to all the smallest states. Moynihan's coalition defeated an alternative proposed by Sen. John Warner (R-Va.), who attempted to build support by increasing benefits to larger states, making it difficult for him to distribute funds broadly enough to garner a majority of senators' votes. By providing benefits to the less populous states,

Moynihan was able to build a majority and to do so efficiently, leaving substantial funds to allocate to New York.

7. Nevada (0.48 percent of the United States population) and Maine (0.49 percent) receive only very small increases under a 0.5 percent minimum. For this reason the difference between a purely population-based distribution and the minimum may be a matter of indifference to the senators from these states.

8. When programs contain minimum allocations they typically require that program funds first be distributed based on the other factors in the formula. Afterward each state falling below a certain level will receive an additional amount to bring it up to the established floor. To pay for the minimum, allocations to all other states are proportionately reduced. See, for example, the funding formula for the Vulnerable Elder Rights Protection Program (CFDA 93.049) in the *U.S. Code,* Title 42, subchapter 11, § 3058b for an example of the standard way for minimum allocations to be included.

9. A list of the categories of recipients eligible for each federal grant-in-aid funded in 1995 reveals that states are direct recipients of 87.2 percent of all formula grants-in-aid (115 out of 133), whereas they are the direct recipients of only 24 percent of project grants (115 out of 479) (Advisory Commission on Intergovernmental Relations 1995).

10. This is exactly the behavior suggested by the distributive politics model, suggesting that the literature's stress on the distributive politics model may stem from the discipline's traditional emphasis on the House.

11. The sum of money to be distributed by funding formulas is not always fixed. At times, bargaining over the formula takes place at the same time as bargaining over the total amount to be authorized for the program. This was the case, for example, during the bargaining over the 1998 transportation reauthorization. Coalition leaders seeking a change in the formula knew they would be likely to succeed only if they were able to secure a large funding increase for the transportation block grant program as a whole, thus making their proposals more acceptable to those states that would receive a smaller proportion of the total funds under the new formula. Even so, senators recognize that conceding on a formula has long-term consequences, even when they do so in the context of increases in dollar amounts received by their states, because a lower percentage guaranteed to their states will mean more painful cuts if the total allocation for the program is reduced in the future.

12. Senator Strom Thurmond (R-S.C.) followed Randolph in speaking and elaborated on this point: "I can visualize where a President in power would use his influence on that Secretary to allocate a larger amount of funds to some particular State in an election year, which would throw the matter into politics, and it would be very bad" (*Congressional Record* 1978, 30570). No senator disputed these points.

13. In compiling its list of grants, the ACIR relies on the *Catalog of Federal Domestic Assistance (CFDA).* The *CFDA* defines a federal program as "any function of a Federal agency that provides assistance or benefits for a State or States, territorial possession, county, city, other political subdivision, grouping, or instrumentality thereof; any domestic profit or nonprofit corporation, institution, or individual, other than an agency of the Federal government" (U.S. General Services Administration 1996, V).

14. Because departments generally administer programs serving roughly similar public policy purposes, the *CFDA* number adequately identifies the broad policy purposes of programs.

15. Excluding these large programs in the name of randomness would actually increase, rather than decrease, error resulting from selection bias. On this subject King, Keohane, and Verba write: "Even when random selection is feasible, it is not necessarily a wise technique to use. . . .Indeed, if we have only a small number of observations, random selection may not solve the problem of selection bias but may even be worse than other methods of selection" (1994, 125–26).

16. The sample of programs examined are listed in appendix D.

17. In recent years the public law's entry in the *Statutes at Large* provides a brief legislative history listing the report numbers for the House and Senate reports. For legislation before this we located the reports using the reference sources from the Congressional Information Service and the annual indexes of the *Monthly Catalog of United States Government Publications*.

18. Appendix E provides data on the characteristics of the programs sampled as well as on the incidence of House-Senate conflict.

19. There is no relationship between the formula factors included in the program and the type or size of the program. Redistributive and distributive, large and small programs are all equally likely to contain population factors and small-state minimums. The one exception here is that redistributive programs are more likely to include a targeted population factor—but this is no surprise since programs are coded as redistributive on this basis (whether or not the program is aimed at assisting poor or needy areas).

20. When the House and Senate passed legislation establishing conflicting funding formulas at least once during a program's history, the program is coded as one in which House-Senate conflict has occurred. One program that meets this definition is coded as nonconflictual, however, because it is clear that the conflict had nothing to do with geographic representation: the National School Lunch Program. In the School Lunch Program, the Senate changed the formula in 1962 in a way that would encourage greater participation in the program. The original formula was simply based on population and a state's per capita income, so states benefited from placing restrictions on which students could receive subsidized lunches. To reward states for higher participation rates in the program, the Senate pressed for a change to grant funds based on the rate of students' participation in the program. Twenty-eight states lost money initially as a result of the change, and there is no pattern in terms of the population sizes of the states either winning or losing under the change. The House receded to the Senate position in conference. Changing the way this program is coded would not affect the overall findings in the chapter, but the House-Senate conflict over this program's formula is unusual in that it is unrelated to geographic distribution.

21. Program size was coded in this way, as a nominal rather than as an interval-level variable, because we are interested not in the effect each unit ($1 million in this case) has on the odds of conflict, but rather in the difference between large and small programs. Including size in the model as an interval-level variable does not increase the number of cases predicted correctly by the model or substantively change the

coefficient. The distribution of the values on program size as well is such that this coding makes sense. The range of values for program size is bimodal, with eighteen cases under $250 million, eighteen cases above $750 million, and only six cases in the middle range. The median value on program size was $350 million. Defining large and small programs using other values ($250 million, $500 million) does not affect the result shown here.

22. Appendix F provides data on the House-Senate conflicts over the sample programs.

23. These conflicts are broadly distributed across the programs sampled: fifteen of the forty-two programs were never conflictual; twelve were conflictual on one occasion; ten were sources of conflict on two occasions; three exhibited three incidents of conflict; and only two programs had more than three incidents of House-Senate conflict.

24. In 1982, as part of the Job Training Partnership Act, the Federal Employment Service (*CFDA* 17.207) was reauthorized. On this occasion the House's formula was different from the Senate's in two respects: it included a factor measuring the relative number of unemployed in the state as well as a small-state minimum of 0.28 percent. The Senate's bill had neither. It is unclear how this should be interpreted. It could mean that the House was anticipating the Senate position, offering the minimum as compensation for including the need factor.

25. Note that in this case a coalition leader from a populous state attempting to secure a formula more generous to his and other large states still included a mechanism, an increased minimum allocation, to encourage senators from the least populous states to join the coalition.

26. This provision was not part of the final version of the bill. Instead, the conference report dismantled the drug abuse and mental health agency and transferred its functions to the National Institutes of Health (*Congressional Quarterly Almanac* 1992, 425).

27. There are reasons to think that these cases are atypical because of the nature of these programs—these reasons are discussed in the next section.

28. The floor fights over interstate construction and the minimum allocation program are discussed in some detail in F. Lee 1997, chapter 5.

29. Under this very complicated formula, a state's share of the total funds was calculated by multiplying state population by a weighting factor called the allotment percentage. The allotment percentage was calculated in the following way. First the ratio of the state's per capita income to the per capita income of all states was calculated and divided in half. Then this dividend was subtracted from 100 percent and the difference squared (except that figure cannot be less than 33.3 percent or greater than 75 percent). Thus states with a relatively low per capita incomes had large allotment percentages, and states with relatively high per capita incomes had relatively small allotment percentages (Vocational Rehabilitation Act).

30. Conflict within the Senate and between the chambers can occur on issues of program design as well as over the geographic distribution of funds. Senator Javits's successor, Sen. Alfonse M. D'Amato (R-N.Y.), experienced a similar frustration with Senate politics during the 1997 Medicare program reauthorization. Even though the House had already taken measures to encourage HMOs to serve rural areas, the Sen-

ate went much further. D'Amato's frustration is evident in his reaction to the Senate's adopted policy: "This is ruinous. This is nonsense. This is greed. This is over-reaching" (Pear 1997).

31. Many of the early efforts in this area were marred by a failure to consider the sequential nature of the legislative process, thus assuming that the chamber winning most of the particular disputes with the other chamber is the "winner" without considering the agenda-setting role of the first chamber (Strom and Rundquist 1977). This problem of sequence is not very great with respect to funding formulas. The Senate does not usually act second on funding formulas, which are written by authorizing committees, as it usually does on appropriations and revenue bills.

32. This is unambiguously the case with the Entitlement Community Development block grants program (*CFDA* 14.218). States can choose, however, to administer the funds under the Nonentitlement Community Development block grants program (*CFDA* 14.228), but the characteristics of the eligible local areas within states determine their levels of funding. In addition, if a state chooses not to administer the program, the funds go to local governments on a competitive basis.

33. Figure 7.1 does not display the curve for discretionary distributive programs because these are project rather than formula grants.

References

Abramowitz, Alan I. 1980. "A Comparison of Voting for U.S. Senator and Representative." *American Political Science Review* 74 : 633 – 40.

———. 1988. "Explaining Senate Election Outcomes." *American Political Science Review* 82 : 385 – 403.

———. 1991. "Incumbency, Campaign Spending, and the Decline of Competition in U.S. House Elections." *Journal of Politics* 53 : 34 – 56.

Abramowitz, Alan I., and Jeffrey A. Segal. 1992. *Senate Elections*. Ann Arbor: University of Michigan Press.

———. 1997. "Constituent Evaluations of U.S. Senators." Paper presented at the annual meeting of the Southern Political Science Association, Norfolk, Va.

Adler, E. Scott, and John S. Lapinski. 1997. "Demand-Side Theory and Congressional Committee Composition." *American Journal of Political Science* 41 : 895 – 918.

Adrian, Charles. 1960. *State and Local Governments*. New York: McGraw-Hill.

Advisory Commission on Intergovernmental Relations. 1995. "Characteristics of Federal Grant-in-Aid Programs to State and Local Governments: Grants Funded FY 1995." Washington, D.C.

Alexander, Herbert E. 1992. *Financing Politics: Money, Elections, and Political Reform*. Washington, D.C.: CQ Press.

Alford, John R., and John R. Hibbing. 1981. "Increased Incumbency Advantage in the House." *Journal of Politics* 43 : 1042 – 61.

Almond, Gabriel. 1960. "Introduction: A Functional Approach to Comparative Politics." In *The Politics of the Developing Areas,* ed. Gabriel Almond and James Coleman. Princeton: Princeton University Press.

Amy, Douglas. 1993. *Real Choices, New Voices*. New York: Columbia University Press.

Anderson, Thornton. 1993. *Creating the Constitution: The Convention of 1787 and the First Congress*. University Park: Pennsylvania State University Press.

Aristotle. 1985. *Nichomachean Ethics*. Trans. Terence Irwin. Indianapolis: Hackett.

Arnold, R. Douglas. 1979. *Congress and the Bureaucracy: A Theory of Influence.* New Haven: Yale University Press.

———. 1981. "The Local Roots of Domestic Policy." In *The New Congress,* ed. Thomas E. Mann and Norman J. Ornstein. Washington, D.C.: American Enterprise Institute for Public Policy Research.

———. 1990. *The Logic of Congressional Action.* New Haven: Yale University Press.

Atlas, Cary M., Thomas W. Gilligan, Robert J. Hendershott, and Mark A. Zupan. 1995. "Slicing the Federal Government Net Spending Pie: Who Wins, Who Loses and Why." *American Economic Review* 85:624–29.

Austin, Rory A. 1998. "Testing the Impact of Electoral Structures on Minority Office-Holding and Local Policies." Ph.D. diss., Rochester University.

Bach, Stanley, and Steven S. Smith. 1988. *Managing Uncertainty in the House of Representatives: Adaptation and Innovation in Special Rules.* Washington, D.C.: Brookings.

Bagehot, Walter. 1873. *The English Constitution.* Boston: Little, Brown.

Baker, Gordon E. 1955a. *The Reapportionment Revolution: Representation, Political Power and the Supreme Court.* New York: Random House.

———. 1955b. *Rural versus Urban Political Power.* Garden City, N.Y.: Doubleday.

Baker, Lynn A., and Samuel H. Dinkin. 1997. "The Senate: An Institution Whose Time Has Gone?" *Journal of Law and Politics* 13:21–102.

Baker, Ross K. 1989. *House and Senate.* New York: Norton.

Banning, Lance. 1987. "The Constitutional Convention." In *The Framing and Ratification of the Constitution,* ed. Leonard W. Levy and Dennis J. Mahoney. New York: Macmillan.

———. 1995. *The Sacred Fire of Liberty: James Madison and the Founding of the Federal Republic.* Ithaca: Cornell University Press.

Beck, Nathaniel, and Jonathan Katz. 1995. "What to Do (and Not to Do) with Time-Series–Cross-Section Data in Comparative Politics." *American Political Science Review* 89:634–47.

Becker, Gary S. 1983. "A Theory of Competition among Pressure Groups for Influence." *Quarterly Journal of Economics* 98:371–400.

Beitz, Charles R. 1989. *Political Equality: An Essay in Democratic Theory.* Princeton: Princeton University Press.

Bensel, Richard Franklin. 1990. *Yankee Leviathan: The Origins of Central State Authority in America, 1859–1877.* Cambridge: Cambridge University Press.

Bernstein, Robert. 1988. "Do Senators Moderate Strategically?" *American Political Science Review* 82:237–41.

Bibby, John F., Cornelius P. Cotter, James L. Gibson, and Robert J. Huckshorn. 1983. "Parties in State Politics." In *Politics in the American States: A Comparative Analysis,* 4th ed., ed. Virginia Gray, Herbert Jacob, and Kenneth N. Vines. Boston: Little, Brown.

———. 1990. "Parties in State Politics." In *Politics in the American States: A Comparative Analysis,* 5th ed., ed. Virginia Gray, Jacob Herbert, and Kenneth N. Vines. Glenview, Ill.: Scott Foresman.

Bickers, Kenneth N., and Robert M. Stein. 1991. *Federal Domestic Outlays, 1983–1990: A Data Book.* Armonk, N.Y.: Sharpe.

———. 1992. *U.S. Domestic Assistance Programs Database.* Computer file.

————. 1996. "The Electoral Dynamics of the Federal Pork Barrel." *American Journal of Political Science* 40:1300–1326.

Binder, Sarah A. 1997. *Minority Rights, Majority Rule: Partisanship and the Development of Congress.* Cambridge: Cambridge University Press.

Binder, Sarah, Forrest Maltzman, and Lee Sigelman. 1998. "Accounting for Senators' Home-State Reputations: Why Do Constituents Love a Bill Cohen So Much More Than an Al D'Amato?" *Legislative Studies Quarterly* 23:545–60.

Binder, Sarah, and Steven S. Smith. 1997. *Politics or Principle? Filibustering in the the United States Senate.* Washington, D.C.: Brookings.

Birkby, Robert H. 1966. "Politics of Accommodation: The Origins of the Supremacy Clause." *Western Political Quarterly* 19:123–35.

Black, Gordon. 1974. "Conflict in the Community: A Theory of the Effects of Community Size." *American Political Science Review* 68:1245–61.

Bloomer, Kristin. 1998. "Leahy Defends Champlain as 'Great Lake.'" *Sunday Rutland Herald–Sunday Times Argus,* 1 March.

Bond, Jon R. 1983. "The Influence of Constituency Diversity on Electoral Competition in Voting for Congress, 1974–1978." *Legislative Studies Quarterly* 2:201–16.

Bowen, Catherine Drinker. 1966. *Miracle at Philadelphia: The Story of the Constitutional Convention, May to September 1787.* Boston: Little, Brown.

Brant, Irving. 1948. *James Madison: The Nationalist, 1780–1787.* New York: Bobbs-Merrill.

————. 1950. *James Madison: Father of the Constitution, 1787–1800.* New York: Bobbs-Merrill.

Brutus. 1985. "Essays of Brutus." In *The Complete Anti-Federalist,* ed. Herbert J. Storing and Murray Dry. Chicago: University of Chicago Press.

Bullock, Charles S., III. 1976. "Motivations for U.S. Congressional Committee Preferences: Freshmen of the 92d Congress." *Legislative Studies Quarterly* 1:201–12.

————. 1994. "Section 2 of the Voting Rights Act, Districting Formats, and the Election of African Americans." *Journal of Politics* 56:1098–1105.

Bullock, Charles S., III, and Susan MacManus. 1987. "Staggered Terms and Black Representation." *Journal of Politics* 49:543–52.

Burgess, John W. 1902. "The Election of United States Senators by Popular Vote." *Political Science Quarterly* 17:650–63.

Burns, James MacGregor. 1963. *The Deadlock of Democracy: Four Party Politics in America.* Englewood Cliffs, N.J.: Prentice-Hall.

Cameron, Charles, David Epstein, and Sharyn O'Halloran. 1996. "Do Majority-Minority Districts Maximize Substantive Black Representation in Congress?" *American Political Science Review* 90:794–812.

Campbell, James E., John R. Alford, and Keith Henry. 1984. "Television Markets and Congressional Elections." *Legislative Studies Quarterly* 9:667–78.

Cantor, Joseph E. 1997. *Out-of-State Money in the Congressional Elections of 1992, 1994 and 1996: Trends and Policy Issues.* Washington, D.C.: Congressional Research Service.

Collie, Melissa P. 1981. "Incumbency, Electoral Safety, and Turnover in the House of Representatives, 1952–1976." *American Political Science Review* 75:119–31.

————. 1988a. "The Legislature and Distributive Policymaking in Formal Perspective." *Legislative Studies Quarterly* 13 : 427–58.

————. 1988b. "Universalism and the Parties in the U.S. House of Representatives, 1921–80." *American Journal of Political Science* 32 : 865–83.

Congressional Quarterly Almanac. 1956–92. Washington, D.C.: Congressional Quarterly.

Congressional Record. 1956–92. Washington, D.C.

"Constitutional Stupidities Symposium." 1995. *Constitutional Commentaries* 12 : 139–226.

Conway, M. Margaret, and Joanne Connor Green. 1995. "Political Action Committees and the Political Process in the 1990s." In *Interest Group Politics,* 4th ed., ed. Burdett A. Loomis and Allan J. Cigler. Washington, D.C.: CQ Press.

Cook, Timothy E. 1989. *Making Laws and Making News: Media Strategies in the U.S. House of Representatives.* Washington, D.C.: Brookings.

Cottrell, Charles, and Arnold Fleischman. 1979. "The Change from At-Large to District Representation and Political Participation of Minority Groups in Fort Worth and San Antonio, Texas." *Urban Affairs Quarterly* 10 : 17–39.

Cover, Albert D. 1977. "One Good Term Deserves Another: The Advantage of Incumbency in Congressional Elections." *American Journal of Political Science* 21 : 523–42.

Cover, Albert D., and David R. Mayhew. 1977. "Congressional Dynamics and the Decline of Competitive Congressional Elections." In *Congress Reconsidered,* ed. Lawrence C. Dodd and Bruce I. Oppenheimer. New York: Praeger.

Crook, Sara Brandes, and John R. Hibbing. 1997. "A Not-So-Distant Mirror: The Seventeenth Amendment and Institutional Change." *American Political Science Review* 91 : 845–54.

Dahl, Robert A. 1956. *A Preface to Democratic Theory.* Chicago: University of Chicago Press.

Dahl, Robert A., and Edward R. Tufte. 1973. *Size and Democracy.* Stanford: Stanford University Press.

Dauer, Manning J., and Robert G. Kelsay. 1955. "Unrepresentative States." *National Municipal Review* 45 : 571–75.

Davidson, Chandler. 1984. *Minority Vote Dilution.* Washington, D.C.: Howard University Press.

Davidson, Chandler, and George Korbel. 1981. "The Effect of At-Large versus District Elections and Minority Group Representation: A Re-examination of Historical and Contemporary Evidence." *Journal of Politics* 43 : 982–1005.

Davidson, Roger H. 1989. "The Senate: If Everyone Leads, Who Follows?" In *Congress Reconsidered,* 4th ed., ed. Lawrence C. Dodd and Bruce I. Oppenheimer. Washington, D.C.: CQ Press.

Davidson, Roger H., and Walter J. Oleszek. 1998. *Congress and Its Members.* 6th ed. Washington, D.C.: CQ Press.

Davis, Joseph A. 1987. "Nevada to Get Nuclear Waste, Everyone Else off the Hook." *Congressional Quarterly Weekly Report,* December 19, 3136–38.

Deckard, Barbara. 1972. "State Party Delegations in the U.S. House of Representatives: A Comparative Study of Group Cohesion." *Journal of Politics* 34 : 199–222.

Demaris, Alfred. 1992. *Logit Modeling: Practical Applications.* Newbury Park, Calif.: Sage.

Dixon, Robert G., Jr. 1968. *Democratic Representation: Reapportionment in Law and Politics.* New York: Oxford University Press.

Dodd, Lawrence C., and Richard L. Schott. 1986. *Congress and the Administrative State.* New York: Macmillan.

Duchacek, Ivo D. 1970. *Comparative Federalism: The Territorial Dimension of Politics.* New York: Holt, Rinehart, and Winston.

Dumas, Kitty. 1991a. "Urban-Rural Debate Expected over Mental Health, Drugs: House and Senate Push Competing Proposals to Allocate Block Grant Funds to States." *Congressional Quarterly Weekly Report,* June 15, 1590–91.

———. 1991b. "Senators Move to Overhaul Mental Health Funding." *Congressional Quarterly Weekly Report,* July 20, 1990.

Duncan, Dayton, and Ken Burns. 1997. *Lewis and Clark.* New York: Knopf.

Duncan, Phil, ed. 1990. *Politics in America.* Washington, D.C.: CQ Press.

———. 1994. *Politics in America.* Washington, D.C.: CQ Press.

Duverger, Maurice. 1984. "'Duverger's Law': Thirty Years Later." In *Electoral Laws and Their Political Consequences,* ed. Bernard Grofman and Arend Lijphart. New York: Agathon. .

Dye, Thomas R. 1966. *Politics, Economics and the Public: Policy Outcomes in the American States.* Chicago: Rand McNally.

Easton, David. 1965. *A Framework for Political Analysis.* Englewood Cliffs, N.J.: Prentice-Hall.

Elazar, Daniel J. 1987a. "'Our Thoroughly Federal Constitution.'" In *How Federal Is the Constitution?* ed. Robert A. Goldwin and William Schambra. Washington, D.C.: American Enterprise Institute for Public Policy Research.

———. 1987b. *Exploring Federalism.* Tuscaloosa: University of Alabama Press.

Elling, Richard C. 1982. "Ideological Change in the U.S. Senate: Time and Electoral Responsiveness." *Legislative Studies Quarterly* 7:75–92.

Endersby, James W., and Karen M. McCurdy. 1996. "Committee Assignments in the U.S. Senate." *Legislative Studies Quarterly* 21:219–33.

England, Paula, Barbara Stanek Kilbourne, George Farkas, and Thomas Dou. 1988. "Explaining Occupational Sex Segregation and Wages: Findings from a Model with Fixed Effects." *American Sociological Review* 53:544–58.

Engstrom, Richard, and Michael McDonald. 1986. "The Effect of At-Large versus District Elections on Racial Representation in U.S. Municipalities." In *Election Laws and Their Political Consequences,* ed. Bernard Grofman and Arend Lijpart. New York: Agathon.

Epstein, David, and Peter Zemsky. 1995. "Money Talks: Deterring Quality Challengers in Congressional Elections." *American Political Science Review* 89:295–308.

Erikson, Robert S. 1971. "The Advantage of Incumbency in Congressional Elections." *Polity* 3:395–405.

———. 1973. "Reapportionment and Policy." *Midwest Journal of Political Science* 15:57–71.

———. 1990. "Roll Calls, Reputations, and Representation in the U.S. Senate." *Legislative Studies Quarterly* 15:623–42.

Erikson, Robert S., and Gerald C. Wright. 1993. "Voters, Candidates, and Issues in Congressional Elections." In *Congress Reconsidered,* 5th ed., ed. Lawrence C. Dodd and Bruce I. Oppenheimer. Washington, D.C.: CQ Press.

Eskridge, William N., Jr. 1995. "The One Senator, One Vote Clause." *Constitutional Commentaries* 12:159–62.

Evans, Diana. 1994. "Policy and Pork: The Use of Pork Barrel Projects to Build Policy Coalitions in the House of Representatives." *American Journal of Political Science* 38:894–917.

Eyestone, Robert, and Heinz Eulau. 1968. "City Councils and Policy Outcomes: Developmental Profiles." In *City Politics and Public Policy,* ed. James Q. Wilson. New York: Wiley.

Farrand, Max, ed. 1937. *The Records of the Federal Convention of 1787.* New Haven: Yale University Press.

———. 1966. *The Records of the Federal Convention of 1787.* Rev. ed. New Haven: Yale University Press.

Feldman, Paul, and James Jondrow. 1984. "Congressional Elections and Local Federal Spending." *American Journal of Political Science* 28:147–63.

Fenno, Richard F., Jr. 1966. *The Power of the Purse: Appropriations Politics in Congress.* Boston: Little, Brown.

———. 1973. *Congressmen in Committees.* Boston: Little, Brown.

———. 1978. *Home Style: House Members in Their Districts.* Boston: Little, Brown.

———. 1982. *The United States Senate: A Bicameral Perspective.* Washington, D.C.: American Enterprise Institute for Public Policy Research.

———. 1986. "Observation, Context, and Sequence in the Study of Politics." *American Political Science Review* 80:3–15.

———. 1991. *The Emergence of a Senate Leader: Pete Domenici and the Reagan Budget.* Washington, D.C.: CQ Press.

———. 1992. *When Incumbency Fails: The Senate Career of Mark Andrews.* Washington, D.C.: CQ Press.

———. 1996. *Senators on the Campaign Trail: The Politics of Representation.* Norman: University of Oklahoma Press.

Ferejohn, John A. 1974. *Pork Barrel Politics.* Stanford: Stanford University Press.

———. 1975. "Who Wins in Conference Committee?" *Journal of Politics* 37:1033–46.

Fessler, Pamela, and Pat Towell. 1989. "'Stealth' Bomber Survives, with Some Conditions, and SDI Narrowly Escapes a Funding Cut." *Congressional Quarterly Weekly Report,* July 29, 1978–86.

Fillipov, Mikhail G. 1996. "Long-Term Representational Determinants of Allocation of Federal Grants to States." Paper presented at the annual meeting of the Midwest Political Science Association, Chicago.

Fiorina, Morris P. 1974. *Representatives, Roll Calls and Constituencies.* Lexington, Mass.: Lexington Books.

———. 1977. "The Case of the Vanishing Marginals: The Bureaucracy Did It." *American Political Science Review* 71:177–81.

———. 1981. "Some Problems in Studying the Effects of Resource Allocation in Congressional Elections." *American Journal of Political Science* 25:543–67.

———. 1989. *Congress: Keystone of the Washington Establishment*. New Haven: Yale University Press.

Foley, Michael. 1980. *The New Senate*. New Haven: Yale University Press.

Forbes, Malcolm S., Jr. 1995. "Fact and Comment." *Forbes,* November 20, 23.

Fowler, Linda L. 1993. *Candidates, Congress, and the American Democracy*. Ann Arbor: University of Michigan Press.

Fowler, Linda L., and Robert D. McClure. 1989. *Political Ambition: Who Decides to Run for Congress*. New Haven: Yale University Press.

Frederickson, H. George, and Yong Hyo Cho. 1974. "Legislative Apportionment and Fiscal Policy in the American States." *Western Political Quarterly* 27:5–31.

Frost, Richard T. 1959. "On Derge's Metropolitan and Outstate Legislative Delegations." *American Political Science Review* 53:792–95.

Frye, Brian, and Richard Winters. 1970. "The Politics of Redistribution." *American Political Science Review* 64:508–22.

Geoghegan, Tom. 1994. "The Infernal Senate." *New Republic,* November 21, 17–23.

Gerber, Alan. 1998. "Estimating the Effect of Campaign Spending on Senate Election Outcomes Using Instrumental Variables." *Amerian Political Science Review* 92:401–11.

Gerber, Elisabeth, Rebecca B. Morton, and Thomas A. Rietz. 1998. "Minority Representation in Multimember Districts." *American Political Science Review* 92:127–44.

Gilmour, John B., and Paul Rothstein. 1994. "Term Limitation in a Dynamic Model of Partisan Balance." *American Journal of Political Science* 38:770–96.

Glennon, Michael J. 1992. *When No Majority Rules: The Electoral College and Presidential Succession*. Washington, D.C.: CQ Press, 1992.

Goldenberg, Edie N., and Michael W. Traugott. 1984. *Campaigning for Congress*. Washington, D.C.: CQ Press.

Gormley, Ken. 1994. *The Pennsylvania Legislative Reapportionment of 1991*. Pennsylvania Legislative Reapportionment Commission: Pennsylvania Bureau of Publications.

Gould, Stephen Jay. 1980. *The Panda's Thumb: More Reflections in Natural History*. New York: Norton.

———. 1991. *Bully for Brontosaurus: Reflections in Natural History*. New York: Norton.

Governmental Affairs Institute. 1992. *America Votes: A Handbook of Contemporary American Election Statistics*. Vol. 20. Washington, D.C.: CQ Press.

Gray, Virginia, and David Lowery. 1993. "The Diversity of State Interest Group Systems." *Political Research Quarterly* 46:81–97.

Greene, William H. 1993. *Econometric Analysis*. 2d ed. New York: Macmillan.

Grier, Kevin B., and Michael C. Munger. 1993. "Comparing Interest Group PAC Contributions to House and Senate Incumbents, 1980–1986." *Journal of Politics* 55:614–43.

Grofman, Bernard, Lisa Handley, and Richard G. Niemi. 1992. *Minority Representation and the Quest for Voting Equality*. New York: Cambridge University Press.

Gronke, Paul. n.d. *Senate versus House or House and Senate? A Unified Approach to Senate and House Elections*. Ann Arbor University of Michigan Press. Forthcoming.

Hall, Richard L. 1993. *Participation in Congress*. New Haven: Yale University Press.

Hall, Richard L., and Bernard Grofman. 1990. "The Committee Assignment Process and the Conditional Nature of Committee Bias." *American Political Science Review* 84:1149–66.

Hamilton, Alexander, John Jay, and James Madison. 1987. *The Federalist Papers*. Ed. Isaac Kramnick. New York: Penguin.

Hanson, Roger A., and Robert E. Crew. 1973. "The Policy Impact of Reapportionment." *Law and Society Review* 8:69–92.

Hardin, Charles. 1974. *Presidential Power and Accountability: Toward a New Constitution*. Chicago: University of Chicago Press.

Harwood, John. 1994. "Political Treadmill: For California Senator, Fundraising Becomes Overwhelming Burden." *Wall Street Journal*, March 2, A1.

Havard, William C., and Loren P. Beth. 1962. *The Politics of Misrepresentation*. Baton Rouge: Louisiana State University Press.

Haynes, George H. 1938. *The Senate of the United States: Its History and Practice*. New York: Russell and Russell.

Herrnson, Paul S. 1997. "Money and Motives: Spending in House Elections." In *Congress Reconsidered*, 6th ed., ed. Lawrence C. Dodd and Bruce I. Oppenheimer. Washington, D.C.: CQ Press.

———. 1998. *Congressional Elections: Campaigning at Home and in Washington*. 2d ed. Washington, D.C.: CQ Press.

Hess, Stephen. 1986. *The Ultimate Insiders: U.S. Senators in the National Media*. Washington, D.C.: Brookings.

———. 1987. "A Note on Senate Press Secretaries and Media Strategies." Brookings Institution Discussion Paper.

Hibbing, John R., and John R. Alford. 1990. "Constituency Population and Representation in the U.S. Senate." *Legislative Studies Quarterly* 15:581–98.

Hibbing, John R., and Sara L. Brandes. 1983. "State Population and the Electoral Success of U.S. Senators." *American Journal of Political Science* 27:808–19.

Hibbing, John R., and Elizabeth Theiss-Morse. 1995. *Congress as Public Enemy: Public Attitudes toward American Political Institutions*. Cambridge: Cambridge University Press.

Hoebeke, C. H. 1995. *The Road to Mass Democracy*. New Brunswick, N.J.: Transaction.

Hoffman, David, and Lou Cannon. 1987. "With Defeat All but Certain, President Raised the Stakes." *Washington Post*, April 3, A1, A6.

Holcombe, Arthur N. 1967. *Our More Perfect Union*. Cambridge: Harvard University Press.

Horn, Stephen. 1970. *Unused Power: the Work of the Senate Committee on Appropriations*. Washington, D.C.: Brookings.

Hsiao, Cheng. 1986. *Analysis of Panel Data*. Cambridge: Cambridge University Press.

Hunt, Albert R. 1981. "Some Senators Say They Were Promised White House Favors to Vote for AWACs." *Wall Street Journal*, October 14, A4.

Inter-University Consortium for Political and Social Research. 1990. *Candidate and Constituency Statistics of Elections in the United States, 1788–1988*. Computer file.

Ann Arbor, Mich.: Center for Political Studies [producer]; Inter-University Consortium for Political and Social Research [distributor].

Inter-University Consortium for Political and Social Research. 1993. *American National Election Study: Pooled Senate Election Study, 1988, 1990, 1992.* Computer file. Ann Arbor, Mich.: Center for Political Studies [producer]; Inter-University Consortium for political and Social Research [distributor].

Jacob, Herbert. 1964. "The Consequences of Malapportionment: A Note of Caution." *Social Forces* 43 : 256–71.

Jacobson, Gary C. 1984. "Money in the 1980 and 1982 Congressional Elections." In *Money and Politics in the United States,* ed. Michael J. Malbin. Chatham, N.J.: Chatham House.

———. 1987. "The Marginals Never Vanished: Incumbency and Competition in Elections to the U.S. House of Representatives." *American Journal of Political Science* 31 : 126–41.

———. 1989. "Parties and PACs in Congressional Elections." In *Congress Reconsidered,* 4th ed., ed. Lawrence C. Dodd and Bruce I. Oppenheimer. Washington, D.C.: CQ Press.

———. 1992. *The Politics of Congressional Elections.* New York: HarperCollins.

———. 1993. "The Misallocation of Resources in House Campaigns." In *Congress Reconsidered,* 5th ed., ed. Lawrence C. Dodd and Bruce I. Oppenheimer. Washington D.C.: CQ Press.

Jacobson, Gary C., and Samuel Kernell. 1983. *Strategy and Choice in Congressional Elections.* New Haven: Yale University Press.

Jefferson, Thomas. 1955. *Notes on the State of Virginia.* Ed. William Peden. New York: Norton.

Jewell, Malcolm E. 1962. *The State Legislature: Politics and Practice.* New York: Random House.

Jillson, Calvin C. 1988. *Constitution Making: Conflict and Consensus in the Federal Convention of 1787.* New York: Agathon.

Johannes, John R. 1984. *To Serve the People: Congress and Constituency Service.* Lincoln: University of Nebraska Press.

Johannes, John R., and John C. McAdams. 1981. "The Congressional Incumbency Effect: Is It Casework, Policy Compatibility, or Something Else?" *American Journal of Political Science* 25 : 512–42.

Johnson, Janet B., and Richard A. Joslyn. 1991. *Political Science Research Methods.* 2d ed. Washington, D.C.: CQ Press.

Judge, George G., R. Carter Hill, William E. Griffiths, Helmut Lütkepohl, and Tsoung-Chao Lee. 1988. *Introduction to the Theory and Practice of Econometrics.* 2d ed. New York: Wiley.

Kamen, Al. 1998. "Creative Geography." *Washington Post,* February 27, A23.

Katz, Jeffrey L. 1995. "Sunbelt Senators Revolt over Welfare Formula." *Congressional Quarterly Weekly Report,* June 24, 1842–44.

Kazee, Thomas A., ed. 1994. *Who Runs for Congress? Ambition, Context, and Candidate Emergence.* Washington, D.C.: CQ Press.

Kenney, Patrick J., and Tom W. Rice. 1985. "Party Composition in the American

States: Clarifying Concepts and Explaining Changes in Partisanship since the 1950s." *Political Behavior* 7 : 33–351.

Key, V. O. 1956. *American State Politics: An Introduction.* New York: Knopf.

King, Gary, Robert O. Keohane, and Sidney Verba. 1994. *Designing Social Inquiry: Scientific Inference in Qualitative Research.* Princeton: Princeton University Press.

King, Ronald F., and Susan Ellis. 1996. "Partisan Advantage and Constitutional Change: The Case of the Seventeenth Amendment." *Studies in American Political Development* 10 : 69–102.

Kingdon, John W. 1989. *Congressmen's Voting Decisions.* 3d ed. Ann Arbor: University of Michigan Press.

Kramnick, Isaac. 1987. Introduction to *The Federalist Papers,* by Alexander Hamilton, John Jay, and James Madison. New York: Penguin.

Krasno, Jon. 1994. *Challengers, Competition and Reelection: Comparing Senate and House Elections.* New Haven: Yale University Press.

Lazare, Daniel. 1996. *The Frozen Republic: How the Constitution Is Paralyzing Democracy.* New York: Harcourt Brace.

Lee, Emery G., III. 1997. "Representation, Virtue, and Political Jealousy in the Brutus-Publius Dialogue." *Journal of Politics* 59 : 1073–95.

Lee, Frances E. 1997. "The Enduring Consequences of the Great Compromise: Senate Apportionment and Congressional Policymaking." Ph.D. diss., Vanderbilt University.

———. 1998. "Representation and Public Policy: The Consequences of Senate Apportionment for the Geographic Distribution of Federal Funds." *Journal of Politics* 60 : 34–62.

Lee, Frances E., and Bruce I. Oppenheimer. 1997. "Senate Apportionment: Competitiveness and Partisan Advantage." *Legislative Studies Quarterly* 22 : 3–24.

Levitt, Steven D., and James M. Snyder Jr. 1995. "Political Parties and the Distribution of Federal Outlays." *American Journal of Political Science* 39 : 958–80.

Levy, Dana, and Peverill Squire. 1994. "Constituency Size and Home Style: A Comparison of Senators and Representatives." Paper presented at the annual meeting of the American Political Science Association, New York.

Levy, Leonard W. 1969. "Introduction." In *Essays on the Making of the Constitution,* ed. Leonard W. Levy. New York: Oxford University Press.

Lijphart, Arend. 1984. *Democracies: Patterns of Majoritarian and Consensus Government in Twenty-one Countries.* New Haven: Yale University Press.

———. 1994. *Electoral Systems and Party Systems: A Study of Twenty-seven Democracies, 1945–1990.* New Haven: Yale University Press.

———. 1998. "Reforming the House: Three Moderately Radical Proposals." *P.S.* 30 : 10–13.

Lijphart, Arend, and Bernard Grofman. 1984. *Choosing an Electoral System: Issues and Alternatives.* New York: Praeger.

Lind, Michael. 1995. "Prescriptions for a New National Democracy." *Political Science Quarterly* 110 : 563–86.

———. 1998. "Seventy-five Stars: How to Restore Democracy in the U.S. Senate (and End the Tyranny of Wyoming)." *Mother Jones,* January–February, 44–49.

Locke, John. 1980. *Second Treatise of Government.* Indianapolis: Hackett.

Longley, Lawrence D., and Walter Oleszek. 1989. *Bicameral Politics: Conference Committees in Congress*. New Haven: Yale University Press.

Lowery, David, and Virginia Gray. 1993. "The Density of State Interest Group Systems." *Journal of Politics* 55:191–206.

———. 1995. "The Population Ecology of Gucci Gulch, or The Natural Regulation of Interest Group Numbers in the American States." *American Journal of Political Science* 39:1–19.

———. 1996. *The Population Ecology of Interest Representation: Lobbying Communities in the American States*. Ann Arbor: University of Michigan Press.

Lowi, Theodore J. 1964. "American Business, Public Policy, Case-Studies, and Political Theory." *World Politics* 16:667–715.

Lublin, David. 1997. *The Paradox of Representation: Racial Gerrymandering and Minority Interests in Congress*. Princeton: Princeton University Press.

Luce, Robert. 1930. *Legislative Principles*. Boston: Houghton Mifflin.

MacFarquhar, Neil. 1996. "In New Jersey, Meeting the Voters Is a Luxury." *New York Times,* November 1, A1.

MacManus, Susan. 1978. "City Council Election Procedures and Minority Representation." *Social Science Quarterly* 59:153–61.

———. 1979. "At Large Elections and Minority Representation: An Adversarial Critique." *Social Science Quarterly* 60:338–40.

Maddala, G. 1977. *Econometrics*. New York: McGraw-Hill.

Magleby, David B., and Candice J. Nelson. 1990. *The Money Chase: Congressional Campaign Finance Reform*. Washington, D.C.: Brookings.

Main, Jackson Turner. 1967. *The Upper House in Revolutionary America, 1763–1788*. Madison: University of Wisconsin Press.

Maisel, L. Sandy, Walter J. Stone, and Cherie Meastas. 1997. "Quality Candidates in Congressional Elections: A Preliminary View from the Candidate Emergence Study." Paper presented at the annual meeting of the American Political Science Association, Washington, D.C.

Malbin, Michael. 1987. "Congress during the Convention and Ratification." In *The Framing and Ratification of the Constitution,* ed. Leonard W. Levy and Dennis J. Mahoney. New York: Macmillan.

Manley, John. 1970. *The Politics of Finance: The House Ways and Means Committee*. Boston: Little, Brown.

March, James G., and Johan Olsen. 1989. *Rediscovering Institutions: The Organizational Basis of Politics*. New York: Free Press.

Matthews, Donald R. 1960. *U.S. Senators and Their World*. Chapel Hill: University of North Carolina Press.

———. 1990. "Senators and the Senate." In *The Changing World of the U.S. Senate,* ed. John R. Hibbing. Berkeley, Calif.: IGS Press.

Matthews, Donald R., and James A. Stimson. 1975. *Yeas and Nays: Normal Decision-Making in the U.S. House of Representatives*. New York: Wiley.

Mayhew, David R. 1974. *Congress: The Electoral Connection*. New Haven: Yale University Press.

McAdams, John C., and John R. Johannes. 1988. "Congressmen, Perquisites, and Elections." *Journal of Politics* 55:412–39.

McCubbins, Matthew D., and Thomas Schwartz. 1988. "Congress, the Courts, and Public Policy: Consequences of the One Man, One Vote Rule." *American Journal of Political Science* 32:388–415.

McDonald, Forrest. 1979. *E Pluribus Unum: The Formation of the American Republic, 1776–1790.* Indianapolis: Liberty Fund.

———. 1985. *Novus Ordo Seclorum: The Intellectual Origins of the Constitution.* Lawrence: University Press of Kansas.

McPherson, Harry. 1972. *A Political Education.* Boston: Little, Brown.

Merriam, Charles Edward. 1931. *The Written Constitution and the Unwritten Attitude.* New York: Richard R. Smith.

Moffett, S. E. 1895. "Is the Senate Unfairly Constituted?" *Political Science Quarterly* 10:248–56.

Mondak, Jeffrey J. 1995. "Elections and Filters: Term Limits and the Composition of the U.S. House." *Political Research Quarterly* 48:701–27.

Morgan, David R., and Laura Ann Wilson. 1990. "Diversity in the American States: Updating the Sullivan Index." *Publius* 20:71–81.

Morley, Felix. 1959. *Freedom and Federalism.* Chicago: Regnery.

Moynihan, Daniel Patrick. 1995. Introduction to *The Federal Budget and the States: Fiscal Year 1994,* by Monica E. Friar and Herman B. Leonard. Cambridge, Mass.: Taubman Center for State and Local Government at the Kennedy School of Government.

Nathan, Richard. 1993. "The Politics of Printouts: The Use of Official Numbers to Allocate Federal Grants-in-Aid." In *American Intergovernmental Relations,* ed. Lawrence O'Toole. 2d ed. Washington, D.C.: CQ Press.

Newcomer, Kathryn E., and Richard J. Hardy. 1980. "Analyzing Political Impact: Selection of a Linear Trend Model." *Policy Studies Journal* 8:928–41.

New York Times. 1998. "Maybe It's an Ocean." Editorial, March 4, A20.

North, Douglass C. 1990. *Institutions, Institutional Change and Economic Performance.* New York: Cambridge University Press.

Oleszek, Walter J. 1996. *Congressional Procedures and the Policy Process.* 4th ed. Washington, D.C.: CQ Press.

Oppenheimer, Bruce I. 1989. "Split Party Control of Congress, 1981–1986: Exploring Electoral and Apportionment Explanations." *American Journal of Political Science* 33:653–69.

———. 1996. "The Representational Experience: The Effect of State Population on Senator-Constituency Linkages." *American Journal of Political Science* 40:1280–99.

Ornstein, Norman J. 1983. "The Open Congress Meets the President." In *Both Ends of the Avenue: The Presidency, the Executive Branch, and Congress in the 1980s,* ed. Anthony King. Washington, D.C.: American Enterprise Institute for Public Policy Research.

Ornstein, Norman J., Thomas E. Mann, and Michael Malbin. 1998. *Vital Statistics on Congress: 1997–1998.* Washington, D.C.: American Enterprise Institute for Public Policy Research.

Overby, L. Marvin, and Kenneth Cosgrove. 1996. "Unintended Consequences? Racial Redistricting and the Representation of Minority Interests." *Journal of Politics* 58:540–50.

Parker, Glenn R., and Suzanne L. Parker. 1985. "Correlates and Effects of Attention to the District by U.S. House Members." *Legislative Studies Quarterly* 10:223–42.

Patterson, Samuel C., and Gregory A. Caldeira. 1984. "The Etiology of Partisan Competition." *American Political Science Review* 78:691–707.

Peabody, Robert L. 1976. *Leadership in Congress: Stability, Succession, and Change.* Boston: Little, Brown.

———. 1981. "Senate Party Leadership: From the 1950s to the 1980s." In *Understanding Congressional Leadership,* ed. Frank H. Mackaman. Washington, D.C.: Congressional Quarterly Press.

Peacock, Anthony A. 1997. *Affirmative Action and Representation: Shaw v. Reno and the Future of Voting Rights.* Durham, N.C.: Carolina Academic Press.

Pear, Robert. 1997. "Medicare Revamp Advances in Vote by Senate Panel." *New York Times,* June 19, B12.

Pearson, Richard. 1990. "Sen. Spark Matsunaga, Hawaii Democrat, Dies." *Washington Post,* April 16, D6.

Peirce, Neal R., and Lawrence D. Longley. 1981. *The People's President: The Electoral College in American History and the Direct Vote Alternative.* New Haven: Yale University Press.

Persons, Georgia A. 1997. *Race and Representation.* New Brunsick, N.J.: Transaction.

Peterson, Paul E. 1995. *Classified by Race.* Princeton: Princeton University Press.

Pitkin, Hannah. 1967. *The Concept of Representation.* Berkeley: University of California Press.

Polsby, Nelson W., and Aaron Wildavsky. 1996. *Presidential Elections: Strategies and Structures of American Politics.* 9th ed. Chatham, N.J.: Chatham House.

Pressman, Jeffrey L. 1966. *House v. Senate: Conflict in the Appropriations Process.* New Haven: Yale University Press.

Price, David E. 1972. *Who Makes the Laws? Creativity and Power in Senate Committees.* Cambridge, Mass.: Schenkman.

Pulsipher, Allan, and James Weatherby. 1968. "Malapportionment, Party Competition and the Functional Distribution of Governmental Expenditures." *American Political Science Review* 62:1207–19.

Rae, Douglas. 1967. *The Political Consequences of Electoral Laws.* New Haven: Yale University Press.

Rakove, Jack N. 1987. "The Great Compromise: Ideas, Interests, and the Politics of Constitution Making." *William and Mary Quarterly* 44:425–57.

Ranney, Austin. 1965. "Parties in State Politics." In *Politics in the American States: A Comparative Analysis,* ed. Herbert Jacob and Kenneth N. Vines. Boston: Little, Brown.

———. 1971. "Parties in State Politics." In *Politics in the American States: A Comparative Analysis,* 2d ed., ed. Herbert Jacob and Kenneth N. Vines. Boston: Little, Brown.

———. 1976. "Parties in State Politics." In *Politics in the American States: A Comparative Analysis,* 3d ed., ed. Herbert Jacob and Kenneth N. Vines. Boston: Little, Brown.

Ranney, Austin, and Willmoore Kendall. 1954. "The American Party Systems." *American Political Science Review* 48:477–85.

Ray, Bruce. 1980. "Congressional Promotion of District Interests: Does Power on the Hill Really Make a Difference?" In *Political Benefits,* ed. Barry S. Rundquist. Lexington, Mass.: Heath.

Reed, W. Robert, and D. Eric Schansberg. 1995. "The House under Term Limits: What Would It Look Like?" *Social Science Quarterly* 76:699–716.

Ripley, Randall B. 1969. *Power in the Senate.* New York: St. Martin's Press.

Ripley, Randall B., and Grace A. Franklin. 1991. *Congress, the Bureaucracy and Public Policy.* 5th ed. Pacific Grove, Calif.: Brooks/Cole.

Robinson, Theodore, and Thomas Dye. 1978. "Reformism and Representation on City Councils." *Social Science Quarterly* 59:133–41.

Roche, John P. 1961. "The Founding Fathers: A Reform Caucus in Action." *American Political Science Review* 55:799–816.

Rogers, Lindsay. 1926. *The American Senate.* New York: Knopf.

Rundquist, Barry S. 1978. "On Testing a Military Industrial Complex Theory." *American Politics Quarterly* 6:29–53.

———. 1980. *Political Benefits: Empirical Studies of American Public Programs.* Lexington, Mass.: Heath.

Rundquist, Barry S., and David E. Griffith. 1976. "An Interrupted Time-Series Test of the Distributive Theory of Military Policy-Making." *Western Political Quarterly* 29:620–26.

Rundquist, Barry, Jeong-Hwa Lee, and Ching-Jyuhn Luor. 1995. "States vs. Districts as Units of Analysis in Distributive Studies: An Exploration." Paper presented at the annual meeting of the Midwest Political Science Association, Chicago.

Sabato, Larry J. 1984. *PAC Power: Inside the World of Political Action Committees.* New York: Norton.

Sayrs, Lois W. 1989. *Pooled Time Series Analysis.* Newbury Park, Calif.: Sage.

Scarrow, Howard A. 1983. *Parties, Elections, and Representation in the State of New York.* New York: New York University Press.

Schattschneider, E. E. 1942. *Party Government.* New York: Farrar and Rinehart.

———. 1960. *The Semi-sovereign People: A Realist's View of Democracy.* New York: Holt, Rinehart and Winston.

Schiller, Wendy J. 1995. "Senators as Political Entrepreneurs: Using Bill Sponsorship to Shape Legislative Agendas." *American Journal of Political Science* 39:186–203.

———. 1997. "Competing for Home Field Advantage: How Senators Attract Interest Group Support." Paper presented at the annual meeting of the Midwest Political Science Association, Chicago.

———. 1998. "Senators and Their Constituents: Can the Media Bridge the Gap?" Paper presented at the annual meeting of the Midwest Political Science Association, Chicago.

Schubert, Glendon, and Charles Press. 1964. "Measuring Malapportionment." *American Political Science Review* 58:302–27.

Seelye, Katharine Q. 1998. "Superior Is Great, Could Champlain Be, Too?" *New York Times,* March 4, A1.

Seiler, Casey. 1998. "Greatness: A State of Mind." *Burlington Free Press,* March 9, A1.

Sharkansky, Ira. 1966. "Voting Behavior of Metropolitan Congressmen: Prospects for Changes with Reapportionment." *Journal of Politics* 28 : 774 – 94.

Shepsle, Kenneth A. 1978. *The Giant Jigsaw Puzzle.* Chicago: University of Chicago Press.

Sinclair, Barbara. 1989. *The Transformation of the U.S. Senate.* Baltimore: Johns Hopkins University Press.

———. 1990. "Washington Behavior and Home-State Reputation: The Impact of National Prominence on Senators' Images." *Legislative Studies Quarterly* 15 : 475 – 94.

———. 1997. *Unorthodox Lawmaking: New Legislative Processes in the U.S. Congress.* Washington, D.C.: CQ Press.

Skocpol, Theda. 1995. *Social Policy in the United States: Future Possibilities in Historical Perspective.* Princeton: Princeton University Press.

———. 1992. *Protecting Soldiers and Mothers: The Political Origins of Social Policy in the United States.* Cambridge: Harvard University Press.

Skowronek, Stephen. 1982. *Building a New American State: The Expansion of National Administrative Capacities, 1877–1920.* Cambridge: Cambridge University Press.

———. 1993. *The Politics Presidents Make: Leadership from John Adams to George Bush.* Cambridge, Mass.: Belknap Press.

Smith, Steven. 1989. *Call to Order: Floor Politics in the House and Senate.* Washington, D.C.: Brookings.

———. 1993. "Forces of Change in Senate Party Leadership and Organization." In *Congress Reconsidered,* 5th ed., ed. Lawrence C. Dodd and Bruce I. Oppenheimer. Washington, D.C.: CQ Press.

Smith, Steven S., and Christopher J. Deering. 1990. *Committees in Congress.* 2d ed. Washington, D.C.: CQ Press.

Snyder, James M., Jr. 1993. "The Market for Campaign Contributions: Evidence for the U.S. Senate, 1980 – 1986." *Economics and Politics* 5 : 219 – 50.

Sorauf, Frank. 1962. *Party and Representation.* New York: Atherton.

Squire, Peverill. 1988. "Who Gets National News Coverage in the U.S. Senate?" *American Politics Quarterly* 16 : 139 – 56.

Starobin, Paul. 1987. "Highway Bill Veto Overridden after Close Call in the Senate." *Congressional Quarterly Weekly Report,* April 4, 604 – 6.

Stein, Robert M., and Kenneth N. Bickers. 1994a. "Congressional Elections and the Pork Barrel." *Journal of Politics* 56 : 377 – 99.

———. 1994b. "Universalism and the Electoral Connection: A Test and Some Doubts." *Political Research Quarterly* 47 : 295 – 317.

———. 1995. *Perpetuating the Pork Barrel: Policy Subsystems and American Democracy.* New York: Cambridge University Press.

Steiner, Gilbert. 1951. *The Congressional Conference Committee: Seventieth to Eightieth Congresses.* Urbana: University of Illinois Press.

Stewart, Charles, and Mark Reynolds. 1990. "Television Markets and U.S. Senate Elections." *Legislative Studies Quarterly* 15 : 495 – 523.

Stewart, Charles, III, and Barry R. Weingast. 1992. "Stacking the Senate, Changing the Nation: Republican Rotten Boroughs, Statehood Politics, and American Political Development." *Studies in American Political Development* 6 : 223 – 71.

Stewart, Joseph, Robert England, and Kenneth J. Meier. 1989. "Black Representation in Urban School Districts: From School Boards to Office to Classroom." *Western Political Quarterly* 42:287–305.

Stimson, James A. 1985. "Regression in Space and Time: A Statistical Essay." *American Journal of Political Science* 29:914–47.

Storing, Herbert J. 1981. "The Federal Convention of 1787." In *The American Founding: Politics, Statesmanship, and the Constitution,* ed. Ralph A. Rossum and Gary L. McDowell. Port Washington, N.Y.: Kennikat Press.

Strom, Gerald S. 1975. "Congressional Policy Making: A Test of a Theory." *Journal of Politics* 37:711–35.

Strom, Gerald S., and Barry S. Rundquist. 1977. "A Revised Theory of Winning in House-Senate Conferences." *American Political Science Review* 71:448–53.

Sundquist, James L. 1986. *Constitutional Reform and Effective Government.* Washington, D.C.: Brookings.

Swift, Elaine K. 1996. *The Making of an American Senate: Reconstitutive Change in Congress, 1787–1841.* Ann Arbor: University of Michigan Press.

Taagepera, Rein, and Matthew Soberg Shugart. 1989. *Seats and Votes: The Effects and Determinants of Electoral Success.* New Haven: Yale University Press.

Taebel, Delbert. 1978. "Minority Representation on City Councils." *Social Science Quarterly* 59:142–53.

Thomas, Martin. 1985. "Election Proximity and Senatorial Roll Call Voting." *American Journal of Political Science* 29:96–111.

Tocqueville, Alexis de. 1990. *Democracy in America.* Trans.Henry Reeve, ed. Francis Bowen and Phillip Bradley. New York: Vintage.

Tsebelis, George, and Jeannette Money. 1997. *Bicameralism.* Cambridge: Cambridge University Press.

U.S. Department of Commerce. Bureau of the Census. 1994. *Where the Growth Will Be—State Population Projections: 1993 to 2020.* Washington, D.C.

———. 1997. *Statistical Abstract of the United States.* Washington, D.C.

U.S. General Services Administration. 1996. *Catalog of Federal Domestic Assistance.* 30th ed. Washington, D.C.

U.S. House. Committee on Economic and Educational Opportunities. 1995. *Hearing before the Subcommittee on Oversight and Investigations to Examine Issues Involved in Consolidating into Block Grants Aid Currently Provided to State and Local Governments through Categorical Programs.* 104th Cong., 1st sess., 9 February.

———. Committee on Education and Labor. 1972. *Older Americans Act Amendments of 1972.* 92d Cong., 2d sess., H. Rept. 1287.

———. 1978. *Rehabilitation, Comprehensive Services, and Developmental Disabilities Amendments of 1978.* 95th Cong., 2d sess., H. Rept. 1780.

———. Committee on Energy and Commerce. 1992. *Alcohol, Drug Abuse and Mental Health Reorganization.* 102d Cong., 2d sess., H. Rept. 546.

U.S. Public Law 73. 89th Cong., 1st sess., 14 July 1965. *Older Americans Act of 1965.*

U.S. Senate. Committee on Labor and Human Resources. 1978. *Rehabilitation, Comprehensive Services, and Developmental Disabilities Amendments of 1978.* 95th Cong., 2d sess., S. Rept. 890.

Uslaner, Eric M. 1976. "The Pitfalls of Per Capita." *American Journal of Political Science* 20:125–33.

Van Beek, Steven D. 1995. *Post-passage Politics: Bicameral Resolution in Congress.* Pittsburgh: University of Pittsburgh Press.

Vogler, David J. 1971. *The Third House: Conference Committees in the U.S. Congress.* Evanston, Ill.: Northwestern University Press.

Weaver, David H., and G. Cleveland Wilhoit. 1974. "News Magazine Visibility of Senators." *Journalism Quarterly* 51:67–72.

———. 1980. "News Media Coverage of U.S. Senators in Four Congresses, 1953–1974." Journalism Monogaphs. Lexington, Mass.: Association for Education in Journalism.

Wehr, Elizabeth. 1985. "Budget Squeaks through Senate Floor." *Congressional Quarterly Weekly Report,* May 11, 871–74.

Weingast, Barry R. 1979. "A Rational Choice Perspective on Congressional Norms." *American Journal of Political Science* 23:245–62.

Weisberg, Herbert F. 1978. "Evaluating Theories of Congressional Roll Call Voting." *American Journal of Political Science* 22:554–77.

Welch, Susan. 1990. "The Impact of At-Large Elections on the Representation of Blacks and Hispanics." *Journal of Politics* 52:1050–76.

Welch, Susan, and Albert Karnig. 1978. "Representation of Blacks on Big City School Boards." *Social Science Quarterly* 59:162–72.

Westlye, Mark C. 1991. *Senate Elections and Campaign Intensity.* Baltimore: Johns Hopkins University Press.

Whitby, Kenny J. 1997. *The Color of Representation: Congressional Behavior and Black Interests.* Ann Arbor: University of Michigan Press.

White, J. T., and N. C. Thomas. 1964. "Urban and Rural Representation and State Legislative Apportionment." *Western Political Quarterly* 17:724–41.

White, William S. 1957. *Citadel: The Story of the U.S. Senate.* New York: Harper.

Wilhoit, G. Cleveland, and Kenneth S. Sherrill. 1968. "Wire Service Visibility of U.S. Senators." *Journalism Quarterly* 45:42–48.

Wilson, James Q. 1973. *Political Organizations.* New York: Basic Books.

Wilson, Rick K. 1986. "What Was It Worth to Be on a Committee in the U.S. House?" *Legislative Studies Quarterly* 11:47–63.

Wilson, Woodrow. 1885. *Congressional Government: A Study in American Politics.* Boston: Houghton Mifflin.

———. 1911. *Constitutional Government.* New York: Columbia University Press.

Wittenberg, Ernest, and Elisabeth Wittenberg. 1989. *How to Win in Washington: Very Practical Advice about Lobbying, the Grassroots, and the Media.* New York: Blackwell.

Wolpe, Bruce C., and Bertram J. Levine. 1996. *Lobbying Congress: How the System Works.* 2d ed. Washington, D.C.: CQ Press.

Wood, Gordon S. 1969. *The Creation of the American Republic, 1776–1787.* Chapel Hill: University of North Carolina Press.

Wooddy, Carroll. 1926. "Is the Senate Unrepresentative?" *Political Science Quarterly* 40:219–39.

Wright, Gerald C., and Michael B. Berkman. 1986. "Candidates and Policy in United States Senate Elections." *American Political Science Review* 80:567–88.

Yack, Bernard. 1993. *The Problems of a Political Animal: Community, Justice, and Conflict in Aristolelian Political Thought.* Berkeley: University of California Press.

Zajonc, Robert B. 1968. "Attitudinal Effects of Mere Exposure." *Journal of Personality and Social Psychology Monograph Supplement* 9:1–27.

Zakaria, Fareed. 1997. "The Rise of Illiberal Democracy." *Foreign Affairs* 76 (November–December): 22–43.

Zimmerman, Joseph F., and Wilma Rule. 1998. "A More Representative United States House of Representatives." *P.S.* 30:5–10.

Index